ISLAMIC PERSPECTIVE ON CHARITY

Khalil Jassemm, Ph.D.

A COMPREHENSIVE GUIDE FOR RUNNING A MUSLIM NONPROFIT IN THE U.S.

Bloomington, IN      Milton Keynes, UK

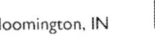
authorHOUSE

AuthorHouse™
1663 Liberty Drive, Suite 200
Bloomington, IN 47403
www.authorhouse.com
Phone: 1-800-839-8640

AuthorHouse™ UK Ltd.
500 Avebury Boulevard
Central Milton Keynes, MK9 2BE
www.authorhouse.co.uk
Phone: 08001974150

First published by AuthorHouse 11/13/2006

ISBN: 978-1-4259-3227-5 (e)
ISBN: 978-1-4259-3160-5 (sc)

Library of Congress Control Number: 2006904636

Printed in the United States of America
Bloomington, Indiana

This book is printed on acid-free paper.

Contents

Foreword

Before September 11, 2001, Muslim charities in the United States conducted their operations channeling Muslim resources into humanitarian disaster relief around the world. Relatively unknown by all but their own baseline of supporters, this handful of organizations discovered themselves wholly unprepared for the disastrous challenges thrown at them in the aftermath of that terrible day.

Regardless of any truths or falsehoods behind the closure of several of the largest of these organizations, all Muslim organizations were victimized or affected in some manner. Even local nonprofits that merely provided religious services to their Muslim communities, never spending a penny overseas did not escape public scrutiny. The doctrine of preventing future attacks led the government to cast a wide net. As a result, individual Muslims suffered immensely as many were interrogated, expelled or imprisoned without due process.

As Muslims feared that performing the third of Islam's five pillars would bring the FBI to their door, charitable donations nose-dived, plunging those communities and individuals that benefited most from the charities' assistance into dire circumstances. Therefore, depriving the poor and needy of vital help, and denying Muslims channels for charity giving.

As Islamic nonprofits currently face greater challenges and scrutiny than ever before, it is vitally important that they be proactive and positive, by increasing their capacity, effectiveness and professionalism, and adopting complete transparency in their everyday operations. Oversights or misunderstood behaviors could quite easily result in disaster not just for a singular organization, but for many others as well. The light of suspicion has yet to dim; therefore, for Islamic nonprofits to successfully carry out their missions, these tempestuous times must be dealt with through professionalism and perseverance. After all, our communities, donors and beneficiaries deserve nothing less.

Another dark residual of the attacks in 2001 is the opinion of many Muslim experts that it may take a decade or longer to rebuild US Islamic nonprofits to capacities realized before 9/11. Even now, more than five years later, those charities that survived, and those newly created, are perceived as guilty until proven otherwise. Charities face many challenges and are suspected mainly because they operate overseas in the Arab and Muslim world with the Arab-Israeli conflict as the political background.

PURPOSE AND AUDIENCE

All charities found themselves in a new political and enforcement environment in the post-9/11 era. The whole nonprofit sector had a new set of challenges to deal with, including new demands for accountability and transparency. More internal controls were required. Governmental and community outreach became not an option, but a must.

Muslim charities face the same set of challenges as those of any nonprofit sector, but with additional challenges relating to donors, recipients, and general operational issues. If the Muslim charities are able to upgrade and increase capacity, they will serve as a model for Muslim and Arab charities worldwide.

The majority of American Muslims are not at all convinced that US Islamic nonprofits have at any time had anything to do with terrorism or the horrific events surrounding September 11, 2001. It is also our hope that some day in the near future, the US government will realize that they were intentionally misled by self-proclaimed 'terrorism experts'. Yet, we must deal with the reality of the situation and thus envision only two choices for the future of Islamic nonprofits in the US:

• Resignation: Become resigned to the notion that there is no possible way Islamic nonprofits can any longer freely operate within the US, and surrender to the powerful special interest groups that have been very persistent in targeting our charities.

• Upgrade Performance: This option involves building capacity, upgrading performance, positive government engagement and public outreach to the rest of society.

Muslim charities are an asset, not a liability. Resignation is not an option, and would have great negative consequences for both the Muslim community and the US government. Muslim charities have a market that only they can serve. Charity is a pillar of their faith, and Muslims must give charity money (Zakat), which is obligated to be spent in ways consistent with the practices of Islam. Only Muslim charities have the know-how to spend these funds in a manner consistent with Islamic religious requirements. For example, the Red Cross and Salvation Army—while they do great work—cannot perform the function of the Muslim charities. Therefore, if the US government closed Muslim charities, those charitable funds would be given with greater frequency through alternative channels, as is happening now. American Muslims would struggle to find trustworthy and able individuals willing to deliver Zakat funds to be spent on charitable causes. For example, a group of individuals would get together, collect money and send it overseas to help a village. Such an arrangement would have no accountability, no checks-and-balances, and no structure for government oversight. With the closing of all Muslim charities, such an arrangement would be the rule, making government enforcement of laws extremely difficult. The Muslim charities also play a vital and unique role in distributing humanitarian assistance throughout the world. While USAID and other American humanitarian assistance agencies spend billions of dollars, they have shown sparse tangible results in enhancing America's image in the Muslim world. Therefore, Muslim charities are an asset and a treasure, not a liability for both the US government and Muslims in the US.

With this text, it is my intent to target several main audiences:

- Intellectual Americans who would like to learn what Islamic charity is all about and how it functions.

- American Muslim leaders and workers who have a desire to improve their nonprofits through strategies and expertise, guiding them to better governance and operations.

- The average citizen with a desire to understand the basic concept and practice of Islamic charity.

- Leaders and decision-makers of Muslim charities outside the US who would like to understand how American charities work.

- Leaders of other nonprofit organizations seeking good operational practices.

ACKNOWLEDGMENTS

This book could not have been completed without the support of Allah (swt). I give my sincerest thanks to Him, Who enabled me to be part of the great work of serving those in need and then delivering my humble experiences to others working in the humanitarian field. I also would not have been able to complete this work without the help, support and encouragement of my dear wife and friend for life Srood.

I thank Miriam Amer for her dedication, patience, and skills. I greatly appreciate the tremendous effort she put into researching, editing and formatting this work, and I ask Allah to reward her for all that she has done.

I would also like to extend extra thanks and appreciation to the staff of LIFE for Relief and Development for their support, hard work, and encouragement.

This book is dedicated to all those who work for or support nonprofit organizations, whether they are leaders, employees, volunteers, or donors. Without their combined efforts, the world would be filled with pain and misery, devoid of spiritual guidance. It is they who provide the education on which our next generation relies, the skills and tools for the needy to be self-reliant, and healthcare for the ill. Through their selfless efforts, sad faces can smile, love is brought to empty hearts, and the world is made a better place in which to live. To all, I dedicate this book.

I also wish to thank the membership and staff of InterAction. As a member of InterAction, I was able to meet a group of professional individuals from the nonprofit world from who I learned a great deal.

Khalil Ibrahim Jassemm, Ph.D.

Southfield, Michigan

February, 2006

Overview of the Contents

This book is a comprehensive guide for nonprofits to grow and prosper. The first three chapters deal with the concepts and principles of Muslim philanthropy, while the others serve as practical guidelines for nonprofits to function professionally.

Chapters 1, 2 and 3: Chapter 1 discusses the concepts of philanthropy in Islam with references to other religious charitable practices to put into comparative context. It examines the size and behaviors of American Muslim philanthropy—how much they give, and to what causes and organizations. Chapter 2 discusses how Islam deals with the issue of poverty, and considers at length the concepts of Zakat and Waqf in Islam. Chapter 3 is an overview of the laws of compliance for American nonprofits post-9/11. It also discusses the backlash from September 11, 2001, and the targeting of Muslim charities. Within this chapter, my research demonstrates that it is in the strategic interest of the US to empower these charities as vital assets to improve America's image abroad, primarily in the Muslim world.

Chapters 4, 5 and 6: These chapters outline how to think strategically, helping the nonprofit to base its entire operation on a focused mission, and working within a clear strategic plan to achieve the desired goal. Chapter 4, 'Defining Your Vision and Mission Statement', discusses the role of the mission statement in nonprofit organizations: how to conceptualize it, and how to implement it in decision making. Chapter 5 deals with strategic planning, from its role in nonprofit management, its formulation, and then its use within the nonprofit's organizational operations. Chapter 6 addresses goals: how to set objectives and goals in light of a strategic plan, and how to achieve these goals.

Chapters 7 and 8: These two chapters deal with the people behind the organization. Chapter 7 approaches the subject of the nonprofit board of directors: their role and responsibilities, and the function of the governance system behind the organization. Chapter 8 addresses the issue of management of staff and volunteers: how to effectively develop and manage your human resources.

Chapters 9, 10, 11, 12 and 13: Fundraising, marketing and building effective relationships are addressed in these chapters. Chapter 9 is an overview of sources of funding. Chapter 10 presents 'The Missing-Link Cycle' as a proven model developed by us for the nonprofit to effectively connect to their donors or potential donors. In Chapter 11, the focus is on successful direct mail solicitation, which is a prominent method of fundraising used by Islamic nonprofits in the US. Chapter 12 outlines how the Internet can be an effective fundraising tool. In Chapter 13, I discuss the vital issues related to donor, community, and government relations.

Chapters 14, 15 and 16: Chapter 14 addresses financial planning: the basic elements every nonprofit should know and apply to plan successfully for their finances. Chapter 15 deals with budgeting, a subject that is overlooked by many nonprofits (especially those that deal in disaster relief) due to the uncertainty surrounding their future programs and services. It is here that I present the practical, easily applied concepts and methods of budgeting for nonprofits. Chapter 16 deals with revenue and expense management. Once an organization plans and budgets its finances, this chapter will demonstrate how to manage not only income as it arrives, but expenses as they are allocated.

In the last section of this book, I offer the reader concluding remarks and final insights into my motivations and goals, while outlining my expectations for those who endeavor to "get between the pages" of this text.

Chapter

1.

Religion and Charity

Each religion or culture has its own history and unique ideals and practices of charitable giving. These differ from individual to individual, from culture to culture, and from time to time—handing a slice of bread to a hungry person, tossing coins into a beggar's cup, spending a few hours a month cleaning up at an animal shelter, or donating to the building of a school or a place of worship.

In this chapter, we will discuss our obligations towards those in need, and how mankind tends to deal with them from religious perspectives. In this chapter, we will discuss the American welfare system and its vast nonprofit sector, as well as the American concept of giving. We will also present a summary comparative study of charity in Islam and the other two monotheistic religions: Christianity and Judaism. Current studies of charitable giving and practices by Muslims in the west in detail are limited; therefore, this chapter will offer a brief theological background on the subject, as well as study current giving behaviors of Muslims within the framework of available data.

Since there is no simple definition of Islamic philanthropy, nor is there a comparative gauge by which to measure its magnitude, this study will attempt to draw a comparison between non-Muslim and Muslim charity and giving practices, highlighting both similarities and differences.

I.   The Social Obligation Debates

The political, theoretical and academic debates about what society's obligations are to those either in the twilight of life or the less fortunate (or both) has been a contentious issue in American politics since before the implementation of Social Security in the Twentieth Century.[1]

SOCIAL SECURITY OR INSECURITY?

Social security is a governmental insurance program that provides workers, and retired workers and their families with a degree of economic cushion through cash payments which substitute for income lost as a result of retirement, unemployment, disability, or death. All industrialized nations as well as many less developed countries have a social security system of some form or another.

The US social security program is financed by employers and workers through payroll taxes, and is required for nearly all workers in the US. Approximately one-sixth of America's population receives Social Security benefits[2] that consist of three primary parts:

- Social Security comprised of old-age, survivors, disability, and hospital insurance

- Unemployment insurance

- Workers' compensation. As a social parachute, major drawbacks (or insecurity) of Social Security for the upcoming generation of retirees are many-fold, including:

  - A solvency issue where the possibility exists that the program may go broke as the proportion of retirees outnumbers workers, leaving future generations without Social Security to fall back on when they retire.

  - One must work at least 40 quarters prior to retirement in order to draw full benefits.

  - Benefits are not drawn equally by all participants.
    Benefits are based on a person's earning capacity during their working years, which can be supplemented by private pensions. Most who rely solely on their Social Security benefits to survive in retirement may find themselves living on severely limited incomes, at or below the poverty level.

SOCIAL SECURITY VS. WELFARE

Welfare, or public assistance, provides aid to those poor who are in need of assistance by providing money, medical care, food, housing, and other necessities. People who receive welfare include children, the aged, the blind, the disabled, and others who cannot adequately provide for themselves and their families.

Social Security should not be confused with public assistance, as its benefits are payable to workers and their families according to their work histories, whether or not they are poor. Most Americans will someday be recipients of Social Security as more than 152 million people who work pay Social Security taxes. Meant to replace about 40 percent of an average wage earner's income after retiring, currently, more than 45 million people receive monthly Social Security benefits.[3] To have a comfortable retirement, Americans need much more than just Social Security. They also need private pensions, savings and investments.[4]

The only criterion for welfare, or public assistance, is poverty. Springing from the 1930s Great Depression, along with Social Security and other New Deal programs, it was designed to be a part of the federal government's safety net of benefits for those who have fallen onto hard times, and was intended primarily to aid widowed or single women and their dependent children.[5]

The Welfare State

In the United States, welfare mainly helps those who live below an imaginary line of wealth established by the federal government called the poverty line, which is adjusted annually to account for inflation. The poor and needy who receive welfare that is financed by citizen and corporate tax dollars are served by federal and state governments through a number of public assistance programs:

- Medicaid

- Cash aid programs

- The Food Stamp Program.

WorldBook Encyclopedia dictionary defines a welfare state as a "state whose government provides for the welfare of its citizens, especially through social security, unemployment insurance, free medical treatment, and other such programs". Before its welfare reform act in 1996,[6] England, France, Sweden and Japan among others joined the United States in their preference for a system based upon this premise of a cold, involuntary and forceful redistribution of the nation's collective wealth. Many economists see the welfare state as society in transition toward a totalitarian civilization where the bureaucracy has control of the public treasury and doles funds out at will. Once the government has taken over charitable distribution, the public is relieved of this "troublesome burden". Since they are crowded out of the loop, voluntary charity and the growth of philanthropic organizations begins to slow. This phenomenon is seen over the last 15 or 20 years in the US where statistics showed that between 1960 and 1976, total voluntary contributions increased from about $8.9 billion to about $29 billion.[7] Although, before 2001 the overall total growth rate for charitable contributions had increased at nearly seven percent annually, personal income expanded at around nine percent a year. These statistics show an overall gap of two percent per year. A significant figure when one takes into account that almost 75 percent of all contributions to charitable organizations come from individuals.[8]

Social Insurance Abroad

Although most countries have some form of welfare, they differ in how much they spend on welfare as compared to social insurance, and in how much they spend on welfare relative to the size of their overall economy. Most European countries have universal programs that provide for their needy mainly through national programs that benefit all their citizens by providing free medical and hospital care, family allowances, and retirement pensions. European countries typically spend a larger share of their economy on welfare and social insurance than do other countries. Some countries like Norway and Kuwait have such comprehensive programs that they are labeled as welfare states. Others like Canada, Australia, New Zealand, and the United Kingdom provide a larger share of their aid through public assistance. These countries have much more generous welfare systems than the United States, and expend a larger share of their economy on aid to the poor. While other nations such as Japan, South Korea, and Singapore rely more on privately funded welfare that comes largely from employers and the families themselves. Governmental welfare expenditures in those countries are low by international standards.

Those nations that are less developed in Africa, Latin America, and Asia have lower welfare budgets than others, although in some of those countries, their welfare systems are quite well-developed. Some examples of this are Uruguay's particularly generous system, and South Africa's comprehensive health care system.

Falling into the Void

The US is not classified as a welfare state because aid that it provides its needy is not as complete and comprehensive as that given in other nations. Although there is a marked breach between amounts of support from government sources and support doled out by charitable causes. By some standards, charity is generally seen as "gap insurance", helping needy persons and families fill in the void left by the lack of government aid for everyday living. Government aid has not kept up with increases in the cost of living; therefore, the chasm has grown wider. According to the 2000 US Census, as of April 1, 2000, 281.4 million people called America home, an increase of 33 million people just in the last decade. As the US population grows, so has the number of Americans living in poverty. According to a US Census Bureau report, as of August 2004, 35.9 million people live below the poverty line in America, including 12.9 million children.[9] Even with the increase in Americans' charitable giving, there are still too many needy falling into the void.

SOCIAL WELFARE VS. VOLUNTARY GIVING

From 1950 to 1976, social welfare payments in the United States raised to more than $260 billion, accounting for more than half of all federal funding, and more than two-thirds of all state and municipal payments. In 1950, payments of social welfare only accounted for about ten percent of personal income payments. In 1977, they accounted for nearly 25 percent of personal income. When compared to the total personal income growth of nine percent, welfare payments skyrocketed [Salamon, 2002].

Welfare to Work

In 1996, welfare reform legislation enacted in the United States moved millions of recipients from welfare to work. Although the social welfare system in the US before welfare reform was quite competent at providing basic care for those in need, it lacked a structure that encouraged self-reliance. The economic boom of the late 1990's allowed the creation of extraordinary employment opportunities for welfare recipients. This lead to a dramatic decrease in the public welfare roles from five million families in 1995 to two million in 2000.[10]

Before the 1996 welfare reforms, the effectiveness of the welfare state was called into question. The theory behind providing welfare is that it is a temporary safety net. The understanding is that individuals would face a crisis at one point in time and need assistance for short periods; however, the way the welfare system operated created dependency. The system did not give recipients incentives to become self-reliant. For example, individuals who received welfare payments faced the threat of losing health insurance if they were gainfully employed, earning an amount of money slightly above a certain level of income. Therefore, the poor had a reason to either not obtain work or to under-report their earnings to stay eligible to receive healthcare and food stamps.

Unlike in 1900 when taxes paid to federal, state and county governments only amounted to nine percent of personal incomes, the level of taxes and government spending now far exceeds this. Moreover, their tax and welfare burden bred indifference and apathy towards charitable contributions, enabling the government to vastly outperform private charitable organizations using the people's own tax dollars!

The majority of money given into charity and the greatest percentage of volunteer hours donated in the US are to hospitals, schools and universities. Private social service agencies also receive the lion's share of their funding from such sources. So, how do social welfare programs compare with voluntary giving? In 1950, philanthropy represented almost 20 percent of total welfare payments. Although the growth of giving varied by sector from 1977 to 1997, philanthropy accounted for only 16 percent of charitable giving.[11]

II.   The American Concept of Giving

When nonprofit giving began in American culture is a highly debated issue. Since the time of its infancy, Americans were tossing coins into the cups of blind beggars on street corners, or quietly slipping a loaf of warm bread on the porch of a needy family. Americans are a kind and generous lot who give more to charitable causes each year than the nations of France, Germany and England combined [Salamon, 2002]. It was a generally accepted notion throughout America that its charities were well organized, responded quickly to disaster, and that the bulk of the money given by Americans for their selected causes went entirely to that cause.

Within two months after the events of 9/11/2001, individuals, corporations, and foundations had contributed an astounding $1.5 billion[12] to a broad spectrum of relief agencies and efforts. Some of these included household names such as the American Red Cross, the Salvation Army, and the United Way. Hundreds of other agencies sprung up across the country to directly or indirectly give aid and channel funds to the victims and their families. According to a survey funded by AFP and conducted by Indiana University, an astonishing 74 percent of those surveyed made contributions in some form or other to help in recovery from this crisis.[13]

The actions of Americans after this tragic event bolstered the world's view of Americans' generosity toward others, and the nation's remarkable spirit and strength; however, the weaknesses of its premier charities were also brought to light. Although private groups of volunteers were quite effective in mobilizing immediate action and relief, the meld of the larger charities was brought into the spotlight. Their inability to handle the enormity of the crisis soon became apparent. Power struggles ensued over their autonomy and coordinated efforts between their agencies or governmental entities. Those who desperately needed help found themselves having to navigate through bureaucratic waste generated by the government and the agencies themselves.[14] Each organization had its own criteria for assistance, along with having their own targeted forms of aid. Some of those who needed the aid the most fell through the cracks, while others benefited from multiple assistance sources, or received more than their fair share. Ultimately, the donations themselves were questioned when donors learned that funds they intended to be given in their totality to help with this disaster were reallocated for longer-term recovery, administrative costs, and other, less visible future disasters.[15]

WHAT IS THE AMERICAN NONPROFIT SECTOR?

In reviewing the first 150 years of America's history, its people have been described as industrious, independent, humane and kind. They are a compassionate people whose society has evolved by setting up a sort of safety net for those in need in the form of personal charitable aid.

Without America's deeply engrained practices of volunteering and charity, the frontier settlers would have found that without the aid of their neighbors, they would have been unable to raise barns, or establish schools and towns. In the early part of the 19th century, French writer and Statesman Alexis de Tocqueville was impressed by the proliferation of such voluntary groups while observing American democracy and individualism. He wrote, "Wherever at the head of some major undertaking you are sure to find the state in France or a person of wealth in England, you will find an association in America."[16]

Nonprofit giving has increased in huge numbers over the years to organizations representing family and children's services, neighborhood development programs, and antipoverty and community health facilities. These also include numerous support organizations, such as foundations and community chests that help to generate financial assistance for these organizations, as well as the traditions of giving, volunteering, and service they help to foster.

The term nonprofit encompasses organizations that are eligible for exemption from federal income taxation under Section 501(c)(3) of the tax code. These also include the closely related "social welfare organizations" eligible for exemption under Section 501(c)(4) of the same code. Included here are organizations that operate "exclusively for religious, charitable, scientific, or educational purposes" and do not distribute any profits to any private shareholder or individual. The 501(c)(3) organizations stand alone among the 26 types of organizations exempted from federal income taxation. These organizations may also receive tax-deductible contributions from individuals and businesses; however, they are expected to serve a broad range of public purposes as opposed to the interests and needs of the members of the organization alone.

AMERICA'S VAST NONPROFIT SECTOR

Although a conservative estimate puts the number of 501(c)(3) and (c)(4) organizations in the US at 1.2 million as of the mid-1990s—including an estimated 350,000 religious congregations—data on even the best known nonprofits is notoriously incomplete. As of 2001, these organizations employed over nine and a half percent of the US work force,[17] and enlisted the equivalent of another 5.7 million full-time employees as volunteers. The paid employment sector of nonprofits alone constitute three times that in agriculture, twice that in wholesale trade, and nearly 50 percent greater than that in both construction and finance, insurance, and real estate.[18]

According to a study done shortly before his death in 1994, George Cornell of the Associated Press concluded that in America alone, religious giving in 1992 totaled $56.7 billion. Contrary to popular belief that Americans spend more on sports than in charitable giving, this figure was 14 times the $4 billion spent on America's three most popular sports: major league baseball, football, and basketball.[19]

The majority of nonprofit employment is concentrated in three fields: health (43 percent), education (22 percent), and social services (18 percent). Official statistics put the total number of religious nonprofit employees at only five percent. If one were to include the volunteers in these figures, healthcare would be 34 percent, while the religious share would take 23 percent. These categories can be further broken down into subcategories such as the 56 sub-fields of arts, culture, and humanities which collectively translate into potentially thousands of different types of nonprofit organizations. Larger organizations can claim the bulk of the employment and economic resources of this sector; however, most of the organizations are quite small, with few or no full-time employees.

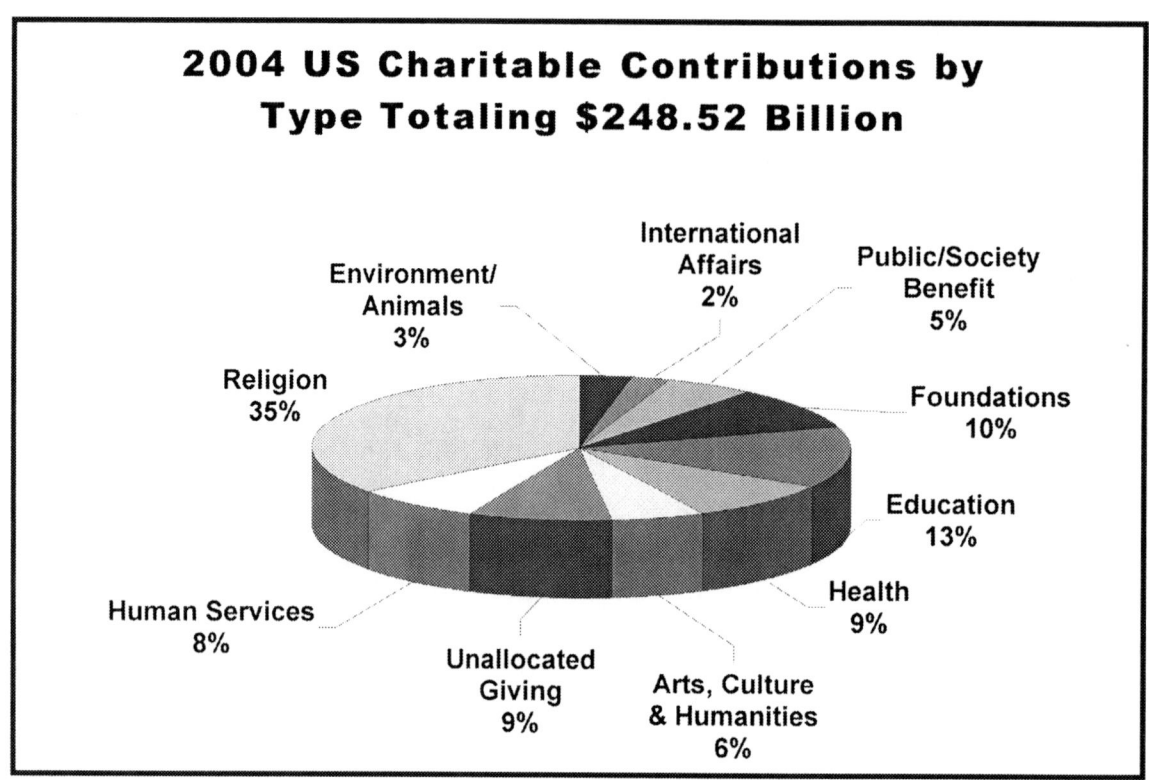

2004 US Charitable Contributions by Type Totaling $248.52 Billion

International Affairs 2%

Public/Society Benefit 5%

Environment/Animals 3%

Religion 35%

Foundations 10%

Education 13%

Human Services 8%

Health 9%

Unallocated Giving 9%

Arts, Culture & Humanities 6%

Figure 1-A

Reversing a Downward Trend

An economic downturn that began in 2001, effectively stagnating charitable giving in the US, was reversed in 2003. When adjusted for inflation, total giving for 2004 rose 2.3 percent over those funds collected in 2003. In dollar figures, this translates to $248.5 billion in 2004, with $187.5 billion coming from individuals alone. Of the remaining donated funds, $19.8 billion came from bequests, $28.8 billion from foundations, and $12 billion from corporations.[20]

So, where did this money go? Research finds that $88.3 billion of this support went to local religious organizations, followed by gifts totaling $33.8 billion to education. In 2004, this increase held true for all but two areas: international affairs groups and human services, which when adjusted for inflation, saw a 1.8 percent and 1.1 percent decline respectively. Although the majority of contributions earmarked for South Asian tsunami relief were given in 2005, and are expected to represent only a fraction of that year's total contributions, those donations made in 2004 totaled less than one-half of one percent of overall giving for that year.[21]

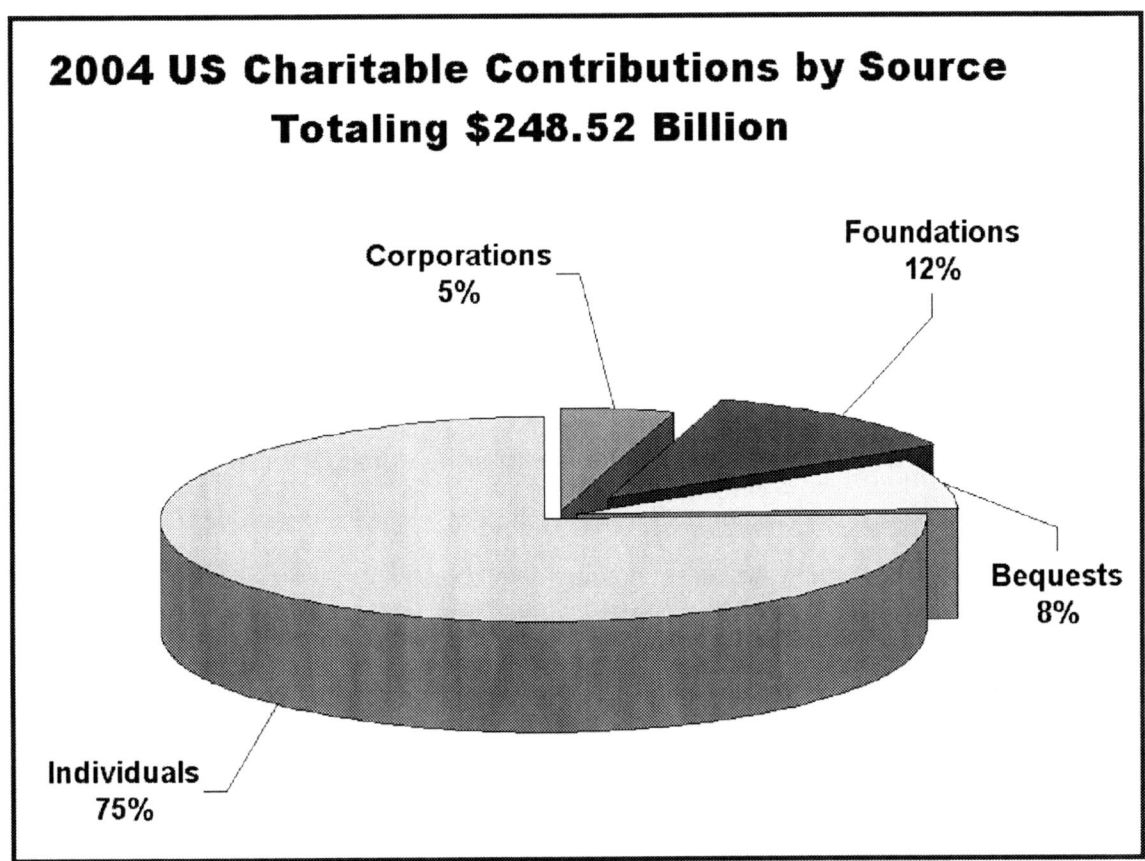

2004 US Charitable Contributions by Source Totaling $248.52 Billion

Corporations 5%

Foundations 12%

Bequests 8%

Individuals 75%

Figure 1-B

What's in it for Me?

Quid pro quo, tit-for-tat, do unto others...These timeless clichés tell the story that not every person has an innate charitable nature. Overlooking the tremendous generosity and kindness that lies at the crux of charitable giving, throughout society in general, there is more than likely to be a few people who ask the questions, "Why should I give?" and "What's in it for me?"

In Islam, as well as in other religions, the answer is quite easy and straightforward: because of a Muslim's obligation to Allah, and Allah's commandment to mankind to care for the poor and needy.

Tax Advantages to Giving

So, why then do Americans give to so many charitable causes each year? Most of those who give do so for truly benevolent reasons—out of the goodness of their hearts, not for what they might reap from the transaction. Yet, although most people do care what becomes of their fellow man, tree, endangered species, etc., they generally do not have the financial wherewithal to be so charitable with their dollars. Setting altruistic reasoning aside, one reason might be summed up in two little words: tax breaks. The federal government encourages and approves of charitable giving, illustrated by Uncle Sam's long term policy of allowing individuals tax deductions for their charitable contributions to qualified organizations.

Dependent upon a taxpayer's bracket, for every dollar donated, a portion of that dollar can be deducted from a person's overall income, thereby reducing their overall tax burden. As a general rule, the higher the tax rates, the lower the "out of pocket" price of giving. If a person in the 20 percent tax bracket gives one dollar, then the true cost of that dollar is really only 80 cents. While for a person in a 35 percent bracket that cost would only be 65 cents, since that person would have to pay 35 cents in taxes if they kept the dollar. Effectively, the federal government pays a portion of the person's charitable contribution. All of the above is notwithstanding the true tax rebel who asks, "Why give to the government what can be put where I want it to go?"

It is important to bear in mind that US tax code changes periodically, and presently only those who itemize their deductions are allowed to actually take a deduction for charitable contributions. Not to mention that the caps for tax exemption by wealthier individuals adjusts as well according to current laws.

III. Charitable Giving in Judaism

In Judaism, the concept of charitable giving is quite similar to that in Islam. The concept of giving in Judaism is directed to aid those in need. "Tzedakah" is the Hebrew word for charity: giving aid, assistance and money to the poor and needy, or to worthwhile causes. It is also the responsibility of the individual to give a portion of one's personal wealth for the common good. However, literally translated, Tzedakah varies from the definition of charity which suggests benevolence and generosity for the benefit of the poor and needy.

Tzedakah is derived from the Hebrew language and means righteousness, fairness or justice. In Judaism, giving to the poor is not viewed as a generous act, but is simply an act of justice, the performance of a duty, giving the poor their due.[22]

AN ENDURING CUSTOM

From early childhood, most Jewish children learn to give charity by depositing Tzedakah coins into the blue and white tin boxes (pushke) present in many Jewish homes. Commonly passed around during prayer services, the pushke links prayer and charity. Through this method, Jewish children learn that it is their responsibility to care for others in need. Through the centuries, this custom has endured and evolved toward a new motivation: to sustain the Jewish people, to enhance the Jewish life and to strengthen the Jewish community for today and the future.

Tzedakah has two aspects: one with the hand and one with the heart. Judaism teaches that donors benefit from Tzedakah as much or more than its beneficiaries. Whereas the poor receive money or other material assistance, the donor receives the merit of sharing the Almighty's work.

The minimum annual contribution of Tzedakah is under $2.00. However, the contribution from a person of adequate means is a suggested ten percent of their income. This includes any accumulation of wealth, plus a one-time contribution of one-tenth of the value of their net assets. As giving too much may cause the generous person to become needy himself, the rabbis limited Tzedakah to giving no more than one-fifth of one's income. However, there are exceptions to this limit, as one may give more for circumstances relating to ransoming a slave, saving a life, supporting Torah scholars and atonement for sin.[23]

A HISTORY OF SUCCESS

Although there are more than 14.5 million Jews worldwide, followers of Judaism comprise only two percent of the US population.[24] Yet, of all the religious charities in the US, the Jewish charities have been the most successful. In 1998 alone, Jewish philanthropy raised nearly two billion dollars in gifts and endowment funds for Jews in the US, Israel and other nations around the world.[25] Clearly these numbers would be miniscule if they were able to be compared to the total volume of giving by Jews to all categories of charities world wide—both Jewish and non-Jewish. But, according to Gary Tobin, director of the Institute for Jewish and Community Research, no comprehensive study of worldwide Jewish philanthropy presently exists to measure these statistics in relation to generic American giving, regardless of whether it is to synagogues or for other purposes.[26]

IV.   Charitable Giving in Christianity

In the Old Testament, Proverbs 21:13 says, "If a man shuts his ears to the cry of the poor, he too will cry out and not be answered."

In Matthew 26:11, Jesus is quoted as saying, "The poor you will always have with you."

For Christians, no set schedule of giving is required. Moralists urge the obligatory giving of charity at the beginning of the moral life when reason has attained its full development, at the point of death, and from time to time during life.

Mankind's possession of free will is one of the fundamental tenets of the Christian church, recognizing that man has control over and is responsible for all his actions. For a Christian to perform an act of charity and to gain the spiritual rewards for this act, it must be performed by the conscious intent of the individual. An act of charity is an act of helping those in need; yet, it can only be a Christian act when it involves the application of free will. Although an individual should have the right to designate how their own property is bestowed in charitable ventures, an individual does not have the right to make this choice for others.

The majority of Christians give aid out of their conviction that human beings are all brothers and it is our duty to help each other. Although for many Christians, charitable acts and giving are a way of helping them to attain a higher level of spirituality, emulating the generosity and life of Jesus.

Christian church members worldwide in 2000 gave $107.9 billion to churches, and another $162.6 billion to parachurch agencies, for a total of $297.6 billion to all causes, including $27.1 billion to secular causes and $270.5 billion to Christian causes.[27] A subset of this is the worldwide figure given by Evangelical Christians, who donate approximately $181 billion per year.[28] These figures can be further broken down into American Protestants versus Catholics, where Protestants donated an average of $1,093 to their churches in 2001, more than double the figure of $495 given by Catholics to their churches.[29]

In the Catholic Church, it is a commonly accepted rule that tithing by parishioners should equal ten percent of their yearly personal income. Although Christians comprise about one-third of the world's population, some sources claim they hold nearly two-thirds of all physical wealth, while their charitable giving amounts to less than three percent of that wealth.[31] The average total Sunday collection for Roman Catholic churches in America is $5.5 billion per week.[32]

The death of Pope John Paul II has renewed interest in the Pontiff's statements about the obligations of society toward the weak and less fortunate. In a 1995 speech in Baltimore, Maryland, the Pope said, "Our commitment to the dignity and value of all human beings is the reason why the ecclesial community establishes such things as soup kitchens, provides shelter for the homeless and medical care for the poor, counsels those addicted to drugs and alcohol, and helps people to participate more fully in the life of society."[33] The majority of Catholics believe that government should help the less fortunate. Some Catholic Diocese leaders feel that the US federal yearly budget spells out where our national priorities lie, but fail the scriptural test of inclusion of relief and aid for all.[34]

V. Charity in Islam

Islam as a religion details the foundations and principles of charitable giving through guidelines set forth in Qur'anic verses and *Hadith* (documented sayings or deeds of the Prophet Mohammed). Islamic philanthropy is built upon a foundation of elaborate sets of rules and institutions which govern those philanthropic efforts. Although it would be politically correct to state that Muslims have practiced their mandated philanthropy with consistency, this would be an inaccurate statement. Like many other aspects of Islam, these practices have varied over time depending on the abilities of Muslim individuals to give, or their level of trust in those who administer charitable giving, whether they are governmental or non-governmental bodies. Also, some of these variations can be attributed to the variances in the ruling religious governments and their schools of jurisprudence—specifically, how they dealt with charitable donations and obligations.

A Hand Up, Not a Handout

Islam outlines a number of viable alternatives to the receiving of charity. The foundation of Islamic giving and administration of charity dictate that those who can work should do so. Those who are employable, but have no skills should be trained and/or given the tools they require to earn a living. Thereby preserving their self-worth, and affording the needy person the opportunity to become self-sufficient. Additionally, those who cannot work are to be supported first by their direct relations, then their far relations, their immediate neighbors, and lastly by strangers. In Islamic teaching, charity is a hand up, not a handout. Whereas the traditional characteristics of charity are based on the opposite concept: welfare states, etc.

Charity is an Obligation

For Muslims, Zakat is one of the required five tenets, or "pillars" of Islam. This is along with fasting during *Ramadan,* maintaining the five daily prayers, pilgrimage to Mecca at least once in an able Muslim's lifetime, and making a declaration of faith that "there is no God but Allah, and Mohammed is His prophet". Muslims are also strongly encouraged to give additional optional charity, called *Sadaqah.*

In Islam, charity is viewed as an obligation to God, and a cleansing of one's wealth. A Muslim's belief in charitable giving goes even further. Islam contends that Allah is the owner of all wealth, and human beings are only His trustees. Wealth belongs to God, not the individual. Man must obey the true owner of this wealth by giving a set portion of it to those in need. Public recognition or credit for giving it is discouraged unless doing so will encourage others to give. This is a belief foreign to most non-Muslims, often creating a great deal of misunderstanding, as the western philosophy to wealth is commonly held to be "what is mine, is mine". In Islam, the concept of one's wealth is very different than that of other religions in that it asserts a person's wealth is only a loan from Allah. Allah is the true owner of all wealth, and mankind is simply a temporary trustee.

ZAKAT

To the world's 1.7 billion Muslims,[35] the giving of charity is not an option. This mandate cannot be erased by simply shutting the doors of Islamic charities, or confiscating Muslim charitable funds. No tax will ever replace it, and no man-made law will ever supersede it; therefore, if prevented from giving through organizational means, Muslims will resort to informal methods.

Types of Islamic Charity

Zakat: One of the five pillars of Islam required by all Muslims. Depending upon the type, Muslims pay from 2.5% to 20% in charity. Zakat means "purification" and "growth." The giving of this obligatory tithing to religious authorities is considered a monetary act of worship.

Sadaqah: A voluntary type of charity that is highly encouraged for Muslims to pay. This type of charity is not always monetary; although in practice voluntary giving in terms of volume greatly exceeds Zakat giving.

Kaffara: A charitable contribution paid in penance for breaking an oath or committing a minor sin.

Khoms: A charitable contribution that is considered to be obligatory for Shi'a Muslims which is calculated to be 20 percent of annual profits, or income above and beyond living expenses.

When Americans pay their taxes to the government, those taxes are based on overall income even before our families are provided for. These sums can be quite staggering, sometimes as much as 50%. In comparison to Christians who are required to pay a "tithe" of a minimum ten percent of their overall annual income, Muslims are required to pay "Zakat", which is one of the five pillars of Islam. Depending upon the type of wealth, Muslims pay from 2.5% to 20% of one's disposable income and property towards this obligation that has specific uses within the Islamic community. Muslims are also strongly encouraged to pay an additional voluntary charity of unlimited amounts, or "Sadaqah", to help any person in need, regardless of their religious beliefs.

Variations in Practice

The two main groups in Islam are the *Sunni* and the *Shi'a,* where the Sunni constitute about 80 percent of Muslims worldwide, with the Shi'a (which is predominantly practiced in Iran and around the Persian Gulf) comprising 20 percent.

In Sunni Islam, there are four main schools of thought based on the studies of renowned scholars who lived in Islam's first three centuries (650-850 CE):

- Hanbali

- Hanafi

- Maliki

- Shafi'e.[36]

One's geographical customs most likely determine which of the four schools of jurisprudence a Sunni Muslim follows. It is not uncommon to find several different schools of jurisprudence practiced side-by-side without any hostility or conflict. While the differences between these four major Sunni schools tend to lie in details rather than principles, there is agreement in the majority of their content, with their imams or founders tending to support each other. When it comes to questions of Zakat, these differences might be as minor as the answers to: "Do you pay Zakat on the money you loaned to others, which is not in your possession?" Or, "how much should we give the poor out of Zakat funds?"

Within Shi'a Islam there are also many differing schools of jurisprudence, with the most common being Ja'afari. Additionally, significant differences in jurisprudence can be found between Sunni and Shi'a.

Modern Standardizing Practices

The trend in modern Islam is towards homogenization of practices and cooperation, and orthodoxy in religious beliefs aided by modern advances in communication and the ease of travel between nations. The effects of such are far reaching in the field of philanthropy. Since Muslims currently give to governmental institutions with immense caution, the outcome of blending the schools of jurisprudence may be bringing local or regional causes to the forefront for all Islamic nations, resulting in unprecedented cooperation and efforts. Additionally, philanthropic practices are becoming more uniform through worldwide media exposure of religious scholars whose learned opinions reach into the homes of millions of Muslims, legitimizing a form of mainstream Islam, while debunking local custom and culture.

PRACTICING ISLAMIC PHILANTHROPY

Historically, most charitable funds come through optional voluntary charity called Sadaqah, not the percentage-limited funds of Zakat. These are the funds that support society's infrastructure:

- Schools

- Orphanages

- Vocational training programs

- Roads

- Water and sewerage systems, etc.

Philanthropy in Islam encompasses a wide range of practices supported by religious doctrine. As such, Islam emphasizes two types of charitable work whose sources are Zakat and Sadaqah:

- Materialistic or tangible charity which deals with providing educational, medical and social services.

- Emotional charity which deals with providing spiritual or non-tangible support such as a smile, a touch on the head of an orphan, a kind word, etc.

Unbreakable Donor Restrictions

Many wealthy Muslims set aside a good portion of their income every year towards charity. The money entrusted to charity is a sacred trust. It is Islamically unlawful for funds that are designated or restricted for a particular cause—such as for an orphanage or meals for the hungry—to be used for something other than what they are specified for by the donor. Throughout Islamic history, there are stories of wealthy men who gave their entire fortune for the sake of Allah (God). Even in recent times, it is not unknown for professionals such as physicians and businessmen who make several hundreds of thousands of dollars a year to give as much as 50 percent of their income for Sadaqah. Most, in fact, give many times more than what they owe in Zakat. For example, although a person may only owe a minimum of $50 in Zakat, they may actually give several thousand dollars during the course of the year. At end of the year, some of these people have given so much in Sadaqah to help others they have left very little for themselves on which they owe Zakat.

Islam as a faith establishes charitable giving through the concepts of governmental institutions such as Zakat, and non-governmental institutions such as Waqf, as we will show in an upcoming chapter. In most Muslim countries, governments control this charitable money. However, because of corruption, mismanagement, and/or ineffectiveness, it carries little effect in resolving the very problems the funds are meant to alleviate. Since this is an unbreakable religious obligation, Muslims around the world will pay their due Zakat no matter what—either through formal organizations, or informally by giving directly to needy causes, and through friends and family members. Charities have structures and reporting requirements, and are held accountable in many institutional ways. This is not true for charity that is given through family and friends. Therefore, it is far better for Muslims and the US government that those funds should be given without fear to recognized American Muslim charities, and distributed according to US government guidelines and donors' restrictions.

Cementing a Community

Islamic philanthropy is a sort of cement within the Islamic culture, linking Muslims to each other and to their obligation to Allah. Their faith helps to build a community and an obligation toward each other, making each Muslim responsible for every other Muslim. This obligation is known as *takafful*, and is bolstered by the concept of Zakat.[37] Muslims are also required to help their non-Muslim community members. Islam clearly instructs that Sadaqah can be paid to a non-Muslim if they are needy.

The notion that charity is a religious ideal is depicted in Islamic-based governments where charity is a keystone for social justice. No Muslims enjoying life within this realm—rich or poor—are exempt from contributing to these efforts. Their leaders are expected to feed the hungry, treat the ill, and house the indigent, the widow and the orphan. Unfortunately, corruption and graft often disallow the fulfillment of this belief.

Anonymous Charity

Islam emphasizes giving while preserving the dignity of the recipient. Contrary to what is acceptable in other traditions, Islam teaches that giving privately is highly favorable over drawing attention to one's charitable acts. Sa'ad related in a Hadith that the Prophet said, "Allah loves the pious rich man, who (in spite of his piety and wealth) is obscure and unknown to fame" (reported by Sahih Muslim).[38]

Occasionally, it is necessary for one to give in the open, thereby encouraging others to part with a portion of their wealth for the sake of others. Regarding this, the Prophet also said, "Whoever starts a good practice will get its reward and the reward of all those who do it after him without that decreasing his reward in the least, and whoever starts a bad practice will get his sin and the sin of all those who do it after him without that decreasing their sin in the least".

The Charity of a Smile

While giving monetary charity is often the norm, a kind word or a smile are also considered to be acts of charity. A Hadith relates that "Your smile to your brother is a charitable act". The Arabic word *tasaddaqah* (to give charity) comes from the root *Sadaqah*, which means to speak the truth or to be sincere. Any good deed or charitable act is known as Sadaqah; ergo, a Muslim demonstrates their sincerity of faith by being generous. However, Sadaqah is more than just a charitable act. It is an act of worship where the doer seeks to become closer to Allah, and the act of Sadaqah is received directly by Allah. This belief is upheld in the Qur'an, "Did you not know that Allah is the One who accepts repentance from His slaves and takes their charities, and that Allah is the ever-Forgiving, the Merciful" (At-Tawba: 104).

Muslims are enjoined to do good things that contribute to the wellbeing of society, while prohibiting evil acts. The simple act of helping another person is the carrying out of this concept. Islam teaches that an act of charity does not necessarily have to come with a dollar sign before it. Therefore, Sadaqah takes on many forms that should be present in a Muslim's daily life. This Sadaqah strengthens their piety, keeping Allah forever on their minds and in their deeds while spreading goodwill and charity throughout their community. In the early days of Islam, the Prophet Mohammed told his followers that "There is a (compulsory) Sadaqah (charity) to be given for every joint of the human body (as a sign of gratitude to Allah) everyday the sun rises. To judge justly between two persons is regarded as Sadaqah. And to help a man mount his animal or by lifting his luggage on to it, is also regarded as Sadaqah. And (saying) a good word is also Sadaqah. And every step taken on one's way to offer the compulsory prayer (in the mosque) is also Sadaqah. And to remove a harmful thing from the road is also Sadaqah" (Reported by Sahih Al-Bukhari and Muslim).[39]

It might seem odd that even those who have no money are obligated to give into charity. For Muslims, there is great reward in doing good deeds accomplished for the sake of Allah, with no expectations of receiving anything in return. A Hadith reports that the Prophet said, "Giving charity is obligatory upon each Muslim". Notice that he did not say, "except for the poor". Additionally, the Prophet was asked, "What do you say of him who does not find (the means) to do so?" He answered, "Let him do manual work, thus doing benefit to himself and give charity". Then he was asked, "What about one who does not have (the means) to do so?" He said, "Then let him assist the needy, the aggrieved". That is the concept of volunteerism to help those in need. Again, he was asked, "What do you say of one who cannot even do this?" He said, "Then he should enjoin what is reputable or what is good". He was then asked, "What if he cannot do that?" The Prophet answered, "He should then abstain from evil, for verily that is charity on his behalf".

The previous passages outline that even simple deeds and righteous actions are acts of Sadaqah. The Messenger of Allah said, "Sadaqah is prescribed for each descendant of Adam every day the sun rises". When asked from what we give Sadaqah every day, the Prophet answered, "The doors of goodness are many...(praising Allah)...enjoining good, forbidding evil, removing harm from the road, listening to the deaf, leading the blind, guiding one to the object of his need, hurrying with the strength of one's legs to one in sorrow who is asking for help, and supporting the feeble with the strength of one's arms—all of these are Sadaqah prescribed for you" (Sahih Ibn Hibban).[40]

Another Hadith is reported in Bukhari, "Your smile for your brother is Sadaqah. Your removal of stones, thorns, or bones from the paths of people is Sadaqah. Your guidance of a person who is lost is Sadaqah". Additionally, Bukhari relates that Prophet Mohammed said: "A Muslim does not plant or sow anything from which a person, an animal, or anything eats but it is considered as Sadaqah from him".

Giving by Proxy

For many people, seeking help from charitable organizations or those who are wealthy is a source of embarrassment. Their pride will not allow them to let others know of their suffering. By the same token, very few people have extra money just lying around to give to others. Therefore, one aspect of Sadaqah is the Muslim's obligation to help those in distress by identifying their need to those who can give necessary funds. When a generous person donates $500 to a needy family because of the efforts of another, then the person who encouraged that donor to give, or who pointed out the poor person's need, receives the same level of reward as the one who gave the money. By bridging the gap between the rich and the poor, the needy received the help they required. Being a "go-between" is a type of charitable giving by proxy, and by doing so also gains this person the pleasure of Allah.

VI.   Volume and Nature of Muslim Giving

Although there are no known hard statistics, worldwide Islamic philanthropy is estimated to be between $250 billion to $1 trillion annually.[41] As for Muslims in the US, generally, if each of America's estimated six million Muslims were to donate at the rate of the average American, their total giving would exceed $5.3 billion annually. The 2003 overall charitable giving by individuals in the US was approximately $240 billion,[42] with the average donation being in the range of $200 each in cash and non-cash donations. In this section, we have made an effort to estimate the volume of giving by Muslims in the US. We arrived at our statistical data by adding up the charitable revenues received by the majority of Muslim charitable organizations in the US. Because we may have inadvertently omitted some of the smaller organizations, we must emphasize that our data is an estimate; yet, these numbers represent figures close to true giving volume.

WHO GIVES AND HOW MUCH?

Because of our in depth observations and long history in this field, we believe that the percentage of Muslims who give to Muslim nonprofit organizations in the US, whether mosques or humanitarian charities, may be less than ten percent. The rest either give to charity informally through personal contacts with the needy—which may include relatives here in the US or overseas—or to non-Muslim organizations. While some may not give at all.

Muslim charitable giving can be categorized into two columns:

- Formal institutionalized charity

- Informal personal charity.

The second can be highly difficult to estimate, if not impossible, because these acts of charity do not go through recognized organizations. A big part of this type of giving is done on an anonymous basis because many donors do not want anyone except Allah to know of their donations. This is best accomplished by giving directly to beneficiaries without intermediaries. The question of why Muslims do this has many reasons.

The first may be a historic mistrust of governments in the original Islamic countries because of lack of democratic rule, corruption and ineffectiveness.

The second may be that those who travel overseas see first-hand who needs their help the most. Thus, they may give the aid to their nearest relatives or to those in their own communities.

Thirdly, as previously mentioned, as faithful Muslims, they may simply wish to remain anonymous. Additionally, a large percentage of those who do not give to Muslim organizations donate within American mainstream organizations. In fact, our analysis clearly showed that charitable donations by Muslims to American non-Islamic organizations far exceed their giving to Islamic organizations.[43] Out of an estimated $5.3 billion given by Muslims in the US, only $478 million went to Muslim organizations. While about six percent of this, or $30 million, was given to causes outside the US.

Seasonal Giving

There are definite seasons for Muslim philanthropy. Most give mainly during the holy month of Ramadan. While many others will give for one or both of the annual holidays: Zakat al-Fitr (or Fitrah) on 'Eid al-Fitr, and Udhiya (or Qurbani) on 'Eid ul-Adha. For humanitarian charities, we have seen that between 40 to 50 percent of annual donations come during the season of Ramadan. Although the monetary Zakat is a minimum of two and one-half percent of one's wealth, those who do give exceed this many fold.

No Typical Giving

We have seen Muslim communities vary greatly in their philanthropic behaviors. Take, for example, two mosques in the same city. Both have more than 5,000 financially capable associated members, and who show a high level of religious devotional behavior in areas such as prayers, fasting and abstaining from forbidden acts. A public event attended by 600 people at one of these mosques raised over $350,000 within an hour. Whereas, another event at the other mosque which hosted the same number of people saw less than $55,000 raised. The same outcome ratio was seen on more than one occasion, and for different causes.

There are several explanations for such dissimilar donation habits. One major factor is whether their community's religious leadership emphasizes and encourages charitable giving. One must also take into consideration whether donors are accustomed to giving charity through institutional mediums such as charitable organizations or mosques, or directly to poor individuals and needy causes. While lesser rationale points to cultural and ethnic customs, level of trust, and fear of giving post-9/11.

WHO RECEIVES WHAT?

The majority of donations by Muslims are contributed for causes similar to those of the average American: educational, medical and social institutions, as well as Islamic community projects such as mosques, and youth and cultural centers. Additionally, a small percentage of these donated funds are earmarked for international relief causes. Muslim donors who give to formal US organizations tend to give to four types of nonprofits:

Local Mosques and Islamic Centers

These centers are now playing larger roles in the lives of Muslims in the US. Some important information to note about these nonprofit recipients according to a comprehensive and thorough study by the Council of American Islamic Relations (CAIR):[44]

- CAIR's study included 1,209 mosques established and operating in the US as of the year 2000. The study pointed out that this figure is not the total number of American mosques; CAIR also stated that many smaller or new mosques were missed in the survey.

- Number of mosques grew from 1994 to 2000 by 25 percent.

- Two million American Muslims are associated with these mosques. On average, 1,625 Muslims have a religious association in some way with each mosque, attending at least twice per year for 'Eid Prayers.

- The average number of regular mosque participants is 340 Muslims. Multiplying this by 1,209 mosques yields an estimated total of 411,060 Muslims regularly participating in mosque activities.

- Thirty percent of all mosques were established in the 1990s.

- At the average mosque, 33 percent of members are of South Asian origin (India, Pakistan, Bangladesh, etc.), 30 percent are African-American, and 25 percent are from the Arabic-speaking world.

- Almost 70 percent of mosques provide some type of assistance for the needy.

- Ninety-two percent of mosques provide cash assistance to needy directly or with the cooperation of another organization.

- Seventy-one percent of mosques have a weekend school, while more than 20 percent of mosques have a full-time school.

- Activities and programs offered by mosques other than worship services are Islamic study classes, sisters' programs, youth programs, Arabic classes, marriage counseling, interfaith dialogues, political awareness and voter registration, social services, financial assistance to needy individuals and families, food pantry, clothing/thrift assistance, and substance abuse programs.

- Mosques typically do not have financial problems; 49 percent of mosques are in excellent to good financial health, and only three percent are in serious financial difficulty.

CAIR's study did not consider the total income per mosque—simply stating that about a quarter of these mosques have annual revenue exceeding $100,000. However, when we estimated the total revenue of American mosques, we found those revenues to be close to $218 million annually.[45]

American Muslim Charities

These groups are known by many as relief organizations or international humanitarian organizations. Some of the characteristics of these charities are:

• Most of these organizations were founded in early 1990s, while very few were founded in the late 1980s.

• They are few in number. Prior to US government closings stemming from the fallout of the September 11, 2001 terrorist attacks, fewer than ten were active national organizations that were not limited to minor or temporary city-level causes. Currently, even fewer are in operation.

• Some of these charities have US headquarters and branches abroad to oversee their operations. In most cases, overseas staff greatly exceeds US staff, ranging from office administrators, relief workers, doctors and medical clerks at clinics and hospitals, as well as teachers at schools, etc.

• These organizations collect charitable donations for an array of causes such as emergency relief, education, healthcare and developmental programs. As well as fulfilling the Muslim religious obligations of Zakat, Udhiya and Fitrah. These play the same role as those of the Christian/Catholic organizations such as the Red Cross, Salvation Army and Catholic Relief, and Jewish organizations like Jewish Relief Agency (JRA) and the Jewish Coalition for Disaster Relief.

• The average Muslim in America views these Islamic charities as highly respected, professional, and experienced institutions. A number of those charities have been closed, such as the Holy Land Foundation (HLF), Global Relief Foundation (GRF), Benevolence International Foundation (BIF), Islamic American Relief Agency (IARA), and Help the Needy, as well as a number of smaller organizations. Others are still in operation, such as Life for Relief and Development, Islamic Relief-USA, and ICNA Relief. This claim of high regard is bolstered by the two million to nine million dollars entrusted to each of these charities annually. The federal crackdown on Islamic charities after September 11, 2001 began with the largest of these organizations. Although there have been a few charities founded post-September 11th, such as KindHearts, KinderUSA and the Zakat Foundation, the federal investigation caused KinderUSA to voluntarily temporarily close their doors because intensive government scrutiny paralyzed their operations. Also, KindHearts was later shut down as well in early 2006.

• Some of these charities have been closed and their data is no longer available; however, our research finds that the total cash revenue of these humanitarian organizations before 2001 was approximately $40 million. After the federal closures began, figures for 2002 showed only $17 million—a staggering loss of $23 million in one year! Moreover, in 2005 the funds collected by these Muslim charities are not expected to reach $30 million, or 75 percent of what it was prior to September 11, 2001. This jolting fall is attributed to two primary factors: the disappearance of most of the first-generation charities, and donor fears of giving to Islamic charities, especially after the heavy-handed approach taken by the government in dealing with these charities and their donors. This stunning drop in philanthropic donations to Islamic charities in the US does not mean that Muslims are giving less into charity. Rather, it means they are giving more into informal charity; that is through friends and families, and to informal entities—a troublesome fact for the charities and government.

• The primary purpose of these charities is to meet the religious needs of the Muslim community in the US. By collecting Zakat and Sadaqah from capable Muslims, they then disburse these funds worldwide to the needy according to the wishes of their donors. Their main program areas are providing humanitarian relief or aid, and developmental programs to communities in distress regardless of their creed and race.

While the majority of American Muslim communities are still young, and have maintained strong ties to their roots for social and religious reasons, only a small portion of these donations go for overseas programs and services. Our research indicates that even at their peak prior to September 11, 2001, the total figure of combined funds from these Muslim charities directed to programs abroad never exceeded $23 million annually! This figure is insignificant when compared to other religious and ethnic minorities in the US who raise billions in support of their brethren outside America.

Just how lopsided this comparison is becomes clear when one considers the level of funds and in-kind donations given each year by Jews to the State of Israel or other Jewish international causes, thought to exceed two billion dollars annually. In 2004, out of the $855 million raised solely by the United Jewish Communities, 31 percent, or $266.4 million, went to Israel and Jewish needs overseas.[46] It therefore seems quite paradoxical that all the fuss surrounding American Muslim charities funding international causes overseas is centered around petty sums collectively spent on an array of diverse programs abroad, as if international giving is simply a Muslim issue. What is more contrary is the logic used to justify the millions of tax dollars the federal government, especially the FBI and Treasury, have expended to investigate where these Islamic nonprofits applied the funding. Although the total bill for investigating these charities is not public knowledge, it is almost a certainty that the costs far outweigh the $23 million taken in by the charities, all without a single allegation coming to fruition in open court.

• The most important lesson learned by those charities that weathered the post-September 11 crackdowns is unmistakable: by allocating more resources to domestic programs, the average American will bear witness to the dedication of Muslims to the giving of charity. Proving beyond a doubt that Islam and Muslims are a part of the American system, not foreign entities as has been implied. By extending more of a giving hand here at home, these Muslim charitable organizations are helping to mainstream Islam in America by leaps and bounds. As witnessed in September 2005 during Hurricane Katrina, when a coalition of Islamic charities formed an emergency task force, collectively pledging $10 million in contributions and other aid to help the victims of this natural disaster that affected millions along America's Gulf coast.

• These charities depend on the donors' compassion and restrictions of their contributions, as they are moved by events such as the exodus of Bosnians, and the devastation caused by the Tsunami. What they see on television directly effects the causes they donate to. Therefore, the charitable organizations are religiously and legally obliged to allocate their contributions accordingly.

• Traditionally, these organizations have been mainly reactive to diverse international emergency situations, whether man-made disasters such as wars resulting in refugees and displacement of people, or natural disasters such as earthquakes and floods. Although it is the desire of most of these organizations to focus on developmental programs, the enormous needs of Muslim communities overseas during the past two decades have prevented these organizations from focusing on developmental programs such as education and vocational training. Rather, the bulk of assistance has gone into immediate relief: providing food aid, shelter, medical care, and orphans and needy families sponsorships. This is also due in part to the wishes of Muslim donors who readily give for emergency relief causes based upon feelings of compassion towards the victims.

• Examples of who the recipients of this aid are, and the areas these funds go to constitutes quite an extensive list:

  - Afghani refugees in Pakistan and Afghanistan who received the aid mainly in the late 1980s and early 1990s. Under the Soviet invasion, they suffered enormous poverty and cruelty.

- In the early 1990s, ethnic cleansing produced catastrophic humanitarian crises for Bosnian refugees, and subsequently for the Kosova refugees in the Balkans.

- Throughout the last few decades, Palestinian refugees in the Middle East have suffered tremendous cruelty and hardship due to the ongoing conflict.

- After their country's invasion of Kuwait in the early 1990s, ordinary Iraqis suffered terribly under the resulting UN economic sanctions, and a ruthless dictator.

- Those suffering from the war in Darfur, Sudan have seen more than their share of tragedy.

- Natural disasters such as frequent floods in Bangladesh, droughts in the Horn of Africa, earthquakes in Iran, Algiers, Turkey, and Pakistan, Tsunami on the coast of Indonesia, and Hurricane Katrina hitting the US.

While considering the donations of two major Muslim charities (without considering their in-kind donations), we found that their cash income from 2002 to 2004 amounted to $12,214,000 from a total of 56,165 donations, with the average donation being $217. However, these donations came from a base of only 23,608 donors. Throughout this period, more than 8,900 donors made multiple contributions. The annual gift per donor varies greatly, from one-time bequests of only $10, to repeat donors who gave multiple times per year, with total individual annual donations reaching over $20,000. Yet, we found that a typical repeat donor (someone who gave more than one time per year) gave on average a total of $483 in 2004; whereas, a typical one-time donor gave an average of $232 that year. These charities rely on a wide base of donors. Furthermore, they are dedicated, with repeat rates of about 38 percent. As previously mentioned, these same donors give to other organizations and mosques as well. As of September 2, 2005, the Salvation Army garnered $24.5 million in donations for Hurricane Katrina relief, receiving $1.7 million through its toll-free telephone line. The average size of those gifts was $205.[47]

Other Muslim Nonprofits

This group is composed of organizations other than mosques, Islamic centers and charities. Some of these organizations work in the US in specialized areas such as:

- National and regional associations

- Civil rights and advocacy organizations

- Legal defense funds

- Political organizations

- Educational institutions

- Media organizations, etc.

Because of overwhelming need, donations to these organizations have increased post-September 11. Many of these organizations employ full-time staff, requiring large annual budgets, many of them in the millions of dollars. Examples of some of these organizations are:

- Islamic Society of North America (ISNA)

- Islamic Circle of North America (ICNA)

- Council on American-Islamic Relations (CAIR) which has 30 chapters in different states

- Muslim American Society (MAS)

- Legal Defense Fund

- Islamicity.com

- Bridges TV.

Among dozens of others throughout the country, these national organizations grew quickly within the last several years, learning to rely on national revenue sources, while providing services and collecting funds throughout the states.

The number of nonprofit organizations working on the local level (such as the hundreds of part- and full-time Islamic schools) has grown tremendously as well. Muslim Student Associations (MSA) currently have 150 registered chapters located on campuses of universities and colleges throughout the US and Canada. The numbers of educational institutions such as Muslim universities, research facilities and think tanks are also swelling. Service organizations geared to providing various programs on the local level such as youth centers, cultural and ethnic Muslim societies, community centers, immigration and refugee service centers are increasing as well. Additionally, there are many new Islamic councils and associations such as the Fiqh Council of North America, the Council of Islamic Organizations of Greater Chicago Area, and other similar organizations in most major cities. Groups such as the Association of Muslim Scientists and Engineers, and other organizations for different types of professions have also been flourishing. While these organizations are either totally or partially funded by charitable contributions, alternative sources of funding may be realized through tuition, membership or service fees. Because of their quantity, breadth of causes, and because of their localization, the exact volume of giving towards these organizations is not known. However, our conservative estimates put their total charitable contributions throughout the US at about $230 million annually.[48]

American Mainstream Nonprofits

This category encompasses the fourth type of Muslim philanthropic giving. Basically, they are the organizations that an average American donates to, such as libraries, educational institutions, healthcare facilities (hospitals and clinics), social service agencies, secular and non-religious charities, etc. According to the previously mentioned CAIR study, two-thirds of Muslims in the US never associate themselves with mosques. The study also shows that only about 7% (411,000 out of 6,000,000) regularly attend mosques. From these statistics, it would be fair to say that 93% of Muslims are not religious, and therefore their charitable giving is directed toward secular, non-religious institutions.

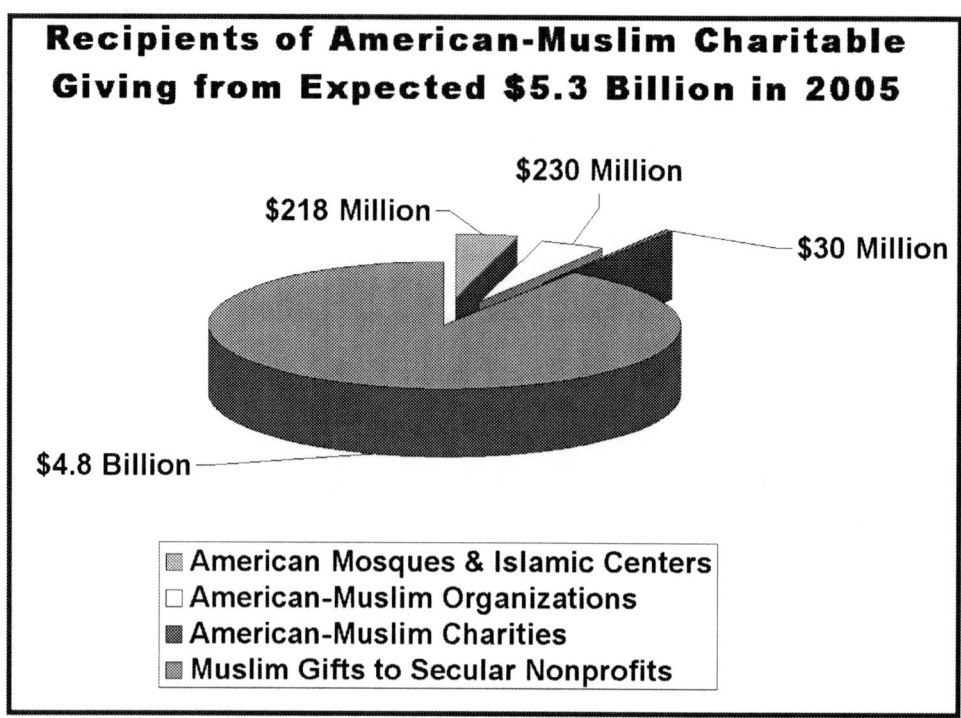

Recipients of American-Muslim Charitable Giving from Expected $5.3 Billion in 2005

$230 Million

$218 Million

$30 Million

$4.8 Billion

- American Mosques & Islamic Centers
- American-Muslim Organizations
- American-Muslim Charities
- Muslim Gifts to Secular Nonprofits

Figure 1-C

Although we cannot begin to determine the level of giving by this category of Muslims, what can be concluded is that unlike devout Muslims, they give not out of religious obligation, but rather out of civic responsibility and compassion. These secular Muslims probably give generously as well because charity is so deeply embedded in their Islamic culture. We have seen many examples of wealthy Muslim individuals contributing large sums of money to various American causes that have no Islamic connection. We are also certain that donations from secular Muslims to American mainstream and non-religious nonprofits far outpace those of observant Muslims to Islamic charities. Thereby constituting the majority of the estimated $5.3 billion to be given in 2005 by Muslims in America. Ergo, as our research indicates, American Muslims will likely donate $478 million to Islamic nonprofit causes in 2005, leaving $4.8 billion for nonprofits without a religious cause.

VII. Religious Giving: What's on the Collection Plate?

Many religions tax their brethren just as the government does. However, not all religions have tithing requirements. The following chart outlines which faiths require a certain amount, and what followers can gain spiritually from their donations.[49]

Religion	Obligation	Spiritual Component
Baha'i	The Baha'i are asked to make voluntary contributions, often as much as 19 percent of their income to Baha'i causes and the Baha'i world center. Contributions are considered a sacred obligation, in order to expand Baha'i spiritual activities.	Several Baha'i writings explain the importance of both generosity and the Baha'i fund.
Buddhist	Buddhism emphasizes the giving of alms or "dana", to Buddhist monks, nuns, and other teachers of the dharma.	Dana is an act of generosity and reverence. Almsgiving is considered a way of cultivating selflessness, compassion, and non-attachment. Buddhist texts encourage giving, but they do not stipulate exact amounts.
Catholic	Most Catholic churches suggest that parishioners contribute ten percent of their income to charity, with five percent going to the local church and five percent going to the parishioner's charity of choice.	The concept of sacrificial giving is very important in Catholicism, both to help those less fortunate and to show gratitude for God's gifts. Catholics follow the Bible's words about tithing and giving. "Active love for the poor" is also emphasized in the catechism's treatment of the commandment "You shall not steal."
Eastern Orthodox	The Orthodox Church emphasizes voluntary stewardship instead of a specific tithe amount. The church sees stewardship as a way for members of the church to participate fully in the church.	The Orthodox concept of stewardship comes from both the Old and New Testaments.
Hindu	There is no official Hindu tithe, but Hindus do pay for pujas and often donate to their temples. Donation is considered a religious duty in Hinduism. Hindus also donate "daan", alms, to holy men and the poor.	Though there is no tithe, giving is still an element in many Hindu sacred texts.

Islam	"Zakat", one of the five pillars of Islam. Depending upon the type, Muslims pay from 2.5% to 20% of certain individual wealth in charity. Zakat means "purification" and "growth." The giving of this obligatory tithing to religious authorities is considered a monetary act of worship. Muslims are also strongly encouraged to pay a voluntary charity of unlimited amounts, or "Sadaqah". In practice, Muslims give far more Sadaqah than the minimum Zakat.	Giving Zakat is one of the five pillars of Islam and is said to purify wealth, as well as enhance it.
Judaism	Jews are obligated to give ten percent of their income to charity. Although Jews are encouraged to give more, the rabbis limited Tzedakah to no more than a fifth of one's income so that no one would impoverish him- or herself by giving to others in need. Synagogues are supported by voluntary donations for membership dues, which are separate from charitable obligations.	Few people today follow the tithing laws outlined in the Torah. Instead, many Jews use Maimonides' Ladder of Charity[50] as a tool for understanding the modern Jewish concept of Tzedakah. Giving "Tzedakah" is considered a sign of righteousness.
Mormon	Mormons are required to tithe ten percent of their income to the church. The tithe is used to pay for the operating costs of the church, as well as the funding of new temples, missionary programs, and more. Mormons consider tithes to be sacred money, and tithing is seen as a duty and a test of faithfulness.	Mormon laws of tithing are outlined in the Latter-day Saints' Doctrine & Covenants.
Protestant	Many Protestant churches follow the biblical exhortation to give ten percent of one's income back to God. The tithe goes to wherever a person receives his or her spiritual teaching.	Many Protestant churches emphasize stewardship as the path to receiving God's blessings and both spiritual and material abundance. Malachi 3:8-10 and many other Bible verses.

VIII. Conclusion

"We are our brother's keeper." From the beginning of time, this term rings true for all who give into charity, those who administer it, and those who receive it.

Religion, faith and values are remarkable devices. Not only do they give humanity justification for its system of laws and morals, but they also provide a rope for mankind to grasp onto in times of despair and hope. The majority of religious and/or spiritual teachings worldwide recognize that every human is a member of the family of mankind, and therefore have an undeniable responsibility for all others, our environment and the creatures that share this earth.

The important thing to grasp is that despite sometimes gaping differences dividing the world's faiths, their philanthropic aims share common ground. Their mutual purpose is to provide for the poor, bring ease to those who suffer, heal the ill, give compassion to those in need, and enrich the lives of those who want.

Endnotes

[1] Social Welfare and Individual Responsibility (For and Against), David Schmidtz. Cambridge University Press, 1998.

[2] U.S. Social Security Administration, http://www.pueblo.gsa.gov/cic_text/fed_prog/ssundben/t_ssundben.html.

[3] Ibid.

[4] Ibid.

[5] Daynes, Byron W., and others, eds., New Deal and Public Policy. St. Martin's, 1998.

[6] In 1996, Congress created legislation to revise the welfare system. Clinton vetoed two bills, claiming they included changes that would harm the poor too much. But he approved a third welfare bill in August 1996, upsetting many in his own party. The bill placed limits on how long people can receive welfare benefits, and it shifted much responsibility for administering welfare from the federal government to the states.

[7] Foundation for Economic Education, Inc., June 1978, Vol. 28, No. 6.

[8] Lester M. Salamon, The State of Nonprofit America. Washington, DC: The Brookings Institution Press, 2002.

[9] US Census Bureau Report issued August 2004 (<http://www.census.gov/hhes/www/income.html).

[10] Danziger, Sheldon H., and others, eds. Confronting Poverty.

[11] Nonprofits and Development Center for Civil Society Studies Institute for Policy Studies, The Johns Hopkins University, Baltimore, MD. "Issues of Democracy", USIA Electronic Journal, Vol. 3, No. 1, January 1998.

[12] The Foundation Center, 2002. The Foundation Center's database contains the most complete record of institutional funding related to September 11, 2001 and its aftermath.

[13] The America Gives Survey, published January 18. 2002 conducted by IU Center on Philanthropy at Indiana University in Indianapolis, the Association of Fundraising Professionals (AFP) and the AFP Foundation for Philanthropy.

[14] Leslie Lenkowsky, Professor of Public Affairs and Philanthropic Studies, Indiana University, "The Politics of Doing Good: Philanthropic Leadership for the 21ST Century", 2003-04 Distinguished Speakers Series, February 19, 2004.

[15] "Meeting the Challenge of Effectively Administering Volunteers and Donations in an Emergency: A White Paper", Emergency Asset Management, April 2002.

[16] Alexis de Tocqueville, Democracy in America, 1835/1840.

[17] The New Nonprofit Almanac and Desk Reference, published in 2002 by the Urban Institute's Center on Nonprofits and Philanthropy, Washington, DC.

[18] US Bureau of Labor Statistics, Washington, DC.

[19] The Philanthropy Magazine, Philanthropy Roundtable, May/June 2001.

[20] Chronicle of Philanthropy, Giving Slowly Rebounds, October 28, 2004, http://philanthropy.com/free/articles/v17/i02/02002601.htm.

[21] Giving USA 2005, The Annual Report on Philanthropy, published by the AAFRC Trust for Philanthropy.

[22] Rabbi Jeff Portman, Agudas Achim Congregation, Iowa City, IA.

[23] Tracey R. Rich, Tzedakah: Charity (Judaism 101).

[24] U.S. Center for World Mission, Global Missions Statistics, 2001.

[25] Charles Schusterman, How Donor Directed Giving Impacts Jewish Philanthropy, speech delivered at the meeting of the Charles and Lynn Schusterman Foundation Advisory Council, Cleveland, Ohio, October 27, 1998.

[26] AAFRC Trust for Philanthropy (2002), p 102.

[27] David B. Barrett and Todd M. Johnson, World Christian Trends AD 30-AD 2000: Interpreting the Annual Christian Megacensus (Pasadena, Calif.: William Carey Library, 2001), p 655.

[28] Misc. Facts and Interesting Information (Houston: ServLife International, n.d.).

[29] George Barna, Americans Were More Generous in 2001 Than in 2000, news release by Barna Research Group, April 9, 2002.

[30] "CAIR Says Exploitation of Tsunami Aid Hurts America's Image", Washington, DC, January 15, 2005.

[31] David Smith, "Forget Me Not", 2001-2003, http://www.surfinthespirit.com.

[32] John Ronsvalle and Sylvia Ronsvalle, An Exploration of Roman Catholic Giving Patterns, The State of Church Giving through 1993. Champaign, Ill.: Empty Tomb, 1995.

[33] Cathedral of Mary Our Queen, Archdiocese of Baltimore, MD 2001. http://cathedralofmary. org/history/papalvisits/100895.htm.

[34] Keith Gottschalk, "Catholics urge government help for poor", Faith and Values, The Gazette, Cedar Rapids, Iowa, April 9, 2005.

[35] US Center For World Mission 1997 Report. Muslim Population is increasing at the rate of 2% annually around the world, for a calculated population in 2003 of 1.70403 billion.

[36] USAID: The Center for Strategic and International Studies, "The Idea of Philanthropy in Muslim Contexts", Jon B. Alterman and Shireen Hunter, Washington, DC. February 2004, p 4.

[37] Definition of Takafful according to the Center for Strategic and International Studies, 1800 K Street, NW, Washington DC, 2005. http://www.csis.org/Mideast/040222_philanthropy.pdf.

[38] The University of Southern California MSA Compendium of Muslim Texts (http://www.usc.edu/ dept/MSA/fundamentals/hadithsunnah/) defines Islamic Hadith and Sunnah as follows: In Islam, the Arabic word Sunnah has come to denote the way Prophet Muhammad, the Messenger of Allah, lived his life. The Sunnah is the second source of Islamic jurisprudence, the first being the Qur'an. Both sources are indispensable; one cannot practice Islam without consulting both of them. The Arabic word Hadith (pl. ahadith) is very similar to Sunnah, but not identical. A Hadith is a narration about the life of the Prophet or what he approved—as opposed to his life itself, which is the Sunnah as already mentioned.

In M. M. Azami's Studies in Hadith Methodology and Literature, the following precise definition of a hadith is given.

According to Muhaddithiin (scholars of Hadith -ed.) it stands for 'what was transmitted on the authority of the Prophet, his deeds, sayings, tacit approval, or description of his sifaat (features) meaning his physical appearance. However, physical appearance of the Prophet is not included in the definition used by the jurists.'

Thus, Hadith literature means the literature which consists of the narrations of the life of the Prophet and the things approved by him. However, the term was used sometimes in much broader sense to cover the narrations about the Companions (of the Prophet -ed.) and Successors (to the Companions -ed.) as well.

[39] Ibid.

[40] Ibid.

[41] The Center for Strategic and International Studies, "The Idea of Philanthropy in Muslim Contexts", Jon B. Alterman and Shireen Hunter, Washington, DC, February 22, 2004.

[42] "U.S. Charitable Giving Surpassed $240 Billion in 2003", Association for Fundraising Professionals, June 21, 2004.

[43] Taken from a Zogby Poll sponsored by Project MAPS: Muslims in the American Public Square, Washington, DC, December 2001.

[44] The Mosque in America: A National Portrait, http://www.cair-net.org/mosquereport/index.html

[45] CAIR's study found that one-fourth of US mosques have annual revenues exceeding $100,000. Of these, most are considered to be major mosques in larger cities, each having employees and basic community services. Some of the largest mosques are known to have incomes greater than $1 million annually. We arrived at our estimate by averaging the income for the top one-fourth of mosques at $275,000 annually, which leads to a combined income for these mosques of $124 million. As for the remainder of these mosques whose annual income is known to be less than $100,000, we estimated the average per mosque income to be about $70,000 annually, covering an imam's salary and the costs of basic utilities. This leads us to a combined income of $94 million; therefore, the estimated total income of all US mosques is $218 million annually.

[46] The findings of the study on the formation of the United Jewish Communities, the largest 20th century merger within the not for profit sector, were released in 2005 by Gerald Bubis, Founding Director of the School of Jewish Communal Service at Hebrew Union College-Jewish Institute of Religion (HUC-JIR) in Los Angeles, and Steven Windmueller, the School's current director, who conducted the study. The study is entitled "Predictability to Chaos? How Jewish Leaders Reinvented Their National Communal System", and is published by Center for Jewish Communities Studies at Baltimore Hebrew University, 5800 Park Heights Avenue, Baltimore, MD.

[47] The Chronicle of Philanthropy, September 2, 2005. http://www.philanthropy.com/free/update/2005/09/2005090201.htm.

[48] This data was extrapolated by calculating the revenue of major national American Muslim organizations (especially the national umbrella associations, major councils, civil rights and advocacy groups, and political organizations), for a total income about $88 million. We also estimated that 25 percent of revenue for all schools comes from charitable donations, and not from tuition. Since there are about 600 American Islamic schools with an estimated average annual income of $435,000, we calculated charitable giving to these schools to be approximately $63 million. A conservative estimate for other localized service organizations (youth centers, ethnic Muslim societies, cultural organizations, etc.), is thought to be about half the number of mosques, for a total of about 900. Our research estimates that each of these has an average annual income of approximately $87,000, for a total estimated charitable income of $79 million yearly. Therefore, we determined that this type of charitable organization receives approximately $230 million annually.

[49] Philanthropy Magazine, "Giving in Different Denominations", Julia Duin. The Philanthropy Roundtable 2001.

[50] Tracey R. Rich, Tzedakah: Charity (Judaism 101).

Chapter

2.

Eliminating

Extreme Poverty:

The Islamic Perspective

Through the ages, the conundrum facing nearly every established religion and the world's deepest thinkers has been how to resolve the plight of poverty, and ease the pain of those who suffer from the condition. Hence, the concept of charity became the primary means developed by society to deal with this all-encompassing problem. Although humanity has depended on charity since its inception so many thousands of years ago, it has not proven to be the sole solution to the dilemma of poverty. To that end, we have developed this study of the how to deal with poverty by specifying what else might be needed to help society reduce poverty to its barest minimum, according to the Islamic faith.

The main point of this chapter is to examine Islam's longstanding history of ideas and practices in dealing with poverty. It is also hoped that a paragon can be established showing that philanthropy is indigenous to Muslim culture, and that Islam is a faith highly concerned with the plight of the poor, offering a plausible solution to poverty. Here, we also point out that using the term "Islamic" is only intended to direct the reader to Muslim religious thought or custom, since defining something as being "Islamic" is an act that can very well be subject to controversy.

I. Poverty: An Ancient and Dangerous Phenomenon

Poverty is not a new problem to the human race. Since the beginning of time, mankind has sought out wealth and its benefits. Sadly, in addition to the concept of affluence has sprung its byproduct: poverty.

According to Islamic faith, wealth is a trust that Allah (The Almighty) has bestowed upon certain people. With that trust, He expects these people who are entrusted with this wealth ("wealthy people") to give a certain portion to the poor. Allah described this in the Qur'an as "cleansing" the wealth. From this wealth, He has also given the poor a measure of rights over the wealth of the prosperous. The Prophet Mohammed's saying (Hadith) states that poverty affects both individuals and society at the same time. In addressing staggering levels of poverty the world over, Muslims can draw from well-defined systems set forth by Islam to collect and give charitable donations. These systems, which are to be given and spent for specific recipients, are controlled through accountability standards that include, and in many cases, exceed current standards.

There is no doubt that poverty is a dangerous disease affecting religious belief. This is particularly true of extreme poverty within a wealthy society—especially if the poor are the ones who work hard, while the rich are idle.

Poverty Affects Human Behavior

As noted above, poverty is not only a danger to religion, but it also affects one's behavior. Surely, a person's behavior would change if they had nothing to eat, and cannot afford as many possessions as his neighbor who lives a comfortable life. This brings to truth the saying that "the stomach's voice is louder than the brain's". Worst of all, a life of extreme poverty may cause the less fortunate person to question why they should keep good behavior if they are only rewarded with poverty, allowing doubt to creep into their religious values.

Poverty is also a common denominator to hunger, crime, deceit, and poor health and education. This concept was evident more than 1,400 years ago when the Prophet Mohammed described how extreme poverty or debts could lead people into dishonesty: "When a man falls under so many debts, he would lie by making a promise he does not fulfill" (as reported by Al-Bukhari).

Poverty Affects Human Thinking

A person's behavior is not the only thing affected by poverty. It might also affect the way he or she thinks. After all, how can a poor person think straight or positively if they are suffering from the pangs of extreme hunger? Imam Abu Haneefa once said, "Don't consult those who have no food in their houses". Being mentally pre-occupied with their growling belly or how they will obtain food is not a good foundation for a person to give wise advice, and would surely affect their opinions and actions.

Poverty's Danger to Families

Poor, unmarried men may find themselves preoccupied with how they might be financially able to support another person; therefore, they would find it harder marry and start a family. Adult males and females who cannot afford to marry may very likely stray into areas of forbidden activity, which further drag downs the society as a whole by contributing to crime rates, out of wedlock births, rape, etc. Additionally, economic pressures are a major factor in marital discourse, possibly leading to abuse and domestic violence. Pressures exerted by poverty are definitely a major component in divorce—brutally shattering families.

Poverty sometimes has an enormous impact on individuals within the family, wringing out the last drop of love between members. One particular Qur'anic verse stands out when addressing the specific issue of poverty and its affects on parents towards their children. Before Islam, female children were less valued than were male children. A child was viewed as a burden in terms of contributing to the family's welfare—females are not as physically strong as males, and lack the ability of equality in labor and raising the family's standard of living. In the early times before Islam, the overwhelming fear of additional need was usually the impetus for parents who killed their children at birth. In the Qur'an, Allah warns mankind of this grievous sin whose shame is borne by all of humanity: "and do not kill your children out of poverty; we will provide for you and for them" (Alana'm: 151). In yet another verse, He says, "And do not kill your children for fear of poverty. We provide for them and for you. Indeed, their killing is ever a great sin" (Al-Noor: 32). The reality of poverty is brought forward in the first Ayah, "from poverty". Further emphasizing this frighteningly grave issue, He mentioned in the second Ayah, "the fear of poverty". These two points illustrate Islam's acknowledgement of the destruction poverty pours down upon mankind, and the connection between economic causes and desperate human behavior.

Societal Dangers of Poverty

Social scientists have long shown that poverty is associated with a host of social ills.

Poverty is not only responsible for destruction within the family unit, but it also affects a host of other conditions, being the catalyst for a domino effect of social ills. Even through a precursory glance, man's timeline throughout history clearly demonstrates that poverty breeds crime. It is no secret that crime levels for certain offenses within poorer neighborhoods far exceed the rate in more affluent neighborhoods. Poverty has a sort of ripple effect, radiating outward from its source (the poor neighborhood). If one were to plot crimes such as thefts, assaults, drug arrests, etc. on a map, the most predominant of these would be at the core of poorer neighborhoods, decreasing the further one travels away from poverty.

Abu Dhar, a companion of the Prophet, once said, "I am surprised that a poor person who cannot find food in his house does not go out holding his sword at the [bodies of the] rich people". Although a simple statement that exposes the dark side of the victims of poverty, it puts forth a powerful supposition that within society, there are two levels of people: those who are rich, and those who are poor. By extrapolation, the hearts of those who are poor should be on fire with hatred towards the more affluent.

A Matter of Health

It does not take too much observation or knowledge to realize that there exists a strong correlation between the level of healthcare a person receives and their economic status. Poverty often prevents those who need it most from seeking medical care, often putting their very lives in grave danger. In today's society, death rates from easily treated ailments in poorer neighborhoods far exceed those in communities where healthcare is accessible and affordable. Rates of more chronic diseases like cancer, diabetes, high blood pressure, and heart disease skyrocket within communities with low economic status. The same can be said for infant mortality and the rate of physical disabilities among children from poorer families.

A Host of Other Dangers

The danger of poverty does not stop at poor health. Poverty breeds poor living conditions as well. Worry, pressure, and anger negatively affect physical and psychological health. Some other common negative byproducts of poverty that affect society as a whole are low body weight or obesity from poor nutrition, low self-esteem, explosive tempers, assorted chemical addictions, homelessness, etc.

Early on in its history, during the early stages of Mecca times from 610 B.D. until 622 B.D., Islam addressed and emphasized the issue of poverty and social injustice directly and encouraged Muslims to deal with it. Below are just a few of many verses that addressed this issue:

Al-Doha, Verse/Ayah 6-11:

(6) "Did He not find thee an orphan and give thee shelter (and care)?

(7) "And He found thee wandering, and He gave thee guidance."

(8) "And He found thee in need, and made thee independent."

(9) "Therefore treat not the orphan with harshness."

(10) Nor repulse the petitioner (unheard)."

(11) But the Bounty of thy Lord: Rehearse and proclaim!"

Al Mutaffifeen Verse/Ayah 1: " Woe to those that deal in Fraud"

Al-Takweer, Verse/Ayah 8-9:

(8) "When the female (infant), buried alive, is questioned,"

(9) " For what crime she was killed"

Al-Maoun, Verse/Ayah 1-3:

(1) "Seest thou one who denies the Judgment (to come)?"

(2) "Then such as the (man) who repulses the orphan (with harshness)"

(3) "And encourages not the feeding of the indigent".

During that period was the initial campaign to eliminate poverty and look after the well being of the less fortunate element of society. The above verses addressed the orphan issue, the extremely needy people, the issue of burying girls alive and the issue of unfair trade practices. These are just a few among numerous verses that addressed many other issues in direct ways and made them part of Islam's ideology and practice.

II.   Islam and Basic Human Needs

From an Islamic perspective, human beings are created equal and each one, both man and woman, is granted the highest dignity by their creator Allah as the Qur'an states in Al-Israa, Verse/Ayah 70:

"We have honored the sons of Adam; provided them with transport on land and sea; given them for sustenance things good and pure; and conferred on them special favors, above a great part of Our Creation."

This verse clearly states that human beings are granted the highest possible respect and that they are better than all other creatures, including the Angels. The Qur'an clearly states in Taha, Verse/Ayah 118-119, that the basic human needs must be maintained and secured for every individual, as Allah is addressing Adam:

"There is therein (enough provision) for thee not to go hungry, not to go naked, Nor to suffer from thirst, nor from the sun's heat."

Every individual in Islam is entitled to all the above basic human needs and natural rights, which in modern-day terminology means:

- Food

- Clothing

- Clean water and sanitation

- Adequate shelter.

In addition, according to Islam, each individual is also entitled to the following:

- Respect and dignity

- Access to education

- Access to health care

- Transportation

- Right to marriage and family.

If an individual is unable to achieve or maintain these needs, assisting them becomes the responsibility of their family and relatives. If the family or relatives are unable to fulfill this responsibility, it is then transferred beyond the family surroundings to society or greater community through Zakat. If Zakat is not enough to aid the individual in securing their basic human needs, the responsibility will then rest with the government, which should exert every effort in securing basic human needs for all people. This should be accomplished by requesting more money from the wealthy, or by allocating additional resources for this purpose—to the extent that governmental resources are shared equally if necessary.

III. Islamically Prescribed Methods of Dealing with Poverty

Early on, Islam announced an all-out war on poverty by strengthening barriers to poverty through forms of charitable giving. Islamic jurisprudence allows for the regulation of poverty from every possible angle, so that it would not present a major danger to the belief of individuals, their behaviors, their families, and society as a whole. The question of how Islam combats poverty does not have a short answer, as Islam prescribes seven main strategies or defenses against it.

METHOD #1: INDIVIDUAL AND FAMILY RESPONSIBILITIES

In Islam, individuals both men and women, have rights and responsibilities. Their primary responsibility is to worship Allah properly. The second responsibility is to take care of themselves and their family. The third responsibility is to look after their immediate relatives. The fourth responsibility is to look after the community at large and the society's well being. The last responsibility is to take care of the world at large. Therefore, individuals are responsible to financially take care of their families by all different means. However, poverty was, is, and will always be part of any society. When a person or a family faces a hardship, they are required to deal with it in the following manner:

Spiritual and Moral Empowerment

In Islam, everyone is subject to various tests. These tests are intended to solidify and purify their beliefs and they can come in the form of happiness or difficulties. Muslims are instructed to be thankful during good times and to be patient during hard times. It is also in the essence of Muslim beliefs that the livelihood and the richness/wealth and poverty are all pre-destined by Allah, but people are required to work as hard as possible to earn their living. In case things did not work out, and an individual or a family continues to suffer, they are required to carry on by seeking work. In the mean time, they should continue to pray while strongly believing that Allah (swt) will provide them with their livelihood, and that both good and hard times may always change.

Believers are required to be patient and have faith that God will see them through. Despair is considered a sign of disbelief and weakness in Islam. It violates the very essence of faith. Muslims are instructed to always be hopeful and look forward to better times, while realizing that by the end of the day, Paradise is the ultimate reward for the believer. A believer has patience and lives by the Qur'anic instructions. These sets of beliefs are deeply rooted in Muslim societies and they are the cornerstone of keeping one's and society's hopes high at all times.

Resource Management and Waste Elimination

Islam makes it very clear that people should manage their livelihood and financial resources in an effective and efficient manner to avoid waste of resources. Individuals who are blessed with wealth are required to spend their money wisely. This wealth is a trust from God and God requires that it be spent according to His commands. That is clearly stated in the Qur'an in Surah Al-Israa Verse/Ayah (26-27):

"And render to the kindred their due rights, as (also) to those in want, and to the wayfarer: but do not squander (your wealth) wastefully." (27) "Verily those who waste (squander) are akin to devils; and the Devil is ungrateful to his Lord."

In the Qur'an, God also orders human beings not to waste. Those who do are deemed akin to demons. Prophet Mohammed also urged the well-to-do believers to be modest in their spending, asking them to not be accustomed to luxury because one's fortune is not eternal.

Seeking Jobs

In an Islamic society, every person is instructed to work, and eat from the fruits of his own labor. Allah said, "It is He who made the earth subservient to you, so walk among its slopes and eat of His provision. And to Him will be the Resurrection" (Al-Mulk: 15). Here, the meaning of the term "work" is the conscious effort that man does alone or with others, to produce something, or to offer a service. As a result, the working man would achieve some form of reward or profit that would fulfill his family's necessities.

It was reported that Omar, the second Caliph, once saw a group of people in the mosque after prayers. These people claimed to rely only on Allah for their livelihood, without the benefit of work. So he told them, "do not neglect working to earn your living, instead saying, 'Oh Allah provide for me, and verily you know that the sky doesn't rain gold and silver'. Rather, Allah commands His servants, 'Then when the [Jumu'ah] prayers have concluded, disperse and go your ways in quest of God's bounty'" (al-Jumu'ah: 10).

Therefore, Islam orders and encourages every person to have a job of some type to advance their economic condition and their spiritual state. Actions as simple as planting and working a garden are considered a kind of hedge against poverty. It is reported in Al-Bukhari that the Prophet said about those who plant a garden, "For any Muslim who has planted a plant, then Allah will bestow on him a blessing equal to the giving of charity for every time a bird, a human or an animal eats from it". It is also reported that the Prophet said, "no man has ever eaten any better than those who eat from his own work" (Al-Bukhari). This means that the best kind of food a person can eat is that food bought with the income earned through his own efforts, be it by back-breaking work in a garden where the food grows, or by paid employment. Yet another Hadith states, "Whoever gets tired working, Allah will erase some of his sins" (Al-Bukhari).

No Job is Undignified

Islam frowns upon those who are not helping themselves by working, and then beg for handouts. As it is reported in Al-Bukhari, the Prophet Mohammed said, "for a man to go [forth] with a robe and [then] returns with wood on his back, and then sells it to fulfill his need, [it] is much better than asking people to give him [charity]". This Hadith illustrates that having a difficult job like collecting wood—which certainly is not profitable—is much better than being lazy by not working, and then asking people for help.

The Prophet actively encouraged those people around him to take any job, no matter how insignificant or simple, to support themselves. He often used the example of those prophets who people looked up to. He said, "No prophet sent by Allah but was a shepherd ". Prophet Mohammed's companions asked, "what about you Prophet of Allah?" He answered, "Yes, I was shepherding animals for Meccans for two *Kirats* (a very little amount of money)" (reported by Al-Bukhari).

Therefore, Islam destroys the warped perception allotting a higher status to those who possess wealth, and does not denigrate those who are poor from legitimate reasons. Islam instead assigns the higher status to those believers with righteous deeds and knowledge.

Migrating to Earn a Living

Islam stresses that the bounty of Allah is not restricted to a specific area; therefore, Islam prescribes migration to other lands for those who cannot find employment. It is much better for them to leave their homes, traveling as far as necessary to obtain work, than to be poor and accept charity. The Prophet said, "Travel and you'll be rich" (reported by Al-Tabori). This implies that if you leave your home to work elsewhere, you will increase your ability to support yourself financially, and not be in need of another's charity. In the Qur'an, Allah says, "He who emigrates (from his home) in the Cause of Allah, will find on earth many dwelling places and plenty to live by..." (an-Nisa': 100).

No Charity for the Able

After all is said about a person's obligation to earn their own livelihood, it must still be recognized that there are people who do not truly care to work. Instead, they would rather sit at home, depending on Zakat and collections of charitable gifts. People such as these are not legitimate recipients of Zakat.

When two people asked the Prophet to give funds to them from the Zakat, the Prophet said, "There is no chance in it for the rich people, and for those strong and able to work" (reported in al-Nasa'ie). The Prophet did not allow lazy people to live off charity. Instead, those physically and mentally able to work must work, and if they chose not to do so, they have no right in Zakat. Additionally, the Prophet made it unlawful to give to such people from Zakat, saying in a Hadith, "Sadaqah is not lawful for the rich and the able man" (reported by Tirmithy).

A Shameful Sign on One's Face

Except for situations of hardship, the Prophet has also warned people against asking for Zakat, as it is contrary to the dignity of a Muslim. In a speech he said, "The higher hand (the giving hand) is better than the lower hand (the receiving hand)" (reported by Ibn Omar in Al-Bukhari and Muslim).

This is illustrated in a story where a poor man from Ansar came to the Prophet asking for help, but the Prophet asked him, "Do you have anything in your home?" "Yes," the man replied. "I have a *hils* (a kind of blanket). We cover ourselves with part of it and sleep on part of it, and I also have a container we drink from". The Prophet said, "Go get me both of them". Once this poor man brought them, the Prophet announced among his companions, "who would buy them?" One man answered, "I will buy them for a dirham". The Prophet said, "who would give more than a dirham?" He repeated this two or three times, and then another man said, "I will take them for two dirhams". Then, the Prophet sold the hils to the other man, and gave the two dirhams to the Ansari man. He then instructed the Ansari man, "Buy food for your family with one dirham, and buy an axe with the other dirham, and bring it to me". The man did so, and returned with an axe to the Prophet. The Prophet took the axe and installed a wooden handle into its end, making certain that it was tight and secure. Then he told the man, "Go. Cut wood with it and sell the wood, and I want to see you in 15 days".

The Ansari man went out and did what the Prophet had ordered him to do. After 15 days of cutting and collecting wood, then selling it, he returned to the Prophet telling him that he made ten dirhams. He also said that he had bought new clothing and some food for his family. The Prophet was happy with the Ansari man. The Prophet told him, "...and this is much better for you than asking others to provide for you, which brings you in the Day of Judgment with a shameful sign on your face" (Reported by Anas bin Malik in Al-Tirmithy).

There is an old Chinese adage that says, "Give a man a fish, and you feed him for a day; but, teach him to fish and you feed him for a lifetime". In the above, the Prophet did not simply advise or lecture the poor man. Nor did he help him with something that would provide temporary relief. Rather, he prescribed a practical solution while imparting an important lesson to him and others around him. He taught the man, who was extremely poor (having only a blanket and a water container) to use all of his available resources, and his energy to earn a simple yet dignified living.

Through this Hadith, it is shown that the Prophet taught this man and his companions that any Halal (lawful) job that provides for a person's needs is dignified work. This is true even if it means going into the forest to cut wood, since it prevents him from the embarrassment of begging.

RESPONSIBILITIES OF FAMILY AND RELATIVES

One of the primary solutions to fighting poverty is for the poor to use a weapon that is already in their own hands—a job. Although this is a perfectly viable solution for those that are able to work, what about people who are not able to work? What about a widow that has lost her husband and has no money? Where does this leave the children and the elderly who are too young or too old to work? What about those people who are chronically sick or handicapped? Naturally, the above conclusion must be dismissed when considering these classes of poor.

Protecting the Dignity of the Unable Poor

In Islam, poverty that is caused by a person's inability to work does not lessen their dignity, and certainly does not skip any of their rights. Islam teaches all members of society—including the poor—that dignity and status do not result from how much wealth a person accumulates, or how much property they own. However, these conditions do come from the level of knowledge a person acquires, and how many good deeds he or she does for humanity. Ultimately, these are reflected by rewards in the Hereafter. Allah said, "Indeed, the most noble of you in the sight of Allah is the most righteous of you" (al-Hujurat: 13). He also said, "Are those who know equal to those who do not know?" (Az-Zumar: 9). This implies that those with advanced levels of knowledge are higher in status than those who know less. The Qur'an also states that "Allah will raise [into the Hereafter] those who have believed among you and those who were given knowledge by degrees" (al-Mujadilah: 11). Additionally, Allah says, "And not equal are the blind and the seeing, nor are those who believe and do righteous deeds and the evil-doer" (Ghafir: 58). In this case, the blind are those who are ignorant with little or no knowledge, and the seeing are those who possess knowledge.

Islam does not desire the humiliation of any person, especially those who truly need help. Instead, it has prescribed a second shield against poverty. That shield is the poor person's relative. Islam prescribes that all of the relatives of these poor people must be united together. They are responsible to provide help for each other. The strong person of a family is obliged to help the weak. The rich relative is responsible to help the poor relative, and the able members of the family must stand by the unable family members. Allah puts mercy in the hearts of close relatives so that they serve one another, and He ordered them to take care of each other as a due right and obligation to one another.

Compelling Claims of Relatives

Every culture knows that a person standing alone is easy prey. Those who cluster in kindred groups support each other through good and bad circumstances. This is the premise for civilization: safety and support in numbers. There is a tradition in the native tribes of North America that states a twig by itself is easy to snap in two; however, bundling many twigs together gives a single twig great strength.

For this reason, Islam emphasizes the rights of relatives towards each other. It is clearly stated in the Qur'an and the teachings of the Prophet that families shall be responsible for one another, while admonishing those who cut off relations with their families. Many verses in the Qur'an bolster this premise. One of these says, "Indeed, Allah orders justice and good conduct and giving to relatives" (an-Nahl: 90). Yet in another verse, the Qur'an says, "Worship Allah and associate nothing with Him. Do good to parents, and to relatives, orphans, the needy, the near neighbor, the neighbor farther away, the companion at your side, the traveler, and those whom your right hands possess. Indeed, Allah does not like those who are self-deluding and boastful" (an-Nisa': 36).

Amongst most Muslim scholars, it is commonly agreed that it is the husband's responsibility to financially support his wife. This same rule dictates that a father must also financially support his young children, and an able son must spend money on his elderly parents and grandparents if they are needy. From this sprouts the question: who is responsible for whom? While the welfare of the remainder of a man's relatives is open to argument by the scholars, a Muslim man indeed has a measure of obligation toward his needy relatives. The nearer in relation the needy relative is to the Muslim man, the greater the man's responsibility. This chain of responsibility is consistently shown through Hadith. One such Hadith relates what the Prophet once said in a speech delivered to his companions, "The giver hand is the higher. Begin with who you must support: your mother and your father, then your sister and your brother, and then the relatives who are closer and closer" (reported by al-Nasa'ie). On yet another occasion the Prophet said, "start with [giving to] yourself in charity. If there is something remaining, give [charity] to your family. Then if something [else] remains, [give] to your close relatives. And, if something remains [after all this, give] to other relatives, and so on" (reported by al-Nasa'ie).

METHOD #2: SOCIETY'S RESPONSE

Takafful Systems, The General Sadaqah

In addition to all of the above dues and obligations, Islam promotes the admirable side of human beings by encouraging them to be merciful to those in need, and to choose to share their wealth with the less fortunate. Islam realizes that not all matters of charitable concern can or should be accomplished through rules, regulations and obligations, but are open to optional, yet highly encouraged noble gestures. No matter how tough governments get in trying to enforce these rules, they are meaningless unless people have the will to apply them. *Takafful* is a well known concept in Muslim World history. The term means that society's members should do their best to look after the well being of one another.

The truth is that people are not machines that can be turned on whenever someone wishes to flip a switch. Humans are not wheels that move and turn at will, but are complicated beings that feel happiness and sadness. Most people will gladly spend to help others simply out of kindness; therefore, Islam emphasizes the human side and encourages people to be benevolent and responsible towards their fellow human beings. These ideas are advanced through many Qur'anic verses stressing good virtues and the great rewards people who give to others will receive in the Afterlife.

Those people who hold the belief that laws, rules, and decisions are the only things that they need in life, are the people that have a very limited understanding of life. A human being is an amazing amalgam consisting of a brain, a soul, and a body that feels, dreams, thinks and reasons. Islam is a religion that brings people towards a higher status of good behavior. It is not content with ethical laws brought and enforced by governments, because one of Islam's objectives is to raise righteous people who strive to please Allah, while seeking their reward in Heaven through helping others in need.

Aside from all of these previously listed rights imparted upon the poor, Islam stresses that a person's will to give must come from their soul. Islam guides Muslims to develop strength of character that would rather give to the poor than spend money on themselves and their own whims. A good Muslim likes for other people what they like for themselves, and gives without a predisposed want for glory. They should be humble in their charity, not drawing attention to what they give in secret. Allah said, "Those who spend their wealth [in Allah's way] by night and by day, secretly and publicly, they will have their reward with their Lord. And no fear will there be concerning them, nor will they grieve" (al-Baqarah: 274). A pious Muslim knows that money is only a road to help them and others, and must not give because they fear a particular leader, or to become famous. They must do it solely for the sake and way of Allah.

So many verses of the Qur'an, and sayings of the Prophet came as giving good tidings or warnings to mankind. These words encouraged and beseeched humanity to freely give Sadaqah, and not waste their money on nonsense things, while teaching them to act honorably, and be generous to others. Allah said, "who is it that would loan Allah a goodly loan so He may multiply it for him many times over? And it is Allah who withholds and grants abundance, and to Him you will be returned" (al-Baqarah: 245). The "loans" mentioned here are gifts given to the poor as well as other good causes. Additionally, Allah said, "The example of those who spend their wealth in the way of Allah is like a seed [of grain] which grows seven spikes; in each spike is a hundred grains. And Allah multiplies [his reward] for whom He wills. And Allah is all encompassing and knowing" (al-Baqarah: 261). In yet another verse He said, "And hasten to forgiveness from your Lord and a garden (i.e. Paradise) as wide as the heavens and earth, prepared for the righteous who spend [in the cause of Allah] during ease and hardship" (Al-Imran: 133-134). Again, the most worthy spending in Allah's way is helping the poor and needy.

Furthermore, Allah commanded mankind to "Believe in Allah and His Messenger and spend of that whereof He has made you trustees. And such of you as believe and spend [in Allah's way], there will be great reward" (Al-Hadeed: 7). As well as, "And spend [in the way of Allah] from what We have provided you before death approaches one of you and he says, 'My Lord, if only You would delay me for a brief term so I would give charity and be among the righteous'" (al-Munafiqun: 10). Elsewhere in the Qur'an, Allah tells us, "But he has attempted to pass on the path that is steep (i.e. the path which will lead to Paradise). And what will make you know the pass that is steep? It is freeing a neck (slave) or giving food in a day of hunger (famine), to an orphan near of kin? Or to a *Miskin* (poor person) cleaving to dust (out of misery). Then he became one of those who believed (in the Islamic Monotheism) and recommended one another to perseverance and patience, and [also] recommended one another to pity and compassion. They are those on the Right Hand (i.e. the dwellers of Paradise)" (Al-Balad: 11-18). These passages are only a few of the literally hundreds and hundreds of Qur'anic verses that encourage people to help those in need, warning them against ignoring Allah's command. Furthermore, Qur'anic passages that address the concepts of Sadaqah/charitable giving far outnumber those passages which refer to Islam's many other obligations such as fasting, Hajj, etc.

Likewise, there are so many Hadith where the Prophet spoke to mankind with the same purpose. In one such Hadith, the Prophet said, "man says 'my money, my money', and yet man owns only three things from his money: what he ate, what he wore in clothing, and what remains from that which he gave away. All the remainder will be spent or will be left for other people to inherit" (reported by Muslim). The meaning of this Hadith is quite clear: money is either spent, or inherited by others after a person's death. The only money a person truly benefits from is that which they give in charity, and which will give the person a greater reward in the Afterlife. A more precise gauge which measures alms-giving is seen in another Hadith where the Prophet said, "Al-Sadaqah erases the sins just like how the water stops the fire" (reported by Abu Ya'ala).

This mean, *Sadaqah*, or general charity, is probably counted as the main source of support in Muslim society. Historically, most charitable funds come through optional voluntary charity, not the percentage-limited funds of Zakat. Many wealthy Muslims set aside the largest portion of their income every year towards charity. Throughout Islamic history, there are stories of wealthy men such as Abu Bakr who gave their entire fortune for the sake of Allah. Even in recent times, it is not unknown for professionals such as physicians and businessmen who earn several hundreds of thousands of dollars a year to give most of it to Sadaqah. Some give as much as 60 percent of their income!

Sadaqah Jariah

One of the most effective kinds of Sadaqah is *Sadaqah Jariah*, which is loosely translated as a continuous charity. Islam emphasizes the giving of this type of Sadaqah, promising its givers rewards that will last even after the person dies. Sadaqah Jariah is a donation that has long-term benefit such as building a house of worship. As long as people pray in that house (even for centuries), the person who established it will continue to receive reward from Allah for their deed.

In an authentic Hadith reported by Imam Bukhari and Imam Muslim, "Whosoever builds for Allah a masjid (mosque), Allah will reward him similar to it in Paradise." In another narration reported by Imam Ahmad, "Whosoever shares in building a masjid for Allah, even if it is as small as a bird's nest, Allah will build for him a house in Paradise."

Sadaqah Jariah is not limited to the building of mosques or schools, but might encompass innumerable things that have some lingering benefit to living beings. This is shown through another Hadith where the Prophet Mohammed said, "Whosoever digs a well will receive reward for that from Allah on the Day of Judgement when anyone amongst jinn, men and birds drink from it ".

A Sadaqah Jariah that is especially emphasized in Hadith is that of producing a source of beneficial knowledge like writing a book, which is useful to people in any aspect of their life. In this case, even if the writer has died, as long as the book is read and benefited from, he or she will continue to receive reward for it while in the Hereafter.

Abu Hurairah documented that the Prophet said, "If a human dies, then his good deeds stop except for three: a Sadaqah Jariah, a beneficial knowledge (an emphasized form of Sadaqah Jariah), or a righteous child who prays for him" (reported by Muslim).

The Waqf Systems

Laying the Foundation of Islamic Endowment

Ibn Omar reported that his father, Omar Bin Al-Khattab, obtained a parcel of land in Khaibar. Omar Bin Al-Khattab asked the Prophet, "O prophet of Allah, I have property in Khaibar, which is the best of my possessions. What do you order me to do with it?" The Prophet said, "You might want to give it as a Sadaqah, but maintain [it for] its original use". Hence, Omar gave the land as a Sadaqah, but with a condition that it was not to be sold, given away, or inherited by anyone. However, [Omar ordered] that the land was to be used and invested for the benefit of the poor, the weak, and traveling strangers, and to free the slaves" (reported by Muslim and Bukhari).

This Hadith is a perfect example of the term *Waqf*: giving something for charity while maintaining it in its original form. This means that giving the land (or something else of value) as an endowment where all its benefits go to the needy, but the land itself stays as is. In this specific Hadith, the Prophet laid the foundation for the concept of Islamic endowment or Waqf. The purposes of *Awqaf* (the plural form of Waqf) can be categorized as follows:

- Social purposes, such as those serving various groups in need of special help. Or, to provide any financial help such as for handicapped, orphans, elderly, blind, deaf, children, widows and divorced, and the unemployed.

- Religious purposes that are mainly for the establishment of mosques and Qur'an schools, or for the sponsorship of imams, teachers and students of Islamic studies.

- Educational purposes that are mainly used for the establishment and operation of schools, libraries and various institutions. For hiring teachers, awarding scholarships, and establishing presses to print books. Historically, there were dedicated facilities which hired writers to hand-copy or translate books for students. This tradition was carried out in universities or schools in a separate wing like a library.

- Environmental purposes dealing mainly with land irrigation, building water tunnels, and planting forests. Recently Awqaf have been established in some Muslim countries that are strictly dedicated to the handling and disposal of waste and garbage.

- For purposes of public service such as establishing wells, streets, public bathrooms, public guesthouses, etc.

Since Waqf is defined as a contribution whose yields or services are restricted for certain beneficiaries, while keeping its origin as is, there are three issues to meet in regards to Waqf:

- It is a contribution.

- The endowment cannot be altered, destroyed or sold.

- Its yield or service is restricted for the benefit of a certain cause or group of people.

For instance, in the case of farmland donated to an organization, the Waqf trustee or administrator cannot sell it. They are required under the terms of Waqf to take care of the land so that it continues to produce. Additionally, the produce yielded from this land is to be given to, or sold for the benefit of, the restricted group of people identified by the donor, such as orphans.

Another model could be that a donor gives a rental property into Waqf. In this case, the rental income is spent for the benefit of the restricted beneficiaries identified by the donor. The Waqf administrator must maintain the building and pay the maintenance costs from the building's income. He cannot sell the building or destroy it, except under very severely limited situations.

One form of Waqf, or endowment, was initiated by Zubaida who was the wife of Caliph Haroun al Rashid. Zubaida's Waterway is a channel she ordered to be dug directing water to the holy city of Mecca. The waterway ensured that pilgrims had free access to water during their pilgrimage.

Another example would be giving the endowment of a farm whose produce is donated every season to the needy. The farm stays as Waqf, but its yields are benefiting the needy for many years.

A third example might be that a donor gives $250,000 as Waqf for the benefit of a school for the blind in Dhaka, Bangladesh. The Waqf administrator could invest this money, yet only the profit generated would be given towards the school. One scenario could be that the administrator buys stocks for the amount of the initial donation, and the income generated from these stocks funds the operation of the school's annual budget for years to come. However, it is important to note here that Muslim scholars warn against investing Waqf money in such a way that the original amount is lost. The numerous restrictions on how to benefit from this type of Waqf minimize the risk of conflict of interest, or the loss of the original money.

In Islam's earlier centuries, a large sector of properties owned by Muslims were given as gifts for the benefit of various needs, creating Waqf models for future Muslims to emulate. These endowments allowed many vulnerable people to find relief through these institutions, whether they were free hospitals, places to earn their living, free schools for those in need, etc. Moreover, the generosity of Muslims came across in many creative ways, as they looked for additional areas of societal need. Endowments were created to benefit people with every sort of handicap, as well as multitudes of additional projects. Muslims gave of their wealth in such numbers to the extent that institutions were set up to care for sick animals, and others to treat lost dogs.

Waqf Case Example:
Kalawoon Hospital

From about 1250 to 1517 CE, Egypt was ruled Islamically by a group of very knowledgeable scholars who were originally slaves. During this time, a wealthy Muslim entrusted an Egyptian hospital as Waqf. The historical paper documenting the Waqf reads, "This document entrusts the Hospital of Kalawoon", where the giver of the property laid out the conditions of the endowment, and was attested to by witnesses. When reading the paper, which we translated from its original Arabic, it is important to remember that it was drawn up when Europe was still in its dark ages, and long before the west began to debate social welfare systems.

To allow the administration of the Awqaf to apply the endowment, the giver specified, "I found this hospital for the treatment of Muslims, men and women. From amongst the able rich and the needy poor, in Cairo and its surroundings. From amongst its residences and visitors, regardless of their races and their different diseases. They shall be permitted to enter it in groups or as individuals, old and young. The patients, men or women, shall be able to stay at the hospital for treatment until completely cured. And they shall receive whatever treatment is available, regardless of any discriminations due to being from the near or far away localities, or for being relatives or strangers, without asking for anything in return.

"All the necessities of the patients shall be funded through this Waqf such as beds, whether made from wood or else, comforters full of cotton, and pillows full of cotton. Every patient should be given what he needs of bed set according to his medical situation. Making sure to treat them in accordance to the obedience of Allah, putting the utmost efforts in understanding them, and every responsible person is responsible for those under him.

"Furthermore, the kitchen at the hospital shall cook for all patients chicken and meat, and every patient shall have a separate plate that no other patient shares it with him. It (the dish) shall be covered until it is delivered to the patient, and every patient shall receive enough nutritious food for his lunches and dinners, and what is recommended for him in the early and late hours.

"As for the funds generated from this Waqf, it shall pay for the hired Muslim doctors who are responsible to treat patients as groups and in turns. They (the doctors) shall ask them about their situations, and whether there are witnessing increase or decreases in their cases, and shall [prescribe for them] what is supposed to benefit their situation from drugs and nutrition. And these doctors shall sleep at the hospitals in groups or in turns, so to care for patients.

"Furthermore, whomever is poor and sick at home shall be allocated what he needs from drugs and other needs, without being so narrow in spending..." [1]

A historical example of this third type of Waqf began shortly after the death of the Prophet, during the rule of Omar (635-645 CE), the second Caliph. Omar invited some of the companions of the Prophet to Khaibar to witness the Waqf. Jaber, another companion, says that when the news broke out about the Waqf, every landowner made certain that Omar put a condition on the Waqf. This contingency stated that the fruits and revenues of their Waqf be given first to their own children and descendants, and only the surplus, if any, should be given to the poor. This kind of Waqf is called a Posterity or Family Waqf. Therefore, Waqf in Islamic society may also be for one's own family and descendants, unlike American foundations that are restricted to religious or philanthropic purposes.

Historical Role of Waqf

Waqf has played an enormously great role in historic and traditionally Islamic societies, especially in the development of various aspects of Muslim communities.

At one time, Waqf assets were the primary support to establish and maintain mosques, schools, institutions, hospitals, orphanages, libraries, shelters, wells, streets, etc. They were the major source of funding for the maintenance and operational expenses to run these projects, as well as from income generated from farms and factories. Additionally, Waqf used to provide full support for scholars so they might commit themselves to research and teaching. Such scholarships were intended for scholars and students to concentrate on their studies, removing the burden of worry about earning their living and furthering education.

Throughout history, one of the most common Waqf has been real estate, whose revenue provides for the maintenance and operational expenses of houses of worship. Its permanent nature resulted in the accumulation of Waqf properties all over the Muslim lands. The variety of its objectives enables support for far-reaching religious and philanthropic activities. The huge numbers of Waqf and their objectives play primary roles in the socio-political existence of Muslim societies and communities.

One recent study extracted information from the registers of Awqaf in Istanbul, Jerusalem, Cairo, and other cities which indicated that Awqaf property covered a considerable proportion of total cultivated area. For example, in the years 1812 and 1813, a survey of land in Egypt showed that Waqf represented 600,000 feddan (a little less than one acre) out of a total of two and one-half million feddan. In 1841, the number of deeds for Awqaf registered with the Grand Mosque in the capital city of Algiers in Algeria was 543 feddan. Additionally, in Turkey about one-third of all land was Awqaf. While up to the middle of the 16th century in Palestine, 233 Waqf deeds were recorded containing 890 properties, in comparison to 92 deeds of private ownership containing 108 properties. However, modern times have seen these numbers dramatically reduced in many countries. This is evident in present-day Damascus, which has witnessed large portions of its Waqf property becoming lost due to missing records, wars, corruption, and changes in its administration.

In Islamic history, the building of the mosque of Quba' in Medina is the first notable religious Waqf. The mosque was built upon the arrival of the Prophet Muhammad in 622, and although it has been enlarged and remodeled, it still stands in the same location today. Six months after the building of the mosque of Quba', the mosque of the Prophet in the center of Medina was built and endowed to Waqf.

Waqf Today

In today's society, the role of Waqf has been very limited; although, it is still very apparent in Muslim countries. For instance, the Kuwait Awqaf Public Foundation, a governmental institution, has redeveloped this sector so donors can find Waqf funds or properties for every conceivable type of charitable cause.

At this time, reviving the traditional Sunnah of Waqf as one of the main pillars of Muslim community development is desperately needed. Although quite prevalent in the Gulf States, such Awqaf development is rarely found in other parts of the Islamic world.

Control of Awqaf

Waqf assets, such as real estate properties or funds, may be administered and controlled by governments. This is why Awqaf ministries can be found in nearly every Muslim country. Although, their roles currently are limited to administering mosques and some Islamic schools. Awqaf ministries were originally established after the fall of the Ottoman Empire, and are currently instituted by governments to manage the vast amounts and types of Waqf in real estate, institutions, farms, and specific funds. The corruption and misuse of Waqf in many countries is primarily due to the untrustworthiness of some government officials. Large portions of Waqf assets were lost until these ministries' roles became limited to assigning imams to mosques, and the funding of mosque operations. In some countries, they changed the name and focus of these departments to "Ministry of Islamic Affairs" to handle issues other than Awqaf.

Islamic jurisprudence also affirms that NGOs, foundations, and family trusts may administer and control Waqf assets. There are many foundations and non-governmental organizations—mainly regional committees or councils—that control numerous types of Waqf funds restricted for specific groups of people or certain causes. However, such foundations usually receive monetary contributions towards funds dedicated as Waqf, such as the Blind Waqf Fund whose income yields support blind people. Then there are those such as the Chinese Muslim Waqf Fund that is dedicated to aid Muslims in China in building mosques and schools, or whatever else is needed there.

In many parts of the Muslim world, many villages have Awqaf committees that are not under governmental control, nor are they formal NGOs. Additionally, there are numerous privately controlled Awqaf. For example, a donor or a family would dedicate a piece of property as a Waqf, all the while the donor continues taking care of it. If the property is farmland, it is kept producing, and the land's yield is given to the needy or a specific group of beneficiaries. Sometimes this is continued as a privately controlled Waqf for many generations.

Another example might be that a family establishes a mosque. Over the years, they would provide for its maintenance, operational costs, etc. These forms of Waqf are sometimes named after the donor or the family.

From a legal standpoint, the ownership of Waqf property after it is entrusted into endowment does not lie with the person who initiated it. Some Muslim jurists argue that it is "for the sake of Allah", while others believe it is publicly owned for the good of the beneficiaries, but administered by trustees. They argue that the beneficiaries' ownership is not complete in the sense that they are not permitted to dispose of the property, or use it in a way different from what was decreed by the founder of the Waqf. Since a foundation's management is able to dispose of or sell its property, this implies that the meaning of eternity is stronger in Waqf than in foundations.

Main Areas of Awqaf

The benefits of Waqf, whether monetary income, products or services, may further any type of public need. Unlike Zakat, it is not restricted to a few kinds of beneficiaries such as the poor and needy, nor is it for the poor and needy alone. For instance, in some parts of the Islamic world, villages or families used to set aside guest houses as a Waqf for travelers or for those who are not necessarily poor. Providing a haven for a weary traveler (Muslim or non-Muslim) who is passing through the village reflects on the generosity of those in the village. In the past, when there were no hotels and motels, traders or travelers had few options. These guesthouses provided a place for them to be welcomed, where they were fed, and given whatever else they needed at no expense.

Throughout history, one can find hundreds of causes where Waqf was established. An excellent example of one such cause were pieces of green land set aside as Waqf for injured or old animals. Islam teaches that charity to animals is as important as to human beings, and these animals (mainly horses) were given a place to live where plants and water were abundant.

History documents Awqaf dedicated towards medical research, and for public kitchens where a hungry person can get a daily meal at no charge. One might also see Waqf dedicated to support the paralyzed or the mentally ill.

Education is another primary recipient of Awqaf. As its financing in the early days of Islam was not limited to religious studies alone, educational Awqaf also includes libraries, books, salaries of teachers and other staff, and stipends to students. This allows not only the freedom of education, but historically helped to create a dedicated educational environment where not only the rich and ruling class received an education, but the poor and slave segments as well. Founded in 972 in Cairo, Al-Azhar University was financed by its enormous Waqf revenues until the government of Muhammad Ali in Egypt took control over the Awqaf in 1812. Muslim and non-Muslim students from every continent used to come to Al-Azhar to study religion, philosophy, literature, medicine, etc. They lived, learned, received stipends, and afterwards returned to their own homelands having benefited immeasurably from Al-Azhar's Waqf.

While mosques are the main beneficiaries of Awqaf in many Muslim countries, even those funds earmarked toward mosques are further sub-restricted towards building and maintaining mosques, and for paying imams' salaries. As well, Qur'an funds are established with many sub-restricted purposes such as printing copies of Qur'an, establishing Qur'anic memorization schools, or for translating Qur'an to other languages.

Waqf for the propagation of Islam, or daw'a, can be subdivided as well for the sponsoring of preachers, and for media projects such as radio stations recently established in mainly Muslim countries, or producing books on daw'a.

Binding Donor Restrictions

As it is true in all types of donations, in Waqf, it is also an obligation to follow the donor's restrictions. The government, foundations or trustees have no power to change the donor's restrictions once the Waqf is set. Scholars say this is true unless the cause no longer exists. This might apply in the event of when a hospital was established for the treatment of a disease that has been eradicated, or for a cause that is no longer needed, or for a restriction that is unlawful. Even in these cases, to change the donor restriction, it would take an edict by a Muslim judge or a scholar.

Forms of Awqaf

Awqaf can come in different forms. Over 1,400 years ago in the first Muslim community of Medina, traditionally the yield from a palm tree farm was given to support the needy. Today, real estate is still one of the most common types of Awqaf. However, it is not in the form of farms, but buildings used for their rent, or those that house a manufacturing plant whose products are sold to benefit a particular cause. The category of real estate can also be large or small institutions, such as hospitals, schools, and shelters. These are usually dedicated as Waqf not for their monetary yield, but for their donated services such as free medical treatment, free schooling, and temporary housing for travelers or the needy.

There are many restrictions when dealing with Waqf properties. For instance, no one can sell them unless under exceptional circumstances, which usually requires a decision by an Islamic court. Throughout history, the products or yields of any Waqf assets—such as fruits from a farm or furniture from a manufacturing company—are sold though publicly held auctions, or through other means to minimize conflict of interest or corruption by following a strict set of restrictions set by Muslim scholars. For modern times, any new rules pertaining to such deals have always required a Fatwa from the scholastic councils of the Muslim world.

Presently, there are tight restrictions on how to deal with Waqf so that no conflicts of interest occur. On some lands, for instance, the property's yield does not need to be sold. One example of this happens quite frequently in Muslim countries. In an olive orchard dedicated for the benefit of the needy, the Awqaf ministry or the property administrator would hire people to collect the olives. The olives are then distributed among the needy families as whole fruit and/or olive oil. In most cases the donated olives and oil last the poor families for a year, while the benefits from the Waqf are received year after year.

Waqf Can Be In-Kind or Monetary

As outlined in the above text, there are two types of Waqf:

- In-kind donations, such as properties or equipment for the benefit of restricted recipients, or

- Monetary contributions for restricted funds, which is a common method for donors whose smaller donations multiply to create a larger fund, which is then invested toward a certain cause.

In the later case, donors are given various restricted funds to donate towards either in a one-time contribution, or in installments such as monthly contributions. Many donors are encouraged to give a small monthly amount that is usually dedicated by the foundation offering the Waqf. For instance, this foundation would have several Waqf funds: one for awarding scholarships to outstanding students, another to a school for the blind, and a third for building mosques in China, etc. Although most donors cannot give large amounts to be set as Waqf and invested for the benefit of these causes, many donors are willing to give $50 a month or less towards the funds they choose. These collected funds accumulate, and then would be used to yield ongoing income to support the above mentioned causes.

A Waqf Benefit Could Be Time-Limited

In the past, a Waqf fund was always set as such for an unlimited time. Although some scholars saw that setting a temporary time-period of 25 to 50 years or more was lawful. According to Islamic scholars, although it is lawful for donors to set their Waqf for a temporary period, it is rarely done. In these cases, properties revert back under the possession and control of the original donor, or to the donor's heirs at the end of the specified period. An example of such a case is that of a wealthy family who gave a piece of land with a deep artesian well for the benefit of farmers to water their plants and animals for 25 years. At the end of this time, the donor family had a need for the well again, so they took it back after the period expired. Since the family members were the owners of the well, and since donors' conditions are always binding, it was lawful for the family to choose to give the well for that period.

Why Donors Give into Waqf

So, why give Waqf in the first place? Waqf is all about the long-term assistance to beneficiaries. It is also much more about getting *Ajir* (reward) from Allah as a result. Two sayings of Prophet Mohammed encourage deeds such as these. The first states that "the most beloved Deeds to Allah are those ongoing, even if they are small". The second Hadith states that "if the son of Adam dies, his [chance for] good deeds are cut except for three:

Sadaqah Jariah, benefit of knowledge (that he left behind), or a benevolent child who prays for him". Waqf is always a Sadaqah Jariah, a continuous or ongoing charity.

METHOD #3: GOVERNMENT ROLES

Government is the safety net of last resort. However, a government's responsibility is quite significant. The government's financial resources come from the Zakat Fund, the state-owned natural resources (oil, minerals, etc.) and additional taxes if needed. In general, the government is required to do the following:

Human Development

Human empowerment and education are the prime means of fighting and eliminating extreme poverty. Therefore, job training, capacity building, creating jobs, micro-economy, loans and other means are the main responsibilities of the government. The story of Moses and the Righteous Man in the Qur'an represents an ideal and successful means of human development and capacity building. Although Moses was young and strong when he had to leave Egypt, he became homeless with no shelter, no family, and no job. Because he had been a prince in Egypt, he had no form of practical training, which meant that at that time, he had no skills to hold any type of meaningful work. The Righteous Man saw an honest and trustworthy person in Moses, realizing his potential and needs. The Righteous Man entered into an agreement in which Moses would marry one of his daughters. In return, Moses would work for the Righteous Man for eight years. In the process, Moses got a job, shelter, and a family, and learned the skills that were necessary for him to be a productive member of society.

The Righteous Man could have easily showed appreciation to Moses by providing him with dinner and a gift, and then sent him on his way. However, there is immense wisdom in the route that the Righteous Man took with Moses. Moses learned significantly from the wisdom and experiences of the old Righteous Man. This example, and others documented throughout Prophet Mohammed's life, set up the standards for the most effective sort of human development. This development utilizes people's abilities, providing them with jobs and the training necessary to do those jobs—an investment in human beings. A hand up, not a hand out.

Zakat Systems

As we have seen, in Islam, every able-bodied person is ordered to work to fulfill the needs of himself and his family. In the event that a person is not able to work, then his wealthier relatives are responsible for their support.

This concept of working to support oneself and those under their care opens a number of questions that demand viable solutions.

- What does a person do should he be unable to work and has no capable relative to support him?

- Who is responsible for the needy, such as orphans, widows, and elderly parents in the event that they do not have someone to take care of them?

- Should we leave such people to suffer alone from poverty while there are rich people that are happily enjoying life?

These questions open an entirely new preposition. Through Zakat, which has been prescribed by Allah, the needy are not forgotten. This third pillar of Islam's five pillars identifies a specific portion of money—a lawful claim by the poor, which is to be paid by those more fortunate. Simply put, Zakat is almsgiving. The main purpose behind Zakat is to help the needy while maintaining their dignity.

Zakat is mainly intended for the poor and needy. On many occasions, the Prophet mentioned only this group of people who were to be the recipients of Zakat. Such was the story when the Prophet sent Mu'az Bin Jabal to Yemen, ordering him to collect money from Yemen's wealthy and give it to their poor. From this example spawned the reasoning that Abu Haneefa Mazhab did not allow Zakat to be paid to anyone except those in poverty who had a need, and to other recipients. This is specified by the Qur'anic verse: "Zakat shall go to the poor, the needy, and those employed to collect (the funds), and to attract the hearts of those who have been inclined (towards Islam); and to free the captives; and for those in debt; and for Allah's cause, and for the wayfarer. Such is Allah's commandment. Allah is Omniscient, Most Wise" (at-Taubah 9: 60).

The Value of Zakat

Ever since the time of the Prophet, Islam has dealt with the dilemma of poverty without requiring the destitute to demand or revolt for their fair share. Islam sees the issue of dealing with poverty as a highly important matter. Therefore, it is no great surprise to find that Zakat is not only the third pillar of Islam, but is also one of its articles of faith. In a well known Hadith, the Prophet said, "Islam was built on five pillars: Knowing that there is no God but Allah, and that Mohamed is His Prophet, performing prayers, giving Zakat, fasting Ramadan, and performing Hajj for the capable".

Performing Zakat: A Condition for Being a Muslim

In Islam, prayer is the main pillar of worship. The next is the giving of Zakat. In the Qur'an and Sunnah, Zakat and prayer are always associated with each other: a person is not considered a Muslim if he or she does not perform each of these. The Qur'an states, "And woe to those who associate others with Allah, those who do not give Zakat, and in the Hereafter, they are disbelievers" (Fussilat: 6-7). This opinion is also documented in Hadith. A learned companion of the Prophet, Abdullah bin Mas'oud, once said, "You were ordered to perform prayer and pay Zakat, so whomever does not pay Zakat, then his prayer is not accepted."[2]

Primarily, the Qur'an outlines that the performance of Zakat is a sign of the good character of Muslims and one proof of being a Muslim. Allah said, "Certainly will the believers have succeeded: They who are during their prayer humbly submissive, and they who turn away from ill speech, and they who are observant of Zakat" (Al-Mu'minun: 1-4). Allah also describes good Muslims as those performing prayers and giving Zakat. He said, "guidance and mercy for the doers of good who establish prayer and give Zakat, and they, of the Hereafter, are certain [in faith]"(Luqman: 3-4). In fact, nearly every time prayer (which is the most important pillar of Islam after the belief in Allah) is mentioned in the Qur'an, it is coupled with Zakat.

Without Zakat, a man would not be among the righteous people as Allah said, "Righteousness is not that you turn your faces toward the east or the west. But [true] righteousness is [in] one who believes in Allah, the Last Day, the angels, the books, and the prophets and gives wealth, in spite of love for it, to relatives, orphans, the needy, the travelers, those who ask [for help], and for freeing slaves; [and who] establishes prayer and gives Zakat" (al-Baqarah 2: 177). Moreover, without giving Zakat, Allah's mercy will not be deserved by those who do not perform it. Allah said, "…but My mercy encompasses all things, so I will decree it [especially] for those who fear Me and give Zakat, and those who believe in Our verses" (al-A'raf: 156).

Furthermore, for those people who do not give Zakat, Islam has promised punishment in the Hereafter. Allah said, "And let not those who [greedily] withhold what Allah has given them of His bounty ever think that it is better for them. Rather, it is worse for them. Their necks will be encircled by what they withheld on the Day of Resurrection" (Ali'Imran: 180).

In an Islamic society, the government legally applies other worldly punishments for those who do not pay their Zakat. The Prophet said, "… and whosoever refuses to give Zakat, I will take half of his money" (reported by Abu Dawood). From this Hadith, scholars outline the permissibility of the ruling government to take up to 50 percent of the Zakatable wealth of a person who refuses to give Zakat, for as many years as is necessary to give the poor their rights.

Giving Zakat: Not an Option

Although Islam encourages the rich to give charity, and help others in general, it does not leave giving charity to a strictly voluntary basis. Rather, Islam regulates such giving by acknowledging that by ignoring the poor and weak in society, and leaving them to the whims of volunteer support, it might make the poor more vulnerable. While looking at the postulate of "if they want to help fine—if not, then they don't have to", one must realize that this might provide a catalyst for events to worsen. This is especially true if the more affluent are hard of heart, and of weak faith. The wealthy may have become selfish, holding onto their love of money above anything (or anyone) else. This is exactly how society was before Islam when Allah said, "Nay! But you treat not the orphans with kindness and generosity…And urge not one another on the feeding of Al-Miskin (the poor)! And you devour the inheritance all with greed. And you love wealth with immense love" (Al-Fajr: 17-20).

A business transaction usually bears two faces. The price of a commodity is an obligation from the buyer's perspective, and it is a right from the seller's perspective. This claim is clarified by two factors:

- When there is a demand for a commodity, then the seller has a right to set his fee, which is an obligation that the buyer must pay to obtain the commodity.

- When the government takes on the duty of enforcing the right of the seller, it also takes on the duty of seeing that the buyer is being charged a fair price for that commodity.

This simple law of commerce can be applied to charity. The needy have a claim given to them by Allah over the wealth of another. This claim must be paid. The needy also have the right to expect that someone in authority demands this claim on their behalf, such as the government. If the claim is not paid, then the government should enforce its collection. Following this method definitely strengthens the position of those less fortunate in society. In short, charity solely by voluntary means is a weak strategy to deal with poverty.

The Right of Poor to Zakat

From an Islamic standpoint, Zakat is a right owed by the wealthy to the poor. As well, it is a known right to a specific percentage of their Zakatable wealth. Allah said, "And from their properties was [given] the right of the [needy] petitioner and the deprived" (Azzari-yat: 19). While in another Surah, in which Allah was talking about the kind of people who deserve to go to Heaven, He said, "And those within whose wealth is a known right for the petitioner and the deprived" (al-Ma'arij: 24-25).

In terms of Zakat, the poor share the wealth of the rich to some limited extent. From an Islamic standpoint, since the groundwork of ownership to wealth is laid out from the beginning, there are no surprises. Islam contends that Allah is the owner of all wealth. He has entrusted those people of His choosing with various amounts and kinds of wealth, while at the same time, He orders them to spend from it towards the benefit of the needy. Allah said, "...and spend out of that in which He has made you trustees" (Al-Hadeed: 7). Therefore, the true owner of wealth and money from a Muslim's perspective is the Creator, and human beings are only guardians for this abundance. Allah creates wealth, and gives it to whomever He wishes. Man must obey the Master of this wealth by giving a set portion of it to those in need.

Substantial Amounts of Zakat

The two and one-half to 20 percent of Zakatable wealth is an enormous source of support for those in need. Taken as a whole, Zakat is no small amount of money.

Concerning the Zakatable amount of agricultural products, the Prophet said, "from the land that is watered by nature one tenth, and from the land that is irrigated by man or tools half of a tenth" (reported by Al-Bukhari). From all plantation produce such as fruit, vegetables, seeds, etc., the Zakatable amount ranges from five to ten percent.

For those products produced in factories and in the manufacturing sector, scholars apply the same set of rules. The amount of two and one-half percent is also set as the Zakat for monetary assets and trade, which covers most business endeavors. Islam also prescribes a certain Zakatable figure for animal production, such as raising cows, sheep, etc. Additionally, the figure prescribed for all "treasures of earth" (like metals and petroleum) is set at 20 percent, which leads to the enormous amounts of Zakat that petroleum producing countries are required to give.

Zakat Has No Substitute

Islamically, it does not matter what country a Muslim lives in, and regardless of whether or not the taxes they pay increase or decrease, there is no substitute for the paying of one's Zakat. Zakat will always be a pillar of their faith, and no tax will ever replace it. Nor will any circumstance ever affect its payment. Allah has made the giving of Zakat to the needy a sign of loyalty to Him on part with belief in God and His messenger. Even though some governments forgive taxes that have remained unpaid after some years, because Zakat is other people's money, unpaid Zakat cannot be forgiven. Islamic scholars such as Ibn Hazem have said that if a person did not pay Zakat for many years, the due Zakat is calculated at its set percentage rate, and then multiplied by the years it was not paid. Even if this consumes all of their wealth, that person must pay the Zakat they owe. Some scholars agree that if a person did not give their Zakat due, they have no right to deal in business. The implication of nonpayment of Zakat dues is so significant that if a contract's Zakatable amount has not been paid, it nullifies the contract.

Furthermore, when a person dies, upon their death, their Zakat due must be paid before anything else. Ibn Hazem stated that if a person dies and has many debts, the first debt to be paid is their Zakat due because this amount is a trust from Allah for those in need. Only after their Zakat is paid, should payment of any remaining debts follow. This holds true as well before the dead person's heirs can collect any inheritance. If this person did not pay their Zakat due from the past year, for instance, the amount due is estimated and distributed among its rightful owners: the poor and needy. Only then may the remaining funds be distributed amongst the deceased's heirs.

Keeping Zakat Funds Separate

It is the tradition and practice to maintain a separate fund for Zakat, known as Zakat Baitul-Mal or Zakat Fund. This implies that all funds collected for Zakat should not be added to other funds collected by the government or other entity.

The reasoning behind this is that Zakat expenditures differ from other funds. Zakat funds are intended for the poor and needy. Any administrative costs associated with their collection and distribution, as well as the pay of those people who manage the Zakat, may also be paid out of the total collected.

Zakat Recipients

The Qur'an puts a great deal of emphasis on how to distribute Zakat, but not much on its collection. This is most probably due to the way it is collected, which might differ in methodology according to geographical areas and type of wealth. Although these methods might vary from time to time, those who may lawfully receive Zakat are clearly defined. Allah did not leave the disbursement of Zakat to the whims of rulers or scholars. Rather, He identified eight specific options or categories as a guideline for those people in charge on where or who the Zakat should be spent. The Qur'an says, "Zakat expenditures are only for the Faqeer (poor), and for the Miskeen (needy), and for those employed to collect [the funds]; and to attract the hearts of those who have been inclined [towards Islam]; and for freeing captives [or slaves]; and for those in debt; and for the cause of Allah, and for the [stranded] traveler—an obligation [imposed] by Allah. And Allah is all Knowing and Wise" (at-Tawbah: 60).

Once a man came up to the Prophet and asked him to give him from the Zakat. In response, the Prophet said, "Allah did not even permit a prophet's judgment in Zakat. So He decided Himself upon it, and permits it into eight categories. So if you belong to any of these categories, I'll give you your right" (Reported by Abu Dawood).

The Most Deserving of Zakat: Poor and Needy

Out of these eight categories, the main recipients are the poor and needy. Scholars and Qur'anic interpreters have argued about the meaning and the difference between *Faqeer* (translated as poor) and *Miskeen* (translated as needy). In short, most scholars say that the poverty level of those in the Faqeer category is worse than Miskeen. Some scholars specifically state that those classified as Faqeer do not have an income, while Miskeen do have incomes that do not fulfill their entire needs. An example of this is when a family needs $2,500 monthly to fulfill its needs, but their monthly income is only $1,300. In any case, Faqeer and Miskeen are poor and needy individuals who do not have enough income to be independent of others.

Moreover, the most deserving of Zakat are those poor and needy who do not ask or beg for help as described by Allah, "An ignorant [person] would think them self-sufficient because of their restraint, but you will know them by their [characteristics] sign. They do not ask people persistently [or at all]" (al-Baqarah: 273).

Scholars say that a person who quits their job to commit themself to full-time worship does not deserve Zakat funds. Contrary to this, a person who is able to work, yet commits himself to seeking knowledge has a right to take from Zakat funds to afford life's expenses.

Zakat Al-Fitr

There is yet another form of Zakat which is conducted at the end of Ramadan, during the time of the 'Eid. One of the purposes of Zakat al-Fitr is to be generous to those in need and provide for them during the holiday so that they may not feel left out, but cared for by others in society.

The one notable thing that sets Zakat al-Fitr apart from the form of Zakat previously discussed, is that it is not an obligation set solely upon the rich. Rather, it is an obligation placed upon every Muslim man and woman, rich or poor, and is incumbent upon them as long as they possess a day's worth of food! During this holiday, every person is required to give. For example, a father might give on behalf of a newborn child.

The value behind this exercise may possibly be to teach all people that no matter how poor one is, there is bound to be someone poorer. Furthermore, any gift—no matter how small—is a valuable gift. Many of those who give to the poor during this time will receive from other people as well, as they themselves may be poor.

Islam has set the minimum amount for Zakat al-Fitr to be very affordable for almost any person so that all might be involved. This minimum amount, as specified by the Prophet is to be a "Sa'a" of mostly dry food whose value is set to be equal to the weight of approximately 2 Kg of dates, raisins, rice, wheat or other commodities. Presently, this amount is valued to be about between five and seven dollars, an amount affordable by almost all. Additionally, scholars argue that an equal value of food may be substituted for the money.

How Much Should Poor Receive?

After a poor person receives enough Zakat funds to last a month or two, once the money is consumed, history repeats itself. Again, they will be in trouble and require help. In this way, Zakat can be compared to an aspirin: taking a pill to kill the pain for a short time will in no way treat the cause of the pain. For this reason, there are two opinions on how much to give the poor out of the Zakat funds.

Opinion #1) Helping the poor to be self-sufficient for life: This particular opinion is shared mainly by the Shafi'e school and says that the poor person should be given enough funding to last for an extended time so that they will not require the receiving of Zakat again. These scholars believe that if a poor person has a skill or profession, then he should be given enough money to acquire the necessary tools for his field so that he might become self-sufficient. The amount this person should receive varies according to the different professions, where they live, the time, etc. For example, a person who knows how to handle animals could be given a few cows to raise. Alternatively, a person who knows masonry might be given the money to buy the necessary tools for his trade, or possibly be given the tools themselves, while a baker could be given pastry ingredients and an oven, and so on.

So, what about a person who does not have a skill? In this case, recent scholars say they should be provided with the necessary training in a specific skill from which they can make a living. For example, a widow might be trained to sew, and can be given a sewing machine and some fabric, etc., from which to earn a livable wage. The same could be true for an older orphan who can be taught auto mechanics so they can support themselves without being a burden on society.

This option is from the school of the second Caliph who said, "If you give, enrich".[3] This philosophical idea means to entirely transform the state of the poor person from poverty to independence so they will no longer have a need for Zakat.

Opinion #2) Give Enough for an Entire Year: Scholars who follow the Imam Malik and Imam Ahmed schools of Fiqh (jurisprudence) encourage the giving of Zakat to the needy and poor to last them until the next season's Zakat—enough to sustain them for an entire year. Since Zakat money is continuous, there is no need to give a poor person enough money at one time to benefit him for his whole life. Zakat is regularly collected each year, and continuously doled out to the ones that deserve it the most.

Which Opinion is Correct?

Each philosophy has its positive measures. There is no doubt that each is applicable and more effective according to individual situations. The first opinion would be more practical for a poor individual who is able to work but lacks the necessary tools, and can be given enough money to buy those tools to be independent. The second would apply to those people who are unable to work because they are handicapped, elderly, or orphans, etc., and can be given enough to sustain them for a year.

Zakat: A Continuous, Timely Support to those in Need

When examining the purpose of Zakat in Islam, we find it mainly as a welfare system to support those in need, specifically for those who cannot work or do not have a self-sufficient income. In such situations, Zakat funds would sponsor the poor person and their family. This is done either by providing for the poor person enough sustenance or funds to last an entire year, or by somehow providing the skills and tools necessary for them to become self-sufficient. It was reported that a needy lady once came to Omar Bin Al-Khattab saying that she was not given Sadaqah for her children. Omar called for Mohammed Bin Muslimah who was responsible for collecting and distributing Zakat. When he came, Omar said, "You chose not to help that lady. What would you say if Allah asks you about her?" Mohammed's eyes started to tear. Then Omar said, "Allah has sent us His Prophet and we believed him, and he did what Allah ordered him to do. So, he prescribed the Sadaqah for those in need". Then, Omar ordered Mohammed to give her Sadaqah on a yearly basis. In addition, he gave her a camel with containers full of oil and flour, and other types of nonperishable foods to correct the wrong the administration had done to her.[4]

This story clearly illustrates how the second Caliph gave Zakat on a yearly basis for those who were unable to work. It also shows that Zakat was a regulated and continuous assistance. So, why is Zakat given on a yearly basis? The answer lies in the fact that Muslims give their Zakat annually. As stated earlier in the second option, if support for the needy is organized on a monthly basis due to the inability of the administrative agency to distribute it yearly, this is still permissible as the purpose is fulfilled.

Geographical Distribution of Zakat

From the beginning, the Prophet ordered his people to collect Zakat from the wealthy, and give it to the poor of their locality. This practice has continued throughout history, as it is better for each locality or community to support its own needy and poor citizens.

Abu Obeid said that all of the Hadith of the Prophet prove that the needy of every society deserve to receive the Zakat collected in that society, until they no longer need it.[5] This means that it is better not to move Zakat collected from one country or one community to another country unless there is not much need for the Zakat in the community from where it was collected.

In cases where the people of one nation are affluent and have little need for Zakat funds, it is permitted to move those funds to another nation where the people are suffering from extreme poverty. Hadith dictates that when extreme poverty appears elsewhere, then Zakat should be given to those poor even if they are far away. Because of Muslim brotherhood, we should favor them more than those who are closer to us, but have less need for it.[6] Sahnoon said that if the imam knows that there is more poverty in another country, then he is allowed to send Zakat collected funds to that country. Moreover, Imam Malik made it clearer by saying that "it is not permitted to move Zakat out unless it more needed in another land".[7]

Zakat: The First Welfare System

Welfare in many countries in Europe, and North and South America is a relatively new thing. Many countries did not institute the system until this last century. To this day, many countries still do not have any form of welfare to aid their less fortunate citizens. In this type of assistance, Zakat is the first known form of welfare regulated as a social support for those in need. Zakat does not depend solely on voluntary charity, but is an obligation from a religious point of view. Additionally, governmental law enforces the collection of Zakat from those who refuse to give it. The intention of Zakat is to cover the basic necessities of life, seeing to it that the disadvantaged receive enough food, clothes, housing, as well as whatever else a family would need to live in some degree of comfort.

It is quite remarkable that this type of welfare system was fully in place over 14 centuries ago. One must realize that when this system was devised and instituted, European civilizations had not come out of their dark ages, and the western continents of North and South America had not yet been discovered. The nations of Europe were embroiled in bitter, violent battles between the rich and the poor, where the poor were fighting valiantly for their rights. It was not until the ends of World Wars I and II that poverty in Europe and elsewhere in the west was effectively addressed.

The validity of this statement is shown in 1941 when England and the United States completed a social welfare system that initiated a worldwide agreement for governments to respect and guarantee the social welfare of individuals. The Arab countries followed their lead in 1952, when a delegation met in Damascus to discuss the social welfare situation in the Arab world.[8]

Going an Extra Mile, Beyond Zakat

In addition to all of the obligations discussed previously, there are other dues that are incumbent upon Muslims. All of which are supportive in one way or another of the poor. Some of these are:

The Rights of Neighbors

Allah ordered Muslims to take care of their neighbors. It is a contradiction to call oneself a Believer while ignoring the rights of one's neighbors. Allah said, "Worship Allah and attach nothing with Him (in worship); and do good to parents, and to relatives, orphans, the poor, the neighbor who is near of kin, the neighbor who is a stranger, the companion by your side, the wayfarer (you meet), and those (slaves) whom your right hands possess. Verily, Allah does not like such as are proud and boastful" (An-Nisa'a: 36). Also, the Prophet said, "Gabriel (the Angel of Revelation) kept instructing me to take care of my neighbors, until I thought that Allah will give my neighbors the right to inherit me" (reported by Ibn Majah). It is reported that the Prophet also said, "He is not a Believer whoever dies full while [he knows that] his neighbor next to him is hungry" (Al-Tabarani). Additionally, Abu Zarr reported that the Prophet told him that "If I cook to increase the food, then give part of it to your neighbors" (Reported by Muslim).

But, who are considered to be one's neighbors? Contrary to what one might think, neighbors are not just the house next door. It was said, "...there are forty houses of neighbors" (Abu Dawood). Some scholars have clarified this statement by explaining it as forty houses each way from the four directions! The "rights" of these neighbors refers to taking care of them when they are in need, being mindful of their situation, and doing kindness unto them even if their actions were to the contrary. In a well-known story, each day a Jewish boy would pick through garbage in front of the Prophet's house, taking what he wanted. One day, the Prophet did not see evidence that the boy had been there, so he asked about the boy's situation. The Prophet was told that the boy was sick at home. Right away, the Prophet went to see the boy and look after his needs during his sickness.

The Obligation of Encouraging Others to Help

Not only are Muslims asked to help those in need, but they are also encouraged to call upon others to do so as well. Allah says, "Indeed, he did not use to believe in Allah, the Most Great, nor did he encourage the feeding of the poor" (al-Haqqah: 33-34). This Surah means that it is a person's obligation to feed the poor, as well as to call upon others to feed them. This is further demonstrated in Surat al-Ma'un, where Allah pronounces one of the signs of denying Islam as not helping orphans and the needy, and not calling upon others to do so. Allah said, "Have you seen the one who denies the Recompense? For that is the one who drives away the orphan and does not encourage the feeding of the poor" (al-Ma'un: 1-3).

In Hadith, Sahl bin Sa'd narrated how the Prophet said, "I and the person who looks after an orphan and provides for him will be in Paradise like this," putting his index and middle fingers together to demonstrate their closeness (Bukhari).

In Surat al-Fajr, Allah spoke to the ignorant in society by saying, "No! But you do not honor the orphan and you do not encourage one another to feed the poor" (al-Fajr: 17-18).

The Ritual of Udhiya

Also known as *Qurbani, Udhiya* is one of the fundamental rituals of Islam performed on the occasion of 'Eid ul-Adha, and is a prescribed obligation not only for the pilgrims performing Hajj, but for all able Muslims. Although the practice of Udhiya began in the time of Prophet Adam (peace be upon him), particular significance is brought to the practice through a specific act of Prophet Ibrahim. According to Islamic belief, the dreams of the prophets are regarded as revelations from Allah. Prophet Ibrahim (peace be upon him) dreamed that Allah commanded him to sacrifice his only son, Prophet Ismail, a child who was a blessing from Allah to Ibrahim in his old age. Prophet Ibrahim told his son of the dream; thus, Ismail entrusted himself to Allah, and agreed to be sacrificed by his father. Because of their absolute faith, humility and dedication, Allah stopped Ibrahim from slaying his beloved son, and sent a ram to be slaughtered in the place of Ismail.

This tradition of sacrifice for the sake of Allah continues even today. On the occasion of 'Eid ul-Adha, faithful Muslims all over the world submit to the Will of Allah and sacrifice a camel, cow, goat or sheep. The meat is then divided into three equal portions: the person who performs the Udhiya retains one part, the second is given to their friends and relatives (whether wealthy or poor), and the third portion is distributed to the poor. Because a camel or cow is enough to feed seven people, some scholars say these are the best sacrifices, followed by sheep and goats.

There are two scholarly opinions on Udhiya. The first is that it is waajib (obligatory). This is the opinion of al-Ozaa'i, al-Layth and Abu Haneefah. It is also one of the two opinions of Imam Ahmad and Imam Malik. Those who favor this opinion take the following verse as evidence: "Therefore turn in prayer to your Lord and sacrifice [to Him only]" (al-Kawthar 108: 2). As this is a command, it implies that something is obligatory. This opinion is also supported by the Hadith: "Whoever can afford to offer a sacrifice but does not do so, let him not approach our place of prayer" (Reported by Ahmad and Ibn Majah).

The second scholarly opinion is that performing Udhiya is a confirmed Sunnah (Sunnah Mu'akkadah). This is the view of al-Shafa'i school, as well as those of Malik and Ahmad. However, most who favor this opinion stated that it is makrooh (disliked) for the one who is able to offer a sacrifice to neglect to do so.

Some scholars say that each point of view has its evidence. To be on the safe side, the one who is able to offer a sacrifice should not neglect to do so because of what is involved in this act of reverence towards Allah. Aishah narrated that the Prophet Muhammad said, "There is nothing dearer to Allah during the days of Qurbani than the sacrificing of animals. The sacrificed animal shall come on the Day of Judgement with its horns, hair, and hooves [to be weighed]. The sacrifice is accepted by Allah before the blood reaches the ground. Therefore sacrifice with an open and happy heart".[9]

Kaffarat

Kaffarat, the expiation of sins or correction of wrongs, comes in many different forms. However, each has one common denominator: seeking the forgiveness of Allah. The following are different types:

- *Kaffarat Al-Yameen:* If someone is unable to fulfill a promise they made—such as swearing an oath to accomplish something—then Islam allows them to correct this by feeding ten poor people for an entire day, or clothe them. Such a solution allows a person to be forgiven for not fulfilling what they have sworn to, while helping someone in need. Allah said, "So it's expiation is the feeding of ten needy people from the average of that which you feed your [own] families, or clothing them or the freeing of a slave" (al-Ma'idah: 89).

- *Kaffarat Al-Si'yam:* For those who are unable to fast during Ramadan due to old age or sickness, Allah allows them to substitute the fast on those days by giving to those in need. The same rule applies for those who are able to fast but with great difficulty (such as a traveler). The traveler must make up for those days missed during Ramadan by fasting an equal number of days during alternative times. The same applies to when the ill person recovers from their sickness. Allah says, "[Observing Sawm (fasts)] for a fixed number of days, but if any of you is ill or on a journey, the same number (should be made up) from other days. And as for those who can fast with difficulty, (e.g. an old man), they have (a choice either to fast or) to feed a Miskin (poor person) (for every day)" (al-Baqarah: 184).

- *Al-Hadey and Kaffarah:* Refer to the slaughter of sheep, cows or camels to distribute meat to the needy. Al-Hadey is performed during Hajj, and Kaffarah is done to seek forgiveness for wrongs or sins someone has committed.

There are many other occasions where seeking forgiveness from Allah through Kaffarah can be applied, such as having sex during the daylight hours in Ramadan, or when a man insults his wife or compares her to her mother. To correct such wrongs, a Muslim might slaughter a specific number of animals and distribute the meat to the poor, or give aid to a specific number of people.

Baitul Mal Systems

Previously, we have shown the reader that Zakat is the first financial source to support people in need who cannot work and have no help from relatives. Nevertheless, Zakat might not be enough to insure all poor are given adequate help. This is where an additional source of funding comes in: *Baitul Mal*, which is the government treasury set up to fund all the remaining welfare and needs. Among these needs are all other forms of governmental spending, such as public employees, schools, hospitals, roads, transportation, and other official services. The sources of Baitul Mal are numerous, and can be from government owned assets, publicly held assets known as Waqf, or special taxes such as those on imported goods, etc. These types of funds should benefit the wellbeing of not only Muslims, but also all non-Muslims living in Muslim lands.

Caliph Omar bin Abdul-Aziz wrote to Oday bin Artat (who was at that time the ruler of Basra), reminding him of some of his duties in this position. When Oday received the letter, he read it to a large audience in Basra. "Look for people that are Christians or Jews that are old, weak, and cannot work. Then give them from Baitul Mal what would fully support them, because it was reported to me that the Caliph Omar Bin Al-Khattab saw an old non-Muslim man knocking at people's doors, begging for money. Then Omar told him, 'we did not treat you justly if we taxed you when you were younger, then we leave you alone when you are old'." Then, Omar allocated for this man a continuous financial support from Baitul Mal that would fully support him.[10]

Moreover, scholars have ruled that if neither Zakat nor Baitul Mal with their various financial resources can eradicate poverty, then Muslim rulers have the right to set an extra taxation on the rich to support the poor. Additionally, some scholars argue that the rulers may raise the percentage of Zakat dues as well.

Social Welfare: A Top Priority in Islam

Islamic historians tell a parable about Omar bin Abdul-Aziz's wife Fatimah who once entered a room where Omar was praying. There, she found Omar with his face buried in his hands, crying. She asked him what was wrong. He replied, "O Fatimah, I was appointed to lead this society. Then I thought of the hungry poor, the ill person, the broken hearted orphan, the lonely widow, the sad victim, the oppressed stranger, the elderly man, the family with numerous children and little money, and many other kinds of people that face similar suffering all around the nation, and I know that Allah will question me about them all in the Day of Judgment. So I felt sorry for myself and cried".[11] This simple story imparts to us that taking care of the welfare of all people under Muslim rule is of such high priority that it should not be taken lightly. For many centuries, this issue was a serious matter for the various rulers of the Muslim lands. This held true for hundreds of years, until later Muslim rulers set aside the welfare of the people in their quests for leadership, control and pleasure.

The following example clarifies the previous statement. Omar bin Al-Khattab preserved a large piece of land close to Medina called Al-Rabtha, which was suitable for shepherding animals. Here, he allowed poor people to freely graze their cattle so they might increase their animals' milk production, and in turn help themselves to become self-sufficient. Omar instructed Hany, the man who was appointed to administer the land, to "help people and you'll be rewarded by Allah for that, and don't let the animals of Ibn Affan and Ibn A'of (two wealthy families) feed there. They have many sources for income. But let the animals of those poor [feed there]. For if their animals die out of feed (starve), they (the poor people) will come to me with their children, and I can't then leave them without care".[12]

These concepts are what prevent society from having two extreme levels: the very poor and the very rich, with an implicit goal to destroy the division between them. As well, such formulas assist the rich in not becoming too stingy and preoccupied with the accumulation of wealth. So, when taken together thoroughly, these systems will help reduce poverty to minimal levels, and may even eradicate it. History supports Islam's method of dealing with poverty by erasing poverty and fear, and fulfilling peoples' safety, freedom and justice.

IV. Practical Applications Made a Difference

Throughout Islamic history, these concepts illustrated through the Qur'anic verses and Hadith did not fall on deaf ears. With the probable exception of the last few centuries—when Muslims found themselves in a different situation—the practical implications of these teachings had an enormous effect. In earlier times, poverty was nearly eradicated from some Muslim societies. This was when the wealthy felt extremely happy and privileged to find needy people who were willing to accept their charity, giving them the opportunity to earn Allah's pleasure. The following text illustrates a few practical examples.

Qur'an interpreters reported that Abdallah bin Mas'oud said, "when the Prophet of Allah received the verse 'Who is he that would loan Allah a goodly loan so He may multiply it for him many times over?' (Al-Baqarah: 245). Abu Addahdah Alansari said, 'O prophet of God, Allah wants to have a loan from us?' The Prophet answered, 'yes O Abu Addahdah'. Then, Abu Addahdah said to the Prophet, 'Give me your hand'. The Prophet did, so he shook his hand and told him excitedly, 'I loaned Allah my farm'. Ibn Mas'oud reported that his farm has 600 palm trees, which was a huge property at that time. And when Abu Addahdah came to his wife while on that farm with their children, he told her, 'O Um Addahdah get out of there, I gave it as a loan to my Lord'".[13] For Addahdah to give his farm as a loan to Allah simply means that he is to distribute its holdings and land among the poor so that they might benefit from it. Certainly, Addahdah trusts that he will receive his loan back from Allah many times over in the Hereafter.

As such, charity of this sort continued between people for years on many different levels. Those who gave their money to help others were surprising role models. The objectives of Islam were for the wealthy to give money to the poor, instead of saving it forever.

People often talked about Imam Al-Laith Bin Sa'd who said that he had a great deal of money. He received 1,000 dinars every day, which was a great deal of money at that time. Yet, he did not have to pay Zakat on it. "Why is this?" one might ask. The answer is that Zakat must be paid if a minimum amount called Nisab (the value of four ounces of pure gold) stays in the possession of a person for an entire year. If the person does not possess the amount of Nisab for that whole year, then they do not owe Zakat on their wealth. The money that Al-Laith had did not stay in his possession for the whole year, as he spent it mostly for the sake of Allah. The story also relates that each day, Al-Laith did not speak until he had given daily Sadaqah to three hundred and sixty poor.

Another story tells of Abdullah Bin Ja'afar who never declined to give aid if someone asked him for help. Some people were surprised when he would interrupt his speech to give those who were needy the help they requested. He said, "Allah has taught me a habit, and I taught His people a habit too. Allah has given me money, and my habit is to give generously to His people of needs. So I am afraid that if I stop my habit, then He would stop His".

NO RESULTS FROM A PARTIAL SOLUTION

Unless a Muslim society applies comprehensive solutions, none of the previous concepts or shields will be enough. Assume that we were to apply the principles of Zakat to all of society in current Muslim countries. Will it solve the poverty issue, if taken separately from all other issues? The answer is no! This is because Zakat must be taken in the context of the complete guidance and guidelines of Islam so that it works. For instance, Islam forbids overspending on luxuries, even if the person is very wealthy. In Islam, owning utensils made of gold and silver, and living in very luxurious homes are forbidden. As is the wearing of gold and silk by men.

Additionally, Islam forbids the earning of interest, inspiring mankind to work for their money, not to simply live off its interest. The rich are also encouraged to employ the poor. If Zakat is not given willingly, then its payment must be enforced. This system does not exist in most countries today, or is corrupted to some degree in those countries that do enforce its collection. It must be established and carried out without becoming bogged down in bureaucracy, ensuring that the deserving needy and poor receive their just dues. Even those wealthy who give their Zakat willingly are not comfortable giving their Zakat to corrupted governmental agencies.

ASTONISHING RESULTS

People tend to believe what they see, more than what they read. History supports Islam's method of dealing with poverty by erasing poverty and fear, and fulfilling peoples' safety, freedom and justice. For this express reason, foundations and NGOs are being established wherever possible to fill this void.

Al-Bukhari reported in the very early days of Islam that the Prophet said, "Give Sadaqah as there will come a time when a man walks with his Sadaqah, but will not find [one] who will accept it. When a man would say: If you came [to me] with it before, then I might have accepted it, but today I don't need anything" (Sahih Al-Bukhari).

This Hadith was at the time of the first generation of Muslims, when most people suffered in poverty. However, such a situation actually took place during the era of Omar Bin Abdul-Aziz. As documented by Al-Baihaqy in his book Al-Dala'el, "Omar Bin Abdul-Aziz ruled Muslims for 30 months. During this time, rich men used to come to Baitul Mal with great amounts of money saying, 'spend these among the poor'. Yet, these men would return home with their money, being told there were 'no poor we know of'".[14]

It is also documented that Yahya bin Saeed said, "Omar Bin Abdul-Aziz sent me to Africa to collect Zakat from the rich and return it to the poor of that land. However, after we collected the due Zakat, we could not find a single poor [person], and we could not find [anyone] who would take this money from us. Omar made all people self-sufficient...so we bought slaves (in Africa) with the Zakat we had collected, and freed them (the slaves)".[15]

At one time, the Zakat system of caring for the poor in Muslim lands was so effective that Al-Amwal noted how Abu Abeed recounted a letter written by Omar bin Abdul-Aziz. In the letter, Omar directed Abdul-Hameed bin Abdurrahman who was collecting Zakat money in Iraq to give the poor people there what they deserved from those funds. Abdul-Hameed bin Abdurrahman wrote Omar bin Abdul-Aziz back saying that he had given to all those who were worthy of the Zakat funds, but there was still a lot of money remaining in Baitul Mal. So, Omar ordered Abdul-Hameed bin Abdurrahman to look for those who had outstanding loans, and give those people Zakat money to help pay off their loans. Abdul-Hameed bin Abdurrahman did this, and wrote back saying "we still have so much money in Baitul Mal". Again, Omar wrote him a letter saying, "look for unmarried men with no money, and whoever wants to get married, pay for their dowries so that they might get married. Then Abdul-Hameed did what Omar had ordered, and wrote back saying, "I have helped every bachelor that asked to get married and got them married, and I still have so much money remaining in Baitul Mal". Finally, Omar ordered Abdul-Hameed to look for those who pay *Kharaj* (a form of taxes based on their land production), and give them loans with which to strengthen their property. "And tell them that we don't want those loans for a year or two years".[16]

Further evidence of the benefits of Zakat is shown by a story that happened several years before the time of Omar bin Abdul-Aziz, when the Prophet sent Mua'th Bin Jabal to Yemen to represent him and rule the Muslims there. The Prophet ordered Mua'th Bin Jabal to specifically take the Zakat due from the rich and return it to the poor. Although Mua'th was appointed during the time of the Prophet, his appointment continued during the rules of Abu Bakr and Omar. After only a few years under Mua'th Bin Jabal's rule, there were no poor who needed the Zakat. Therefore, Mua'th Bin Jabal had no choice but to send the money to Medina, the Khilafa headquarters during the time of Caliph Omar Bin Al-Khattab. Once Omar received the remaining Zakat money from Yemen, he became upset and told Mua'th, "We did not send you as a tax collector, but to take from the rich their dues and to return them to their poor". Mua'th responded, "I would not have sent you anything if I could find [anyone] who would take money from me". The amount Mua'th sent to Medina was nearly one-third of what was collected. Three years after this incident, Mua'th reported to Omar that "I could not find any single person willing to take anything from me". The entire amount of Zakat collected by Baitul Mal in Yemen was sent to Medina, the capital of the Khilafa.[17]

The previous examples are only a few of the cases where Zakat is allowed to be spent on recipients other than the poor. These alternative beneficiaries are designated from amongst the eight categories specified in the Qur'an, such as freeing slaves. Any remaining Zakat money would be expended in this manner until all funds are depleted: spending on those with overdue loans, on travelers who are away from their wealth, and in the cause of Allah as seen fit by the Muslim rulers.

During these early years, people lived in abundance without seeking excess wealth. This continued for centuries, as poverty was nearly eradicated to minimal or negligible levels, where people lived in justice, and were satisfied with what they had.

V.   Conclusion

Islam has clearly outlined a viable plan for the eradication of poverty. However, as is plainly seen from the terrible conditions of present day countries run by so-called Muslim governments, these strategies are not incorporated. Poverty, disease, corruption, war and selfishness seem to reign without check.

Today's global society is witnessing amazing technological advances in transportation, logistics and communications making the world a more intimate environment where relief and personnel can be on the other side of the globe in a matter of hours. At the same time, amazing progress in agriculture, the harvesting of natural resources and medical procedure should ensure that no person goes hungry, survives without shelter, or suffers from illness or disease without some form of treatment.

In the past, it took years for news of a disaster to reach the masses. Today, devastating events are witnessed around the world in a matter of seconds. Frankly, with present technology, ignorance is no excuse.

If implemented and adhered to, Islam's blueprint could and would certainly make a significant dent in the number of poor and needy the world over.

Endnotes

[1] Mohammed Al-Ghazali, Laisa Mina al-Islam, p 24-25.

[2] Al-Amwal, p 596.

[3] Ibid.

[4] Al-Amwal, p 599.

[5] Al-Amwal, p 598.

[6] Al-Mudawana Al-Kubra, vol. 1, p 246.

[7] Al-Amwal, p 595.

[8] Third United Nations Social Welfare Seminar for Arab States in the Middle-East, Damascus, 8-20 December 1952, 1953.

[9] Tirmithi p 275, Vol. 1.

[10] Al-Amwal, p 46.

[11] Al-BidAyahh and Al-NihAyahh, Ibn Katheer, Vol. 9, p 201.

[12] Al-Amwal, Abu Obeid, p 299.

[13] Tafseer Ibn Katheer, Vol. 1, p 299.

[14] Omdat Al-Qari', Vol. 16, p 135.

[15] Sirat Omar Bin Abdul-Aziz, Ibn Abdul-Hakam, p 59.

[16] Al-Amwal, p 256.

[17] Al-Amwal, p 596.

Chapter

3.

Charities:

US and International Law

In this chapter, we will attempt to give some basic guidance through the legal minefield charities must now navigate in order to remain in operation, or comply with regulations. Within these pages, we will touch on state and federal issues, as well as international humanitarian law. Also addressed is the necessity of building a partnership between Islamic nonprofits and the US government in order to bring effective aid on the ground overseas. It is important to remind the reader that this chapter is not intended as, and in no way should be substituted for, sound and specialized legal advice.

I.   Charities and Legal Compliance: An Overview[1]

"A lawyer representing nonprofit organizations faces, on a daily basis, a barrage of questions about the rules governing the organizations' formation, administration, operation, and management. Some of these questions may be answered using state law rules, while some may be answered with federal law rules. More frequently than non-lawyers might suspect, there is no law on this particular point."[2]

"What is the legal standard by which a nonprofit organization should be operated?

"The legal standard is highest for a tax-exempt charitable organization. In general, the standard is easy to articulate, but often difficult to implement."[3]

Nonprofit organizations do not operate in a vacuum. They exist in a sea of laws and regulations that they are presumed to know and abide by. Currently, there are more than one and a half million nonprofit organizations in the US, and it is assumed that all of them know every law that is pertinent to their work. No one would be surprised if one of these nonprofit organizations, knowingly or unknowingly, violated the law in some technical way. The risk of detection of a technical violation is relatively small since, realistically, the government has limited resources and the use of these limited resources is focused on areas of presumed need. While all charities are well advised to update their knowledge about the law and adopt policies to conform to the laws and regulations, it is vitally important to Muslim charities, particularly those involved in international operations, to make the necessary changes because they are an enforcement priority.

In a perfect world, every nonprofit organization would have an attorney responsible for navigating the sea of laws and regulations, making sure the organization is fully complying with all pertinent laws. However, we do not live in a perfect world. Nonprofit organizations, especially Muslim organizations, are typically too small to be able to afford an in-house counsel. Therefore, it is incumbent on the chief executive officer and the directors of the organization to educate themselves about the pertinent laws and regulations. This education, coupled with having outside counsel to consult with on a regular basis, is probably a good safeguard against violating the many laws and regulations affecting charities.

THE LAWS OF THE UNITED STATES

Every person residing in the US, as well as every organization is categorized as a legal person, living under the rule of a number of laws. The supreme law of the land is the US Constitution. The following is a ranking of laws from highest to lowest:

- US Constitution

- Federal Statutes, Regulations and Executive Orders, Treaties

- State Constitutions

- State Statutes

- Local Ordinances

The US Constitution is the supreme law of the land. Any law that conflicts with the US Constitution is null and void. If a provision in a state constitution conflicts with a federal statute, the federal statute is controlling. For example, Alabama's 104-year old state constitution still calls for school segregation.[4] Obviously, this state constitutional provision conflicts with federal law and therefore it is null and void. An international treaty ratified by the Congress or executed by the President as an executive agreement has the same legal weights as a federal statute. In the case of a conflict between a federal statute and a treaty, the last in time controls.

In addition to the list of laws above, nonprofit organizations are governed by their mission statement, articles and bylaws. It is not unusual for a charity to be sued by a board member for an action that violates its articles or bylaws. Additionally, the top law enforcer in the state of incorporation, the attorney general, can sue to enforce the bylaws and the articles of the organization.

State Law

Most of the matters that affect our life are state regulated. Think of birth, marriage, adoption, buying or selling a house, getting a driver's license, and inheritance. They are all state matters. A nonprofit organization is a creature of the state. It is formed by its filing of the articles of incorporation with the state where it is to be located. In addition to incorporation in the state, the charity has to file for a license to solicit funds as well. If the charity wants to engage in soliciting funds in other states, the charity has to be licensed to do business and raise funds in the other states as well. Moreover, the "professional fundraisers" that a charity uses must be registered in the state where the fundraising is to occur. State law should be carefully studied to determine who qualifies as a "professional fundraiser."

A nonprofit organization is supposed to act in a "reasonable" and "prudent" manner. The actions must be "reasonable" and the people running it have to be "prudent." Engaging in unreasonable activity or unreasonable expenditure can revoke the status. At the state level, unreasonable behavior can lead to investigation by the state attorney general.

Traditionally, states have not closely regulated charities. However, in the aftermath of 9/11 and the reaction to corporate scandals, a number of states are moving to impose more regulations on nonprofits. An example of such a state is California's Nonprofit Integrity Act of 2004, of which the key provisions are:[5]

Registry/Filing of Articles of Incorporation–Charitable corporations have 30 days, rather than six months, to register and file the Articles of Incorporation. The effective date of the Act is January 1, 2005; therefore, initial registration was due January 30, 2005.

Independent Audits–Charitable Corporations and unincorporated associations with gross revenues of $2 million or more must prepare annual financial statements audited by an independent certified public accountant. Audited financial statements must be made available for inspection by the attorney general and the public no later than nine months after the close of the fiscal year. The $2 million gross annual revenue threshold excludes government grants that require an accounting of how those funds are used.

Audit Committees–Audit Committee provisions are applicable to entities at the $2 million gross annual revenue threshold, exclusive of government grants. The governing board must appoint an audit committee, which may include persons who are not members of the governing board. Members of the finance committee may serve on the audit committee, but must comprise 50 percent or less of the audit committee.

Executive Compensation–Governing boards of charitable organizations and unincorporated associations must review and approve the compensation (including benefits) of the CEO and CFO to ensure such compensation is just and reasonable. The governing board has the authority to define just and reasonable compensation. The review process must occur at initial hiring, when the term is renewed or extended, or when the compensation is modified.

The focus of this state legislation is on the financial side of the business operation. It is meant to pre-empt the corrupt practices that led to the failure of Enron and WorldCom.

Federal Law

IRS Rules and Regulations: A 501(c)(3) status is the most privileged tax status possible. A charity applies for this recognition with the Internal Revenue Service (IRS). Once recognized, the donations to the charity are tax deductible and the charity is exempt from paying taxes on the funds raised. A charity is not allowed to spend its resources on non-charitable purposes. In 2003, Congress amended the Tax Code to provide for the "automatic, retroactive suspension of tax-exempt status for an organization designated as a terrorist organization under any relevant legal authority."[6]

Sarbanes-Oxley Act: The American Competitiveness and Corporate Accountability Act of 2002, commonly known as the Sarbanes-Oxley Act, is a major piece of legislation intended to regulate the publicly traded corporations. This law came in the aftermath of a number of corporate scandals that shocked the American public and spurred Congress to action in this area. This act was designed to improve corporate governance and ensure that corporate corruption similar to the Enron and WorldCom scandals do not recur in the future. The Sarbanes-Oxley act does not target nonprofits. In fact, only two provisions of the act, the document destruction provision and the whistle-blower provision, apply to the nonprofit sector. However, it has been wisely suggested that the nonprofit sector be proactive on this issue and voluntarily adopt the governance mandates laid out in the act.[7]

To help members comply with the document retention and the whistleblower provisions, InterAction set two voluntary standards for members:[8]

- **Standard 3.7 [Document Retention and Destruction Policies]**–The organization will have policies for document retention and destruction that ensure protection of documents during an official investigation.

- **Standard 6.3.2 [Grievance Procedures]**–The organization will have policies to address complaints and prohibit realization against whistleblowers.

Nonprofits do not have to comply with the other provisions of the act, but it has been recommended that they do. Independent Sector neatly summarized the act's requirements in the form of a checklist:

Insider Transactions and Conflicts of Interest: Understand and fully comply with all laws regarding compensation and benefits provided to directors and executives (including "intermediate sanctions" and "self-dealing laws").

- Do not provide personal loans to directors and executives.

- In cases in which the board feels it is necessary to provide a loan, however, all terms should be disclosed and formally approved by the board, the process should be documented, and the terms and the value of the loan should be publicly disclosed.

- Establish a conflict of interest policy, as well as a regular and rigorous means of enforcing it.

Independent and Competent Audit Committee: Conduct an annual external financial audit (the boards of very small organizations, for whom the cost of an external audit may be too burdensome, should at least evaluate carefully whether an audit would be valuable.)

- Establish a separate audit committee of the board.

- Board members on the audit committee should be free from conflicts of interest and should not receive any compensation for their service on the committee.

- Include at least one "financial expert" on the audit committee.

- The audit committee should select and oversee the auditing company and review the audit.

- Require full board to approve audit results.

- Provide financial literacy training to all board members.

Responsibilities of Auditors:

- Rotate auditor or lead partner at least every five years.

- Avoid any conflict of interest in staff exchange between audit firm and organization.

- Do not use auditing firm for non-auditing services except tax form preparation with pre-approval from audit committee.

- Require disclosure to audit committee of critical accounting policies and practices.

- Use audit committee to oversee and enforce conflict-of-interest policy.

Certified Financial Statements:

- CEO and CFO should sign off on all financial statements (either formally or in practice), including Form 990 tax returns, to ensure they are accurate, complete, and filed on time.

- The board should review and approve financial statements and Form 990 tax returns for completeness and accuracy.

Disclosure:

- Disclose Form 990 and 990-PF in a current and easily accessible way (also required of all nonprofit organizations by IRS law).

- File 990 and 990-PF Forms in a timely manner, without use of extensions unless required by unusual circumstances.

- Disclose audited financial statements.

- Move to electronic filing of Form 990 and 990-PF.

Whistle-Blower Protection:

- Develop, adopt, and disclose a formal process to deal with complaints and prevent retaliation.

- Investigate employee complaints, and correct any problems or explain why corrections are not necessary.

Document Destruction:

- Have a written, mandatory document retention and periodic destruction policy for electronic files and voicemail, which includes guidelines.

- If an official investigation is underway (or even suspected), stop any document purging in order to avoid criminal obstruction.[9]

II.   Executive Order 13224 and The PATRIOT Act

The President is the head of the executive branch of government. He is in charge of enforcing the laws passed by Congress. One of the lesser known powers of the President is the ability to issue executive orders. An executive order has the weight of law.

No executive order affected charities like Executive Order 13224 issued by President Bush in the aftermath of the 9/11 attacks. Executive Order 13224, issued by President Bush on September 23, 2001 "prohibits US persons from transacting or dealing with individuals and entities owned or controlled by, acting for or on behalf of, assisting or supporting, or otherwise associated with, persons listed in the Executive Order." Those designated and listed under the Executive Order are known as 'Specially Designated Global Terrorists' (SDGTs)."[10]

This Executive Order prohibits transactions with individuals and entities deemed to be associated with terrorism. The definition of terrorism is a controversial issue in the public policy domain. However, this Executive Order defines it as: "an activity that (1) involves a violent act or an act dangerous to human life, property or infrastructure; and (2) appears to be intended (A) to intimidate or coerce a civilian population; (B) to influence the policy of a government by intimidation or coercion; or (C) to affect the conduct of a government by mass destruction, assassination, kidnapping, or hostage taking."[11] "Transactions" include financial support, in-kind donations and technical assistance. This Executive Order gave the executive branch the authority to freeze the assets of organizations or individuals identified as "terrorists, supporters of terrorists or otherwise associated with terrorists." This freezing of assets can occur while an investigation is ongoing, which can have a devastating effect on a charity, even if it were eventually cleared of charges.

CIVIL LIBERTIES VS. EXECUTIVE ORDER

The 9/11 attacks had a profound and, so far, lasting effect on American law and government. The Bush administration lobbied for legislation that expanded the government's ability to combat terrorism. The Bush administration was able to have congress pass a major piece of legislation that shifted the balance between civil liberties and security in favor of security. This legislation is the PATRIOT Act, which became law on October 26, 2001. This law greatly strengthened prior laws that fight terrorism. The act imposed significant fines and imprisonment for any entity that provides "material support" to terrorist acts or to foreign terrorist organizations.

In the criminal justice system, to determine guilt, the government has to prove its case beyond any reasonable doubt. In a civil case, the plaintiff has to prove his case with a preponderance of the evidence. In administrative law, the standard for making a case is much more relaxed. Hearsay is admissible. The level of proof is more likely than not. The freezing of assets, the equivalent of the death penalty in criminal law, can be imposed while an investigation is ongoing. The evidence that is the basis of the freezing can be classified, and the target of the investigation has no right to see it. Therefore, not only is the government able to freeze assets on the basis of mere suspicion, the target of the freezing realistically has no real opportunity to defend itself. Richard Newcomb, then Director of the Office of Foreign Assets Control (OFAC), at a hearing before the House Financial Services Subcommittee on Oversight and Investigations stated: The USA PATRIOT Act of 2001 has enhanced OFAC's ability to implement sanctions and to coordinate with other agencies by clarifying OFAC's authorities to block assets of suspect entities prior to a formal designation in 'aid of an investigation' In addition, the PATRIOT Act explicitly authorizes submission of classified information to a court, in camera and ex parte, upon a legal challenge to a designation. This new PATRIOT Act authority has greatly enhanced our ability to make and defend designations by making it absolutely clear that OFAC *may use classified information in making designations without turning the material over to an entity or individual that challenges its designation.* (emphasis added)[12]

This power is not theoretical. There are many laws on the books that are not enforced. These provisions have been used by the executive branch and, not surprisingly, they were used against Muslim charities that had no chance to defend themselves. Two Illinois based Muslim charities had their assets frozen while an investigation was ongoing of their possible ties to terrorism. According to the Monograph on Terrorist Financing presented to the National Commission on Terrorist Attacks upon the United States in August 2004, "This provision lets the government shut down an organization without any formal determination of wrongdoing. It requires a single piece of paper, signed by a midlevel government official. Although in practice, a number of agencies typically review and agree to the action, there is no formal administrative process, *let alone any adjudication of guilt"* (emphasis added)..."The administrative record needed to justify a designation can include newspaper articles and other hearsay normally deemed too unreliable for a court of law. A designated entity can challenge the designation in court, but its chances of success are limited. The legal standard for overturning the designation is favorable to the government and the government can rely on classified evidence that it shows to the judge but not defense counsel, depriving the designated entity of the usual right to confront the evidence against it."[13]

OMB Watch Report states that the independent commission investigating the 9/11 attacks raised "substantial civil liberty concerns" regarding the government's shutdown in December 2001 of two Chicago-area Islamic charities.[14] Since then, the government has neither proven either group was guilty of any terrorism-related crimes, nor convicted anyone involved.

Authorities closed the Global Relief Foundation (GRF) of Bridgeview and Benevolence International Foundation (BIF) of Palos Hills before any official finding that they were aiding terrorist organizations. The OMB report concludes: "...these cases demonstrate the government's dramatic shift from pre-9/11 investigating and monitoring terrorist financing to actively disrupting suspect entities through freezing their assets. It also found many suspects are denied due process and organizations have been closed without formal evidence that they actually funded al-Qaeda or other terrorist groups. The question becomes what is the threshold of information for the government to take disruptive action against suspect charities."[15]

WHO IS ON THE LIST?

In no other area of the law is the process so extremely in favor of the government. Given the degree of danger to the charity's very existence, the organization must do all it can to avoid transacting with suspected terrorists. It falls upon the nonprofit to consistently search against the number of available databases and lists of suspected terrorists. The United Nations, the European Union and several US governmental agencies maintain their own lists. The Treasury Department's Office of Foreign Assets Control (OFAQ) maintains the most extensive index, the Special Designated Nationals List (SDN List). Since names are added almost daily, these lists should be searched frequently to avoid noncompliance with federal law. Additionally, many commercial services allow the user to search a number of public lookout databases. One example of these is Bridger Insight, an online subscription program that is constantly updated, enabling the subscriber to access a number of different worldwide databases.[16]

EMBARGOES AND TRADE SANCTIONS

Charities also have to be aware of embargoes and trade sanctions, which are primarily maintained by the Treasury Department. The US currently imposes embargoes and trade sanctions on a number of countries. The Treasury Department website has a list of the embargoed countries, of which Cuba is a perennial member. Transacting with an entity that is the target of sanctions is punishable by civil and criminal penalties. Usually, there are exemptions to providing "humanitarian aid" to embargoed entities. In some cases, a charity needs to get a license from Treasury or Commerce before sending humanitarian aid to a listed entity.

III.   Treasury Voluntary Best Practices Guidelines

In November 2002, "Anti-Terrorist Financing Guidelines: Voluntary Best Practices for US-Based Charities" was issued by the US Department of Treasury to provide guidance for charities on how to comply with Executive Order 13224 and the PATRIOT Act. These guidelines deal with the governance of the charity, disclosure and transparency in governance and finances, financial practices, accountability, and anti-terrorist financing procedures. These guidelines have been criticized in the charity circles as too onerous—demanding extensive due diligence not only on grantees but on vendors and financial institutions used in carrying out foreign grant-making and programming."[17] For example, before any charitable funds are provided to a foreign recipient, the November 2002 guidelines advise: "The charity should collect the following basic information about a foreign recipient organization:

- The foreign recipient organization's name in English, in the language of origin, and any acronym or other names used to identify the foreign recipient organization.

- The jurisdictions in which the foreign recipient organization maintains physical presence.

- The jurisdiction in which the foreign recipient organization is incorporated or formed.

- The address and telephone number of any place of business of the foreign recipient organization.

- The principal purpose of the foreign recipient organization, including a detailed report of the recipient's projects and goals.

- The names and addresses of organizations to which the foreign recipient organization currently provides or proposes to provide funding, services, or material support, to the extent known, as applicable.

- The names and addresses of any subcontracting organization utilized by the foreign recipient organization.

- Copies of any public filings or releases made by the foreign recipient organization, including most recent official registry documents, annual reports, and annual filing with the pertinent government, as applicable.

- The foreign recipient organization's existing sources of income, such as official grants, private endowments, and commercial activities."

SETTING THE STANDARD

For charities that operate in the US, collection of such information is relatively easy. However, for international charities working in such extremely challenging environments such as Iraq, these requirements are extremely difficult to satisfy. Treasury's guidelines are onerous but helpful in understanding the requirements of the laws and regulations on charitable work. Initially, there was excitement about the voluntary guidelines from individuals with no experience in the field of global charity work. This was due to lack of practical field experience and what compliance with the guidelines would entail. However, charities are free to adopt these guidelines as operating rules for themselves. But once this happens, then the standard that a charity would be held to would be the standard it has set for itself. Therefore, no organization should adopt these guidelines without a thorough review of the guidelines and the charity's ability to abide by them. However, the fact that some parts of the guidelines are too burdensome does not mean that these guidelines are not useful and therefore should be ignored. In fact, many of these guidelines are sound business practices. For example, the guidelines on governance and conflict of interest are already required by either state and/or federal law.

These guidelines were revised in December 2005 to "improve their usefulness and effectiveness."[20] Treasury states in the introduction to the revised guidelines, "Treasury recognizes the vital importance of the charitable community in providing essential services around the world. Treasury also understands the difficulty of providing assistance to those in need, often in remote and inaccessible regions, and applauds the efforts of the charitable community to meet such needs. The goal of these Guidelines is to protect the integrity of the charitable sector by offering the sector *ways to minimize* (emphasis added) the threat of well-intentioned donations not reaching their intended beneficiaries and to combat the abuse of charities by terrorists and their support networks."[21]

The following are the revised guidelines, without footnotes in the original Treasury Department text.[18]

The guidelines focus on financial controls and the vetting of potential foreign recipients. They provide for rigorous financial oversight and, importantly, high levels of disclosure and transparency that will enhance donor community confidence in the professionalism and bona fides of the domestic charity. The guidelines are consistent with the principles espoused in both the private and international public sectors, e.g., the Better Business Bureau, the Evangelical Council for Financial Accountability and, most recently, the Financial Action Task Force, an international organization dedicated to combating money laundering through enhanced transparency in international financial transactions. By implementing the guidelines with sufficient resources, diligently adhering to them in practice, and immediately severing all ties to any foreign recipient associated with a terrorist organization (whether designated as such by the US Government or discovered to be such by the domestic charity exercising due diligence), the domestic charity can enhance donor confidence and significantly reduce the risk of a blocking order.[19]

FUNDAMENTAL PRINCIPLES OF GOOD CHARITABLE PRACTICE

• Charitable organizations must comply with the laws of the United States.

• Charitable organizations are encouraged to adopt practices in addition to those required by law that provide additional assurances that all assets are used exclusively for charitable or other legitimate purposes.

• Individuals acting in a fiduciary capacity for any charitable organization should exercise due care in the performance of their responsibilities, consistent with applicable common law as well as local, state and federal statues and regulations.

• Fiscal responsibility is an essential component of charitable work and must be reflected at every level of a charitable organization.

Governance

Governing Instruments: Charitable organizations should operate in accordance with governing instruments, e.g., charter, articles of incorporation, bylaws, etc. The governing instruments should:

• Delineate the charity's basic goal(s) and purpose(s);

• Define the structure of the charity, including the composition of the board, how the board is selected and replaced, and the authority and responsibilities of the board;

• Set forth requirements concerning financial reporting, accountability and practices for solicitation and distribution of funds; and

• State that the charity shall comply with all applicable local, state, and federal laws and regulations.

Board of Directors: Charitable organizations should be governed by a board of directors ("board") consisting of at least three (3) members.

• The board should be an active governing body.

• The board of each individual charitable organization is responsible for that organization's compliance with relevant laws, and it should adopt and implement practices consistent with the principles contained herein. The board of each charitable organization should oversee implementation of the governance practices to be followed by that organization in a manner consistent with this Section III.

• The board should be an independent governing body, exercising effective and independent oversight of the charity's operations. The charity should establish a conflict of interest policy for board members and employees. That policy should establish procedures to be followed if a board member or employee has a conflict of interest or a perceived conflict of interest.

• The board should maintain records of all decisions made. When appropriate, these records should immediately be made available for inspection by the appropriate regulatory/supervisory and law enforcement authorities.

FINANCIAL PRACTICE/ACCOUNTABILITY

• The charity should have a budget, adopted in advance on an annual basis, and approved and overseen by the board.

• The board should appoint one individual to serve as the financial/accounting officer who should be responsible for day-to-day control over the charity's assets.

• If the charity's total annual gross income exceeds $250,000, the board should select an independent certified public accounting firm to audit the finances of the charity and to issue a yearly audited financial statement. The yearly audited financial statement should be available for public inspection.

Receipt and Disbursement of Funds

• The charity should account for all funds received and disbursed in accordance with generally accepted accounting principles and the requirements of the Internal Revenue Code. The charity should maintain records of the salaries it pays and the expenses it incurs (domestically and internationally).

• The charity should include in its accounting of all charitable disbursements the name of each recipient, the amount disbursed, and the date of the disbursement.

• The charity, after recording, should promptly deposit all received funds into an account maintained by the charity at a financial institution. In particular, all currency donated should be promptly deposited into the charity's financial institution account.

• The charity should make disbursements by check or wire transfer rather than in currency whenever such financial arrangements are reasonably available. Where normal financial services do not exist or other exigencies require making disbursements in currency (as in the case of humanitarian assistance provided in rural areas of many developing countries), the charity should disburse the currency in smaller increments sufficient to meet immediate and short-term needs rather than in large sums intended to cover needs over an extended time frame, and it should exercise oversight regarding the use of the currency for the intended charitable purposes, including keeping detailed internal records of such currency disbursements.

DISCLOSURE/TRANSPARENCY IN GOVERNANCE AND FINANCES

Board of Directors/Trustees

• Charities should maintain and make publicly available a current list of their board members or trustees and the salaries they are paid.

• While fully respecting individual privacy rights, charities should maintain records containing additional identifying information about their board members, such as home address, social security number, citizenship, etc.

• While fully respecting individual privacy rights, charities should maintain records containing identifying information for the board members of any subsidiaries or affiliates receiving funds from them.

Key Employees

• Charities should maintain and make publicly available a current list of their five highest paid or most influential employees (the key employees), and the salaries and/or direct or indirect benefits they receive.

• While fully respecting individual privacy rights, charities should maintain records containing identifying information (such as home address, social security or their taxpayer identification number, citizenship, etc.) about their key, non-US employees working abroad. Such information should be similar to that maintained by charities in the normal course of operations about all US employees, wherever employed, and foreign employees working in the United States.

• While fully respecting individual privacy rights, charities should maintain records containing identifying information for the key employees of any subsidiaries or affiliates receiving funds from them.

Mechanisms for Public Disclosure of Distribution of Resources and Services

• The charity should maintain and make publicly available a current list of any branches, subsidiaries and/or affiliates that receive resources and services from the charity.

• The charity should make publicly available or provide to any member of the general public, upon request, an annual report. The annual report should describe the charity's purpose(s), programs, activities, tax-exempt status, the structure and responsibility of the governing body of the charity, and financial information.

• The charity should make publicly available or provide to any member of the general public, upon request, complete annual financial statements, including a summary of the results of the charity's most recent audit. The financial statements should present the overall financial condition of the charity and its financial activities in accordance with generally accepted accounting principles and reporting practices.

Supplying Resources

When supplying charitable resources (monetary and in-kind contributions), fiscal responsibility on the part of a charity should include:

• The determination that the potential recipient of monetary or in-kind contributions has the ability to both accomplish the charitable purpose of the grant and protect the resources from diversion to non-charitable purposes, including any activity that supports terrorism;

• The reduction of the terms of the grant to a written assignment signed by both the charity and the recipient;

• Ongoing monitoring of the recipient and the activities funded under the grant for the term of the grant; and

• The correction of any misuse of resources by the recipient, and the termination of the relationship should misuse continue.

Supplying Services

When supplying charitable services, fiscal responsibility on the part of a charity should include:

• Appropriate measures to reduce the risk that its assets would be used for non-charitable purposes, including any activity that supports terrorism; and

• Sufficient auditing or accounting controls to trace services or commodities between delivery by the charity and/or service provider and use by the recipient.

Solicitations for Funds

• The charity should clearly state its goals for and purposes of solicitation funds so that anyone examining its disbursement of funds can determine whether the charity is adhering to those goals.

• Solicitations for donations should accurately and transparently tell donors how and where their donations are going to be expended.

• The charity should substantiate a request that solicitations and informational materials, distributed by any means, are accurate, truthful, and not misleading, in whole or in part.

• The charity should fully, immediately, and publicly disclose whenever it makes a determination that circumstances justify applying funds for a charitable purpose different from the purpose for which they were contributed.

ANTI-TERRORIST FINANCING BEST PRACTICES

Charities should consider taking the following steps before distributing any charitable funds (and in-kind contributions). As explained in Section I, when taking these steps, charities should apply a risk-based approach, particularly with respect to foreign recipients due to the increased risks associated with overseas charitable activity.

The charity should collect the following basic information about recipients:

• The recipient's name in English, in the language of origin, and any acronym or other names used to identify the recipient.

• The jurisdictions in which a recipient maintains a physical presence;

• Any reasonably available historical information about the recipient that assures the charity of the recipient's identity and integrity, including: (1) the jurisdiction in which a recipient organization is incorporating or formed; (2) copies of incorporating or other governing instruments; (3) information on the individuals who formed the organization; an (4) information relating to the recipient's operating history;

• The address and phone number of each place of business of a recipient;

• A statement of the principal purpose of the recipient, including a detailed report of the recipient's projects and goals;

• The names and addresses of individuals, entities, or organizations to which the recipient currently provides or proposes to provide funding, services, or material support, to the extent reasonably discoverable;

• The names and addresses of any subcontracting organizations utilized by the recipient;

• Copies of any public filings or releases made by the recipient, including the most recent official registry documents, annual reports, and annual filings with the pertinent government, as applicable; and

• The recipient's sources of income, such as official grants, private endowments, and commercial activities.

The charity should conduct basic vetting of recipients as follows:

• The charity should conduct a reasonable search of public information, including information available via the Internet, to determine whether the recipient is suspected of activity relating to terrorism, including terrorist financing or other support (see Part D of this Section VI for guidance on communicating suspicious information to the appropriate authorities).

• As US persons, US-based charities must comply with all Office of Foreign Assets Control ("OFAC") administered sanctions programs. Among other precautions, the charity should assure itself that recipients do not appear on OFAC's master list of Specially Designated Nationals (the "SDN List"), maintained on OFAC's website at www.treas.gov/offices/enforcement/ofac/sdn/.

• With respect to key employees, board members, or other senior management at a recipient's principal place of business, and for key employees at the recipient's other business locations, the charity should obtain the full name in English, in the language of origin, and any acronym or other names used; nationality; citizenship; current country of residence; and place and date of birth. The charity should assure itself that none of these individuals is sanctioned by OFAC. Moreover, charities should be aware that other nations may have their own lists of designated terrorist-related individuals, entities, or organizations pursuant of national obligations arising from United Nations Security Council Resolution 1373 (2001).

• With respect to the key employees, board members, or other senior management described in the preceding paragraph, the charity should also consider, on the basis of risk, consulting publicly available information (e.g. through public database or Internet searches) to ensure that such parties are not suspected of activity relating to terrorism, including terrorist financing or other support (see Part D of this Section VI for guidance on communicating suspicious information to the appropriate authorities); and

• The charity should require recipients to certify that they do not imply, transact with, provide services to, or otherwise deal with any individuals, entities, or groups that are sanctioned by OFAC, or with any persons known to the recipient to support terrorism.

The charity should conduct basic vetting of its own key employees as follows:

• The charity should consult publicly available information, including information available via the Internet, to determine whether any of its key employees is suspected of activity relating to terrorism, including terrorist financing or other support; and

• The charity should assure itself that none of its key employees is sanctioned by OFAC.

Should a charity's vetting practices lead to a finding that any of its own key employees, any of its recipients, or any of the key employees, board members, or other senior management of its recipients is suspected of activity relating to terrorism, including terrorist financing or other support, the charity should act as follows:

• If there is a valid or potentially valid match between the name of one of the individuals or organizations listed above and a name on the SDN List, the charity should immediately report this match to OFAC and seek further guidance. Charities should report the match through OFAC's hotline at 1-800-540-6322; and

• The charity can provide information on any suspicious activity that does not directly involve an OFAC match through a referral from available on Treasury's website at http://www.treas.gov/offices/enforcement/key-issues/protecting/index.shtml. In addition, a charity should simultaneously report suspicious activity to the Federal Bureau of Investigation through it local field offices. A list of the locations and telephone numbers of the FBI's field offices is available at http://www.fbi.gov/contract/fo/fo.htm.

The charity should review the financial and programmatic operations of each recipient as follows:

• The charity should require periodic reports from recipients on their operational activities and their use of the disbursed funds;

• The charity should require recipients to take reasonable steps to ensure that funds provided by the charity are not distributed to terrorists or their support networks. Periodically, a recipient should apprise the charity of the steps it has taken to meet this goal; and

• The charity should perform routine, on-site audits of recipients to the extent possible—consistent with the size of the disbursement, the cost of the audit, and the risks of diversion or abuse of charitable resources—to ensure that the recipient has taken adequate measures to protect its charitable resource from diversion to, or abuse by, terrorists or their support networks.

Charities should give careful thought to these revised guidelines and consider adopting at least some of the guidelines. Many of the principles are already part of state and federal law. The most troubling guideline is that of the vetting of recipients, ongoing monitoring of recipient, and vendors. These revised guidelines are open for comment until February 2006. It remains to be seen what becomes of them.

AN ONGOING PROCESS

The work of charities is by its nature challenging. The post-9/11 changes in the political and legal environment have added much complexity and difficulty to the world of charities. The least enviable position is that of Muslim charities that operate globally in troubled areas. Being informed about the law and setting up policies that make sure those charities conform to laws and regulations are a must. However, given that the law in this area is in flux, charities need to stay current and be aware that compliance is an ongoing process and not a one-time event. Charities cannot learn about the law and devise policies on their own. It is highly advisable to join groups that have the expertise and resources to aid charities in the learning and compliance process. InterAction is such an organization.[22] Access to Boardsource and Independent Sector is also crucial.

IV. International Humanitarian Law

Charities not only have to abide by US laws and regulations, they also have to be aware of and operate within the existing International Humanitarian Principles and Humanitarian Action Principles. These principles shape the concepts and the purpose of the organizational existence. It also shapes its operating methodologies, organizational structures and priorities all when working in the International Relief Arena. It is important to be aware of these international humanitarian principles and follow them in practice.

THE HUMANITARIAN PRINCIPLES

Humanitarian principles are devised to guide the work of the relief agencies in conflict-ridden situations. Guiding the work of the relief agencies by these principles is alternatively termed "Principles of Humanitarian Action". A good example of these principles is the Red Cross/NGO Code of Conduct. This Code of Conduct, or the set of principles which address the broader concern of the international humanitarian law, include the Ground Rule (in southern Sudan) and the Humanitarian Charter draft (the Sphere Project). They contain statements of support for non-combatant immunity (the Sphere Project) in addition to the manner of relief delivery.

The fundamental human rights and non-combatant immunity are principles included in international law. However, the legal position of the Principles of Humanitarian Action is more ambiguous.

INTERNATIONAL HUMANITARIAN LAW

International Humanitarian Law is often divided into two strands: The "Geneva" and "Hague" laws.

Hague law concerns the conduct of hostilities, coded in a series of declarations and treaties following the first Hague Peace Conference in 1899. The most significant principle of Hague law is the unlimited right of belligerents to adopt means of injuring the enemy. The principle of distinction between civilians and military targets also has its roots in this branch of the law. Article 25 of the Regulations prohibits "The attack or bombardment, by whatever means, of towns, villages, dwellings or buildings which are undefended".

The four Geneva Conventions of 1949 are the most complete statement of Geneva law, but they contain nothing about the conduct of hostilities. They are concerned with the treatment of victims of war and are more relevant to international charities than the Hague Conventions. The first two Geneva Conventions concern the treatment of wounded and sick members of the armed forces. Convention I deals with war on land, and Convention II with war at sea. Convention III concerns the treatment of prisoners of war. Convention IV concerns civilians that are under the power of the enemy. Article 3, common to all four Conventions, prescribes the minimum standard of treatment to be afforded persons taking no active part in the hostilities (which covers all the above categories).

The two 1977 Additional Protocols to the Geneva Conventions combine aspects of Geneva and Hague law. The Provision of Relief to the Civilian Population falls within the scope of the fourth Geneva Convention, the two Additional Protocols and Common Article 3. There are a total of 289 separate articles, but only 22 that relate to the Provision of Relief (Mackintosh 2000).

INTERNATIONAL HUMANITARIAN LAW AND ITS RELEVANCE TO RELIEF AGENCIES

It is very important to be aware of the rights that relief organizations have under international law. The Geneva Conventions are addressed to states, and they are binding on states that ratified the Conventions. The Geneva Conventions describe the situations in which states must allow humanitarian relief assistance to be delivered to civilians in their jurisdiction, and the conditions that they can impose on delivery. This is a very important law which gives international relief agencies access to populations in need and provides guidance on how to operate in conflict situations.

Provisions of these Conventions reflect "customary international law", are binding on all states, whether they are parties to the Conventions or not. According to legal doctrine, when a state has ratified the Conventions or Protocols, the provisions relating to internal wars are also binding on non-state party to the conflict.

The Geneva Conventions simply do not address the humanitarian agencies explicitly as actors, and so we cannot strictly say that they confer rights or impose obligations upon these humanitarian agencies. The articles of the Conventions which concern civilian relief describe the situations in which states must allow such assistance to be delivered to the civilians in their jurisdiction and the conditions which they are entitled to impose on such delivery.

THE PRINCIPLES OF HUMANITARIAN ACTION

The Principles of Humanitarian Action appear as conditions for access for relief operations under the Geneva Conventions and their Additional Protocols. Three terms appear repeatedly in the Geneva Conventions and Protocols to qualify legitimate relief activities. These are "Humanitarian", "Impartial" and "without adverse distinction". Humanity, impartiality and non-discrimination fundamental principles appear in the International Committee of the Red Cross (ICRC)/Non-Governmental Organizations (NGO) Code of conduct. It also appears among the principles of the Ground Rules of Southern Sudan. These principles are humanitarian, impartiality, consent, and neutrality.

Humanitarian

The ICRC commentary to the Geneva Conventions defines humanitarian as "being concerned with the condition of man considered solely as human being, regardless of his value as a military, political, professional or other unit, and not affected by any political or military consideration" (Pictet, 1958: 96).

There does not in fact appear to be a simple requirement that assistance be given to victims on all sides in a conflict in order to satisfy the definition of "Humanitarian" under international law. Perhaps no more can be deduced from this term than the very basic Red Cross definition of the principle of humanity: Preventing and alleviating human suffering.

Impartial

The fundamental principles of the Red Cross isolates three elements of impartiality. The first is non-discrimination. This is the absence of objective discrimination on the basis of membership of a social 'group'.

The second element of impartiality is the principle of proportionality, or that assistance will be afforded according to need. This is echoed in all of the charters of principles currently in use or under consideration by relief agencies, and can be said to be a principle firmly embedded in international humanitarian law. If the need is equal on two sides, the principle of impartiality should operate to ensure that humanitarian assistance is offered to both.

The third element of impartiality is that there should be no subjective distinctions: no individual decisions on whether the recipient is innocent or guilty, good or bad, and hence deserving or undeserving of assistance on any basis other than need. An interesting contrast can be drawn from the international refugee law. Under the statute of UNHCR, that organization is prohibited from assisting those accused of international crimes.

Neutral

Neutrality is often cited as a principle of humanitarian action. However, it is not mentioned in the Geneva Conventions. Neutrality is nonetheless one of the fundamental principles of the Red Cross, and so is brought within the Conventions by reference to it. It contains two aspects: ideological neutrality, presumably as expressed through comment or operation, and non-participation in hostilities, direct or indirect.

Conditionality

To conform to the principles of the Geneva Conventions, humanitarian assistance must be intended to relieve human suffering, and must be motivated by the condition of individuals as human beings. Relief should not be conditioned on the recipient's value as military, political, professional or other units. Allocation of relief is on the basis of need only.

Consent

The Geneva Conventions always provide that the delivery of relief is subject to the consent of the relevant party to the conflict. The Guiding Principles annexed to the resolution creating the UN Department of Humanitarian Affairs declare that: 'Humanitarian assistance should be provided with the consent of the affected country and in principle on the basis of an appeal by the affected country' (General Assembly Resolution 46/182, Dec. 1991). In certain situations, relief agencies operate without the permission of the country's government.

If a state is ordered to accept the operations of humanitarian agencies on its territory, those agencies no longer need to win access by operating according to international humanitarian law (See UN Security Council Resolutions 688 (Iraq); 771 (former Yugoslavia); 758 (Bosnia and Herzegovina), etc.).

HUMANITARIAN PRINCIPLES IN A CHANGING WORLD

The humanitarian impulse may be universal and timeless, but the rules and institutions through which it is expressed, and the extent to which these are respected, are historically determined. Humanitarian principles can best be seen as a compromise between soldiers and the people they fight over. As such, they are one part of the broader set of the 'rules of war'.

The number of NGOs operating now is much larger than at the time of the passage of the Conventions. The world is also more complex. There is now a greater variety of agencies working in conflict zones than ever before. There are a number of projects designed to improve the work of international relief organizations. Examples of such projects are

The Sphere Project, The Active Learning Network on Accountability and Performance (ALNAP), and The Humanitarian Ombudsman Project.

The Humanitarian Charter and Minimum Standards in Disaster Response, also known as the Sphere Project, is a project of SCHR and InterAction, supported by ICRC, VOICE and ICVA. It aims to promote the rights of people affected by disasters through specifying minimum standards in disaster response that those providing humanitarian relief should aim to uphold (Sphere Project, 1998). The Active Learning Network on Accountability and Performance (ALNAP) is a network that aims to improve the quality and accountability of humanitarian assistance by providing a forum for the identification and dissemination of best practices, and the building of consensus on common approaches. The Humanitarian Ombudsman project is a non-governmental, inter-agency initiated to establish a Humanitarian Ombudsman to act as an impartial and independent voice for people affected by disaster and conflict.

Common to all of these approaches, however, is the desire to develop 'a principled approach', in other words a practical ethical framework for humanitarian action suitable for the current political context. Hence the recent rediscovery by many humanitarian agencies and academics of the original Red Cross principles and the debate about their meaning and significance. It is important for international NGOs to get their staff involved in one of these projects, especially the Sphere Project. Many grants require that the staff of the NGO receive training on international work. The Sphere Project training is often singled out as a requirement.

EXISTING GUIDELINES FOR THE USE OF MILITARY IN CIVILIAN HUMANITARIAN RELIEF (OSLO GUIDELINES)

In 1994, OCHA published the Oslo Guidelines, a non-binding document outlining the use of military and civilian defense assets in natural and technological disasters. The draft guidelines state that military and civil defense assets supporting UN humanitarian activities will normally not be used in the direct delivery of assistance. When possible, the supported agencies will try to use military and civil defense assets in a manner that limits their visibility, and no tasks that do not call into question the neutrality or impartiality of the agency, implementing partners or other humanitarian actors. The paper sets out three core operational principles for the use of military and civil defense assets, as follows:

Complementary: Military and civil defense assets are means of last resort in responding to a humanitarian emergency. UN agencies will not request these assets unless they are urgently needed, and civilian assets are not available.

Civilian Control: Military and civilian defense assets employed in the support of UN humanitarian activities will be under the supervision and control of a responsible authority, such as the UN humanitarian coordinator.

No Cost: Military and civilian defense assets, as with all other humanitarian assistance, are provided at no cost to the affected population or the receiving state. States sending such assets should not attempt to recover these costs through other planned and programmed assistance, such as development aid. States providing military or civilian defense assets must not exploit these missions to gather intelligence, or to undertake psychological operations.

Finally, these assets must be used within a limited time-frame. The humanitarian coordinator should plan for the earliest possible release of any military or civilian defense assets provided to support humanitarian activities, and avoid developing any dependencies on these assets once the emergency has passed (Secretariat of the Oslo Guidelines Process, 2001).

SUMMARY

International Humanitarian Law (IHL) governs the way in which armed conflict is conducted, setting limits and making specific provisions for the protection of non-combatants. The International Humanitarian community succeeded in establishing a Code of Conduct and Humanitarian Action Principles that were derived from the International Laws and the consensus of the NGO actors.

V.   Rebuilding Relations Post-9/11

As the missions of Islamic charities have focused on the wellbeing and development of people in third world and Muslim countries, it is quite clear that these NGOs have collectively become an integral cog in the wheel of American foreign policy. Through their years of operation and interaction, Islamic charities are regarded as American Muslim organizations working on behalf of the American government and people, becoming essential public relations representatives for the US on the ground. By rendering assistance to the needy, providing educational opportunities and job training, supporting orphans and widows, supplying medical care to the ill, feeding the starving, drilling safe water wells and providing clean drinking water, and delivering relief to victims of war and natural disaster, American Muslim charities are enhancing America's image and strengthening good will the world over. These charities are demonstrating that the US's negative image burned into the collective consciousness of the Muslim world is false. Public opinion of the United States and its administration has taken a nosedive around the world since the first day it began moving towards war with Iraq.

This section was written with genuine optimism for the future of the US image and perception in the Muslim world. Additionally, it is presented as an opportunity to afford insight as to how the American Muslim charities are presently, and can become unique, professional, and reliable partners in reversing this unfavorable image to win the hearts and minds of the Muslim world, while enhancing goodwill and cooperation.

THE NUMBERS TELL IT ALL

Before September 11, 2001, public and political feelings in the vast majority of Arab and Muslim countries across the globe toward the US were tepid. Since then, opinions of the United States have grown downright chilly—in some countries, to the point of open hostility. This is shaped largely by a climate of fear from the fall-out of post-September 11, and America's invasion of and subsequent war in Iraq.

In June 2004, Zogby International polled Arab men and women in Saudi Arabia, Egypt,

Jordan, Lebanon, Morocco and the United Arab Emirates regarding their feelings toward the United States. The Zogby poll shows that views of the United States have deteriorated to such an extent that the populations of long-time allies such as Egypt register a 98 percent unfavorable opinion of America. A similar poll taken in 2002 by Zogby International found that 76 percent of Egyptians registered negative feelings towards the US. The same trend upheld for Morocco where 61 percent viewed the US unfavorably in 2002, but jumped to 88 percent two years later. Attitudes in Saudi Arabia went from 87 percent to 94 percent, while Lebanon did not see much of a change. Only the UAE had a positive shift, going from 87 percent unfavorable in 2002 to 73 percent in 2004. Those adults polled said their opinions were formulated by American policies, rather than by values or culture.[23] "In 2002, the single policy issue that drove opinion was the Palestinians; now it's Iraq and America's treatment, here and abroad, of Arabs and Muslims," said James Zogby, who commissioned the report with the Arab American Institute.[24]

Views of America: U.S. Approval Ratings[29]					
USIA*	1999/2000	Summer 2002	March 2003	May 2003	March 2004
Britain	83	75	48	70	58
France	62	63	31	43	37
Germany	78	61	25	45	38
Italy	76	70	34	60	—
Spain	50	—	14	38	—
Russia	37	61	28	36	47
Canada	71	72	—	63	—
Brazil	56	52	—	34	—
Japan	77	72	—	—	—
Indonesia	75	61	—	15	—
South Korea	58	53	—	46	—
Turkey	52	30	12	15	30
Nigeria	46	77	—	61	—
Pakistan	23	10	—	13	21
Jordan	—	25	—	1	5
Morocco	77	—	—	27	27
*(United States Image Attitudes survey for listed countries)					

Unfortunately for America, this negative sentiment exists not only in the Arab and Muslim countries, but in the rest of the world as well. Statistics tell a tale of not much having changed since 1983 when a poll conducted by Newsweek magazine showed only one-fourth of France's population approved of American foreign policies, with only slightly better responses from Germany and Japan.[25] The chasm between America and the rest of the world has spread deeper and broader now than at any time in modern history. Europeans are reminded of their own weakness in a world where America is the sole superpower. European citizens express that the American Administration fails to recognize the authority of the international community. A Channel 4 television poll in the UK said that Britons regard the US as the biggest threat to peace today, not Iraq or North Korea.[26]

Numbers published in February 2005 by a Pew Research Center report should be a wake-up call to the American administration. Although the report draws numbers from Europe to Asia, from South America to Africa, nowhere is the gap more apparent than in the Muslim countries. The Pew Research report's findings reflect the concerns raised by the September 11 Commission report released in 2004, which emphasized a losing battle for public opinion. "Support for the United States has plummeted," the commissioners wrote.[27]

Although the majority of the world admires America's democratic values and way of life, they still hold overwhelming negative assessments about whether or not the US administration takes into account the interests of other countries when it decides its foreign policy, and its even-handedness in meting out world justice. In 2002, the Pew Global Attitudes Project began measuring global attitudes through a series of surveys of nearly 75,000 people conducted in a total of 49 populations and the Palestinian Authority.[28] It seems that post-September 11 sympathy has waned tremendously in light of these numbers. The one thread that continued to weave its way through the statistics was the enmity the remainder of the global community had towards the US, and America's opinion of itself atop that community. Although Americans are known to be a generous and giving people, they have not helped their own image in the Muslim and Arab world—appearing to be aloof and even arrogant toward the plight of the rest of the world's ills. Additionally, Americans continue to be fairly consistent in how they view their own country on a global scale, and pretty much unconcerned about how the remainder of the world's inhabitants view America.

Although animosity for American policy softened a bit in the Muslim nations after 9/11, the US wars in Iraq and Afghanistan have tempered that sympathy. Most in the Muslim and Arab world have found reinforcing fodder in their debate that the US government is anti-Arab and anti-Muslim in its policies through the US government's own actions. The war in Iraq has badly frayed international unity, leading most to question America's honesty and motives for the war. Muslims are skeptical of US sincerity, and its tactics in the war on terrorism. The US image plummeted when a survey conducted in October 2003 by Eurobarometer in the European Union compared America with Iran as a threat to world peace. The majority believes that the US covets Middle East oil, and that it wishes to dominate the world, while targeting Muslim nations to protect Israel.[31] Even in Great Britain—America's most trusted ally—55 percent agreed with this contention.

A MORAL DILEMMA

As the war unfolded on television, American Muslims were wringing their hands in sadness and concern. Dozens of Islamic charities and foundations that Muslims entrusted millions of dollars a year to had been abruptly shutdown, their assets frozen or seized. At a time when those requiring humanitarian aid needed help the most, many Muslims say they feared giving to the Muslim charities that collect Zakat funds. Although Muslims also contribute to secular and community organizations, religious Muslims are far more comfortable giving to American Muslim charities the same as many Christians and Jews prefer giving to charities affiliated with their own religious groups.

Large portions of the funds given to fulfill one of the five pillars of Muslims' faith were completely lost with the government shutdowns. The allegations alone had a chilling effect on Islamic giving. Fear and bewilderment became the emotion du jour among Muslims in America. Rather than give their dollars to the needy through charities and foundations, many sent lesser amounts through friends or family who were traveling abroad, or gave to their local mosque. A Chicago-based attorney who advises more than 30 American Muslim charities said that for the groups he represents, there has been an estimated 40 percent reduction in financial support since 9/11.[32] Organizations whose aim is to assist impoverished peoples in regions such as the West Bank and Gaza, Iraq, Bangladesh, Sudan, Kosovo, Afghanistan, and the tsunami-ravished regions of Asia are struggling to hold on to their support base.

REJECTING A SAFE LIST

In 2003, Iowa Republican Senator Charles Grassley, chair of the Senate Finance Committee, indicated that his committee had begun its own investigation into American Islamic charities, operating on the premise that these and other Islamic nonprofits were potentially involved with funding terrorism. Senator Grassley's public comments did not deviate from the standard in assuming the organizations are suspect, and therefore presumed guilty, simply because they are Muslims, despite sponsoring a hearing in June 2004 entitled, "Charity Oversight and Reform: Keeping Bad Things from Happening to Good Charities".

After intense lobbying by Muslim organizations and others, a resolution sponsored by Jacqueline Y. Collins, and co-sponsored by Christine Radogno and Martin A. Sandoval was introduced in 2005 to the 94th General Assembly of the Illinois Senate. The Bill, SR0178, urges development of a list by federal agencies of charitable organizations, including Muslim organizations, that are safe for all Americans to contribute to without fear of prosecution and with assurance that their contributions will be used for their intended purposes. A copy of this resolution is included in the appendix at the end of this chapter.

To date, according to the September 11 Commission report, no evidence has been met that any Muslim charities in the US supported terrorism.[33] Additionally, the majority of the post-9/11 allegations have been unfounded, and most of those arrested have never been charged with anything connected to terrorism. Yet, the aura of suspicion still lingers over the charities. Since most of the major Islamic charities shuttered by the federal government were accused of funding terrorism, the Muslim faithful requested the Justice Department provide them with a "safe" list of organizations to which they could give their Zakat funds. The Justice Department rejected their request, saying it was impossible to fulfill.[34] Hence, the majority of American Muslims feel that they are trapped in a situation of Catch-22.

As noted previously in this chapter, some of the Treasury Department's published guidelines for charities are simple commonsense accounting methods; however, those who have studied the guidelines say they are beyond the capacity of most donors and even many foundations. The red-tape created by the guidelines is prohibitive, as they require detailed information, including the names and legal status of groups and staff members overseas who administer the contributions.[35] While these guidelines are being followed, innocent people will be suffering.

FEELINGS OF BETRAYAL

America's Muslims generally feel betrayed by their own government. Additionally, they feel that punishment has been doled out in an uneven, wide swath.

The weakness of the evidence used to arrest or indict Muslims and their charities is quite alarming, as is the administration's crude approach to fighting terror. Not only has the White House made enemies of organizations that once were their staunchest allies in the Muslim world, but also they have drawn some bizarre links that are yet to be proven beyond doubt. The majority of the post-9/11 allegations have been groundless, and most of those arrested have never been charged with anything connected to terrorism. A senior government official who led the government's efforts against terrorist financing from September 11, 2001 until late 2003 believed the efforts against the Islamic charities were less than a full success because no charity has been publicly proved to support terrorism.[36]

One recent positive step towards combating America's negative image propagated in many parts of the world has been achieved by the Bush Administration. In March 2005, former White House counselor Karen Hughes was named to lead the Administration's effort to improve the US image abroad, particularly in the Muslim world.[37] Needless to say, Hughes has her work cut out for her.

MUSLIMS UNDER SUSPICION

For a government that is frantic to add notches to its belt in a war on terror that has so far proven to bear little fruit, Muslim charities are attractive targets. By relying on tenuous bonds as rationale for confiscating millions of dollars in funds meant to help the poor and needy, the US government has amputated its ties with those groups best able to help in its war on terror: the Muslim charities. Just as in World War II when the Red Cross was given accusatory looks for their work within the Nazi prison camps, Muslim charities sometimes find it necessary to enter into agreements with conflicting parties so they might provide aid to those who are caught in the midst of fighting.

Since all of this began, President Bush and his administration have gone to extraordinary lengths to assure Muslims around the world that this is a war on terror, and not Islam. Unfortunately, mostly due to the US response post-September 11, these statements have not done much to allay the fears of Muslims around the world. Additionally, concern among donors is still widespread that Islamic charities with global operations are still under heavy scrutiny by law enforcement agencies. By the same token, putting choking restrictions on the agencies themselves during times of humanitarian crisis is irrational. Although the guidelines mentioned earlier are voluntary, the government has taken a passive-aggressive stance in promoting their usage. Any charity that does not comply fully is subject to closure under the International Emergency and Economic Powers Act. The PATRIOT Act requires a "knowing" standard before action can be taken against an entity, while the Executive Order does not. These expanded legal powers give the federal government the right to seize or freeze assets of a nonprofit "pending an investigation", without the opportunity for the nonprofit to learn the evidence against it or effectively challenge the designation. Additionally, there is no way to know whether these actions are justified because of the secrecy surrounding the decisions.[38]

Organizations such as a Texas-based charity formed in early 2002 in response to the deteriorating humanitarian picture in Palestine enacted a voucher program to address the problem of aid distribution to Palestinians in the West Bank and Gaza Strip. The vouchers were limited to individual recipients who could use them to purchase food, household products and other necessary daily items, which ensured funds were directed towards hungry families, not political or military activities. While the NGO painstakingly applied the Treasury Department's guidelines, even though they found these guidelines far too difficult. The NGO suspended operations in January 2005 after learning it was being targeted by the federal government despite their totally diligent efforts to work within the laws and guidelines put forth, and maintaining a totally open-book policy with full disclosure.

Muslim communities find it extremely troubling that only Islamic organizations in the US are targeted, and denied due process. The US administration's actions seem to operate on the assumption that all Muslim charitable donations are basically intentionally or unintentionally corrupted, and therefore, all acts of Muslim charitable giving are suspect. The most prominent flaw in this theory is that to date, the government has not been able to demonstrate an absolute 'money trail' confirming their accusations that American Muslim charitable funds have been used to finance terrorism.[39]

CHARITIES RESPOND TO NEED

From 1999 to 2003, more than 35,000 nonprofit groups focusing on religious activities received charity status from the IRS. While Christian groups accounted for about half, more than 1,000 new Buddhist and Islamic charities were created. Of these two groups, Muslims cited discomfort in seeking charitable services from organizations that serve other faiths. They also expressed a need to come together more as a community to give themselves a voice in response to heightened threats towards Muslim interests following the 2001 terrorist attacks.[40]

Islamic philanthropic organizations across the US have garnered numerous honors, awards and plaudits throughout the years for the work they have done and are doing inside the US and around the world, regardless of the recipients' religious beliefs. This recognition has come via television, radio, written articles and through other media.

A few of the programs American Muslim charities have implemented for people of all faiths are partnerships with Habitat for Humanity, free medical clinics, soup kitchens and food pantries. They have also undertaken work within America's inner cities: after-school programs, drug rehabilitation and neighborhood revitalization projects. In the 1990s, Philadelphia's Mayor Ed Rendell applauded the efforts of the local mosque and Muslims for cleaning up one of the worst drug and prostitution affected areas in the city through their outreach and social programs. Likewise, Muslim nonprofits' efforts abroad bring much needed relief to populations that are stricken by war, famine, poverty and natural disaster. Islamic charities were the first to respond with aid for the refugees fleeing war in Bosnia and Kosovo, and those escaping the grip of the Taliban in Afghanistan.

Traditionally, Muslim charities have successfully operated in areas that other western charities were unable or feared to serve because of dangerous situations, violence, kidnappings for ransom, etc. American Muslim charities find this success through the ethnic diversity of their staffs, and knowledge of the lands, cultures, languages, and religious practices.

VI. Partnership with American Muslim Charities

Most people around the world are well aware of the 8.9 magnitude earthquake and subsequent tsunamis that struck nations in the Indian Ocean on December 26, 2004, wiping entire towns off the map, and claiming more than 200,000 lives. In the tsunamis' wake, tens of thousands were left homeless, and threats of disease outbreaks, including cholera, loomed over the survivors.

Muslim charities were primary responders to the devastation caused by the December 2004 catastrophe. Because they have been quite successful working in these regions previously, they know how to implement programs there, and have earned tremendous respect and trust from the governments and indigenous peoples.

Although the US administration initially pledged $15 million in aid towards the disaster, it later reassessed the situation after sharp criticism that the US was being "stingy", and pledged

$350 million in assistance. The US Pacific Command dispatched men, aircraft and materials to Thailand and Sri Lanka, two of the hardest-hit countries.[41] Despite US Agency for International Development (USAID) Administrator Andrew S. Natsios' glowing speech in January 2005 before the House Subcommittee on Foreign Operations concerning the US response[42], without the help of Muslim charities, USAID efforts cannot be fully effective and mindful to Muslims' needs in implementing relief efforts in the mostly Muslim-affected areas.

REGULATIONS AND REQUIREMENTS

Having a 501 (c)(3) status, and abiding by all pertinent laws and regulations, does not guarantee that a charity would be able to get funding from governmental or even non-governmental sources. Institutional donors can have additional requirements that recipients are obligated to meet. For example, USAID has its own compliance regulations that charities applying for grants must fulfill.[43] A charity that aspires to obtain government grants does well by complying with all the aforementioned laws and regulations. However, compliance with all these laws and regulations is not enough to ensure ability to get USAID grants.[44] Institutional donors have additional requirements that charities need to satisfy to become eligible to receive assistance.

THE NEED FOR PARTNERSHIP

As demonstrated through the most recent statistics illustrating how America's image has suffered around the world, the US administration needs partners on the ground that intimately know the situation in the Muslim countries. Whether local or American, Islamic charitable NGOs are these perfect partners.

The humanitarian work conducted by American Muslims puts forth a strong statement within the Muslim world. By allying with USAID, the goodwill built by these charities will strengthen the message that the US is indeed concerned with the plight of the rest of the world. This vital partnership will further redeem the American image abroad, declaring that the US still stands for those values of freedom and plurality on which it was founded.

In forming USAID in 1961, President Kennedy recognized that widespread poverty and chaos in the world's weaker nations would endanger our own security. The USAID "was established to unify assistance efforts, to provide a new focus on the needs of a changing world, and to assist other countries in maintaining their independence and become self-supporting".[45]

It would be disastrous in terms of both national security and economically for us as a nation to fail to live up to those obligations set forth by the USAID. At the same time, by incorporating those principles in partnerships with American Muslim charities, America will be shoring up our nation's security by building a foundation of trust and mutual respect within the Muslim world. The result is deflating those arguments terrorists use to garner support and sympathy. Additionally, by collaborating with American Muslim charities that normally partner with other nonprofit organizations in the Muslim world, western international NGOs will benefit greatly from the enormous annual contributions given to charity by Muslims around the world, especially those funds given by Muslims in the Gulf States.

People tend to believe what they see, more than what they read or hear. By reaching out to the Muslim world with generosity, evenhandedness, and caring, the US Administration can repair the severe damage done to America's image. A valuable example of this is shown through a poll commissioned by the nonprofit group "Terror Free Tomorrow" which recorded a substantial positive shift in Muslim world public opinion since the beginning of the war on terrorism. In Indonesia alone, because of US relief efforts in the tsunami-ravaged areas of the Indian Ocean, support for al-Qaeda has dropped significantly, while favorable opinion of the US has increased.[46]

VII. Conclusion: Where Do We Go From Here?

The assertion that Muslims hate America for its values and culture could not be further from the truth. On the contrary, studies show that most of the Muslim world respect and strive for many of America's values of democracy, civic and religious freedom, diversity, tolerance, self-determination and pluralism. Many also insist that these values are not only consistent with Islam, but were the bedrock of Islam's glorious past civilization. Instead, they point to US foreign policy that is seen as oppressive and hostile to Muslims.[47]

For the US Administration, empowering and partnering with American Muslim charities and NGOs is a very critical strategy that will effectively win the hearts and minds of Muslims worldwide, ultimately regaining America's lost respect.

POINTS TO PONDER

What are some of the perceived problems in the US government's approach?

- Lack of respectful government interaction with American Muslims.

- Limited participation by Muslims in policy making on issues related to Islam and Muslims, resulting in ineffective public outreach.

- Not engaging Muslim and Arab charities and community leaders in a constructive, respectful manner from all levels.

- The Administration operates on the assumption of automatic guilt by association.

- Muslims should be treated fairly and openly to dispel distrust and fear of cooperation.

- The use of inaccurate intelligence information related to Muslim concerns demonstrated by the targeting and destruction of so many Muslim charities without proof of terrorist related activities or involvement by the charities. As well as the imprisonment and/or deportation of thousands of Muslims.

What are some of the strategies that the US Administration can implement to combat its negative image in the Muslim mind?

- Empowering the American Muslim charities to give humanitarian aid to needy Muslims will build trust and mutual respect.

- American Muslim charities are in a better position to know the culture, language and customs of the indigenous peoples, thereby winning over their hearts and minds. So, these American charities are assets, not liabilities, and can greatly enhance the American image abroad.

- Buying airtime or establishing TV stations to enhance the American image will not help. The messages imparted will be labeled as propaganda once the people surmise where the station receives its funding. The majority of these nations are already accustomed to these tactics from their dictatorial leadership. The wise strategy is to act compassionately at the ground level, amongst the needy, through humanitarian programs and services that speak louder than TV stations.

- Despite the fact that the US Administration is contributing large sums of financial resources for overseas programs, this has not been proven effective in improving its image. To the contrary, these entities are viewed by people abroad as mere ineffective bureaucracies or corrupted institutions, generating negative results. Therefore, cooperating and partnering with American Muslim charities as well as forming coalitions that bring together these charities, international NGOs and USAID to implement and deliver humanitarian assistance abroad will no doubt produce desirable results.

There are still many American Muslim NGOs and charities continuing to work tirelessly overseas in mainly Muslim countries where they represent the best of what America has to offer: a caring and giving culture. Problems stemming from ignorance, great poverty, lack of freedom and development plague these third world countries. For this reason, it is vital that the US assists the poor in Muslim countries where anti-American feelings are bred, leading to hatred and violence. Additionally, when American Muslims provide humanitarian aid to needy Muslims around the world, we lend credibility to the US, diffusing suspicions of America's motives and actions.

The bottom line is that American Muslim charities are assets in America's quest for better relations around the world and the war on terror, not liabilities. Respect and trust is a two-way street. As the old adage says, "give and you shall receive."

Appendix

Acronyms:

ALNAP	Active Learning Network on Accountability and Performance
CARE	Catholic Relief Services
CRC	Convention on the Rights of the Child
HPU	Humanitarian Principles Unit
ICRC	International Committee of the Red Cross
ICVA	International Council of Voluntary Agencies
IHL	International Humanitarian Law
INGO	International Non-Governmental Organization
IRC	International Rescue Committee
JPO	Joint Policy of Operation
LoU	Letter of Understanding
MSF	Medecins Sans Frontiers
NGO	Non-Governmental Organizations
OCHA	Office for the Coordination of Humanitarian Affairs
OFDA	Office of US Foreign Disaster Assistance
OLS	Operation Lifeline Sudan
OTI	Office for Transition Initiatives
Oxfam	"Oxford Committee for Famine Relief " Oxfam International is an internationalconfederation, comprised of 12 independent non-government organizations
PPHO	Principles and Protocols of Humanitarian Operation
PCVC	Program Compliance Violation Committee
PRM	State Department's Bureau for Population, Refugees and Migration

SCHR	Steering Committee for Humanitarian Response
SCF	Save the Children
SPLM/A	Sudan People's Liberation Movement/Army
SRRA	Sudan Relief and Rehabilitation Association
UNHACO	United Nations Humanitarian Assistance Coordination Office (for Liberia)
UNHCR	UN High Commissioner for Refugees
UNICEF	United Nations Children's Fund
USAID	US Agency for International Development
WFP	World Food Program

Charity Without Fear
State of Illinois
Senate Resolution 178 (SR0178)

WHEREAS, The United States is a nation of immigrants from around the world, with a wide diversity of cultures and faiths; and

WHEREAS, Every faith tradition has a basic tenet that its followers contribute to charity to aid the poor and sick; and

WHEREAS, One of the five pillars of Islam is the principle of Zakat, commanding Muslims to give to charity; and

WHEREAS, Muslims also follow the principle of Sadaqah, which asks that they give voluntarily to charity; and

WHEREAS, Devout Muslims comply with this principle by giving to charities that provide educational, medical, and other humanitarian assistance; and

WHEREAS, The civil rights and liberties of American Muslims and the operational intent of Muslim charitable organizations have come under intense governmental scrutiny since the 9/11 terrorist attacks; several charitable organizations based in Illinois have been targeted for investigation and prosecution based on alleged ties to terrorist activity; during the course of these investigations and prosecutions, the federal government has frozen the assets of these organizations, which total in the millions of dollars; and

WHEREAS, Good-faith and legitimate contributions made to these organizations by devout Muslims have gone unused for charitable purposes, contrary to the intentions of the contributors; and

WHEREAS, American Muslim contributors have become increasingly concerned not only that their contributions will go unused, but that past contributions may be used against them retroactively in criminal or immigration prosecutions if the specific charitable organization in question is, in a future investigation, suspected of having ties to terrorist activity that the contributor was not aware of at the time of contribution; and

WHEREAS, Congress is currently considering the REAL ID bill (HR 1268) which, among other provisions, would threaten immigrant contributors to charitable organizations with deportation ex post facto of a good faith contribution to a charity that was in good standing at the time of contribution; and

WHEREAS, Americans giving charity to Muslim charities need assurance that the charitable contributions they make in good faith to charities in good standing will indeed go to humanitarian purposes and will not give rise to potential retroactive criminal or immigration prosecution; therefore, be it

RESOLVED, BY THE SENATE OF THE NINETY-FOURTH GENERAL ASSEMBLY OF THE STATE OF ILLINOIS, that we urge the US Department of Treasury, US Department of Justice, and US Department of Homeland Security to develop a list of charitable organizations, including Muslim charitable organizations, that provide international relief and are safe for Americans of all ethnic and faith backgrounds to contribute to without fear of personal prosecution and with assurance that their contributions will indeed be used for their intended charitable purposes; and be it further

RESOLVED, That a copy of this resolution be sent to the US Department of Treasury, US Department of Justice, US Department of Homeland Security, and every member of the Illinois Congressional Delegation.

References

Anderson, M. (1996) Do No Harm: Supporting Local Capacities for Peace, Cambridge for Peace Project, The Collaborative for Development Action, Inc.

Borton, J., Nicholds, N., Benson, C. and Dhiri, S. (1994) NGOs and Relief Operations: Trends and Policy Implications. ODI (Overseas Development Institute), London.

De Waal, A. (1996) Contemporary Warfare in Africa: Changing Context Changing Strategies. IDS Bulletin 27, pp6-16.

De Waal, A. (1997) Famine Crimes: Politics and the Disaster Relief Industry in Africa, Oxford: James Currey.

Harmer, A., Macrae, J. (2003) Humanitarian action and the 'Global war on terror': a review of trends and issues. ODI, London.

ICRC von Flue, C. (Ed.) (1997a) Humanitarian Law and Protection: Report of the workshop, November 1996, pp18-20. Geneva: ICRC.

ICRC (1997b) Report on the Wolfsberg Humanitarian Forum. Anonymous Geneva: International Committee of the Red Cross.

ICRC (1998) Protection: Toward Professional Standards. Geneva: International Committee of the Red Cross.

Keen, D. (1998) The Economic Functions of Violence in Civil Wars, London: International Institute for Strategic Studies.

Macrae, J., and Zwi, A. (1994) War and Hunger: Rethinking international responses to complex political emergencies. London: Zed Books.

Mackintosh, K. (2000) The Principles of Humanitarian Action in International Humanitarian Law. Study four in The Politics of Principle: the principles of humanitarian action in practice. London: Overseas Development Institute.

Moorehead, C. (1999) Dunant's Dream: War, Switzerland and the History of the Red

Cross. London, Harper Collins.

MSF-H (1998) Workshop on the Protection of Civilians, Internally Displaced Persons and Refugees: final report of the Workshop held in Soesterberg, The Netherlands, 20 May 1998. Amsterdam: Medecins sans Frontieres-Holland.

OECD, (1999) Guidance for Evaluating Humanitarian Assistance in Complex Emergencies. Paris: Organization for Economic Cooperation and Development.

Pictet, J. (1958) The Geneva Conventions of 12 August 1949: Commentary/published under the general editorship of Jean S. Pictet, director for the general affairs of the International Committee of the Red Cross. Geneva : International Committee of the Red Cross, 1959-60.

Pictet, J. (1979) The Fundamental Principles of the Red Cross: Henry Dunant Institute.

Short, C. (1998) Opening Address by the Rt. Hon. Clare Short MP, Secretary of State for International Development. Anonymous Report on the Conference on the Promotion of Human Rights in Acute Crisis, Colchester: Human Rights Centre, University of Essex.

UN (1998a) Humanitarian Assistance in Liberia: Principles and Protocols for Operation. UN (1998b) Strategic Framework for Afghanistan, Towards a Principled Approach to Peace and Reconstruction. Islamabad: UN.

Endnotes

[1] This chapter is not intended as legal advice. Readers are advised to consult experienced and specialized legal counsel regarding specific legal situations.

[2] Bruce R. Hopkins. 1996. The Legal Answer Book for Nonprofit Organizations. John Wiley & Son, Inc.

[3] Ibid, p8.

[4] Jeffrey Zaslow, "Replacing Superman: How to Go Forward After a Charismatic Founder Dies,"

The Wall Street Journal, December 7, 2005, pD-1.

[5] Summary of the California Nonprofit Integrity Act, prepared by InterAction.

[6] Handbook on Counter-Terrorism Measures: What U.S. Nonprofits and Grantmakers need to Know. A publication of Day, Berry & Howard Foundation Inc., p vi.

[7] For a full discussion of Sarbanes-Oxley, its implications for nonprofit organizations and practice recommendations, see "The Sarbanes-Oxley Act and Implications for Nonprofit Organizations," Board Source and Independent Sector, 2003.

[8] InterAction defines itself as "the largest alliance of US-based inter-national development and humanitarian non-governmental organizations. With more than 160 members operating in every developing country, we work to overcome poverty, exclusion and suffering by advancing social justice and basic dignity for all." For more information, see www.interaction.org.

[9] Learning from Sarbanes-Oxley: A Checklist for Nonprofits and Foundations, www.independentsector.org.

[10] Dr. Laila Al-Marayati, American Muslim Charities: Easy Targets in the War on terror. Pace University School of Law Symposium "Anti-Terrorist Financing Guidelines: The Impact on International Philanthropy." December 3, 2004.

[11] Exec. Order No. 13224 Section 3d; 31 CFR Section 594.311.

[12] As quoted by Al-Marayati.

[13] As cited by Al-Marayati.

[14] Commission Finds Muslim Charities Shutdown Without Cause." http://www.ombwatch.org

[15] Ibid.

[16] The website for Bridger Insight is http://bridgerinsight.choicepoint.com.

[17] Handbook on Counter-Terrorism Measures: What U.S. Nonprofits and Grantmakers need to Know. A publication of Day, Berry & Howard Foundation Inc., p vii.

[18] "US Department of the Treasury Anti-Terrorist Financing Guidelines: Voluntary Best practices for US-Based Charities,"www.treas.gov/offices/enforcement/key-issues/protecting/charities-intro.shtml

[19] The guidelines are available on Treasury website, http://www.treas.gov/offices/enforcement/key-issues/protecting/charities-intro.shtml

[20] "US Department of the Treasury Anti-Terrorist Financing Guidelines: Voluntary Best practices for US-Based Charities,"www.treas.gov/offices/enforcement/key-issues/protecting/charities-intro.shtml, pp2-3.

[21] Department of Treasury press release: http://www.ustreas.gov/press/releases/po3607.htm.

[22] For more information, see www.interaction.org.

[23] Impressions of America 2004: How Arabs View America, Zogby International poll, Washington, DC.

[24] Dafna Linzer, "Poll Shows Growing Arab Rancor at US", Washington Post, July 23, 2004, pA26.

[25] Ibid.

[26] CNN Report, February 14, 2003 <www.cnn.com>.

[27] September 11 Commission Report, 2004.

[28] Complete reports and top-lines on all surveys are available at <www.pewglobal.org>. The surveys have examined public attitudes on a variety of topics, including economic globalization; democracy and governance; social, cultural and religious values, security and terrorism.

[29] Source: Pew Global Attitudes, except as noted:

- *Countries where 1999/2000 survey data are available.

- Trends provided by the Office of Research, U.S. Department of State

- Canada trend by Environics International, now Globescan.

[30] Global Perception Gap on American Unilateralism, Pew Global Attitudes, Washington, DC, March 2004.

[31] Trends 2005, Pew Research Center for the People and the Press, Washington, DC, 2004, p110.

[32] Benjamin Duncan, American Muslim Voice, <http://www.amuslimvoice.org>, March 6, 2005, "US Islamic charities in trouble", Washington, DC.

[33] September 11 Commission Report, 2004.

[34] Allison Hantschel, "Local Muslims Denied List of 'Safe' Charities", Daily Southtown, October 21, 2004.

[35] Laurie Goodstein, "Muslims Hesitating on Gifts as U.S. Scrutinizes Charities", MPACNews, <http://www.mpacnews.org>, Thursday, April 17, 2003.

[36] September 11 Commission Report, 2004, p111.

[37] Peter Baker, "Karen Hughes to Work on the World's View of U.S.", Washington Post, March 12, 2005, pA3.

[38] The government's authority to shut down organizations and freeze assets comes under the International Emergency and Economic Powers Act, which was expanded by the Patriot Act and Executive Order 13224, signed by President Bush in September 2001.

[39] September 11 Commission Report, 2004.

[40] Harvy Lipman, "Religion and Education Groups Grew the Most", The Chronicle of Philanthropy, January 6, 2005.

[41] Yahoo News, "US boosts tsunami aid to 35 million dollars; says it's not 'stingy'", Washington, DC, December 2004.

[42] US Agency for International Development Administrator Andrew S. Natsios, "US Relief

Efforts to Tsunami-Affected Countries", Testimony before the Subcommittee on Foreign Operations, Appropriations Committee, U.S. House of Representatives, Washington, D.C., January 26, 2005. <www.USAID.org/press/speeches/2005>.

[43] See for example, USAID Acquisition & Assistance Directive on "Implementation of the United States Leadership Against HIV/AIDS, Tuberculosis and Malaria Act of 2003- Eligibility Limitation on the Use of Funds and Opposition to Prostitution and Sex Trafficking, issued June 9, 2005.

[44] USAID is an acronym for United States Agency for International Development.

[45] <www.USAID.gov>.

[46] Lee Hamilton, "Shifts in Muslim Opinion Possible", Christian Science Monitor, March 21, 2005.

[47] Shibley Telhami, "U.S. Policy and the Arab and Muslim World: The Need for Public Diplomacy", The Brookings Review, Summer 2002, Vol.20 No.3, pp47-48.

Chapter

4.

Defining Your

Vision and Mission

Many nonprofit organizations are motivated to provide help to those in need; however, those needs may be quite numerous, coming in many forms. Trying to accomplish it all is the wrong path; as is settling one issue now and another later. For these reasons, we strongly emphasize the importance of the mission statement.

A mission is the primary purpose for the existence of an organization. It is the response to the question: why were we founded? The mission statement clarifies the organization's direction, why it does what it does, and how it conducts itself in the nonprofit arena. Articulating the answer to "why" through a clear statement and then abiding by it will focus our efforts and provide for a nonprofit's unmistakable direction.

In this chapter, we will look into Vision, Mission, and Values as the viable cornerstones in philanthropic organizations. Additionally, we will present a specific seven-step procedure to help your organization develop its mission statement, outlining how to keep it alive and useful throughout the life of your organization.

As usual, at the end of the chapter we will end up with a group of assessment questions that will help you evaluate the situation of your organization in regards to what this chapter presents.

I. Role of the Nonprofit's Mission Statement

A mission statement's primary reason for being is to remind people why the organization exists, to connect with the things they value, and to inspire them to become involved. All too often they end up expressing the "what" the organization does without explaining "why" its services are necessary.

"Why do we exist?" is a question organizations should identify without using infinitive forms of the verbs to educate, to provide, to counsel, etc. Asked to define "why", the answer should be "we exist because..." California Pacific Medical Center's motto presents an excellent example of the why statement: "we exist because life is precious". Another effective solution comes from a food bank, which was struggling with too much description of what: "We exist because hunger hurts".

Moreover, mission statements focus efforts and resources on a specific direction to meet specific need(s), so it provides a "focus" on the organization's human and financial resources. A nonprofit organization is founded to meet a specific need. This need is the organization's mission, and the mission is what draws donors who supply funding, and volunteers who give their time. It is also what potential board members identify with.

DEFINING YOUR PURPOSE WITH A MISSION STATEMENT

The mission statement not only is legally binding, but it gives an organization a sense of direction or focus. There is no doubt that the needs of our Muslim communities are too overwhelming to articulate. Reacting to meet every single need is not realistic, and ultimately is a mistake. American Muslim charities have fallen, willingly or not, into this trap. Few vital factors cause this pitfall to be clearly recognized, especially when it comes to gaining the support of their communities. These organizations' purpose is to help those in need. While those Muslims in need are scattered all over the world, their needs vary widely: the need for food aid, education, healthcare, shelter, vocational training, etc. Hence, these organizations found themselves trying to "do" it all, which is very challenging and sometimes ineffective. Even for such organizations, their mission statements might be vague or include many varied focuses or humanitarian fields. Spreading themselves so thin might be possible if they were unquestionably strong organizations, or were mature enough or have been in operation for many decades such as Red Cross/Red Crescent Society, CARE and Oxfam. However, for such organizations in their first decade of life, doing this is quite ineffective and not easy to pull off.

An explicit mission statement brings excellence and effectiveness to an organization, even if that statement is quite short. In the US, there are several small Muslim charities that focus on specific geographical areas or within a specific area of humanitarian aid, such as focusing on providing emergency aid in Somalia or Da'wa inside prisons. In most Muslim countries, many charities are offshoots of larger umbrella charities that specialize in a specific charitable area, including assisting the unmarried, financing mosque construction, printing Qur'ans, and Internet development. Although these organizations are small with limited resources, each is relatively effective at what it does, as an effective mission statement distinguishes one charity from another.

KEYS TO THE MISSION AND ITS STATEMENT

The following are three keys to know about working with the mission, and the development of the mission statement:

- The mission reflects the values, reason, and sustaining passion of the organization's very being. Discussions about mission may become quite polarized and emotional.

- The mission is felt more than known. Sometimes it is difficult to distill a mission into a purpose that is easily expressed in a simple statement.

- Because of the importance given to succinct expression of the mission, organizations may struggle at length with their mission statement, its meaning, wording, use, evaluation, and implementation, even if their sense of mission is clear.

As the mission must state a dynamic expression important to society, nonprofits must be able to identify those needs, and then meet, create, advance, and articulate their mission that moves towards solving and serving those issues.

Moreover, the mission statement should be able to be easily used as a marketing tool to convey its values in a way that is memorable and grabs the interest. Although some organizations may have an aversion to doing this because it might sound too emotional or soft, nonprofits have a legitimate claim to value-based expressions of their purpose and reason for existence. Nonprofits are often shy about using emotion to draw their customer base—unlike corporations who are normally much bolder about attracting and retaining customers, using value-based marketing to lure customers into buying their products and services. Like the statement "because life is precious", powerful mission statements motivate by combining crisp language within a short, flowing phrase.

```
┌─────────────────────────────────────────────────────────────────┐
│                                                                   │
│      Nonprofit Mission Statement is about Why and What...         │
│                                                                   │
│              •   Why do you exist?                                │
│              •   Why are your services are necessary?             │
│              •   Why should we support you?                       │
│              •   What need(s) do you meet?                        │
│              •   What is your focus?                              │
│              •   What solutions do you offer?                     │
│              •   What have you done with our donations?           │
│                                                                   │
└─────────────────────────────────────────────────────────────────┘
```

II.   The Mission Statement: the "Why" and the "What"

There is a definite difference between an organization's mission and its mission statement. To simplify this difference, think of the mission as the "why" the organization exists and the mission statement as the "expression of the why". A mission is felt, acted on, and used as a compass for navigating uncertain times, and the basis for decision-making. The mission statement is a description of the need and "what" the organization is doing to meet that need. A rare and greatly desired mission statement is one which inspires involvement, and keeps the board, staff, donors and volunteers motivated. A compelling mission statement involves ten characteristics:

1.   *The language is bold, clear and memorable.*

2.   *It conveys the organization's values both implicitly and explicitly.*

3.   *There is both an emotional and national impact in it.*

4.   *It combines both a "why" statement and a "what" statement.*

5.   *The need being met is described in positive not negative terms.*

6.   *It uses verbs that are active, not passive.*

7.   *It inspires people to act, give, join, serve, and learn more.*

8.   *It is adaptable for both marketing and fundraising.*

9.   *It succinctly summarizes the mission.*

10. *It is specific enough to guide major decisions.*

Radius Health Programs in Eureka, California created one of the best-expressed "why" mission statements more than a decade ago. Written during a class at Indiana University Center on Philanthropy, it provides a powerful example of combing the "why" and the "what". To understand their mission statement, it is elemental to know that Radius Health Programs works with individuals who have sustained hand injuries. Their Mission Statement reads as follows:

Next to the human face, hands are our most expressive feature. We talk with them. We play with them. We comfort and love with them. An injury to a hand affects a person professionally and personally. At Radius Health Programs, we give people back the use of their hands.

CORPORATE VS. EMOTIONAL

Often those with a corporate background disagree that a mission statement is about the "why". Rather, they usually argue that it should be more about the "what": "The mission of XYZ organization is to provide programs and services for those who suffer from hunger". The previous statement is corporate and to the point.

When a person donates to a nonprofit, it is generally acknowledged and accepted that the donor receives nothing in return—save the knowledge that they were able to help or make a difference. This begs the question: "why?" When added to the "what", the result usually satisfies the needs of those who want to see a more traditional corporate statement.

III. Relating Mission to the Vision and Values

There is a fine line of definition between the words mission and values, and although they are often confused with each other, these words are not interchangeable. A mission defines the organization's true direction, as opposed to vision that defines its destination. Organizations are often described as "mission driven", "mission focused", and "value based". Being mission driven or mission focused means that an organization should be motivated in their programs, activities, and decision making with a basis on why they exist in the first place. To be value based essentially means that the organization has deeply held beliefs, which guide it; for instance, respect fiscal responsibility and accessibility.

Vision, mission and values are the givens in establishing the framework for involvement, and advancement of nonprofits. An organization's mission statement captures the reason and the need, and adds a simple, powerful statement of what the organization is doing to meet those needs.

Mission and Vision Example

The mission and vision of a Midwest interfaith group comprised of 55 houses of worship representing 17 separate faiths are intertwined in their intent, yet different in their meaning. The group's vision states:

"Our vision is to promote understanding, compassion, and acceptance of each other and our beliefs. And to foster a caring community in which honesty, respect and responsibility are celebrated".

While their mission statement reads: "The mission of the Inter-Religious Council of Linn County is to provide means for people of all faiths to promote understanding and respect for one another, and to work with the community for the spiritual, moral, social and civic welfare of Linn County".

An organization's dream is its vision. It has also been described as what the organization wants to look like, feel like, and be like in the future. Vision may be two pronged: the vision for the organization and the vision for what their work will accomplish. Both vision and mission are the basis for philanthropy; each possessing embedded values, an implicit part of mission statements.

ORGANIZATIONAL VALUES

Although there is a reported increase in publicized statements of organizational philosophy or creed, they usually only reflect the values, aspirations, and commitment with no uniformity in their content. While these are adapted to the nature of the organization's business, they are designed to represent the organization's public image, and are often the cornerstone of the organization's overall method of operation. These values inspire and guide action in the form of planning, fundraising, marketing, good governance and sound management. Components of the organization's value statement include key interests to be satisfied and balanced by their devotion to public interest and community, to its board, its donors, and its employees, as well as quality and excellence in its service. The philosophy of an entity that deals in resale of rehabilitated donated goods while employing the mentally and physically disabled "seeks efficiency to provide low cost, high productivity, and value for the money received". Additionally, it states that "it is a good place to work, provides excellent opportunity for advancement, is a fair organization to deal with, it emphasizes teamwork, and the leadership supports its staff and develops their employees".

Although an organization may have as many as ten values, they are the main principles the organization would like to commit its operation to. While each value is typically expressed by a single word followed by an explanation, many organizations include their values as part of, or followed by, the mission statement.

Sample Value Statement

The value statement of one international nonprofit organization expresses their philosophy by stating, "We believe that the money we collect must be spent directly on the people who need it most. To do that, we keep our administration costs to a bare minimum".

IV.   Developing Your Mission Statement

The development stage of a nonprofit organization is the single most important challenge faced by that organization at the beginning of their life. This should not be done behind closed doors by a few senior management. It requires reflection on the basic questions behind the organization's existence, wide involvement of people, and professional help to write it. It is probably better not to develop the mission statement at the very beginning of the organization's operation; rather a year or two later.

ENGAGING THE BOARD AND STAFF IN THE MISSION

It is the primarily role of the board to define and advance the mission of an organization. Most board members are clear in their role of keeping the mission, but are not clear in their method of how to do it. However, they are usually very aware of the importance of the overall mission through marketing, fundraising, management, and program development of the organization.

Total Inclusion is Critical

Everyone knows that the board's key job is to determine and advance the mission. Involving the senior staff, and preferably key beneficiaries and donors in tasks around mission development is critical. The staff's role in mission development processes should be a pivotal role since staff—whether paid or volunteer—implement the mission and make daily decisions about programs and services that reflect the mission. A board that operates without staff input severely limits themselves in implementing the mission, not to mention the ultimate rising of resentment from being excluded. Staff brings a critical internal perspective to the process by possessing practical knowledge and experience, including familiarity with the organization's beneficiaries, members, or constituents. Staff input complements and helps to sharpen and refine the way in which the mission is expressed.

By the same token, board members also bring their own form of uniqueness to the process. Representing the community allows them to bring a vital vision that helps to determine whether the organization is meeting needs. Some board members will be closely involved, while others will provide feedback, giving a critique on the final process. Board members who take charge of the mission development process should be keenly interested in the process and the product.

Neglecting to Include International Staff

In the event that a Muslim charity has international branches, it is very beneficial to involve not only headquarters staff, but also managers of regional or country branches. This would include educating all those on what a mission statement is, giving them actual statements for well-known organizations, and then requesting their answers to a detailed questionnaire as to reflect on their main values and top priorities. Later on, discussing the summary of what they wrote will bring about a deeper look into answering the questions of "why do we exist?" "What do we want to provide?"

Involvement Equals Commitment

Once all key staff and board involved in the process arrive at a mission statement, and preferably the statement of values, they feel that they own this mission. They will feel more a part of the organization, while their senses of involvement and commitment will be at a higher level than before.

Earlier, we witnessed an example where an organization involved all of its staff, not just senior management. Every branch manager at the headquarters and at its branches was responsible to meet with their staff to follow a specific process to come up with a proposed mission statement. Then, all international managers, staff, and board members met at the headquarters to discuss various proposals and the results of the questionnaires they had filled out. After considerable discussion and reflection, staff left contemplating basic questions they neglected to ask themselves.

The process was concluded when the final mission statement was compiled by a professional writer based upon input from the organization's staff and other representatives. Since everyone collaborated in the mission process, they had a right to feel that "this is my mission" and "my organization". All of this resulted in a growth of commitment to the organization, which grew so much that management did not have to worry about following up on different staff's responsibilities. Moreover, staff did not think of their jobs as simply being part of a "9-to-5 routine". Rather, they felt part of the organization's development. After all, it was their mission that they were working towards fulfilling.

BEGIN WITH A COMMON UNDERSTANDING

To develop a mission statement, it is essential to begin by focusing your board and staff on the mission first, without writing anything. Take a long, hard look at the community and its needs. Determine what population the organization will serve and why, what the population needs, and what kinds of programs will be developed to meet those needs. One land conservation organization that was making a major transition in leadership initiated its planning process by doing a market survey and then evaluated its mission statement based upon what the community was saying. After evaluating everything, the organization decided to keep its original name, but changed its mission statement, significantly improving it and rededicating itself.

Board members and key staff must agree on the mission. Confusion, dissension, disaffection and turmoil usually earmark dysfunctional nonprofits. Having a common understanding of the mission is essential because mission should be the ultimate definer for program development, decision making, policy setting, fundraising, strategy, and all other related actions of the board. Problems arise when the mission is not used enough in these decisions and evaluations.

ARTICULATING THE MISSION STATEMENT IS A SEVEN-STEP PROCESS

It is one thing to feel what an organization's mission is. It is quite another to be able to put that mission into words, and getting everyone else to agree to that wording. What tone should a mission statement take? Just as there are countless experts to help write a mission statement, there are countless ways to write it. As stated earlier, some organizations lean towards corporate-sounding mission statements that are direct, devoid of character and quite frankly, as dry as the Sahara. Take Radius's statement prior to the re-written version: "The mission of Radius Health Program is to provide surgery, treatment, and therapy for people who have sustained injuries to their hands". Although this statement may be to the organization's liking, it does not explicitly answer the question of "why", or raise emotions or inspire people to learn more about the organization. Only after a consensus has been reached on which key points to convey in a mission expression is it time to begin writing the mission statement. The following are a suggested process, which outlines the single most challenging job any nonprofit, may face:

1. *Identifying or reaffirming the values that guide your mission.* Board and staff should be involved in this process where each is asked to write down three values he or she believes are vital to the organization. This step may also be presented in the form of a questionnaire where they are asked to state the top priorities the organization needs to meet and

the main values it must abide by.

2. *Discuss these values in meetings so that the meaning of each word or phrase is thoroughly understood by everyone, allowing each person to provide an explanation.* Often the explanation is richer than the word or words themselves. See what might be missing from the list, and add to it if necessary. Try to build a consensus on core points that reflect why the organization should exist. Any conflicting items should be eliminated through further discussion, while retaining all expressions that are agreed on.

3. *If creating a mission statement for the first time, assign a team of creative thinkers and writers to use those chosen words to compile a few short, powerful mission statements that embody the key values, which have been identified.* Direct those assigned with this task to read other mission statements, which are both poetic and colorful, and more corporate in nature to further enhance their grasp of a style appropriate for your organization.

4. *Present the first drafts—preferably three versions—to the board and key staff at a meeting to hash out the intent, tone and general message.* If you do not ask for feedback about what they like and what they do not, and about the overall language in both verbally and written form, any delayed input will defer the process.

5. *Using that feedback, assign the writing of the mission statement to a professional who specializes in mission statement development.* It is important to obtain the involvement of a professional writer even from the earliest stage to guide the process and finalize your efforts. A professional's involvement will serve as providing an unbiased professional opinion, which is very important when different views and political dynamics among board members comes into play in accepting one version of the statement over another. The chosen consultant will also be helpful in asking questions, and may bring views closer to a common ground by building consensus. It is preferred that the consultant conduct any meetings related to mission development allowing all views to be taken equally so that the process is not affected by the personal opinions of the chairman or president.

6. *When a final version has been drafted, be certain to seek preliminary approval from the board.* Further meetings can be held to a minimum   as any additional input or changes can be posted by circulating the draft. Be quite certain that the final draft upholds the original mission and values, and that the words do not stray from the intended content.

7. *Lastly, the board must approve the new mission statement.* New feedback may be given after the statement is put into use, and can be retained for use at a later date whenever the statement is re-evaluated.

This is a tried and true process with positive results. Using this process provides for the clarifying of values and promoting ownership of the final product and ensuring board participation at an appropriate level. The time this process should take is usually several months depending upon the type of organization. For local nonprofits such as a social agency, a mosque or a school, it should take three to six months. For an international charity to complete the process of arriving at a written mission and value statement, the timeframe should fall between six months and a year.

V. The Mission Statement is Written… Now What?

Once the mission statement is complete, the board and staff must work at devising ways of keeping the mission fresh. One method of accomplishing this is through evaluation, and ways to use it in planning and decision-making.

It is the board's task to keep it visible, robust, active, and relevant. To keep the mission on track, it should be reviewed regularly at every board meeting in a suggested "brief mission moments". In addition, it is also recommended to offer opportunities for mission board/staff retreats where the leadership of the organization interacts to evaluate their achievements and develop their strategic plan. The mission should also be conveyed at community events to inspire the public, and lay the groundwork for mission-based advocacy, fundraising and outreach. Using the mission as a basis for tough decision-making is yet another method to get and keep board members consciously connected with the mission.

The Mission and Strategic Planning

Since it defines the organization's direction, strategic planning is one of the most visible uses of the mission within the organization, whereas the plan is a roadmap.

Vision and mission stimulate goals and programs. One example of this can be drawn from a senior care facility, Hillside Community that provides day care for adults afflicted with Alzheimer's disease. Hillside's vision is "to become the premier provider of senior services in our community". One of their goals is "to create Alzheimer day care centers in neighborhoods not currently served".

When considering the previous points, it is important to remember that primary internal uses of the mission are to inspire the board and staff, and to serve as a guide and measurable device in the organization's strategic planning.

The Role of Mission in Donor and Fund Development

No one likes to feel like a beggar. Historically, the fundraising arm of any nonprofit (be it a mosque, church, charity, school, etc.) has the hardest time of all when it comes to finding the volunteers whose job it is to twist arms and turn people upside down to collect the spare change that falls from their pockets.

The standard shakedown methods are usually no longer necessary when people see the actual accomplishments from their donated money or time. This miniscule technique allows an organization to shift from being a beggar with needs, and instead shows that they are meeting needs. For most organizations, the focus is no longer on being poor and needy, and instead becomes an opportunity to invest in community changes and differences that have a valid impact, showing results and success. A religious school in the Midwest found that raising the $150,000 to expand their facility with six classrooms and a gymnasium was nearly impossible. After nearly four years and tens of pleas to their community, they were no closer to raising the money needed for the project. Members of their community had tired of the board's constant begging for dollars and lack of visible progress. Donations had slowed to a trickle. So, the foundation decided to take a bold gamble: they took the funds they had previously collected, cleared the land and broke ground. The board was hoping that the sight of actual work being done would spur the membership into giving the remaining funds necessary to complete the project. Their gamble paid off. The remaining dollars poured in, and the project was completed in record time.

Developing a Positive Connection

Through effective visual marketing, an organization is able to demonstrate that it is now a powerful community partner in their mission whether the fight is against hunger, poor education or healthcare, the environment, or the myriad of other struggles nonprofit missions seek to challenge. With a subtle change in language, attitude and positioning, an organization can significantly increase their boards' and volunteers' investment, keeping those individuals involved in donor development. They will now better understand the importance of taking time to develop a values-based and issues-focused relationship with a potential donor. Not simply by asking for money, but by exposing them to the organization's programs and their impact, showing visible community connection and benefits. Doing this replaces the transaction of asking for money with a commitment to engaging the donor in a long-term relationship based on shared values and understanding of mission.

Giving Donors a Rate of Return

Once a donation is made, the relationship is not over. Only by maintaining a strong sense of stewardship can the relationship stay strong. As board members become more dedicated to the mission, their sense of accomplishment is reinforced when they engage others, developing a nurturing relationship with the donors. Their experiences and ability to impart the organization's successes will keep the donors feeling as though the return on their investment is a very high one indeed. Additionally, donors are convinced to continue giving (possibly increasing their gifts) when they see the organization so committed to its mission through its programs and achievements.

Promote your Mission within the Community

People donate not just money, but also valuable time to organizations. This is not because of the organization's need for money, but because the organization meets the needs of others. Therefore, a clearly worded and descriptive mission statement is an invaluable asset towards gaining both funds and volunteers.

Although there are a number of venues where the mission can be launched to gain public support, the following are both effective examples:

- *Website*–most organizations now post their mission statement on their website. As well, people like to see results, and showing any positive impact the organization has on their community could very well be one of the most effective strategies.

- *Printed materials*–even though we have entered the 21st century, not everyone has access to or is comfortable surfing in cyberspace. For this reason, old-fashioned paper is still an effective way to reach potential donors and volunteers.

MODIFICATION OF THE MISSION STATEMENT

Since an organization's mission is its most enduring aspect, tampering with it should not be taken lightly. Any modification should encompass the involvement of the board, staff, key donors, and respective members of the community, and via a thorough review from the entire organization.

Why Would a Nonprofit Change the Course of their Mission Statement?

The case of the March of Dimes is a well-known example of why an organization was faced with the altering of its original mission statement. The March of Dimes was originally founded to provide funding for the research and treatment of infantile paralysis (polio myelitis/polio). After the Salk and Sabine vaccines were developed, polio was nearly eradicated, making the March of Dimes' original mission statement obsolete. This situation forced them into redefining their reason for being—or go out of business. After research identified a need for the eradication of birth defects, the March of Dimes reinvented itself into its present-day, hugely successful organization whose new mission and goal raises large amounts of money yearly.

VI.   Assessing Your Situation

In order to reasonably benefit from this chapter, please consider the situation of your organization, in light of what we have presented here. By answering these questions, you would be assessing your situation as well as identifying the areas where corrections are needed. Additionally, you are encouraged to go back to review the specific materials of the chapter for clarification on some questions.

- *Does your organization have a Mission Statement (MS)?*

- *Does the MS express clearly "why" your organization exists and "what" its primary focus is?*

- *Does your organization's MS clearly distinguish your organization from other Muslim organizations?*

- *Does your MS inspire advancement of your organization, as well as motivate involvement of people to act, give and serve?*

- *Does your organization have a Statement of Values that articulates the top several principles that guide your entire operation?*

- *Who was involved in the development of your MS?*

- *Is your MS able to be recited by every board and management staff member?*

- *Do you feel that your board, donors, employees, volunteers, community members and beneficiaries are clear concerning the main reason(s) for your organization's existence and the need(s) it intends to meet?*

- *If your organization has a well-articulated MS, when was the last time your organization reviewed it and evaluated the organization's operations in light of that mission?*

- *Does your board have a "Brief Mission Moment" at every board meeting and an annual "Mission Board-Staff Retreat"?*

- *If your organization does not have a useful MS, when and by what process will your organization follow to develop one?*

- *Do you find your MS and Statement of Values being plainly visible and relevant during times of strategic planning, major decision-making, goal setting and fund allocation and development?*

- *Are your MS, and possibly your Vision and Values, being publicized amongst your constituencies and donors through publications, website and public events?*

Chapter

5.

Strategic Planning

I.   *Strategic Management*

  - *What Strategic Management Aims to Accomplish*

  - *CEO as Organizational Strategist*

  - *Practices of Successful Leaders*

  - *Roles of Program Executives in Strategic Management*

II. *Strategic Planning*

  - *Why Develop a Strategic Plan?*

  - *The Goals Approach*

  - *Strategic Planning and Budgeting*

  - *How to Design a Realistic Planning Process*

  - *Tips for Drafting Strategic Plans*

III. *Strategic Assessment*

  - *The Purpose of Strategic Assessment*

IV. *Assessing Your Situation*

It is critical for charities to appreciate the importance of strategic management. While the word "strategizing" means to devise a strategy or strategies, to lay out careful plans for the future, the word "strategy" refers to the skillful planning and management of anything. This chapter concerns both planning for the present and the future: knowing where your organization is presently, and where you want it to be.

This chapter is also about standardizing strategic thinking. As well as addressing the strategic management concept: what your organization's leadership aims to accomplish, and the actual roles and practices your organization's leaders must take to assure future success.

We will also discuss the strategic planning process as the main tool to bridge the present with the future, and map the way that leads you there, ensuring a feasible and realistic approach to reach that future state. In this chapter, we discuss how to successfully conceive and set about planning the Goals Approach and Strategic Assessment that will lead to your stated goals. This chapter also considers other useful concepts and tools to aid in an intelligent approach to your desired outcome.

I.   Strategic Management

In order to better understand the nature of the strategic management process, there are several elements that should be considered. Strategic management is a process that sets long-term or strategic goals for an organization's future by assessing its present situation. In order to bring about those future goals, initiatives are identified and adjusted as needed by the organization's management. This also allows management to make choices that can become the basis for current decision making, while options can be indicated for future flexible alternative courses of action that identify opportunities, threats or constraints to exploit or avoid.

Strategic management is about seeing the big picture without getting bogged down in details. It can be envisioned as a sort of master plan (the future) drawn out on an erasable plastic overlay that sits over a base sheet (the present). The overlay can be lifted up to view each plan individually, or laid atop the base to envision the plan's overall design. Whenever necessary, the overlay can be adjusted by simply erasing or adjusting goals, resulting in an appended design for the future without altering the present. Changing back and forth between the present and the future allows the strategic mind to cope with change. Being able to shift rapidly from dilemma to reparatory response is integral to effective management performance, and is in no way replaced by strategic planning even when issues cannot be supported in exact quantitative conditions.

For strategic management efforts to be effective, it must be taken as a continuous cumulative process. It must also be self-improving by being an organized process of methodical questioning and directed transformation, responding to fluctuating external conditions. By continuously revising and reorganizing itself, the plan will never suffer obsolescence. Although it does not do the actual operational planning, strategic management produces the guiding basis for managerial functions such as program design, program budgeting, organizational structure, and human resource development. It also demands smart application of skill and discipline to navigate the choppy waters of indecision and ambiguous data. Because educated guesses allowed for too many mistakes, public, private and nonprofit organizations are increasingly turning to strategic management because of its substantial payoff in terms of its impact on their future.

WHAT STRATEGIC MANAGEMENT AIMS TO ACCOMPLISH

Strategic management's main intent is to map out where individuals working together are going, and what they hope to accomplish when they get there. In order for strategic management to work, it must not only provide a direction that sets these goals, but it must also indicate where to concentrate resources and talents by focusing on key result areas. It must also highlight upper-level and organization-wide visibility and mindfulness to the objectives and initiatives being sought. Because unlimited open-ended funding is certainly very rare indeed, managers must conceive intelligent plans that make wise use of limited resources. Moreover, by carefully monitoring and measuring progress, managers can facilitate and assure effective implementation of strategic initiatives and programs. Sometimes Murphy's Law takes over and the most carefully thought out plans can go awry. By having built in flexibility, a strategic planning method can be helpful in reducing the risks associated with future uncertainties and change by turning a negative into a positive. The basis for strategic management is establishing directional goals, new strategic initiatives, and indicators of progress. This allows for keeping your organization on track, establishing proactive reaction to problems, and providing a reliable measure for accomplishments. Without these guideposts, there is no objective basis for control and evaluation.

CEO AS ORGANIZATIONAL STRATEGIST

As the president or executive director, the chief executive has the authority to manage the organization individually, or they may share it with one other officer such as a deputy or executive vice president. Just as a ship's captain who fails to command will find their vessel dashed upon the rocks or wandering in open seas, a chief executive officer (CEO) that passively sits back in his/her ivory tower will soon find their organization floundering or failing. Modern management methods now stress that an organization cannot be successful unless the CEO comes out of isolation, providing solidly consistent support to effective strategic performance, while making certain that others within the organization recognize the importance of his or her direction.

The rules of the game are set by those who run the strategic management system, as a powerful means to standardize strategic thinking and action everywhere in the organization. Although not usually known for quickly responding to change, nonprofit leaders are beginning to realize this, and are learning to deal with the changing demands placed upon them by boards, legislatures, and beneficiaries. Their CEOs are taking on a multitude of strategies that are formulated, executed and evaluated throughout the organization via a host of managerial instruments: systems, task forces, meetings and forums, decision and policy support structures, and strategic plans.

PRACTICES OF SUCCESSFUL LEADERS

Management research has outlined five essential practices containing two commitments each, enabling leaders to accomplish extraordinary achievements.

1. Challenging Procedure

Successful leaders are not stagnant. They seek out change by experimenting and creating innovative ways for accomplishing outstanding goals. They never take defeat without putting up a fight; instead, they create new ideas, reformulate old ones, and learn from their mistakes.

- *Seek Challenging Opportunities to Evolve, Advance, Innovate, and Improve.* In management, those who are considered to be leaders have achieved significant changes in product, quality or customer service, cost or processes. They may have opened new doors of opportunity for employees to maximize their skills and abilities, or face new challenges. Leaders are inspired, committed, excited and feel rewarded with their achievements and those of their followers, and instill those same feelings in their staff.

- *Experiment Boldly and Learn from Mistakes.* Leaders reformulate old ideas, and experiment with new ones by means of collaboration through meetings, status reports, retreats, and going to where the organization's foremost applications are being utilized. To diminish risk and gain experience, they experiment, set up pilot projects and use demonstrations, while rewarding and supporting those willing to think outside the box.

2. Inspiring a Shared Mission

Leaders know that what can be visualized, often can be realized. They know that by working together for a shared vision, achieving much more is possibλε.

- *Visualize a Glorious Future.* Keeping an eye out for an ideal and unique future gives an organization direction and purpose. Documenting a mission for tomorrow on paper, and testing and challenging it allows an organization to know what it wants and which way to go to get tηεre.

- *Recruit Others in a Shared Mission by Appealing to Their Interests, Goals and Beliefs.* An organization should know its constituents intimately enough to be able to focus on what appeals to them. Effective communication with them will allow the organization to share with them their interests and aspirations. It is vital for the organization to be confident, hopeful and openly honest with them.

3. Enabling Others to Act

Leaders know that they cannot do the job alone. They are good at delegating authority, and in seeking partners in the planning and execution of a project. Good leaders are considerate of others, and give the mutual respect that they anticipate receiving back.

- *Encourage Partnership by Promoting Cooperative Goals and Building Trust.* By sharing the credit and being inclusive in interactions and problem-solving, leaders garner a climate of trust and openness. Their staff feels secure and positive in theiρ *goals.*

- *Strengthen Bonds by Sharing Information and Power, and Increasing Discretion and Prominence.* Leaders know their staff, are sensitive to their needs, and create trusting bonds with them. They also know that by sharing power, offering praise, and including them in decision-making, and by keeping their staff informed, they will strengthen those bonds of trust.

4. Showing the Way

Good leaders seem instinctively to know the way, and are good guides along that path. They are good at demonstrating their philosophy, and imparting their high standards through methods that make their organizations σ*tand out.*

- *Set an Example Consistent with Stated Values.* An organization should impart the fundamental values through a manner consistent with their values that put the message across. It must somehow show the intensity of an organization's commitment.

- *Plan Small Achievements that Foster Commitment.* By joining forces with others to achieve exceptional results, a plan can be broken down into manageable pieces that are easily accomplished. Highlighting milestones and allowing people to make choices will provide positive momentum, commitment and ownership.

5. *Encouraging the Heart*

Support, encouragement, recognition, and reward are all words in the leader's vocabulary. They show pride in their work and that of their staff, and they show their appreciation for a project's successful completion.

- *Reward Individual Contributions to Every Successful Project.* Develop measurable fulfillment standards to show a job well done, and institute a formal process for rewarding positive performance.

- *Regularly Celebrate Team Accomplishments.* By highlighting a team's accomplishments, their efforts will be rewarded, which will foster positive feelings of belonging to a greater organization.

ROLES OF PROGRAM EXECUTIVES IN STRATEGIC MANAGEMENT

Program management is what organizations do, and program managers are the ones who manage the development and delivery of service and products within an organization. Program or project managers are usually in charge of a program, project, service, or product and may exist at all levels of an organization. Despite their jobs including many managerial functions, they may not at all consider themselves as managers.

Although a program manager's primary capacity is to be a central point of administration and accountability for the quality delivery of a distinct service and product to specific beneficiaries, they can wear many hats. From the initial design idea, to approval, execution, and final project assessment, the program manager is crucial to setting levels of quality, cost, and timing, and how well the product and service are provided.

Since they are on the upper echelon of an organization, managers—and the organization itself—are very much at the mercy of how well the various individual program managers below them do their jobs. Therefore, there are six vital functions for successful *program executives.*

Six Central Managerial Functions of Program Executives

Program management work is comprised of six central managerial functions:

1. *Strategizing*–A methodical process for defining organizational goals, performing varied strategic situation analyses aimed at performance and environment, making strategic decisions and developing the plans required to reach the strategic goals or long-term directions of the organization.

2. *Structuring*–The method of determining, dividing, and setting up program and organizational subdivisions into lines of command, responsibility, and relationships.

3. *Program Budgeting*–A management approach to budgeting that presents the purpose and objectives for which funds are requested, estimates the costs of the proposed programs, and specifies the directives for measuring the accomplishments and work performed under each program.

4. *Program Planning*–A management tool for establishing a program and ensuring that it is designed clear enough to guide a manager to implement its defined milestones and tasks.

5. *Monitoring and Control*–A series of gauges designed to provide a timely alert for an organization when it is about to get into trouble so that it might take constructive action. They also establish contingency plans or alternatives to handle the matters that do go wrong.

6. *Evaluating*–A systematic means for determining how well an organization is doing the things they set out to do, and the probable reasons for their success or failure.

Key managerial functions are integral and interdependent, constituting an integrated management system, which provides the framework for telling program managers what to do in sequence as they guide their program through these six steps. In a smaller organization, the program manager could very well be responsible for all these managerial functions alone; however, they may draw upon talent from other parts of the organization or from outside the community, such as hiring a consultant.

II.   Strategic Planning

Strategic plan—just the words can cause unnecessary anxiety. Despite being enigmatic words for an uncomplicated process, they need not invoke fear in anyone who does not hold an M.B.A. or a Ph.D. in Management Science.

Strategic planning is the process of determining what and how an organization intends to accomplish its strategic goals over the coming years. Setting such a plan usually involves defining fundamental choices:

- The mission the organization will pursue

- The organization's role in the community

- Who or what it will serve

- The types of services, programs or products the organization will offer

- The necessary resources to reach success (people, funding, expertise, relationships, facilities, etc.)

- How to best combine these resources, programs, and relationships to accomplish the organization's mission.

Strategic planning should not be confused with operational or short-range planning. Short-range planning is what nonprofit organizations do when they develop yearly work plans and budgets. These are often more narrow in scope and focus on a shorter time period such as one year instead of three or five, and they tend to be more detailed. Although both types of plans are quite useful, strategic planning can be used to lay out the organization's long-term goals. Operational planning covers the immediate route which will be taken to reach those goals.

So how long should a strategic plan cover? A simple answer would be long enough to make major shifts in an organization's direction without being unrealistic. Of course, the environment in which the nonprofit works would dictate this. Organizations that operate in quickly changing environments, such as disaster relief could set their plan over a course of two to three years, while those that operate in less volatile circumstances could set a longer course. An organization's size can also be another factor that determines the required length of time. In order to make major changes, larger organizations may require longer lead time of three to ten years.

The ebb and flow of world circumstances dictates that there is never a perfect strategic plan. Most organizations simply use their plan to determine where they generally would like to be headed, while mapping out the primary steps or paths to take them there. The strategic plan is a shared mission of a nonprofit's future and how to make the vision happen, keeping the people and the programs moving towards that goal. All the while filtering out that which works from that which does not.

WHY DEVELOP A STRATEGIC PLAN?

Despite the old adage that a long journey begins with a single step, setting out on a long journey without a road map is foolhardy. Anyone who does not know where they are going is bound to get lost—or in the least, find themselves wandering aimlessly.

The same flaw can be found in an organization that has a general idea of its goals, but does not specifically state them. Setting a mission and goals, and effectively planning for them positively influence an organization's performance. Studies have shown that even small businesses that draw up an effective plan outperform their counterparts who have no such plan.

Strategic planning is crucial for knowing at any point of time where we are and where we are heading; otherwise, the organization will waste its resources on unfocused directions that do not effectively address the reason for its being. Losing focus by becoming preoccupied with an organization's day-to-day affairs can be disastrous for a nonprofit. Effective strategic planning forces the organization to look forward and build a commitment to its goals, metamorphosing it from an organization that simply reacts to one that achieves.

HOW TO DEVELOP A STRATEGIC PLAN

No two nonprofits are alike. Each has distinctive situations and styles; therefore, developing a strategic plan for an organization should be a specific process that is tailored to the organization and its context. Simply appending the planning process used by another organization which operates in a different field, sector or situation may become the source of future problems.

Basic Elements of Developing Your Strategic Plan

    i.   Organize the planning process
    ii.   Analyze your situation
    iii. Set your future direction
    iv. Adopt your strategic plan
    v.   Start implanting your plan
    vi. Evaluate and update your plan

Figure 5-A

Much research has lead to the development of the following five steps which may be adapted to fit the needs, situation and style of any organization. Naturally, these steps apply only when taking into account supplementary factors such as planning experience, an organization's size and the issues it is faced with, available timeframe, leadership considerations, and the number of people and groups which will be involved.

Step #1: Organize the Planning Process

The first task for this step is determining why a plan is being made and note any concerns. Then, select a person or steering committee to keep the planning on track, and decide which people and groups will be involved. Next, determine if a consultant or other resource people are needed, and outline the planning process that fits the organization. Other than in meetings, there are a number of ways that a consultant or facilitator can help the organization such as:

- Assist in designing and leading through the entire strategic planning process

- Orient or train participants

- Assist in the gathering and analyzing data

- Coach the steering committee or person who is leading the process

- Advise on questions specific to technical issues such as the plan format, making financial projections, and how to investigate new options

- Provide process advice or other assistance.

Organize the Planning Effort

Instructions

Indicate how each of the following issues will be handled. Then outline the steps, responsibilities, and timelines for developing your strategic plan.

- You are developing a strategic plan for:
  - ☐ Your total organization
  - ☐ Total organization, plus each major program or division
  - ☐ Only part of your organization (a department or program)
  - ☐ A multi-organization initiative or coalition
  - ☐ Other:

- For what time period are you planning?
  - ☐ Next two years
  - ☐ Next three years
  - ☐ Next four years
  - ☐ Next five years
  - ☐ Other (specify):

- Who will manage the planning effort and keep it on track (suggested members)?
  - ☐ An individual:
  - ☐ A steering committee:
  - ☐ Other:

- Are you going to use a consultant or other resource person(s) in developing the plan?
  - ☐ Yes
  - ☐ No
  - ☐ Unsure

  If so, what kind of help do you need?
  - ☐ Advice on the design of the planning process.
  - ☐ Help in gathering and summarizing information before a planning retreat.
  - ☐ Facilitation of the planning retreat and follow-up meetings.
  - ☐ Assist the executive director in developing first draft of plan if needed.

Figure 5-B

Using a consultant or facilitator in one or more of the above ways can free organizational leaders to participate in meetings without having to manage the agenda or discussion. Additionally, rather than hiring an expensive, skilled consultant, it is prudent to ask a qualified professional to volunteer their time.

There are three main stages to the Situation Analysis

1. Putting together all background information necessary to hold a good discussion about the organization's situation, such as determining what would be useful and the best ways to collect it. This can include:
   - information garnered from conversations, interviews, or group discussions, worksheets or questionnaires;
   - analysis of existing information;
   - organizational strategic assessments and program site visits.
2. Holding as many planning meetings as necessary to discuss the nonprofit's past, present and future, focusing on history, recent progress, mission, internal strengths and weaknesses, and external threats and opportunities.
3. Finalizing the process by hammering out an agreement on the most critical issues or regarding the strategic directions for the future of the organization. If your organization uses the goals approach, then at this point you set strategic goals that guide the completion of the planning process.

Figure 5-C

Lastly, get a commitment and consensus from key people to proceed. Poor groundwork in this step can result in wasted time, frustration, and low-quality plans. The following can guide this process:

- *Regarding mission:* Are mission and desired impact clear? Is this the right mission for the future? If not, how should it be changed?

- *Regarding program strategies:* Is the organization playing the right role or roles in their community? Are the current program strategies effective? Are programs well implemented? If not, what changes are needed?

- *Regarding resources and support:* Does the organization have the resources and assistance it needs to support the mission and programs? Are these assets being engaged in a practical way? If not, what needs to change?

> ## QUESTIONNAIRE
>
> Preliminary Questions for the board and staff to consider prior to attending the planning retreat:
>
> 1) What are your image and overall impressions of the organization?
>
> 2) What do you see us doing well? What are our strengths?
>
> 3) Where do we need to improve?
>
> 4) What opportunities or challenges can you imagine the organization pursuing in coming months and years?
>
> 5) What role(s), initiatives, or programs can you imagine the organization pursuing in coming months and years?
>
> 6) What relationships may be important for us to develop or nurture?
>
> 7) Are there any other ideas or issues that we should consider in our planning?

Figure 5-D

Step #2: Analyze the Situation

Organizations should take a hard look at their history and current situation. If done well, the organization's planning discussion in this step will result in a clear, common understanding of the strategic issues and choices the organization faces.

Set the Direction

This step is left up to the organization's leaders to determine the best direction for the organization. This is done by developing a first draft of the strategic plan based on the conducted strategic assessment or situation analysis of the organization. The draft ordinarily includes the organization's future mission, and major goals and strategies for moving the organization in the desired direction. Some of these plans also detail more information related to future services, finances, staffing, other key issues, and implementation.

- Develop a vision of your organization's future by outlining a goals approach

- Determine how to move the organization toward this future

- Develop a first draft of the plan.

Step #3: Refine and Adopt the Plan

Do this by tuning up the draft plan and securing the necessary approvals. If the first draft is generally on target, by sharpening it the organization increases the likelihood of successful implementation and ensuring broad-based commitment. Although, the plan's draft is usually initially reviewed only by the board and senior staff, allowing a broader review process could be quite helpful. This helps to fine-tune it before the final plan is written.

Whether only the organization's board and key staff or a number of constituents review the plan, adequate time should be given to review it, while encouraging an honest discourse. The following agenda often works well in review meetings:

- Overview of the plan.

- What is the general reaction to the plan? Is it within the expected range?

- What specific likes, vague areas, omissions or problems concerning each section of the plan does each reviewer see?

- What specific suggestions can be made to strengthen or improve the plan?

- What are the next steps to complete the plan?

- Have the plan reviewed and approved by the organization's appropriate decision makers (usually the board of directors). Some organizations also have key staff or other groups formally indicate their support of the plan before it goes to the board.

Step #4: Start Implementing the Plan

An organization does itself a tremendous service by not assuming that once the strategic plan is adopted, the planning is complete. After all, why go to all the trouble of developing a strategic plan, and adopting it if that is where all the work stops? Good strategic plans need good implementation. While the plan is being implemented, it must be periodically monitored for progress and updated with any required adjustments being made usually every year. Additionally, the executive director or a designated group should provide general supervision. Assuring that the initial implementation is going smoothly can be accomplished by using the following six steps.

- *Adhering to Steps 1-4 in Strategic Planning will ensure success.* Getting organized, taking stock, setting direction, and refining and adopting the plan most often makes implementing the plan much easier. If those who are responsible for implementing the plan have contributed their ideas and counsel throughout the planning process, this makes for more effective strategic planning. Implementing the plan is largely a matter of hard work and keeping a continued focus on the set goals.

- *Translating the strategic plan into goals, work plans and budgets for the coming year with everyone involved clear about their role and responsibilities.* Making certain that enough resources are allocated to implement the new goals and directions, and that programs, financial and other reporting systems give enough information to track progress toward those goals.

- *Good implementers do not stray from the larger picture.* Learn what does and does not work, but be flexible enough to know that original plans are often enhanced by new opportunities, seeing what emerges.

- *Do not let changes derail the strategic plan's direction.* Jobs may need to change, and new skills may need to be acquired, while an existing program may need to be discontinued or adapted to accomplish new goals.

- *Letting others who are important to the organization's future course know about the plan.* They can be critical allies in implementing the plan.

- *Monitoring the plan's progress periodically should be done yearly, quarterly or monthly, setting particular points:*

  - What has most contributed to or hindered progress. What has been learned?

  - Do the mission, goals and specific strategies still seem viable? If not, what adjustments should be made?

North American Da'wa Institute Case Study

NADI is an institute which writes and distributes materials introducing and explaining Islam, and provides internationally recognized Muslim speakers for religious and media events. The new board and president of NADI recognized that they needed a clearer strategy for equipping and training people to speak on matters of da'wa.

After a complete situation analysis, the institute leadership laid out several critical issues and strategic goals to guide the institute, a more detailed planning process was set in place that covered the next ten years. They drafted a document that stressed their marks of excellence in the institute's commitment of forwarding Islamic education, and then stated five strategic goals for the next period:

- To inaugurate a revised educational program for excellence well into the 21st century.

- To achieve a stable population of 450 high-quality students from diverse backgrounds, ages and vocations.

- To build a community of living, learning and worship which prepares qualified persons who are excellent for da'wa.

- To ensure the financial strength and stability of the institution.

- To strengthen the bond of brotherhood between the institution and those it serves.

The document also outlined the year-long process for reshaping the institute around these marks of excellence and strategic goals. In addition, it noted how the progress towards these goals would be monitored. The draft document was reviewed with the board, administration, other constituents, faculty and students. After several changes, the board approved the plan, which set a general direction for the institute over the next ten years. Subsequently, the institute's administration was restructured around these strategic goals, and teams were established to further develop and implement parts of the plan by revising the institute's educational programs, modifying recruitment and the hiring of scholars, and refocusing fundraising efforts.

Figure 5-E   Case Study and Planning Process

Step #5: Update the Plan

Before they plan and budget for the coming year, most organizations update their strategic plans yearly.

- Use a planning questionnaire, worksheets or other methods; reassess opportunities and threats, strengths and weaknesses and other issues critical to the strategic plan.

- Study whether the organization's basic strategies still make sense and outline what adjustments, if any, are needed.

- Revise the plan by including any new services, staffing or financial projections, and steps for implementing them.

- Translate the revised strategic plan into the objectives, budgets and priorities for the coming year.

N.A.D.I.'s Strategic Planning Process

Step	Responsible	Before
1. Select a steering group.	Board chair and Executive director	Feb. 1
2. Select a consultant to assist in design and facilitation of this process	Steering group	Feb. 15
3. Get agreement on the planning steps, responsibilities, and resources required	Steering group, consultant	Feb. 25
4. Gather information via a questionnaire from board members, staff, and others familiar with NADI regarding strengths, weaknesses, opportunities, and critical issues, hopes for future and issues that need attention	Consultant, staff, steering group	March 20
5. At a six-hour planning retreat with board and staff: • Using timetable, review NADI's history and accomplishments since inception. • Review progress toward mission and goals over past year. • Review summary of questionnaire responses. • Determine NADI's future direction, using Goal Approach • Review steps to complete strategic plan	Participants, consultant	April 1
6. Summarize the retreat	Consultant, executive director	April 12
7. At two 2-hour follow-up meetings, develop a draft of the strategic plan. The executive director will develop the initial draft for discussion and refinement with the steering group.	Steering group, consultant as needed	May 15
8. Review the draft with staff and board. Make needed revisions based on these reviews.	Steering group, consultant as needed	June 10
9. Approve the plan.	Board	June 25
10. Start implementing the plan.	Those indicated	July 1
11. Monitor the progress at six months and update the plan yearly.	Steering group	Feb. 1

Required monthly time: Approximately 18 to 20 hours for steps one through eight, plus staff work in preparing for the retreat and drafting the plan.

THE GOALS APPROACH

A goals approach has been found to be the preferred strategy by organizations that want several core principles, values or strategic goals to guide the planning for all of their divisions or programs. This is done by setting several major goals or guidelines which directs the program or division planning so that each develops a course for how it will achieve or contribute to these goals. A strategic plan for the entire organization is then drafted which incorporates those plans.

Establishing Strategic Goals

Sometimes called strategic directions, strategic goals are keys to future directions of change that describe the organization's desired attainable future within a specified time span of two to five years. The functions of these goals is to provide an explicit direction for the entire organization, a major portion of it, or a single program, and is based on, or are compatible with, the organization's mission or basic purpose. More specific than the mission statement, they also serve as the basis for uniting the efforts of operating units and persons into a total, more cohesive organizational effort while encouraging creativity and innovation. Strategic goals set new directions that are critical instruments for guiding the undertaking of the desired changes. These desired changes are chosen—or discarded—according to previously determined strategic assessments and their implications, where needs, benefits or demands are greater.

What Do Goals Accomplish?

When they work, strategic goals are the keys to excellence and success for an organization. Their aim is to achieve several different things:

- Focusing on innovation by doing something completely new, by doing things significantly better, expanding or eliminating current practices, modernizing technology or equipment, or focusing on a new market segment.

- Helping define an organization's direction, while emphasizing expectations or desired actions.

- Setting clear priorities on which to concentrate investments of time, talent, and resources.

STRATEGIC PLANNING AND BUDGETING

Management needs mission. Without it, an organization becomes stagnant, and may possibly fail. Vision is a quality that great managers possess, inspiring their organizations to move forward and excel. What are its strategic goals? Why does it want to achieve these goals? How does it attain them? Through strategic planning and budgeting, an organization can define the direction it wants to go for several years ahead, not simply drift along with the tide.

A strategic plan is a written and defined broad set of goals for the organization, which maps out the primary approaches to achieve these goals. A good example of this is that a soup kitchen's primary mission is to supply an adequate supply of nutritious food for the homeless. There are a number of different approaches the kitchen could take to achieve this mission:

- It could be a lobbying organization, raising money and using that money to pressure for legislation requiring the government to provide nutritious food for the homeless.

- It could solicit donations of food and money, which would then be used to prepare and serve meals directly to the homeless.

In addition to having a strategy, the strategic plan should also have goals. Among other things for example, given its strategy to directly provide meals, the soup kitchen might adopt the following goals:

- Increase the target population served by 60 percent within five years.

- Expand funding sources to cover the increase in services.

Once you have a strategic plan that identifies your strategies and goals, the next step is to translate the goals of the strategic plan into attainable objectives. One of the strategic goals for the soup kitchen is to increase the number of meals served by 60 percent of the target population. In all probability, this cannot be achieved through its day-to-day operations, and however must be met through long-term planning.

The kitchen's managers determine how to achieve this goal (60% increase) by adding three new locations and four more vehicles. More money will be required to buy equipment and vehicles, pay the rent, buy food, and hire additional staff. The long-range plan will also have to take into consideration how this money can be raised, and how to spend it. The soup kitchen's reasonable long-term goals might appear as follows:

Year 1: Establish and begin fundraising campaign to open a new site at the cost of $200K.

Year 2: Add a food distribution/soup kitchen at a new location at the cost of $200K. Raise additional money to acquire and operate a vehicle for food delivery at a cost of $60K. Solicit additional leftover food from more restaurants.

Year 3: Add a food distribution/soup kitchen at a new location at a cost of $200K. Raise additional money to acquire and operate a vehicle for food delivery for $60K. Solicit additional leftover food from other restaurants.

Year 4: Add a food distribution/soup kitchen at a new location for $200K. Raise additional money to acquire and operate a vehicle for food delivery for $60K. Solicit additional leftover food from other restaurants.

Year 5: Add two new vehicles for $120K. Raise extra funds to begin replacement of old kitchen equipment and older vehicles at the cost of $270K. Gain additional contributions to stabilize finances so replacements can be made whenever needed.

As shown above, thinking ahead from the first year is critical to the success of all the following years. Without the funds acquired during that time, the goals of the remaining years are not possible. These objectives outlined in the long-range plan are qualified targets relating to both input and output, making the creation of a detailed budget possible in financial terms.

HOW TO DESIGN A REALISTIC PLANNING PROCESS

Designing a planning process that is unrealistic for an organization could lead to the organization becoming lost or sidetracked. To plan a viable process, the following factors should be taken into account:

- *Planning Experience:* Having someone with experience in developing a strategic plan can be an essential ingredient for an organization's success. An organization should use as many resources as possible when developing their plan. This can be done by reading other texts on the topic, getting help from someone with experience in creating such a plan, or attending courses or workshops on the subject. It is suggested that those who are new to the process should use a relatively simple, straightforward process to develop their first plan. The second time, usually a year or two later, may involve a more involved approach which will become refined with experience.

- *Available Time:* Be realistic when setting time aside for designing the planning process. The key to an effective strategic planning meeting is preparation—it is best to do the bulk of this before and between meeting times. Setting aside ten to 15 hours of meeting time is quite reasonable. Sometimes this is all that a board and staff can muster, while larger organizations that consist of many managerial tiers or broad-based constituencies prefer a slower, more deliberate process. This is something that must be decided on a case-by-case basis, making adjustments as necessary.

- *Leadership:* Strategic planning often requires a few layers of leadership. These can fall into such categories as a steering committee or person who will keep the overall plan on track, an executive and staff who direct future program options and financial strategies, board members who suggest and evaluate major course shifts, and consultants who are charged with suggesting appropriate planning methods or facilitating meetings. Determining an effective chain of command will be invaluable in facilitating each step. Anticipating future problems and dealing with them beforehand makes the process flow more evenly. A committed leader who develops and implements a good strategic plan is critical.

- *Who Should Be Involved:* Most nonprofits involve people from across their entire spectrum (board members, staff, beneficiaries, community members, major donors, partners, etc.) in developing their strategic plan. Doing this allows for the building of a sense of teamwork, promoting learning and a stronger sense of contribution, and growth of commitment. While taking into consideration that involvement by a wider spectrum of participants can greatly contribute to the quality of the plan, it is also a detriment from the perspective that such involvement usually adds time, expense and complexity to the planning process. Involving a capable consultant is a must if the organization did not go through this process before. Even if they did, a professional consultant will contribute positively to the overall process.

• *Mini-Plans:* Most nonprofits develop one strategic plan for their organization that is "one-size-fits-all". Often, other organizations like to develop plans that are tailor-made to each of their programs or major divisions which tie into their overall plan. Usually this is true when each program or division functions slightly independent. So, consider having a mini-plan for each program or division separately so that the development and implementation of these mini-plans are easier and more feasible.

• *Focus on Critical Issues:* One crucial point that must not be forgotten is to keep the planning focused on the critical issues or choices facing the organization. Often, large quantities of time are wasted on issues and information that are not central to the organization's future. Keeping people's attention focused on the most promising ideas and the most critical issues should be a priority, and to do this would require effective leadership.

TIPS FOR DRAFTING STRATEGIC PLANS

1. *Select a person to do the drafting:* Once the future direction of the organization is reasonably clear, designate the party responsible for developing the strategic plan's first draft. This task usually falls to the executive director.

2. *Agree on a format:* Before the plan is drafted, a format should be chosen that is agreed upon by all. This format should include the general length and major section headings. It should also include several basic sections such as a mission statement, major goals for the future and strategies related to those goals with other sections listed below. Although no one includes all of these elements in their strategic plans, it is important to keep in mind that the plan's format is influenced largely by its major goal(s). For example, an organization's major goal is to construct a new building, and the strategic plan might include a section on facilities.

• *Executive summary:* A summary of an organization's overall plan.

- *Mission statement:* A statement of what the organization hopes to accomplish or the reason it exists for.

- *History:* How the nonprofit got started, how it has developed, and what it has accomplished to date.

- *Organizational profile:* Basic facts and figures, current programs, and so on.

- *Situation analysis:* A brief summary of major strengths and weaknesses, opportunities and threats, and critical issues for the future. Some plans include a separate section on critical issues that include the proposed solution for each issue.

- *Goals and strategies:* Strategic goals for the future, plus specific strategies to accomplish each goal. Some planners like to divide these into program goals and supporting goals (also called management or infrastructure goals).

- *Service levels:* A summary of the levels of service planned for each of the next few years. For example, the number of people to be served, the number of training sessions to be held, the number of housing units to be developed, etc.

- *Staffing levels:* A summary of the number and type of staff projected over the next few years. Some organizations include volunteers in this section.

- *Financial plans:* A projected operating budget showing sources of revenue and projected expenses by year. If the organization has capital requirements, they want to note how much will be needed and where the funds will come from.

- *Implementation plan:* A section, or separate document, showing who has the responsibility for advancing each major goal. Some organizations list major tasks or objectives for the coming year, showing who is responsible for each, and the date by which each task must be accomplished.

- *Mini-plans:* Larger nonprofits with many sub-units may include smaller strategic plans for each division or major program.

- *Other specific dimensions critical to an organization's future:* Additional sections on governance, facilities, evaluation plans, marketing strategy, target markets, alliances or key relationships, administrative systems and support, and how and when the strategic plan will be monitored.

- *Appendices:* Additional material that supports the plan. Some organizations include some of the above sections in the appendices.

3. Develop the first draft: Although the first draft is rarely perfect, the task of doing it usually falls to one person with the refining of it done through consultation with others. Another alternative is for several people to be responsible for individual sections, and then the final draft being combined by one person. As this is being done, new issues are bound to be raised, which should be dealt with according to their importance.

4. Detailed plans can be developed separately: Some organizations prefer to add an implementation section in their strategic plans, while others prefer to address implementation issues in a separate document or in their yearly objectives, work plans, and budgets. Also, after a strategic plan has been approved, more detailed or separate plans for marketing, fundraising programs, etc. are often developed.

III. Strategic Situation Assessment

Strategic situation audit or assessment is a process by which managers learn how to make necessary program and operations changes to counter negative affects, or exploit an emerging opportunity in a timely manner. Operationally, it is an analysis of performance and whatever seriously affects that performance. The aim is to make a significant improvement in the way that an organization provides quality product and service.

Although there is no defined content for the strategic assessment, there are three important areas from which an organization might tailor a design that is most appropriate for them: performance, environmental impact, and strategic implications. To be the most effective, an audit should be targeted to a specific unit or program, or at several of these within an organization. To maximize analytical ability to get things done, never analyze the entire organization at once. If you intend to do that, do it separately for different programs or divisions such as one for administrative operation, another for the Social Services

Center, as an example, and a third for finances, etc.

Strategic Assessment Process

Strategic assessment is a recurring process that must be staffed, scheduled and organized so that it is made a regular part of program management work. The series of steps that must be planned and implemented when they are performed are summarized as follows:
- undertake performance analysis
- conduct an environmental scan
- build a strategic data base
- perform a strategic implications analysis
- determine a set of strategic planning or critical issues
- set strategic goals to direct modifications into these critical issues.

Figure 5-F

Strategic audits can be done on a formal, systematic basis that is structured and prescribed, or on an informal basis by individual managers talking with their colleagues and staff in an open manner. Many organizations blend these approaches simultaneously to arrive at the preparation of a strategic plan.

THE PURPOSE OF STRATEGIC ASSESSMENT

The strategic assessment provides a detailed snapshot of how well an organization is doing at a specific time and what may happen in the future in relationship to the outside world. Its main purpose is to identify and analyze the key external events and trends before their serious impact is felt. Although no organization can recognize every piece of information that influences its strategic decisions, they can learn to search for those factors in the changing environment that will have the greatest interest for them, or yield the greatest impact.

A secondary aim is to provide a venue for sharing and debating conflicting views about the noted changes, clarifying their ambiguities and possible impact. While a third objective is to guide the quality of intelligent ideas associated with the strategic audit so that the process does not dissolve into a habitual managerial exercise that results in a great deal of analytical paperwork, and not much else. The most prudent character for strategic leadership to play is that of creating a climate favorable to creative change, stimulating staff to do their best to find exciting answers to pestering questions through three diagnostic elements:

- *Performance*–An analysis of data concerning past and present performance, and any available forecasts and projections. These might include an analysis of institutional and managerial support, such as structure, system, and top management commitment.

- *Environmental Context*–Where trends, forces, and events having a potential impact on the formulation and implementation of strategic directions and initiatives are identified.

- *Strategic Implications*–An analysis of an organization's strengths and weaknesses, and the threats and opportunities that exist in the organization's environment.

IV. Assessing Your Situation

In order to practically benefit from this chapter to maximize your organization's strategic effort, please consider the situation of the organization you are part of, in light of what we have presented here. By answering these questions, you would be assessing your organization, as well as identifying the areas where corrections are needed. Additionally, you are encouraged to go back to review the specific materials of the chapter for clarification on some questions.

- *Does your Chief Executive, whether President or Executive Director, function as your organization strategist or do they take the role of the micro-manager and problem-solver of the organization?*

- *When was the last time your organization performed a situation analysis or strategic assessment, taking into consideration all external and internal factors affecting the organization?*

- *Once you conduct a situation analysis, does your organization identify its critical issues for next period, and then set strategic goals to address these issues?*

- *Does your organization institute a procedure for conducting the strategic planning process by outlining timelines, identifying the responsible parties, and funding allocations before starting this process?*

- *Does your organization distinguish between its strategic plan and its operational (or work) plan when it conducts its planning process?*

- *Does your organization document clearly its specific strategic or directional goals for the next three to five years?*

- *Does your organization involve leadership, staff and other parties, who will execute the plan, in the strategic planning process, or is the process limited to upper-level management?*

- *Have you ever sought help from a professional consultant(s) to aid in the development of the strategic plan?*

- *Does your organization reaffirm its explicit mission statement and values every time it conducts its planning process?*

- *Once you have a strategic plan, does your organization translate it into specific goals, work plans and budgets for every program or division of your organization, with clear responsibilities of those involved?*

- *Once your organization adopted its strategic plan, does it periodically monitor its execution, and update it according to the accomplishments in achieving its milestones?*

- *Does your organization have a set of progress indicators to self-evaluate and measure its performance at specific time intervals?*

Chapter

6.

Setting & Accomplishing

Your Goals

I.   *Three Levels of Organizational Priorities*

     - Mission

     - Objectives

     - Goals

II. *The Goal-Oriented Approach*

     - Benefits of the Goal-Oriented Approach

     - The Power of Goal Setting

     - Setting SMART Goals

III. *How to Set and Accomplish Your Goals*

IV. *Action Planning*

     - What the Action Plan Determines

     - Preparing Action Steps

     - Status Reporting

V.   *Charting your Plans*

     - The Gantt Chart

     - The Work Breakdown Structure

     - Project Management Software

VI. *Assessing Your Case*

In the two previous chapters we presented the vital role of strategic direction, knowing your mission clearly, and setting a long-term strategic plan. Still, unless you transfer your strategic directions into short-term goals and action plans, they will not be implemented. Even when you are clear about your long-term objectives, you must be specific and clear enough to know what the short-term desired results are: your goals. In this chapter, we will be more specific—from identifying strategic direction and long-term objectives to setting goals. We will then go into more details of how to achieve these goals through action planning. Goal setting addresses where the organization is now and where it wants to be. Planning addresses how to reach these goals. Both of these strategies are scientific, sensitive skills.

For many organizations, the greatest roadblock to strategic planning is that their strategic plan is not implemented. Commonly, planners have become fatigued from completing the earlier phase of planning; therefore, action planning may seem detailed and tedious compared to the earlier phase that may have seemed creative in nature. Consequently, action planning is too often ignored, leaving the strategic plan as useless philosophical statements with no grounding in the day-to-day realities of the organization. For successful organizations, their commitment to strategic planning is commensurate to the extent that the organization completes action plans to reach each of their goals.

I.   Three Levels of Organizational Priorities

There are three levels of strategic directions or priorities that successful nonprofits must at all times consider clearly. One has to do with its reason for existence, known as its Mission. The second level deals with its long-term priorities, known as Objectives, while the third has to do with its short-term priorities, known as Goals. Determining these priorities is a key to the effectiveness and success of any organization.

MISSION

An organization's mission is the reason behind its founding. In short, it tells why the organization exists in a broad statement that does not change from year to year. Many nonprofit organizations have an official mission that is expressed through a purpose statement from the time they were registered as a viable entity. Although an organization's mission may occasionally be reviewed, it is vital for a nonprofit to have a practical mission statement that is centered on the organization's entire operation.

In addition to the original mission statement, some organizations effectively have varied mission statements for different departments or committees. This idea is discussed at length in a previous chapter.

OBJECTIVES

Objectives are statements of broad intent that often arise out of the mission statement. For instance, a humanitarian charity with a mission to provide preventive initiatives and medical care to HIV-positive patients in Africa may have several main objectives in their five-year strategic plans. Each of these objectives represents an area of concentration during this five-year period. One of these could be to launch a five-year preventive educational program targeting teens in all high schools of West Africa. Another would be to team-up with a major pharmacological firm to provide HIV medications to medical centers and hospitals in the same area. While a third would be to establish HIV testing units in the most affected areas. For some nonprofits, their objectives do not change because they are part of their mission statement, or they clarify their mission statement. For others, these objectives change whenever they do their strategic planning.

GOALS

A goal may be defined as a specific desired future accomplishment over a defined period of time. Goals are statements describing the "what" your organization wishes to reach, stemming from its mission and objectives. Goals are the "ends" toward that which your efforts will be directed, and often change from term to term or year to year, depending on the nature of the nonprofit. An organizational decision to be the best may be admirable, but it is not a goal. It is a desire, a wish. Maybe even a dream. To make any desirable idea into a goal, it must be expressed in a quantitative term with a deadline.

II.   The Goal-Oriented Approach

"If you don't know where you are going, any road will get you there." This is true for many organizations and companies. Organizations cannot survive and flourish without some basic goals. Goals give an organization a specific, practical direction to move towards throughout the entire year. Organizations today are seeing the value of a goal-oriented approach because it provides clearer directions, and helps concentrate all their energies and resources into moving toward specific goals. Setting specific directions through goal setting often leads to better and more effective programs and services. This approach also becomes a tool to measure progress, and to help define future directions. Though it is true that setting and accomplishing organizational goals will not guarantee success for any organization, not having and accomplishing organizational goals will almost certainly ensure long-term failure.

Benefits of the Goal-Oriented Approach

The goal-oriented manager reaps a series of advantages by setting goals...

- It forces the manager to determine what concrete results need to be accomplished in measurable, time-specific terms.

- It is geared to quantifiable results; thus enabling the organization to assess the effectiveness in terms of what is accomplished.

- It pinpoints each person's responsibility for measurable results, so that everyone is able to clearly see whether performance is above or below expectations.

- It provides continuity by having officially approved objectives and goals.

- It helps focusing on an organization's potential and future plans.

A goal-oriented approach is one of the most prominent and basic tools used by both individuals and organizations to assist in setting their directions and in accomplishing them. Successful nonprofit organizations often set both long- and short-term goals, not only for program and service development but also for improving quality, preserving resources through becoming more focused, and garnering better funding. Goal setting is a very powerful technique that can yield strong returns in all areas of your organization.

In effect, goals are concrete and operational, and have several standout features. They are statements of targets, and are achievable accomplishments. Additionally, they are concrete indicators of attainable outcomes that usually take place within a framework of goals. Their timeframe is usually within a year, and are often accompanied by action steps to carry them out. They represent a joint commitment between managers and their subordinates, and encourage managers to progress beyond levels of excellence.

At its simplest level, the goal-oriented approach, through the process of setting specific goals and focusing on their achievements, helps you to choose where you want to go in your organization and how to get there. By knowing precisely what you want to achieve, you know what you have to concentrate on, and when something is merely a distraction. Goal setting gives you long-term vision and short-term motivation. Once goals are set, action plans specify how to achieve them. The usual timeframe for action plans is from one to twelve months.

THE POWER OF GOAL SETTING

Goal setting works wonders! More is accomplished when you have specific goals to concentrate your efforts on than when you do not. Goal setting and goal achievement have tremendous organizational value. It is a simple, though not always easy, concept that can change fundamentally the way in which organizations do their work. Goals give clear direction to the collective effort of all the parts of an organization, and they provide a truly motivational and accountability tool to all its members. Additionally, they raise the commitment level of all those involved by helping the organization to achieve them. Therefore, there are at least four major benefits of goal setting:

Focused Effort–Every action is subject to the question "How does it help us accomplish our goals?" The question brings about a rethinking of how the organization runs. It reveals actions that are not important and can be dropped, key tasks that need to be done more productively, and procedures that need to be revised to ensure that the most important things are getting done first. Even the definition of what's most important can be changed when a goal exists. The goals themselves determine what is important and what is not. They provide the focus for the organization's operations.

Better Resource Management–When planning goals, consideration must be given to how much time, money and effort is needed to accomplish each of them. Resources such as employees' time, uses of technology and so on must be aligned properly behind the goal. Tasks that are irrelevant or redundant can be eliminated or refocused based on how they contribute to the goal. Therefore, when employees have clear goals before them, they tend to go straight for them, rather than wasting their efforts and their organization's resources on different unnecessary tasks.

Measurement of Success–Goals let you know how you are doing. They are a way to measure success. They are also a way to measure and correct failure. Publicizing an organization's movement toward its goals can spur people on to even greater heights. If the organization is getting off track at any time along the way, pointing to the goals is a way to get it to adjust and get back on track. Some organizations even keep daily tabs on progress toward a goal, and post them for all to see. This is a subtle way of asking everyone to measure their daily success by how much they contributed to the goal at their organization.

Performance Enhancement–Goals also enhance an individual's performance and collective workplace performance. As employees see progress toward the goals, they tend to put even greater effort into them. They are willing to go that "extra mile" to make sure the goal is accomplished. The department's or program's goals also can become a part of each employee's annual or semiannual performance review. A portion of the review can be devoted to a discussion of a question such as: "How did you do in accomplishing our goals?" And, "how can you help bring about our goals over the next six months (or year)?" A manager can spell out expectations clearly and even change employee job descriptions to reflect more accurately their specific contribution to the department's goals. This lets them know that the manager is serious about shifting the organization's efforts from "business as usual" to goal setting and goal achievement.

SETTING SMART GOALS

Because staff do not know what is expected of them, their productivity becomes low. Management usually provides vague objectives, since neither management nor staff knows if and when these objectives have been met. Setting effective goals is as important as reaching them. This means that not only how to accomplish their goals is significant, but more importantly, the way you express the goals you want to accomplish. When you set goals, remember to:

- Be time limited. A target date or time period should be clearly stated.

- Be measurable, tangible, or verifiable.

- Be challenging. Set goals that generate a high energy level for your organization.

- Be realistic—within the scope of your organization.

- Be relevant. As time and resources are limited, goals should be worth pursuing.

- Be visible. Make your goals visible by posting them.

Nonprofit managers must learn how to set effective goals and how to accomplish them. Effective goals are expressed in specific, measurable, attainable, relevant, and time-trackable terms. An easy way to remember these criteria is to set SMART Goals:

- *Specific*–Anyone reading the goal will easily understand what outcome is expected.

- *Measurable*–Able to measure improvement towards reaching the goal and know when it is accomplished.

- *Attainable*–Many goals fail because they are not realistic in the first place. Good management does not set unrealistic goals that are too big to achieve given the current resources (money, staff and time).

- *Relevant*–That is to be aligned with the organization's mission and current priorities. These priorities are usually identified during the process of strategic planning, and they are expressed as critical issues or objectives.

- *Time-trackable*–Every goal must be bound by two dates: a beginning date and an ending date. Stating specific deadlines increases the productivity of staff and enhance the effectiveness of performance evaluation.

III. How to Set and Accomplish Your Goals

It is more effective to set goals as a team, not only to motivate people, but also to conceive better goals. This course of action is more likely to realize greater positive results because people support what they help to create. With team goal setting, you can expect:

- A greater level of commitment

- Increased motivation among employees and volunteers

- Enhanced understanding of the goals

- More effective goals by involving varied opinions.

The recommended procedure to formulate your department, your program, or your organizational goals is as follows:

- Brainstorm goals as a team. People support what they create, and they will more easily accept the responsibility for it. Goals must be aligned with your organizational, or departmental strategic plan. Therefore, it is very important for the team to generate their goals per the strategic directions and objectives spelled out in the strategic plan.

- Choose those goals you wish to attend to from the brainstormed list. Prioritize them as a team so that you end up with the most important goals that the whole team agrees to. In most situations, any brainstorming session generates many important goals; yet, not all of them are attainable at the same time, so you would choose those with top priority and are within the possible reach of your organization. Those goals finally extracted must be expressed as SMART goals in a very specific and measurable format as described above.

- Get organized and delegate each goal to a specific individual, committee or department. The result of this step is to have the same team involved in setting these goals end up with the responsibilities of accomplishing them. For instance, if your result is ten goals, you might delegate three goals to committee A and two goals to committee B, one goal to committee C, and each remaining goal to a different individual.

- Determine the plan of action for each goal. This is to draft the action plan for every goal by the person or group responsible for it. The end result of action planning is to know what tasks and resources are required to accomplish each goal, in addition to who does what tasks, by when, and how. Ideally, you should develop an overall top-level action plan that depicts how all goals will be reached. This document presents all action plans in one major plan without too many details. Senior managers use a document like this to track and evaluate the plan's progress. An action plan's format depends on the nature of the goal, its complexity, and the organization's needs. Different formats of action planning are described below.

- Move into the implementation phase for every goal. This is accomplished by executing the action plan steps or tasks according to the timetable, and those spelled out in the action plan. Managers or essential individuals responsible for each goal must follow up and follow through to make sure the implementation phase is being executed in accordance with the plans.

- Continually evaluate your progress. Those responsible for the goals must meet frequently to evaluate progress until each goal is accomplished. For all goals, the evaluation phase must be completed by senior management, and by different teams for their delegated goals. Even after the goal is accomplished, there should be an evaluation of how well it was achieved, what was done exceptionally good or bad, and what we learned for next time.

Case Example:
Orphans Sponsorship Program

The goal is to increase orphan sponsorship dues for the needy. After careful consideration of the current situation, and the number of orphans waiting for sponsors, the following situation was found:

GOAL: To sponsor 2000 orphans by June 2007.

From previous experience and data analysis, and after studying your marketing options, you expect to reach this goal through the four major methods, explaining each with their estimated cost, timetable and expected return.

1. Brochure

    a. Brochure Insert with receipts: From previous experience, you know that once a donor gets a receipt for a contribution they have made along with an insert (brochure or flier) promoting a certain project, it is very likely they will pay closer attention, and might very well donate towards the cause. Since your charity processes receipts for about 10,000 donors—many of whom donate more than once per year—at least 20,000 receipts are to be issued within the next 12 months. Therefore, a brochure promoting this program and a return envelope will be inserted in the same envelope with every receipt. If the estimated return is only two percent, a return of approximately 400 sponsorships should be expected. A minimal cost of $800 for printing 20,000 brochures would be incurred. Timing: will be done each time receipts are processed. Delegated to: Communications Manager.

    b. Direct Mailings: Mailing the brochure to all donors one time within the specified timeframe. If such a mailing were sent to 12,000 donors, the return would be expected to be approximately three percent, or about 360 sponsorships. The maximum cost expected is estimated to be $4,000. Timing: Accomplished during Ramadan. Delegated to: Communications Manager.

2. Internet

    a. Online Sponsorship: Having a well-presented page on your website to promote this program and enable sponsors to select whom to sponsor. The online sponsorship program will be promoted effectively on the Internet and in all of the charity's publications and mailings.

    b. E-mail blast: Sending to all contacts on the e-mail list an e-mail blast to promote this program, with a link to its page on your website. Timing: Every four months.

c. Banner Advertisements: Promoting this program through banner ads on other related websites to generate traffic to your website. Budget allocated for that is $10,000. Timing: Mainly during Ramadan. All three tasks delegated to: Website Administrator.

It is forecasted that 450 orphan sponsorships will be generated from the above strategies.

3. Advertisement

a. TV infomercials: You decided to dedicate two infomercials on the ethnic xyz station during Ramadan for this program, at an approximate cost of about $9,000. This may bring about 350 new sponsorships per infomercial. Timing: First and fourth week of Ramadan. Delegated to: Media Coordinator.

4. Public Relations Events

a. Dedicated public fundraising events: Since the charity has frequent fundraising programs at mosques, you decided to dedicate three events for promoting the orphan sponsorship program during the summer. No less than 50 new sponsorships per event is expected. Delegated to: PR Manager.

Additionally, a system is set in place to follow up on sponsors and collect sponsorship gifts, disbursing them to orphans through your representatives. As well as keeping this program up-to-date by renewing expired sponsorships.

IV.   Action Planning

A strategic plan should be followed or accompanied by an action, or operational plan that describes the specific actions that must be taken to achieve the individual targets identified in the strategic plan. While the strategic plan focuses on the "what", the action plan will focus on the "how" by providing a real guide to action to reach specific goals. These plans are a link between the strategic plan and the day-to-day activities of the organization.

Once your organization has written its goals, it is time to take this task one step further by developing an Action Plan for each goal. This is an actual detailed map of what is to be accomplished within a specific time framework for each goal.

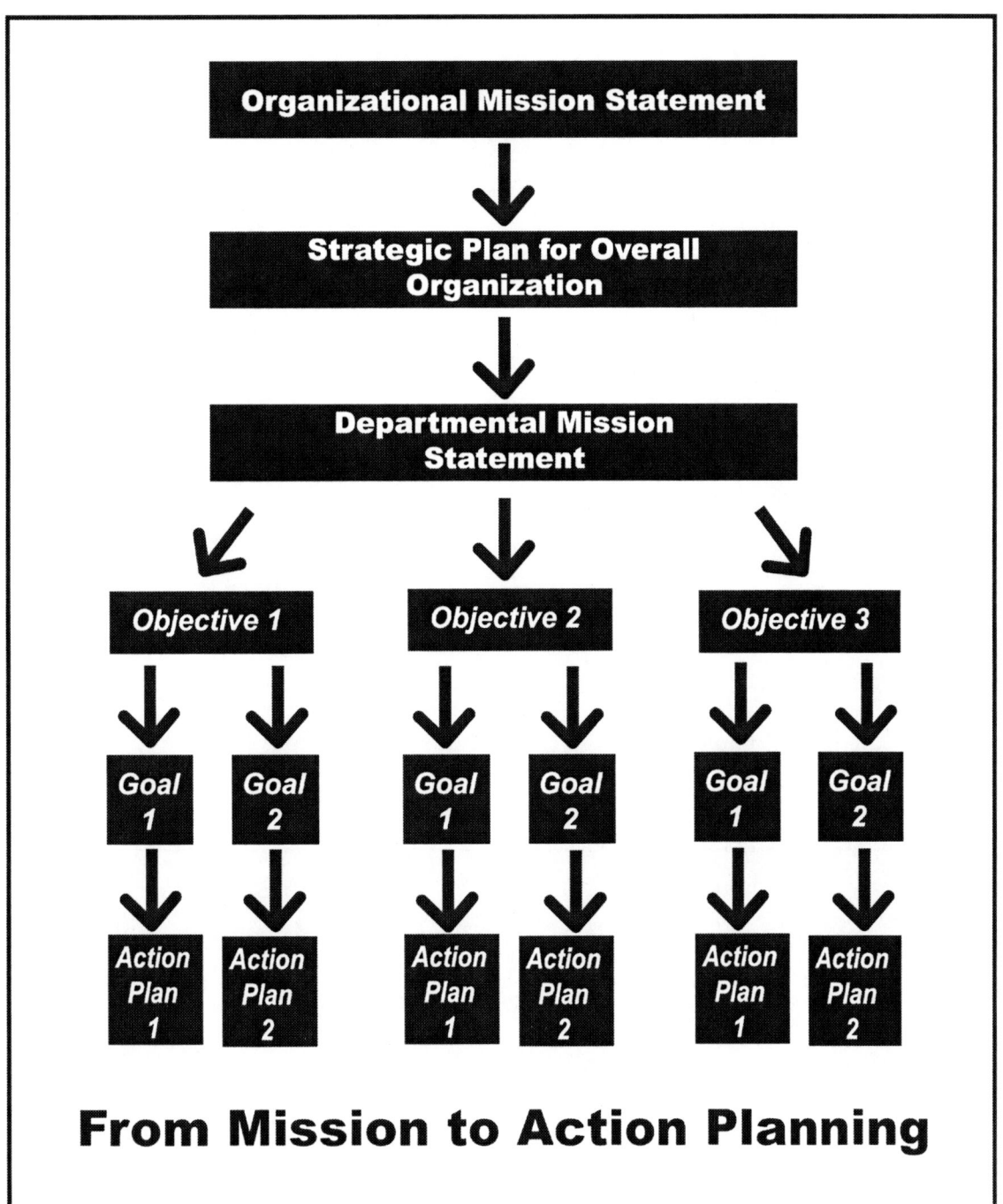

From Mission to Action Planning

Figure 6-A

BASICS OF ACTION PLANNING

As mentioned earlier, action planning typically includes deciding who is going to do what, by when, and in what order for the organization to reach its goals. As well, the design and implementation of the action planning depend on the nature and needs of the organization. Typically, every goal requires a set of tasks to be completed. To map out a certain goal's action plan, one must first identify all the tasks involved. Secondly, determine who is responsible for every task, its beginning and ending times, and how to measure the results. These issues can be clarified through meetings, reports, or other relevant means.

- Action Plan/Task1:

    - How Results will be Measured:

    - Person Responsible:

    - Date to be Started:

    - Date to be Completed:

- Action Plan/Task2:

    - How Results will be Measured:

    - Person Responsible:

    - Date to be Started:

    - Date to be Completed:

    - Etc.

What the Action Plan Determines

- What is to be done (the goal)?
- What are the required resources (staff, budget, etc.)?
- How will it be accomplished (the required tasks)?
- Who is responsible for completing each task?
- When will it be accomplished?
- How will we evaluate the improvement?

PREPARING ACTION STEPS

To develop an action plan, one must begin with a stated goal, while taking care to put the plan in writing to avoid confusion and misunderstanding later on. It is also important to report relevant progress and problems. For example, if the goal is to "conduct a three-day activist training conference involving 200 youth activists by May 14," the following action steps might be set up to accomplish this goal:

ACTION STEPS	COMPLETION DATE	RESPONSIBLE PERSON
Discuss conference with high school officials; request education board president to appoint a planning committee.	1/15	JK
Contact host hotel, check for availability and costs.	1/24	JK
Meet with planning committee chair to develop tentative agenda and set dates for committee meetings to plan conference.	1/31	JK
Arrange with planning committee to set conference schedule and invite speakers.	2/15	DG
Hold and manage conference.	4/11-13	DG

STATUS REPORTING

In order to stay on track with a goal or project, it is helpful to use a project management program to produce reports for gathering regular report information. If an organization does not use a group software reporting system on a computer network that reminds staff of status reports and other administrative requirements, they can rely on good old-fashioned paper systems. By supplying staff with preprinted forms to fill out their weekly and monthly progress, and requiring them to advise management of any encountered problems, they are more likely to submit their completed updates on time. This is especially true when the reports are routinely collected at a specified time and date. When everyone uses the same form, it simplifies the process. The reports should provide the following information:

- Tasks completed (including the date completed)

- Tasks in progress with expected completion dates

- Tasks planned with expected completion dates

- Budget expenditures

- Issues that need attention

- Recommendations for project improvements or changes.

V.   Charting Your Plans

There are several schedule-charting formats to choose from, with the best format being the one that best fits the project.

- *Listings:* These are useful for most small projects. They are basically to-do list of tasks required to accomplish a goal laid out in a table format, specifying who does them and by what date, as in the previous example.

- *Calendar Charts:* Annotated calendars can be extremely useful for keeping track of schedules for many small projects. The calendar chart is adaptable to color-code multiple projects tracking on a washable board, and is a good communication tool when displayed in a central location.

- *Gantt Charts:* These are best used as a visual overview of project timelines; however, they do not show task relationships and should not be a substitute for a network diagram. This tool is discussed in more details below.

- *Milestone Charts:* These can be assigned to summarize major paths on a network, and can also be used to chart an overall project schedule.

- *Work Breakdown Structures:* These are very useful to break a large project into pieces that are easily accomplished. There are many formats to present the breaking up of a project, and this will be covered further later in this chapter.

For current purposes, we will concentrate more on the Gantt chart and Work Breakdown Structure. These important goal or project management tools are used for charting action plans and evaluating their progress.

THE GANTT CHART

A Gantt chart, also known as a project timeline, is a horizontal bar chart developed as a production control that is frequently used in project management. A Gantt chart provides a graphical illustration of a schedule helping to plan, coordinate, and track specific tasks in a project. Gantt charts may be simple renderings created on graph paper, or more complicated computerized versions created using software such as Microsoft Project.

A Gantt chart is constructed with a horizontal *X-axis* representing the total time span of the project which is broken down into increments representing days, weeks, or months, and a vertical *Y-axis* representing the tasks that make up the project.

For example, if an organization's project is to buy a new computer system and software, the major tasks involved in the purchase would be laid out on the Y-axis: conduct research, choose hardware, choose appropriate software, purchase systems, set-up hardware, and install software. Horizontal bars representing the sequences, timing, and time span for each task would be drawn in lengths that vary according to the timeframe each function is expected to take.

Gantt charts clearly show a project's status, but one cannot surmise how a task that is falling behind schedule affects other tasks. Electronically created Gantt charts allow for the storage of additional task information, such as the individuals assigned to specific tasks, and notes about the procedures. They also offer the benefit of being easily updated or changed, and may be adjusted regularly to reflect the actual status of project tasks as they swerve from the original plan. Since each level of tasks has its own Gantt timeline, they can be worked on as a subset of the entire project, and updates to sub-task timelines are immediately shown in the overall project timeline. Actual hours invested and data illustrating a project's percent of completion are available at any level in the project hierarchy. Additionally, every task can be divided into an unlimited number of sub-tasks.

THE WORK BREAKDOWN STRUCTURE

One of the most useful tools of project management is the work breakdown structure, or WBS, that is the heart and framework on which the project is built. It can fit all sorts of purposes and takes many forms, and when done right, is the basis for project planning, scheduling, budgeting, and controlling. A WBS is not the only way to plan a project, but despite it getting little attention, it can be used quite successfully as a project management tool.

What is a WBS?

The WBS is a structured way of breaking a project down to its skeleton or individual components, providing the basis of a plan for successful completion of its objectives. This decomposition should continue only to the level that is required to identify the task or subtask as a natural subdivision of a cost account, or work package. This work package is a job assignment that is identifiable with a person, a job or a budget number, and is where the actual project work is accomplished. The successive layers of a project's details are referred to as its levels with the first being its name. The WBS is rarely developed below the fifth level, and although the work package usually happens at the fifth level, it can occur anywhere below the first level. In a WBS, some projects may require as few as three layers. Others require as many as ten or more layers, or require a WBS for each subproject or milestone within the WBS. The project as relatively simple as a newsletter could have as few as three layers, versus seven or more for creating a new corporate division. Since the WBS is based on the category of tasks, there is no magic formula for organizing a WBS. The following levels are for use in breaking down the work in a project of any size:

- The total project

- Subprojects or milestones

- Major tasks

- Subtasks

- Work packages or work elements.

WBS Formats

It is helpful to think of the WBS process as a reverse flowchart that begins with the project and decomposes it into smaller and smaller elements until the smallest level of detail is achieved. Like a normal flowchart, the process is linear and requires that each successive step be sequential, logical, and at the appropriate level of detail to make the project's components easier to identify. There are two common forms of WBS presentation. The first, and most popular one used by all of the project management software packages is the indented format which is similar to a text outline with each project level indented to set it apart from the previous level. The graphical or tree form is the second type and resembles a traditional organizational chart. Although this presentation form takes a lot of space to develop, it is an effective format for those who work better from visual presentations of data. Scheduling for a large project is more accurate when this type of diagram is used.

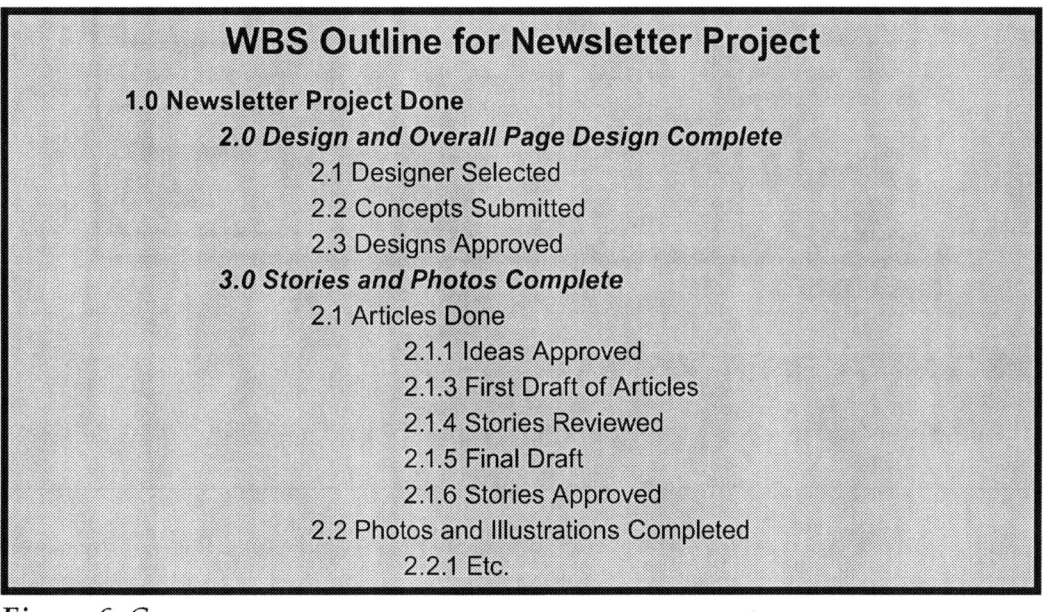

Indented WBS Format

1.0 Project
    1.1 Major Project Subsystem 1
        1.1.1 Task 1
            1.1.1.1 Subtask 1
                1.1.1.1.1 Work Package 1
        1.1.2 Task 2
            1.1.2.2 Subtask 1
                1.1.2.2.1 Work Package 1
                1.1.2.2.2 Work Package 2
    1.2 Major Project Subsystem 2
        1.2.1 Task 1
            1.2.1.1 Subtask 1
                1.2.1.1.1 Work Package 1
                    1.2.1.1.1.1 Components
    1.3 Major Project Subsystem 3

Figure 6-B

Using the example of creating a newsletter, all tasks should be divided into disparate functions, such as writing stories, shooting photos, and printing and production. Once the milestone structure of the project is created, the real work breakdown begins. Without breaking master work into smaller projects, larger projects would be simply too complex to manage.

WBS Outline for Newsletter Project

1.0 Newsletter Project Done
    2.0 Design and Overall Page Design Complete
        2.1 Designer Selected
        2.2 Concepts Submitted
        2.3 Designs Approved
    3.0 Stories and Photos Complete
        2.1 Articles Done
            2.1.1 Ideas Approved
            2.1.3 First Draft of Articles
            2.1.4 Stories Reviewed
            2.1.5 Final Draft
            2.1.6 Stories Approved
        2.2 Photos and Illustrations Completed
            2.2.1 Etc.

Figure 6-C

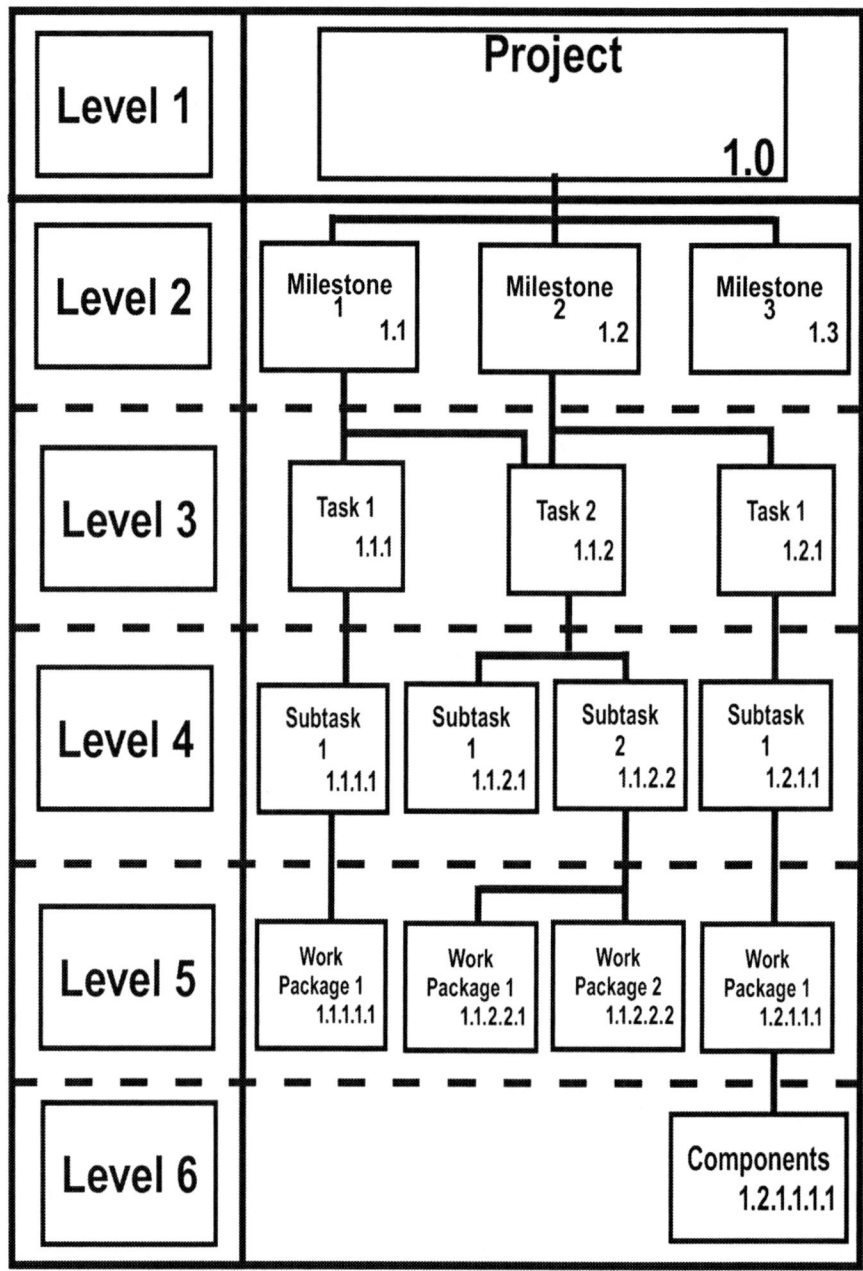

Figure 6-D

PROJECT MANAGEMENT SOFTWARE

If a manager has to do all the graphing, changing and reporting manually, project management would be an extremely tiring and frustrating experience. It is for this reason that the benefits of software programs are too important to overlook. Project management programs range in capabilities from simple scheduling programs that produce Gantt charts to huge mainframe applications integrated into the corporation's budgeting, marketing, personnel, and other information management systems.

A wide variety of project management applications also help to produce standard and custom reports, graph costs, and track interrelated variables, resources, and tasks. They also maintain resource and project calendars that record the availability of staff and equipment, and schedule work elements. The tracking and scheduling of multiple projects at the same time minimizes problems and inconsistencies, and allows multiple people to access, input, and report on project data at the same time. Displaying alternative schedules, task assignments, and cost criteria allows the immediate impact to schedules, sequence, and resource changes to be evaluated.

Easy-to-use project management software like Microsoft Project is relatively inexpensive, and can be mastered in a matter of hours. Computers and software are changing and improving on a daily basis in this technological world; however, not even the most sophisticated software package, or the fastest computer is a substitute for competent leadership and skilled decision making. Even these programs by themselves cannot correct any task-related problems or human-centered conflicts.

VI.   Assessing Your Case

In light of what we have presented here, and in order to practically benefit from this chapter, please consider your particular organization's situation. By answering these questions, you would be assessing your circumstances as well as identifying the areas where corrections are required. Additionally, you are encouraged to go back to review the specific materials of the chapter for clarification on some questions.

- *Does your organization distinguish between objectives and goals?*

- *Does every department, or committee, at your organization have written goals to accomplish during the year?*

- *Do all members of every department know exactly what these goals are, as well as the status of their accomplishments?*

- *Are these goals specific enough to be quantitatively measurable, and each possess a targeted completion date?*

- *Do you see these goals as relevant to your organization's mission and current priorities?*

- *Can you find a document that clearly states the current year's goals for all segments of your organization?*

- *Does your organization, or the committee you are a part of, set their goals as a team, or does senior management set these goals alone?*

- *Does your organization refer to its strategic directions and objectives that are spelled out in their strategic plan when meeting to generate goals?*

- *Once goals are set, do you draft a plan of action to accomplish each goal?*

- *Does your action plan determine clearly who is going to do what tasks, by what dates, and in what order?*

- *Do committees, or departments' teams, meet frequently to evaluate progress during the implementation phase of action plans?*

- *Do you have a weekly or monthly reporting system in place to generate status reports on the action plans being implemented?*

- *What method is used to chart your plans?*

- *Do you use project management software to organize and schedule tasks, and evaluate progress?*

Chapter

7.

Organizational Governance:

Establishing an

Effective Board

I. *Governing Boards*

  - *Types of Boards*

II. *Roles and Responsibilities of Governing Board Members*

  - *Ten Duties of the Nonprofit Board*

III. *Board Selection*

  - *Three Board Selection Models*

IV. *Effective Board-Staff Relationships*

  - *Avoiding Potential Areas of Conflict*

  - *The Executive Director's Role*

  - *Roles and Responsibilities of Chief Elected Officer*

V. *Roles of Committees*

  - *Governance Committees*

  - *Successful Committees*

  - *Committee Problems to Avoid*

VI. *Assessing Your Case*

Governance boards are the ultimate leadership of any nonprofit. They can make or break their organization. We have seen in most nonprofits that although they have good intentions, board members sometimes become so caught up in micro-managing the organization's affairs or basic activities, they neglect their intended roles. Many times this happens because they either are not aware of their obligations as board members, or they are not qualified to carry out those responsibilities. A good example of this is when one finds a board member holding a donation basket or directing traffic at an Islamic center. Although this can be a very humbling task for them, it clearly shows that the Islamic center lacks policies, long-term goals and a plan; while at the same time, the board member's efforts are spent in the wrong areas.

This chapter will discuss what governing boards are all about, and what they should do to become more effective and efficient. We will also present a few board selection models that will help to develop more effective board/staff relationships. Furthermore, we will discuss the roles of committees in this process.

I.   Governing Boards

A governing board is defined as a group of people organized with the collective authority to direct and foster an institution which usually is administered by a qualified executive and staff. The ultimate accountability for organizational accomplishment falls upon the shoulders of the governing board. Being on the board is a privilege and a responsibility.

Governing board members are volunteers, and like most volunteers, they give their time to serve on the board for a variety of reasons. Five of these motivations have been identified as:

- *Service*–To fulfill a sense of civic responsibility or religious obligation.

- *Solidary*–Such as socializing, a sense of group membership, status, and a sense of involvement.

- *Purpose*–Such as the satisfaction of working toward the stated goals of the organization.

- *Developmental*–The ability to acquire knowledge geared to improving or using one's capabilities.

- *Material*–Such as the opportunity to advance politically or the opportunity to make professional contacts.

TYPES OF BOARDS

Nonprofits have various types of boards, ranging from the "Don't Bother Us Board", to the "Micro-Managing Board". From our experience with boards in Muslim organizations, the most common forms are:

Controlling Board–Controlling boards like to micro-manage the organization, although in reality no board can effectively do this. Such a board focuses on minor problems, leaving the bigger issues aside. It acts as if everything must pass through them. As a result, it effectively slows down the entire operation of the organization, wasting a great deal of time on minor issues, especially during painfully long meetings.

PR Board–This type of board is usually compromised of well-known individuals whose names are recognizable to the average potential donor of the organization. They mainly sign off on a yearly budget and annual report at a once-a-year meeting. They have no real influence in setting the mission and goals of the organization.

Fundraising Board–The members of such a board mainly raise funds. They pay detailed attention to how to raise more funds, but fail to give enough attention to setting policies on how to spend the funds. Such a board does not usually have long-term strategies, except in dollar sign goals.

Incapable Board–Usually members of this kind of board are sincere, want to produce, but are not qualified to serve as board members, which might be the case in many nonprofits. They usually lack proper understanding of the roles and responsibilities of the board, lack fundamental understanding of organizational behavior, and usually are reactive according to arisen problems and world events. The solution in this case is to seek training for its members to develop the required skills for these board members who are potentially effective, and replace the others who are not trainable

Types of Boards

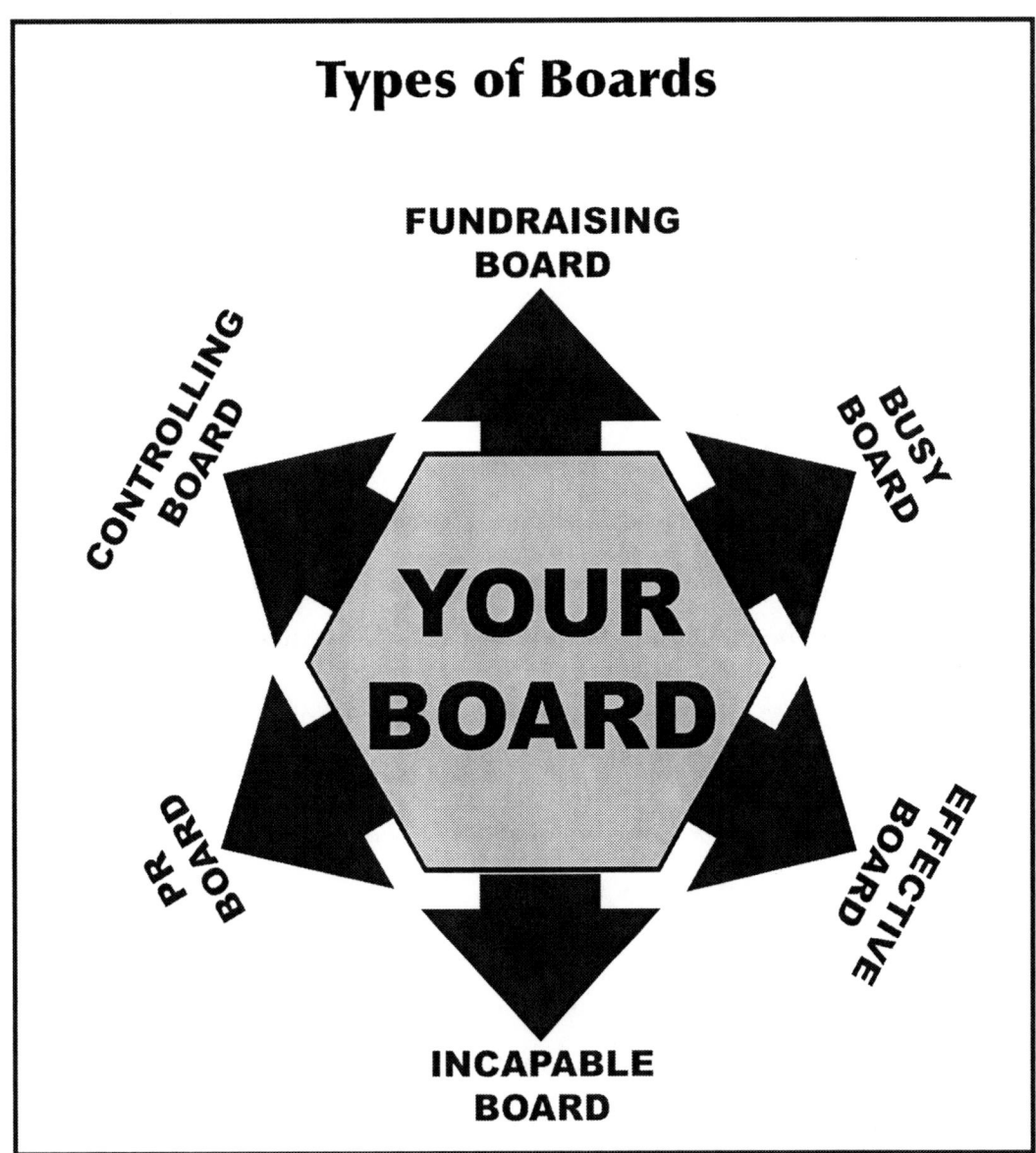

Figure 7-A

Capable Busy Board–Members of this kind of board are capable leaders, but very much involved in many other organizations. Because they have sincere intentions, they are willing to serve as board members of several organizations. They have the vision and qualifications needed, but often times due to time constraints, they are unable to really invest their experience and time. We have seen this in many local Muslim nonprofits, as well in international charities.

Effective Boards–These no doubt exist in Muslim nonprofits, but unfortunately are not very common. Members of effective boards have two qualifications: being willing to invest the time and effort, and able to play an effective role as board members. The first has to do with the ability to volunteer, as serving on boards is a form of volunteering. The second qualification has to do with possessing the leadership qualities and skills to positively affect the organization.

II.   Roles and Responsibilities of Governing Board Members

Islamic organizations must always make an effort to train new members concerning the real roles of boards—which could be the most common problem in Muslim nonprofits. Most board members are sincere; they volunteer their time and expend a great deal of effort for the organization; although, not in responsibilities and efforts related to their positions as board members.

It is widely known that the board of directors is responsible for applying and amending the Bylaws of the organizations. In fact, the first thing that must be drafted after the Mission Statement when forming any organization is the Bylaws which state the mission and main objectives of the organization. They also affirm its founders and/or board members, their roles and responsibilities, and how long they are to serve. Because they are legal documents, items such as Bylaws are normally drafted by an attorney and endorsed by the organization's founding members. However, the roles and responsibilities of boards go beyond that. An effective board functions within its expected role of leadership within the organization. Additionally, it is important that Muslim-run nonprofits pay special attention to who serves on their boards.

TEN DUTIES OF THE NONPROFIT BOARD

The main duties of boards are summarized as below.

1. Determine the organization's mission. It is the board's responsibility to create the organization's mission statement. This document articulates their reason for existing, and defines those primary constituents they will serve. Additionally, it is their duty to ensure that the mission statement is carried out.

2. Select the chief executive. Boards must reach consensus on the chief executive's responsibilities and undertake a careful search to find the most qualified individual for the position.

3. Provide proper financial oversight. The board must assist in developing the annual budget while ensuring that proper financial controls are in place.

4. Secure adequate resources. One of the board's foremost responsibilities is to provide adequate resources for the organization to fulfill its mission, and guarantee that resources are effectively managed.

5. Ensure legal and ethical integrity and maintain accountability. The board is ultimately responsible for guaranteeing adherence to legal standards and ethical norms.

6. Ensure effective organizational planning. Boards must actively participate in the strategic planning process to establish the future course of the organization and assist in implementing and monitoring the plans.

7. Recruit and orient new board members and assess board performance. All boards have a responsibility to articulate prerequisites for candidates, orient new members, and periodically and comprehensively evaluate its own performance.

8. Enhance the organization's public image. The board should clearly articulate the organization's mission, accomplishments, and goals to the public and garner support from the community.

9. Determine, monitor, and strengthen the organization's programs and services. It is the board's responsibility to determine which programs are consistent with the organization's mission and to monitor their effectiveness.

10. Support the chief executive and assess his or her performance. The board should ensure that the chief executive has the moral and professional support he or she needs to further the goals of the organization.

Additionally, members of boards are also responsible to maintain board confidentiality, avoid conflict of interest, maintain appropriate lines of communication, and conduct fundraising activities. Occasionally, the board serves as a court of appeal for employees with a grievance.

Case Study

The following is a case study which utilizes such a grid to match present and potential board members for a particular nonprofit.

The board of this nonprofit agency currently has fifteen members serving three-year terms. By examining the members with expiring terms, it can be determined which characteristics are needed to balance out the board member grid. After reviewing the knowledge, skills, abilities, and other characteristics needed by new board members, the names of possible new members can be identified. These names might be retrieved from a list of people previously considered as board members, professional people whose names are submitted by other agencies, other volunteers, or individuals providing professional services to the agency. People associated with nonprofits, such as beneficiaries, donors, employees, or present board members often recommend prospective board members. Organizations should be vigilant about who they recruit, being certain that those who are chosen will be serving in the organization's best interests. Nonprofits need to seek out those whose special skills will enhance their mission and goals. For example, if an agency has a problem with their budget analysis, they might wish to recruit a person who has a financial background and possesses the ability to review their financial statements.

Statutes and bylaws usually specify the nomination procedures that should be followed, as well as the selection process; therefore, each organization should refer to their own relevant policies and procedures for this process.

III. Board Selection

To be effective, a nonprofit needs a strong board that is the guardian of the organization's mission, making certain that the nonprofit lives up to its commitment and that its management is competent. One of the crucial main responsibilities delegated to the members of a nonprofit's governing board is that of selecting the organization's future leaders. After all, they intimately know the true expertise required to replace them in their roles as fundraisers, strategic planners, policymakers, controllers, mentors, etc.

What should an organization look for when appointing a board member? Not only should the prospective board member bring some specific quality that will enhance the policymaking and oversight responsibilities of the board as a whole, but they should bring certain other qualifications as well. The nominating committee or the existing board should identify these qualities to include a distribution in age, gender, education, ethnic background and location of residence. Additionally, the selection process should consider candidates from the constituency served by the agency, those with expertise, and training in the following areas: personnel, finance, law, fundraising, and public relations. Each candidate should also possess the knowledge, skills, abilities, and other characteristics that relate to the organization's mission and objectives, which can be evaluated using a grid system that identifies specific criteria.

BOARD SELECTION MODELS

While there are three selection models for boards, not all models work equally well.

Model #1: The membership body of an organization, or board members whose term has expired, elects the board.

Model #2: The current board selects new members.

Model #3: The board members are appointed by a higher authority of which the organization is a sub-entity of, or which has a certain authority over it.

It is commonly believed that a strong board is usually one where the board members are chosen through a nominating process which is based on the needed qualifications at the board level. To illustrate this point, co-op boards are rarely considered to be strong since they are elected by their membership. In this instance, the chairperson and the CEO usually have no say in the board's selection, opening the door for problems to arise.

Each of these three models has advantages and disadvantages.

Elected Board

ADVANTAGES:

- Direct constituency control of selection process
- Direct accountability of the board to its electorate

DISADVANTAGES:

- Members of organization usually lack understanding governing board needs.

- Members who campaigned for a certain agenda elect its backers regardless of qualifications

- Election of nonqualified members

- Politicized and divided board

- Lack of fair representation of all sectors and various needed expertise.

- Inability to remove a dysfunctional member easily.

Appointed Board

ADVANTAGES:

- The power given to the appointing authority that is neither a full membership body nor current board

- Ability to appoint all board members with similar views and values to advance specific agenda

DISADVANTAGES:

- Appointing may be subjective

- Appointing may be politically motivated

- Inability to make major decisions not in the interest of the appointing authority

- May blur responsibility.

Self-Perpetuating Board

ADVANTAGES:

- Allows the board to control the continuity of its membership

- Allows the right mix of skills and qualifications

- Tailor the selection process to match changing conditions and needs

- Easy to remove members from the office when necessary

DISADVANTAGES:

- Using this model without an objective, criteria-based selection and term renewal process will turn the board into homogeneous, inbred, and ineffective

- The board may become isolated from the stakeholders it serves such as its community, beneficiaries and donors.

NEW BOARD MEMBERS' ORIENTATION

After the new board members have been selected, regardless of how experienced or professional the new board members are, they should be given a thorough orientation. This orientation involves outlining their responsibilities, and informing them of the organization's mission, objectives, and administrative structures. Among other things, new members should also be provided with the organization's constitution and bylaws, its strategic and long-term plans, its annual report, budget and financial report, program descriptions and its current goals. Additionally they should receive an organizational chart showing all staff names and contact information, a list of all committees associated with the nonprofit and their goals, such as fundraising expectations and commitments, and public relations strategies. Also, they should receive the nonprofit's personnel handbook, and a list of all board members including their names and contact information, meeting information and attendance requirements. They should also receive the minutes from meetings for the previous fiscal year, any appropriate procedures governing conduct of the meetings, and any evaluations conducted during the previous year.

Studies have shown that when people from the for-profit sector join a nonprofit board, they are at a disadvantage because they often lack an appropriate frame of reference of the nature of the mission served by nonprofits. For example, when a businessman from a large corporation joined the board of a small religious organization, he insisted on double digit growth no matter what the implications were for the nonprofit's capacity to fulfill its mission.

IV. Effective Board-Staff Relationships

One of the most basic differences between nonprofit organizations and businesses is that the typical nonprofit has so many more relationships that are vitally important. Each nonprofit has a multitude of constituencies and must work out the relationship with each of them. The bottom line is not the dollar amount raised or spent.

While the board in most businesses takes little interest in the organization until there is a crisis, nonprofit boards are active and committed. Indeed, many nonprofit organizations' staff and management complain that their boards meddle too much, blurring the line between board function and executive management. An area of particular concern for many executives is the blurring of the line between the board's role as policymaker and the executive staff's role as administrators.

AVOIDING POTENTIAL AREAS OF CONFLICT

There are two potential areas where conflict may occur between the board and the executive staff. The first has to do with improper communication channels, while the other has to do with crossing responsibility or authority boundaries. An illustration of the first potential area of conflict might be if the board chairperson delegates a task to a particular staff member without going through the executive director. An example of the second case may arise when the executive director sets major policies or modifies the annual budget without approval from the board.

To have effective board/staff relationships, the board must back the chief executive staff, while providing oversight and thorough annual or semi-annual evaluation of his or her performance. However, they can never micro-manage any administrative matters or interfere in the way he or she manages his responsibilities and his staff at the organization. Also, the chief executive staff must recognize the role of the board as the body he or she is accountable to, and keep the board informed about the overall operations and achievements of the organization through systematic reporting.

There are two basic preventive means to facilitate effective relationships between the board the executive body: when the role of each is clearly known and defined, and when communications of the board go through its chairperson to the executive director, and vise versa.

THE EXECUTIVE DIRECTOR'S ROLE

Although the title and responsibilities of the chief executive vary by agency, this person is generally identified as the executive director. It is this person's role to provide guidance to the governing board, manage all aspects of the organization, and speak on behalf of the organization as delegated by the elected president and governing board.

A good executive director will be familiar with all aspects of the organization. Relying on intuition, management skills, and interpersonal relations are usually the best way for this person to tackle their role. By effectively managing the organization, the executive director has the opportunity to help shape the policy directions by providing meaningful information for the board. Developing good rapport requires a measure of respect for the talents, experience and perspectives of the members of the governing board. It has found that a monthly or quarterly detailed report outlining the organization's activities and accomplishments can be quite helpful in keeping the board informed.

On the other hand, the chairperson of the board has his or her separate responsibilities to provide leadership and oversight to the organization, with full appreciation and support to the executive body. The following outline provides a sample position description for the chairperson, or president, as the chief elected officer of an organization. Similar descriptive outlines should also be done for other officer positions such as vice president, secretary, and treasurer, along with a generic position description for a board director so that each knows exactly their expected roles within the organization.

ROLES AND RESPONSIBILITIES OF CHIEF ELECTED OFFICER

Primary Responsibilities:

- Ensure that the organization abides by its bylaws and established policies.

- Serve as chairperson of the board of directors and the executive committee.

- Preside over all meetings of the board of directors and executive committee, and the annual assembly meeting of the organization, if any.

- Support the executive director of the organization.

- Prepare agendas for all meetings of the board of directors in collaboration with the executive director.

- Report to the membership body, if any.

- Represent the nonprofit to other agencies, the media, and the public.

- Appoint and charge committees in full consultation with the board.

Additional Responsibilities:

- Regularly communicate with the executive director.

- Periodically report to the board of directors.

- Train and otherwise prepare the president-elect for the responsibilities of the presidency.

- Serve as ex officio member of all committees, with the exception of elected committees.

- Receive reports from all officers and committees.

V.   Roles of Committees

Because boards have a great deal of work to do, it makes sense to divide the work among members of the board. Thus, committees are formed. The function of committees is to assist the board and staff with the work of the organization. When committees fulfill their charges, the agency's strategic plan can be realized, advancing the nonprofit's mission. When committees fail, work does not get accomplished and expectations are shattered, frustrating board members, staff and committee members.

Governing boards determine the types and sizes of committees that will assist in the conduct of the organization's programs and services. Normally, the chairperson and members of committees are nominated by the president and approved by the board, but sometimes they are directly appointed by the president. Although their terms may vary, the usual appointment is for one to two years, with the opportunity for reappointment for a second or third term. The nonprofit's bylaws should only include standing committees which relate to the governance of the organization such as the executive committee, the finance committee, and the nominations committee. Other committees such as the education committee, the planning committee, and the fundraising committee, etc. are referred to as special or functional committees, which do not relate to governance issues, and should not be included in the bylaws. In addition, many nonprofits will also appoint ad hoc committees or task forces that are given specific assignments to be completed within a specified timeframe.

GOVERNANCE COMMITTEES

Executive Committee: Their role is to provide guidance for the nonprofit organization between meetings of the governing board. They are explicitly forbidden to make policy except in emergency situations. They are a useful instrument of the board, but should be careful not to assume the board's responsibilities. The main roles of this committee is to assist the boards in emergency situations requiring action where it is impossible to convene the whole board, and executing management performance improvement, including the director's evaluation. This committee also usually sets strategic plans and goals subject to board approval, and is responsible for planning all board meetings. This committee is the only one that is empowered to act with the authority of the full board.

Finance Committee: This committee should work closely with the executive board in the critical role of organizational financial oversight, advising the board on issues related to the nonprofit's budget and financial affairs. The finance committee is usually chaired by the treasurer, and includes other members from the executive committee.

Nominations Committee: This committee's role is a critical one leading to identifying the organization's future leaders. It is directed by a tightly controlled set of bylaws.

This committee is often elected by the nonprofit's board; although, sometimes they are appointed by the president.

Other Committees: Depending on the size, number of volunteers and resources of an organization, these committees will vary. Organizations often have a program planning committee to design and promote the annual meeting of the organization. Other committees may be organized to include audit, fund development, membership, public relations, marketing, etc. Again, dependent upon the needs of the organization, these committees may be long-term and ongoing, and appointed on a yearly basis by the president in consultation with the board of directors.

SUCCESSFUL COMMITTEES

There is a definite recipe for the creation of a successful committee. Some of these criteria include clearly defining the goals or responsibilities that need to be accomplished, setting established timelines, a committed chair who has the time to pursue the goals and prepare concise reports for the board on the committee's accomplishments, and committee members who are also willing to spend the necessary time to accomplish the goals. Additionally, those willing to serve must also be willing to meet as required, work within a budget allocated by the board, and work with a board member liaison who will act as both an advisor and as an advocate.

COMMITTEE PROBLEMS TO AVOID

The following summarizes some of the sundry common problems committees may face.

• *An overabundance of board committees:* This includes those committees whose members must be from the executive board. This results in each member of the board having to serve on too many committees, which is unproductive. A board is unable to fulfill its responsibilities because each member serves on three to five committees which makes them unable to devote their time fully to their appointed task.

- *Small projects or tasks are complicated by unnecessary committees:* It is inappropriate to form a three-member committee to write a press release, for instance. It is customary amongst some boards to form a committee or a task force for any arisen problem or project, no matter how small it is.

- *Uninformed Committees:* Committees are formed or nominated without being given proper mission and goals, and without follow up by the president until the end of the year when the annual report is due.

- *Committees are given clear responsibilities but no budget or authority:* A good example of this might be when a maintenance committee that is responsible for the repair or maintenance of the organization's property and equipment has to go back to the board to request a budget for every expenditure. This is especially ineffective when an emergency situation occurs. When a heater is not functioning, or when a building experiences flooding, nothing should delay a prompt and effective solution.

- *A committee with more than seven members is too large:* The size of a committee varies by the skills needed and its responsibilities. We believe effective committees should be three to five members only. A large committee defeats the intended purpose and makes it hard to meet, make decisions, and implement its responsibilities effectively.

VI. Assessing Your Case

In order to practically benefit from this chapter, please consider the situation of the organization you are a part of, in light of what we have presented here. By answering these questions, you would be assessing your situation as well as identifying the areas where corrections are needed. Additionally, you are encouraged to go back to review the specific materials of the chapter for clarification on some questions.

- *Do you consider your board members as the actual strategic planners and the policy makers of your organization?*

- *What type of board do you characterize that of your organization?*

- *Do you see your board as actively busy while your organization lacks proper plans, budgets and policies?*

- *Can you say that your board is clearly focused on ensuring that your organization's mission is carried out effectively, with the availability of adequate resources?*

- *Does your board select and perform an annual performance review for your executive director?*

- *Does your board assist in public relations and fundraising efforts?*

- *What selection model does your organization incorporate to select new board members?*

- *Do you identify specific criteria when selecting new board members to ensure always having members with expertise in various areas such as Islamic studies, personnel, finance, law, organizational behavior, etc.?*

- *Does your current board provide sufficient orientation for new board members?*

- *Do your board members and executive staff maintain appropriate lines of communication within your organization?*

- *Are there any conflicts of authority and responsibility between the chief elected officer and the chief executive officer at your organization?*

- *Does your executive director keep the board fully informed about the organization's achievements and operations?*

- *How many governance and functional committees does your organization have?*

- *Does every committee have a mission statement or clearly defined role at your organization, including specific goals to accomplish?*

Chapter

8.

Human Resources:

Assembling the

Winning Team

I.   *Vitality of HR Development*

    – *Muslim Nonprofits Lack HR Development*

    – *Financial vs. Human Resources*

    – *Better HR Leads to a Better Organization*

II.   *Human Resources Planning*

    – *Strategic Human Resource Management*

    – *The Need for Diversity*

III.   *Human Resources Needs Analysis*

    – *Changes in Technology Effects on HR Needs*

    – *Three Factors Affecting HR Needs for Nonprofits*

    – *A Practical Case Example*

IV.   *Job Analysis*

    – *Job Analysis Information*

    – *Methods of Collecting Job Data*

    – *Job Descriptions*

V.   *Recruitment & Selection*

    – *Staff Recruitment*

    – *Getting the Word Out*

    – *Screening Applicants*

    – *Staff Selection*

VI.   *Performance Evaluation*

    – *Developing an Evaluation Program*

    – *Evaluating Chief Executives*

    – *Performance/Relationship Link*

VII.   *Compensation and Benefits*

    – *Salary and Benefits*

VIII. *Training and Development*

The greatest resource of any nonprofit agency is their Human Resources. Paid staff costs represent as much as 60 percent of many nonprofit's operational budget, illustrating how valuable human resource management is to your organization. Staff determines the performance capacity of an organization. In an increasingly tight employment market, issues related to attract, retain, motivate, and supervise employees are critical to the nonprofit organization's success.

Employees play a strategic role, their contributions are key to an organization's success. They are a major contributor to the strategic planning and policy development process, guiding and supporting agency efforts as attempts are made to meet the demands imposed on the agency from its external and internal environments.

This chapter is about staffing requirements, the identification of employee training needs and career opportunities, and the development of benefit packages and evaluation instruments. The quality of an organization's human resource decisions largely determine whether it is being run sincerely, whether its mission, values and objectives are genuine and hold meaning, rather than just being public relations and rhetoric.

I.   Vitality of HR Development

One of the most effective ways to increase the productivity of any organization is to improve its human resources. The level of qualifications and skills possessed by the HR of an organization reflects its success level, future growth and effectiveness. The human factor of an organization is like its driving engine for all its operations and programs. An organization depends mainly on the individuals behind it—its leadership and management team, as well as the staff and volunteers working for the organization.

No matter how great the internal system an organization might have, it will fail if the HR behind it is weak and incapable. The delivery of programs will suffer and the financial resources, even if very large, will to some extent be wasted because the quality of both the human resources and internal management system are vital for the success of an organization.

MUSLIM NONPROFITS LACK HR DEVELOPMENT

Muslim nonprofits are generally so busy that leadership is failing to pay attention to taking care of their backbone: their staff. There are clear weaknesses in their current staff, and in their lack of training and development. Because most of these organizations are small, they do not have dedicated HR departments or management to focus on understanding their needs, improving their skills and motivating them. Muslim-run nonprofits also lack the designated management to analyze the job needs as a whole, and draft useful job descriptions, and Policy and Procedure handbooks. What is worse, there is not enough time and effort put into proper recruitment, and too many unwise selections are made when it comes to finding people to fill jobs. There are also shortcomings in developing internal policies, procedures, motivational programs, and reasonable compensation systems; although to be fair, recent improvements have taken place.

FINANCIAL RESOURCES VS. HUMAN RESOURCES

Many people measure the success of a nonprofit organization by the amount of contributions received per year, which are an indication of its size and no doubt the level of success in its fundraising efforts. Overall, organizational strength is better evaluated by the strength of its HR, not only its financial resources. There is no doubt that both financial and human resources are interrelated. The availability of enough money enables the organization to have highly qualified staff. The opposite is also valid: the availability of highly qualified staff can raise good amounts of money. Although it is true that income level is important, it is not the whole story. The single most important element that every aspect of the organization depends on is the people working within the organization.

BETTER HR LEADS TO BETTER ORGANIZATION

Management should provide reasonable salaries and a productive environment, along with needed technical and work items, to receive the full potential of their human resources. Staff should be well trained to conduct their particular job effectively, while understanding their roles and responsibilities clearly. Staff who are motivated, happy and convinced of the mission, and are involved in setting the mission, goals, and objectives will show greater professional conduct. This will lead to an organization harvesting more donors and larger donations, culminating in greater financial resources, more effective programs with higher productivity and continuous growth, resulting in a better organization.

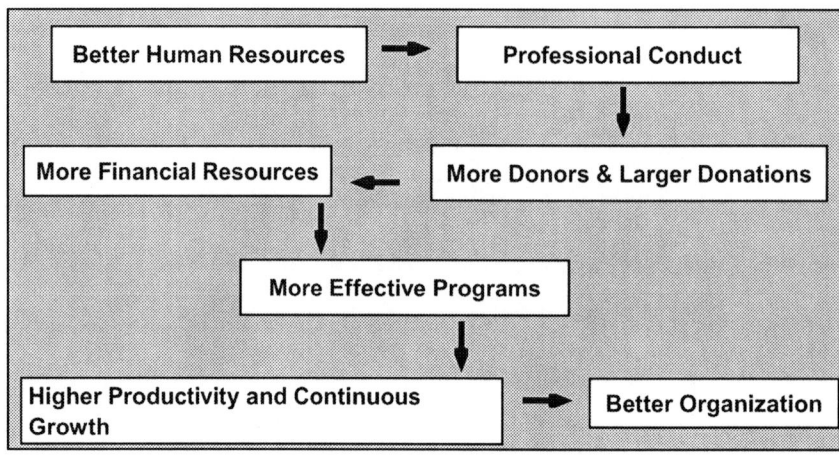

Figure 8-A

II.   Human Resource Planning

The start-up of a nonprofit may be more spontaneous than designed. As it grows, even if the organization cannot yet afford its entire projected staff, it will become necessary to identify the staff needed to reach its goals. Creative use of staff can offset any lack of funding.

Nonprofit sector organizations often are not proactive. Rather than having a strategic focus, too often they find themselves having to deal with crises, and coping with changes rather than planning for them. Human resources planning is a way for nonprofit sector organizations to develop a strategic approach to prevent problems. These agencies need to anticipate their personnel requirements so that they are prepared to deal with changing situations.

STRATEGIC HUMAN RESOURCE MANAGEMENT

Strategic Human Resource Management (SHRM) forces managers to identify future organizational needs, reviewing the demand for, and the readily available supply of skills within the organization and its workforce. SHRM can also assist in the development of programs. An immediate outcome of strategic human resources planning could help an organization to shift from being reactive to proactive. SHRM is a critical component of human resources planning, being the process of analyzing and identifying the need for the availability of human resources to meet the agency's objectives. An organization needs to consider both the internal and the external supply of qualified candidates.

THE NEED FOR DIVERSITY

Changes in society and the workplace have resulted in diversity becoming an important issue for strategic human resources management. Current personnel systems and an organization's culture must be reviewed to produce and retain a diverse workplace. When all workers are valued and included, an organization is seen as well managed, resulting in a productive work environment that is supportive and nurturing, and where employee contributions are appreciated.

One illustration of lack of diversity is quite prevalent among some Islamic charities. These organizations have a tendency to exclude women when hiring employees because of religious constraints or cultural prejudices. As well, other Islamic charities tend to hire only Muslims, or people who share the same cultural background (i.e. all Arabs, Pakistanis or Indians). Unfortunately, all of these instances may be seen in the legal arena as a form of discrimination.

Diversity leads to employees' enhanced interpersonal communication, responsiveness to social and demographic changes, and a climate of fairness and equality. Employees who differ in race, religion, ethnic background and so on are likely to distinguish problems differently, hence developing alternative solutions; therefore, they offer a wider range of ideas.

III.   HR Needs Analysis

Each organization has its own requirements. No two are alike; therefore, this is an issue that is best handled by the organization's careful reflection and analysis of their individual needs. This simple process, which is better done by an outside entity, is to study and evaluate the HR needs of an organization.

CHANGES IN TECHNOLOGY EFFECTS ON HR NEEDS

Information technology is rapidly evolving, with the greater need occurring in personnel systems. The increased use of computer databases, telecommunications, and networking are resulting in the evolution of organizational structure, as well as how work is organized and managed. The use of technology can be quite exciting as today's jobs in both the public and nonprofit sectors are becoming increasingly technological in nature, requiring expanded knowledge and education. Computers and automation currently play a dominant role in the redesign of traditionally routine jobs, and are expected to be a major factor in future productivity. In order to remain competitive, it is critical for organizations to acquire workers who possess those skills, or risk stagnation.

All of this opens a whole new arena of standards for judging performance. Two of these are *efficiency*, which is the ability to produce higher volume with the same or fewer resources, and *quality*, which is matching products or services to a human need with a consistent homogeneity to standards. Regardless of position, these new performance standards require improved skills and competencies for employees throughout the organization. Not only must employees demonstrate proficiency in basic skills such as reading, writing, and elementary mathematical skills, the employee must also have a measure of social and communication skills, and the ability to listen and communicate clearly. Influencing or leadership abilities are also a definite advantage.

THREE FACTORS AFFECTING HR NEEDS FOR NONPROFITS

HR requirements for nonprofit organizations vary from one to another depending on three factors:

1.   How centralized is the organization? The more centralized an organization is, the less staff it requires. For instance, maintaining one location in an organization's headquarters with all operations being directed from there requires fewer staff than having three

different branch offices in three different states. Moreover, regional offices, branches and field offices require more staff, especially for international humanitarian NGOs.

2. What is the organization's level of outsourcing? Many organizations with a smaller core staff outsource responsibilities and tasks. Outsourcing is a sensitive issue for NGOs since they have so much to do in so many different areas of expertise, and without the HR necessary to do the jobs themselves. Many NGOs tend to outsource too much because it is the easiest way to get a job done professionally. However, the negative aspects of such outsourcing are two: first, outsourcing is expensive; and second it prevents the organization from gaining experience by doing it themselves. Outsourcing should not be done unless the organization needs a service that is not frequently required, or they need highly technical skills that they lack.

3. What type of nonprofit is it? A funding or grant allocation organization needs different and fewer staff than an implementing agency in a field that handles all kinds of logistics to deliver the services needed.

IV. Job Analysis

A job analysis is a systematic process of collecting data for determining the knowledge, skills, abilities, and other characteristics required to successfully perform a job and to make judgments about the nature of a specific job. A job analysis also examines the context in which the job is performed, and the personal requirements necessary to perform a job, such as personality, interests, physical characteristics, aptitudes, and job-related knowledge and skills. Each position is also analyzed in relation to other positions in the organization. Job analysis provides the foundation for most HR management activities and are characterized by specific areas of activity such as recruitment and selection, developing compensation systems, human resources planning, career development, and training, performance evaluation, and risk management.

A PRACTICAL CASE EXAMPLE

One international humanitarian organization we examined implements various types of programs in several countries in the areas of emergency relief, and social, healthcare, education and developmental programs. This organization has an annual budget of seven million dollars. It is funded publicly through its national campaigns, and it implements its own programs. Furthermore, it maintains field offices in five of the countries where most of their work is concentrated. Upon careful examination, we determined the human resources that met their needs are:

- Overseas—about 160 staff members consisting mainly of relief workers at field offices and program establishments. Some are administrative staff; but most are field workers, doctors, teachers, and others in clinics, schools, and vocational centers in several countries.

- USA—one office with ten staff members and four public relations members working from home. The head office staff is comprised of:

    - An executive director.

    - An assistant director who helps with the director's responsibilities.

    - A business officer who is an experienced accountant who is in charge of all financial issues such as payroll, payables, receivables, and consolidation of funds. He is also responsible for the tax requirements.

    - Two program officers who manage overseas programs and coordinate their activities.

    - An administration assistant who processes receipts, files documents, and acts as the receptionist.

    - A media manager who coordinates all aspects of marketing, advertisements, and promotional programs ranging from the website, CD production, newsletters, mailings, etc., while aiming to inform the public about the programs, as well as raise funds.

    - A media assistant who helps the above staff.

    - A communications manager that coordinates all internal communications within the organization. This person's main responsibility is processing the field reports from all branches.

    - A donations processor whose responsibility it is to receive all checks and credit card donations, and process them according to procedure.

    - An IT Manager who takes care of the organization's database, analyzes data, and maintains the website, issues the weekly e-mail newsletter, and provides technical support to all staff members.

    - Four PR staff who act as fundraisers by giving presentations and khutbas at mosques, centers and public events to raise funds for the organization.

JOB ANALYSIS INFORMATION

The first steps in conducting a job analysis are to define the purpose behind the analysis and then to determine what information is required. The information most commonly collected are data on job activities, educational requirements, types of equipment or tools required to do the job, working conditions, supervisory or management responsibilities, interpersonal or communication skills, agency contacts, and external contacts. The specific observable competencies required to perform the particular tasks of the position are their skills. These can be a secretary's typing speed, or his/her ability to input data accurately. A worker's skills can also be defined like a system manager's ability to diagnose and repair an organization's personal computers. The applicant's aptitudes for performing particular tasks are their abilities—what the applicant is able to do and how well. Other characteristics include such things as attitudes, personality factors, or physical and mental traits needed to perform the job.

METHODS OF COLLECTING JOB DATA

Job analysis information can be obtained through a variety of methods. Data collection depends on the nature of the positions, the number of employees, and supervisors of the positions being analyzed. As well as the geographical dispersion of jobs, available time, the type of information needed, and the purpose of the analysis. The most common methods of data collection are:

- *Interview*—the analyst interviews the employee performing the job, the immediate supervisor, or another subject matter expert, or a combination of all three, about the essential functions of the position.

- *Questionnaire*—not solely reserved for applicants, questionnaires are also used as an analysis tool for each position and current employees who are already doing the job. The subjects are asked to complete a questionnaire where they list their essential duties or tasks, how frequently they perform each one, and the percentage of time or number of hours daily they devote to these tasks.

For each question, three responses are required:

A. Indicate the **frequency** with which this function is performed in this position.

B. Indicate how **important** this function is to the position.

C. Indicate whether **knowledge** of this function is essential for a newly hired employee in this position.

A	B	C
Frequency	*Importance*	*Knowledge*
0=Never	0=Not applicable	0=Not required for job
1=Rarely	1=Not important	1=Essential for newly hired employee
2=Sometimes	2=Somewhat important	2=Not essential at hire, can learn on the job
3=Often	3=Important	
4=Very Often	4=Very important	

Typing

A	B	C
Frequency	*Importance*	*Knowledge*
0 1 2 3 4	0 1 2 3 4	0 1 2

1. Type/keyboard letters from handwritten rough drafts.
2. Type/keyboard letters to students, faculty, staff, applicants or outside individuals or companies.
3. Type/keyboard inventory reports or budget reports.
4. Type/keyboard monthly status reports.
5. Type/keyboard general office forms (such as purchase requisitions, work orders, travel vouchers, printing requisitions).
6. Type course materials, transparencies, syllabi, or tests for faculty.
7. Compose various letters or memos without written instructions.
8. Compose letters and memos from simple written outline or verbal instructions.
9. Proofread for spelling, grammar, and punctuation on all correspondence and reports.
10. Type/keyboard or edit manuscripts or drafts for supervisor.
11. Prepare manuscripts for publication, including correction of errors and consultation on other editing matters.
12. Layout format and spacing for tables, charts, or other illustrations in preparation for typing.

Figure 8-B   Job Analysis Questionnaire Sample

• *Diary/Log*—in this procedure, employees are asked to keep track of and record their daily activities and the time spent on each.

- *Combination of methods*—Depending on the purpose of the job analysis and the targeted jobs it may be necessary to use a combination of two or more of the methods introduced here. The analyst may use different methods of data collection for different positions.

JOB DESCRIPTIONS

Jobs are arranged around a set of work activities designed to enable the organization to carry out its mission. External and internal changes, however, often force organizations to rearrange or restructure work activities.

Many professional analysts suggest moving away from a traditional job description in which specific job duties and tasks are itemized. They suggest focusing instead on a level of general characteristics important for success in the organization's culture, and for dealing with change.

Job Descriptions Fit Positions, Not Specific Candidates

Job descriptions must be drafted to a particular position, not custom made to a particular person. The job description should outline the responsibilities of the position. If the individual hired to fill the position falls short of this, then orientation and training are the normal solutions.

V. Recruitment & Selections

The recruitment and selection of qualified and competent employees is critical for public sector and nonprofit agencies. This is because they are mission driven entities that are reliant upon their staffs' specialized skills, delivering programs and services expected by their beneficiaries, their board of directors and the public.

THE NEED FOR A VARIETY OF SKILLED HR

So that Islamic organizations continue to grow and improve their operations, they need various elements of the Muslim society or community to get involved in their organizations. This includes professional men and women for their expertise, wealthy individuals for their financial contributions, and the youth to volunteer in delivering programs and services, etc. Moreover, Islamic nonprofits have programs that differ in nature from those in other nonprofits—in what they need, and in their geographic distributions. Therefore, they need different human resources for different programs such as fundraising, management, social and educational programs, economic revitalization efforts, and healthcare.

STAFF RECRUITMENT

Recruitment is the process of attracting qualified individuals to apply for vacant positions within an organization. Selection is the final stage of the recruitment process when decisions are made as to who will be selected for the vacant positions. The organization must determine its immediate objectives and future direction, and it must forecast its employment needs so that those needs are aligned with the organization's strategies.

To fill positions, agencies have a variety of options. They can recruit new employees, or promote or transfer employees who possess the skills needed to do the job. An agency's recruitment must be tied to its mission.

Try not to overlook the integration of internships, and on-the-job training into the recruitment and selection process. Such limited employees often bring valuable skills and enthusiasm to the job, and allow a great deal of room for growth for both the employee and the agency. Cause-related agencies may find two very different prospective employees: those who have empathy for the cause but lack of experience, and those with the desired skills and experience but less personal commitment.

Getting the Word Out

With the explosion in information technology, seeking prospective employees is easier than ever. Technology has made information more accessible to job seekers as well. Advertisements in newspapers generally bring good response. When seeking someone with highly specific skills, placing an ad in a professional journal or with professional organizations is quite effective. For those agencies seeking workers for a particular region, posting ads within a defined cultural neighborhood or community centers, or on specialized language television or radio stations is usually a good way to spread the word.

When an advertisement is part of the recruiting process, it should be written in a manner that will attract responses from qualified individuals, discouraging responses from those who are not qualified. To comply with ADA (Americans with Disabilities Act) guidelines, the advertisement should clearly inform applicants that the hiring process includes specific selection procedures. For example, a written test, demonstration of job skills such as typing, or making a presentation, and an interview.

Screening Applicants

Employment applications are often the first step in the screening process. When an advertisement is initially placed, it should be stated within the ad that resumes are to be sent to, or applications may be filled out, at a specific location. The ad should also state whether or not telephone calls about the position are acceptable.

During the actual screening process, applicants can be asked to respond to a variety of questions which will aid the employer in selecting those applicants best fitting the position. In order to reduce the number of applicants to those most qualified, it is important to have pre-established criteria to facilitate the screening. The use of a resume screening checklist can aid in streamlining this process.

Pre-employment testing is generally administered to measure applicants' skills and predict their ability to perform a task. Another form of pre-employment screening is to administer structured oral exams to evaluate job requirements that are not easily assessed by paper-and-pencil measures. In such an exam, the questions used should be job-related and all applicants should be asked the same questions.

Work sample or performance tests can also be used when an applicant must demonstrate that they possess the necessary skills to perform the job. For example, a clerk-typist might well be asked to take a typing test; while a graphic designer or artist might be asked to supply a portfolio, or demonstrate their level of expertise in some computer graphics program using the employer's computer system.

Organizations must be vigilant that their recruitment and selection procedures do not violate federal or state equal employment opportunity laws; therefore, it is the duty of human resources staff to know these laws, and to adhere to them diligently.

Staff Selection

The selection process of staff affects productivity, the organization's image, and long-term organizational survival. When properly done, the selection process begins with an assignment, not merely a job description. Selecting the right person for the job definitely should never be an impulsive decision, but should be one of careful reflection after screening a number of candidates. Additionally, a focus should be kept on performance by asking "How have these people done in their last three assignments? Have they come through?" Only after these things have been carefully considered should their personality and specific strengths be added to the equation.

At this point, although the selection has been made, the process is not over. It is imperative that the elected individual be asked to give themselves a review after a trial period of ninety days. After the trial period, a self evaluation should be completed to allow the employee to evaluate his/her performance. This will contribute to management's decision to hire them as a permanent staff member.

Staff Selection According to the Qur'an

Being able to trust one's staff is a huge issue, especially in today's political climate and consumer materialistic society. Allah (swt) prescribes, "Verily, the best of men for you to hire is the strong, the trustworthy" (Al-Qur'an 28:26). Strength has to do with skills and capability, both mentally and physically. Here, trustworthiness is a personal qualification—an inner willingness to give. This quality also means that the person possesses motivation, responsibility, and loyalty. They also have a fearfulness of Allah, knowing that He is watching all that they do, so that they will protect their employers' property and resources, and will not waste time or their effort.

Muslim nonprofits require a qualified team possessing these qualities, which includes sharing the organization's mission, being highly motivated, willing and able to learn and develop the necessary skills to perform their tasks, and is loyal to the organization.

VI. Performance Evaluation

Performance evaluations are instruments used to measure employee performance. They should be objective, job related, and consistent with the organization's mission. This is a critical component of strategic human resources management in public and nonprofit agencies, and the information obtained from an effective evaluation system can be invaluable in assisting an agency to accomplish their mission. Performance evaluations provide management with essential information for making strategic decisions about employee advancement, planning, compensation or rewards, retention, or separation. It also links training and development with career planning and the agency's long-term human resources needs.

DEVELOPING AN EVALUATION PROGRAM

Every organization should have its own system for performance evaluation, varying widely across federal, state, and local governments, and nonprofit organizations. Generally, yearly evaluation programs determine pay increases and/or bonuses. Formal appraisal systems usually do not exist in many Muslim-run nonprofits.

Many organizations leave the evaluation up to the employees in the form of a self-evaluation, which is used in a comparison of evaluations by supervisors. This usually culminates in a meeting where differences in perceptions and expectations are clarified, and strategies for future performance improvement or development of career goals are discussed. For each person to take responsibility for his or her own contribution and for being understood requires standards; therefore, standards must be firmly in place. They should also be set high with ambitious, yet attainable goals. The nonprofit must therefore work hard at putting people to work in areas where they can perform to the best of their abilities. As well, workers—especially volunteers—need to know how they have performed.

EVALUATING CHIEF EXECUTIVES

The evaluation of presidents and executive directors of nonprofits is typically performed by the board of directors or a subcommittee. Usually, their review process is stipulated in their contract; however, the simplest approach is to specify an annual review and performance evaluation based on agreed upon standards. The evaluation should target their critical responsibilities such as budget management, supervision, personnel management, leadership, execution of policy, and community reputation. Each board must decide which procedures will better serve the agency; however, there are some general methods of assessment that have been identified:

- *Periodic reports*—this method is used mostly in small organizations, and are intermittent observations such as quarterly reports of the chief executive to the board of directors, or the chairperson of the board.

- *Periodic assessment*—by the board's chairperson or other board members, and should reflect the chief executive's performance over the previous year.

- *Annual board committee reviews*—designed to assess the state of the agency and the chief executive's performance. This is a formal review of the chief executive's goals and accomplishments, and is conducted by either the executive committee, the personnel committee, or an ad hoc committee.

Evaluation Review

During the evaluation period, those doing the rating should discuss both positive and negative aspects. It is important that employees receive feedback throughout the evaluation cycle, not only when it is time to review the formal evaluation.

Employees should be allowed to play a critical role in the process by reviewing their performance appraisal along with the raters. Giving the employee advance notice of the review's schedule will allow the employee to prepare by bringing along any documentation they feel is relevant, such as letters of commendation or records of accomplished objectives. An appraisal should always begin with what the worker has done well, as performance can only be based on strengths. As a final step, the evaluator—usually the supervisor—should hand in a written evaluation result.

PERFORMANCE/RELATIONSHIP LINK

Two-way relationships are symbiotic: everyone benefits from the outstanding performance of a few. An effective nonprofit executive starts by building a two-way relationship with their staff, the board, volunteers, donors, and the community. The true test of a two-way relationship is not that it can solve problems, but that it can function despite problems. Although the problems do not become irrelevant, they also do not get in the way of what is important. People require clear assignments.

This theory holds true for volunteers who represent the agency within the community, the employed staff and the board. All of these players need to know what the agency expects of them. It is up to the nonprofit executive to impart this by working both with employed staff and volunteers to chart a clear path through their contribution, and evolve by joint discussion a specific work plan, goals and deadlines, and be willing to take the responsibility for their performance. The key here is the flow of information because a nonprofit organization must be a compassionate and learning organization. Staff owes performance, and the executive owes them compassion.

VII. Compensation and Benefits

The design, implementation and maintenance of compensation systems are important parts of strategic human resources management. Decisions about salaries, incentives, benefits, and quality-of-life issues are important in attracting, retaining, and motivating employees.

SALARY AND BENEFITS

Compensation is one of the major topics that concern most employees. In order to compete in the marketplace to attract and keep the most qualified and competent applicants, an organization must make strategic decisions about pay levels, pay structures, job evaluation, and incentive pay systems. The fact is most people expect to be well compensated for the services they perform, and to be treated fairly; yet, they lack a basic understanding of the factors which affect that compensation. The expectations and perception of fairness by employees, competitive labor market wages, the extent of other provided benefits, the organization's ability to pay, and federal and state laws dictate these factors.

Comparable Worth

Comparable worth is the idea that each job has an inherent value or worth that can be compared to different types of positions across the organization. The fact is that nonprofits cannot and should not compete with the for-profit world when it comes to compensation. In terms of HR, nonprofits are faced with two major obstacles:

- The availability of experienced staff for the nonprofit market is very anemic.

- Qualified staff is hard to retain if their compensation is not competitive.

Opponents of comparable worth argue that pay disparities are the result of supply and demand, and are dictated by the market, while advocates believe that labor market rates are not entirely objective. Nonprofits more than likely cannot match the level of professional wages in the for-profit sector, and therefore must recruit staff based not only on their experience, but on their motivation as well.

Attracting Employees with Meaningful Benefits

Wages are only part of the compensation system. While the importance of pay should not be underestimated, the emphasis should be on the total compensation package. An attractive package can assist in the recruitment and retention of qualified employees.

Every employer, whether for-profit or nonprofit, faces the challenge of attracting and retaining qualified employees. Nonprofits are notorious for offering lower salaries than their corporate counterparts. In these recent times of the "me generation", however, younger job seekers have been less interested in benefits and more interested in salary. Most of these materialistic young people yearn to be put on the fast-track to promotions and pay increases. Because of funding constraints, nonprofits are hard pressed to respond to these demands.

Not all employees place equal value on particular benefits. Take health insurance, for example. For future employees who are young and fresh out of college, this benefit means relatively little. Older prospective employees may value health insurance above all other benefits and since the shared cost of most insurance plans is rising steadily, this caliper of employee will appreciate it when an employer bears most of the cost. Life and accidental death insurance are benefits whose attractiveness for Muslims is tempered by religious beliefs, and are therefore not generally an issue in an Islamic-based organization. While pension plans and tuition assistance have a more universal appeal than one might expect. To assure some sort of employee retention, the employer must consider a waiting period before eligibility for both benefits, and the relation an advanced degree has to the employee's work.

Some other creative ways to provide much-needed employee benefits is to provide free or reduced fee on-site daycare, free parking passes or vouchers for public transportation, or health and fitness facilities nearby or on site free of charge, or for a reduced fee.

Promotions, Raises and Rewards

If an employee becomes complacent and needs a new challenge, being reassigned can be beneficial to them. Additionally, promotions can be good compensation to honor seniority, overcome salary caps and reward performance. Generally, organizations have a pay range tacked to a particular position, allowing for some growth within that position. With the exception of occasional cost of living raises, budget constraints, however, may temper an organization's ability to reward their employees. Those employees who are truly committed to the agency's mission may be willing to delay or forego any raises in pay during lean years, opting instead for some form of special recognition, extra paid time off or a promotion.

Volunteers do not receive pay; therefore, special recognition for a job well done will have to suffice. This recognition can take the form of special awards, certificates of merit, mention to the local press or an awards luncheon.

VIII. Training and Development

Any organization develops people either by helping them to grow, or stunting them. Advancement of an agency requires training at all levels and in all skills. Agencies that wish to remain viable must develop strategies to maximize their human resources. Training and development are intrinsic components of strategic human resources management, and seek to change the skills, knowledge, and/or attitudes of employees. Two obvious mistakes are not focusing on people's strengths instead of their weaknesses, and taking a shortsighted and narrow view of their development, by importing society's class system into its own operation such as limiting the advancement of those without an ivy league education. Performance is what counts. Making the mission clear and simple is another priority. Every person within the organization should be made to feel that they have not lived in vain, and they have made a difference.

Programs may be focused on improving an individual employee's level of self-awareness, increasing their competence in one or more areas of expertise, or increasing their motivation to perform their job well. One of the most important ways to develop people is to use them as teachers, which is a practical method to get them to expand their own knowledge while imparting on them effective recognition.

TRAINING NEEDS ASSESSMENT

Determining the specific training needs faced by an organization is the first step in needs assessment, which can be defined by the difference between what currently is being done and what needs to be done. Organizations can determine training needs through a variety of techniques:

- A strategic job analysis performed prior to the needs assessment.

- Surveys and interviews with employees and managers.

- Performance evaluations that identify performance deficiencies.

- Criticisms or complaints from beneficiaries of agency programs, clients, staff, or personnel in agencies working with your employees.

- Changes in regulations or operating procedures.

- Requests for additional training

DEVELOPING TRAINING OBJECTIVES

The statements that specify the desired skills employees need to possess at the end of training are called training objectives. These objectives provide the measurement standard for what has been accomplished, and determine the level of accomplishment. They also must be a collaborative effort incorporating input from management, supervisors, workers, and trainers to ensure they are realistic and reasonable.

Curriculum Development

A training curriculum must be refined after assessing the training needs and developing objectives. When doing this, there are a number of factors to take into consideration about the participants:

- level of education

- expectations

- knowledge levels, attitudes, and relationships towards each other

- preparedness to receive technical instruction.

A primary decision to be made is whether to provide training on-the-job, in a classroom environment, or a combination of the two. Some other common forms of training techniques are lectures, video-conferencing, demonstrations, and community resources. Some tools that might be found to be useful in developing an organization's Human Resources could be short one- to three-day seminars, and incorporating a training library with audio- and videotapes, and books. As well, by coordinating trips to the field, program coordinators will become acquainted with the nature of relief delivery if they experience it firsthand by staying for a time in the field where the programs are implemented.

Training Delivery

In addition to curriculum, other issues must be addressed such as how many hours over how many days, and what size group should be involved? Unfortunately, there is no one answer to every situation, and failing to consider any of these factors could negatively affect the outcome. Most public sector and nonprofits can ill afford such waste. Employees from a well-organized work place understand what the training objectives are, and what to expect to obtain from them. The role of the training instructors is to facilitate learning, and for this reason, they are commonly referred to as "facilitators". It is their duty to use many and varied questions, guide the trainees, and encourage a two-way dialogue between the instructor and trainees, as well as productive communications among all participants.

Training Evaluation

At the conclusion of the training session, participants should be surveyed. Whether or not the training program accomplished its objectives can be determined by an evaluation of the data which, by providing feedback, helps the trainers, participants, and managers improve the overall training program.

CAREER DEVELOPMENT

To be successful, training must result in a change of behavior, such as the use of a newly acquired skill or knowledge. Career development provides the employee with knowledge and skills that are intended to be used on the job to meet future agency needs, thereby ensuring the organization's survival. It is also used to improve the skill levels of and provide long-term opportunities for the organization's present workforce to advance within the organization, ensuring a loyal and stable employee. Taking the time and spending resources to develop employees is a sign that their employer values their work and their presence. It is important that once their career development programs have been developed, organizations maintain their programs and revive them with new initiatives. Nonprofits need leaders with the vision to direct and guide their agencies. Technical experience and competence are no longer enough to guide their agencies into the twenty-first century.

DON'T FORGET SELF-DEVELOPMENT

From the chief executive of a nonprofit all the way through the ranks of paid staff and volunteers, the person with the most responsibility for an individual's development is the individual. The first priority for the nonprofit staffs' own development is to strive for excellence, resulting in satisfaction and self-respect. One's own workmanship counts. This can be seen when comparing the attitude of someone who does their job simply to "get by", and the person who takes pride in their work. Self-development is deeply rooted into the mission of the nonprofit through the belief that the work that is being done matters. Lack of money, people, resources or time are not excuses for doing shoddy work.

In all human affairs, there is a constant relationship between the performance and achievement of the leaders, the record setters, and the remainder. The leaders are not the only ones to set the vision and standard. A critical factor for achieving success is for each person to hold himself or herself accountable, asking, "What can I do to make a difference?" , and by taking their job seriously. They should also work toward effectiveness by deciding their priorities, and working within their own strengths—growing with their job by maintaining or enhancing their skills.

A major key to building a successful nonprofit is making everyone feel essential. Those who share in the nonprofit's vision and core beliefs often are happy in their jobs. Since volunteers do not receive a paycheck, they must get more out of being involved. Those who no longer believe in the vision should not, and probably will not, stay with the organization.

IX. Motivation and Dedication to the Mission

It is difficult to get highly qualified staff. It is even more difficult to retain them within the organization without being able to compete in wages with for-profit corporate America. It is our opinion that nonprofits can not and should not compete with the for-profit world when it comes to compensation. To further complicate matters, there are not many people who are trained well enough, and have viable experience doing relief work in third world countries, are good fundraisers, and are effective nonprofit media coordinators among other things. In fact, there are only two universities in the United States that offer Master's degrees in Philanthropy. When their curriculums are examined, they are found to be highly theoretical, and very unpractical.

This brings the realization that to recruit capable staff; an organization must base their hiring not only on qualifications, but also on motivation and dedication to the organization's mission. A highly motivated candidate with potential to learn can be provided with training. This does not mean that staff should be underpaid. However, it does mean that nonprofits must provide an environment where staff members grow in their skills, get connected to the cause not only the salary, and participate in the organization's development and growth.

Most, if not all staff, need training in a few highly important professional skills to increase their effectiveness, benefiting from subjects like time management, Project Management, managing multiple tasks and deadlines, writing, specialized computer programs, interpersonal communication, and organizing the workplace. Most importantly, the leadership of the organization should promote the concept of training and skill development. This additional training could be in the form of a mini-session that could be conducted by a selected staff member who summarizes and presents some form of training or self-study that they participated in. Additionally, having a good audio/video training library, as well as books, that employees are required to watch or read on a continuous basis can be a great help.

More importantly, management should pay attention to maintaining the staff's dedication to the mission. This is usually done by allowing everyone to participate in the development of the mission statement and the overall objectives of the organizations, and by carefully listening to each and every staff member. Dedicated staff should not only receive delegated tasks and projects, but they should be involved in developing them. Experience has shown that staff dedicated to their organization's mission does not just want to leave at five o'clock. They come in on the weekends, and fail to take a few days off because they were so motivated towards the organization's success. It is important to have higher echelon employees get out into the field on a routine basis. Additionally, regularly rotating staff out of office positions and into the field is quite effective. Adopting these two strategies will remind them of the agency's mission and results.

A quick reminder for international relief organizations: do not forget overseas staff. Their dedication means resources are placed more efficiently and effectively with those in need, and provide more careful implementing of programs.

NOT MERELY A 9-TO-5 JOB

Just as in any other industry, an individual who takes a position at a nonprofit as a 9-to-5 chore, solely for the salary most probably is not there to do an effective job. Generally, he or she will not be assertive or act as a self-starter, and will wait to be told what to do. Traditionally, these individuals are not loyal to the organization, and will leave the job if they find a better-paid one, even if only at a slightly higher rate. While not concerned with the outcome of their work, they will give only minimum effort to meet with minimum approval, performing only at a baseline standard just to keep their superior happy. Unless future personnel are carefully screened for motivation and dedication to the mission, there are bound to be one or two slackers in an organization who simply do not care about their job or the mission, and are "just there for the paycheck".

Moreover, mistreated employees tend to have greater rates of absenteeism and, when possible, will seek other employment opportunities. A supportive environment in which employees can contribute and achieve their fullest potential is necessary.

CHARACTERISTICS OF ISLAMIC NONPROFIT STAFF

Those who work for Islamic nonprofits usually possess sincerity in all that they do. Their work is not merely to obtain worldly gains or fame, but to serve humanity for the sake of Allah.

Muslims should be self-conscious at all times about their conduct, how they spend their time, and perform their vocation with 'Itqan' (excellence and completeness). As the Prophet (pbuh) said, "Allah (swt) loves the person who does his work with excellence".

They should also be team players who help others fulfill their responsibilities, and tempers their own conduct in a way that will help them to gain better understanding and insight. The Islamic charity worker should have a positive attitude, demonstrate perseverance, and show gratitude to Allah for being allowed to take part in such noble work. Working in a nonprofit field, they might have to deal with juggling multiple projects at once, limited resources, and emergency situations and crises, which could lead to a great deal of pressure. These situations are usually the norm in most Muslim-run charities. Therefore, they should be patient and focus instead on the final results, remembering that no matter what their area of work, they must execute their job skillfully, always striving to improve themselves in their field.

EFFECTIVE STAFF GIVE UNBIASED EFFORTS

It is important for Muslim nonprofits not to take sides for or against any particular political position or ideology. This should not affect their decisions regarding where programs are implemented, or who they help. Giving should be done without discrimination. Surely, any nonprofit with the mentality of "we will not help because these are not our people" or "they don't agree with us" is an unwise stance, which severely limits itself. Nonprofits must be broad and mainstream in the way they target all potential donors and implement programs. Although political situations change, the mission of helping those in need is universal and unchanging. Therefore, the only acceptable policy should be to help those in need without conditions or strings attached.

Opponents of Muslim nonprofits focused on aid given to a small number of children who had a parent that have committed a suicide bombing, alleging that Muslim nonprofits support violence. However, this allegation is false and defamatory. Humanitarian standards require that aid be given on the basis of need only. Even in the US, hypothetically, the children of a monstrous criminal such as Jeffrey Dahmer are eligible to get public aid. Needy children, regardless of what their parents did, are given public aid. It would be immoral and against international humanitarian standards to deny a child aid on the basis of the actions of their parents. A needy child is a needy child.

X.   Volunteers and Volunteerism

Whenever nonprofit organizations are discussed, one term is always associated with them: volunteers. Because of the many activities connected to nonprofits, these agencies have come to rely heavily on volunteers. In the US, there is a long tradition of volunteerism that began in its earliest times through religious organizations.

WHAT IS VOLUNTEERISM?

Volunteers assist paid staff in meeting an organization's mission and goals, are a valuable asset to the agency they serve, and an important part of strategic human resources management. Currently, vast ranges of nonprofit and public sector organizations provide a wide array of volunteer opportunities ranging from public service to serving on boards of nonprofit organizations. Although these organizations also provide training related to the recruitment and use of these valuable assets, nonprofits should give specific attention to the recruitment, selection, training, evaluation, and management of volunteers as they bring with them a whole new bag of HR management challenges.

THE USE AND CARE OF VOLUNTEERS

The use of volunteers allows nonprofit agencies to spread their already tight funding a bit further. As well, volunteers cost little and bring with them a vast range of talents and abilities, which can be harvested and implemented by nonprofits, freeing up more skilled and paid staff for other responsibilities. They also provide an extra cushion of personnel in times of emergency and peak services needs, expanding the agency's level of service without a high financial consideration. Volunteerism is important for the following reasons:

- It gives a human touch to many labor-intensive tasks, such as delivering relief goods.

- It saves financial resources by reducing payroll expenses.

- It promotes the organization's causes.

- Volunteers receive specialized training so they become more productive elements within their community.

- It directs human effort to benefit society.

- Positions lacking paid staff can be filled.

- Volunteers fill the void in times of emergency or in busy seasons since Muslim-run organizations usually lack full-time paid staff, and are often not ready to handle such situations.

ATTRACTING VOLUNTEERS

In this uncertain economic climate, the demand by nonprofits for volunteers is increasing exponentially. After all, why would someone donate their time? There are many answers to this cosmic question; however, most of those who volunteer express the feelings of satisfaction and sense of accomplishment that giving freely of their time brings them. For the majority of Muslims, it is seeking *"ajir"* (reward) from Allah—not worldly *ajir* from people, as stated in the Qur'an in Surah al-Baqarah (The Cow), verse 158: *"…And whoever does good voluntarily, then verily, Allah is All-Recognizer, All-Knower"*. Additionally, it is the zeal to benefit one's own society or community.

Some volunteers use the opportunity to expand their professional skills or for exploration of career and personal development, such as polishing their grant writing or public relations skills, preparing budgets or making new professional contacts. Others volunteer because they value the goals of the nonprofit.

Communication is the key to finding volunteers. Islamic nonprofits must actively recruit volunteers through advertisements and other means, and strive to keep them productive and happy until the end of their term. Although unpaid, they should be treated as any other staff by being given a written job description that outlines their responsibilities and completing applications to identify their interests, special skills and preferred working days and times.

MANAGING VOLUNTEERS

There are a few obstacles to volunteerism. For the volunteers, there is a lack of permanence in the commitment. Occasionally, there is a lack of accountability where the volunteer feels that they are donating their time, therefore they do not have to be held responsible or dedicated to the cause. For the organization, these impediments can manifest themselves when there is no organized volunteer recruitment and no dedicated management to handle them properly when they do volunteer. Management of volunteer programs requires the development of personnel policies and procedures to assist with the integration of volunteers into the agencies' everyday operations. Before an agency brings a volunteer aboard, there should be a series of testing processes, including an interview. The number of hours a volunteer dedicates can be quite flexible, although they should be driven by the agency's needs, and arranged according to the individual's availability. However, in the US, it is customarily accepted to be no less than twelve hours a month.

Volunteers must be clearly apprised of the agency's hierarchy and where they fit into the organization. An organization should decide early on whether or not to employ a volunteer coordinator to administer their volunteer program to develop, provide orientation, keep track of volunteers' attendance and expenses, monitor and evaluate their performance, and motivate them. Moreover, to successfully integrate their volunteers while minimizing mistakes, they must receive training specific to their assigned responsibilities, and should be oriented to the agency's mission, history, accomplishments, fiscal goals, and strategic plan. Additionally, it is important they should be recognized for their efforts, and their dedication.

WOMEN'S ROLES WITHIN NONPROFITS

There is a common misconception that women have more time than their male counterparts. However, ask any woman, and they will tell you that the old adage "a man works from sun to sun, but a woman's work is never done" is very true. Women comprise one half of society, but volunteer twice as often. Even in the earlier years of Islam, women contributed a great deal to Muslim society, taking care of the sick, and the elderly and orphans. Many nonprofit organizations in the Muslim world currently have departments dedicated to sisters who volunteer, and are run by female managers. Additionally, other organizations have formed women's committees staffed by dedicated chairwomen and members whose sole responsibilities are the recruiting and coordinating of female volunteers. In many cases, if they are provided with a suitable system and the right environment, women volunteers are more effective than their male counterparts. Women are not only effectual in the field as social workers helping disadvantaged children and women in poor societies, but they are creative in fundraising work. Overall, women are an invaluable asset that should not be overlooked or set aside because of cultural prejudices and skewed religious constraints.

XI. Personnel Handbook

One of the major keys for stability and professional conduct of an organization is to build its Personnel Handbook, also known as Policies and Procedures manual (P&P manual). This is a time consuming and dynamic process. Sample handbooks are available from nonprofit publishers that an organization can have tailored to their own needs, while making certain that state and federal regulations are being followed.

An organization's P&P manual is a system that governs and organizes how the organization runs. For many organizations, these handbooks also include the mission statement, the organizational structure, as well as everything related to HR such as compensation, benefits, work ethics and vacations. With written policies that outline the process of how work must be conducted, even new staff will know exactly what is expected of them, and what they can expect from the organization in return.

Many Islamic organizations either do not have P&P manuals that outline policies, procedures for the staff, and job related issues, or they have one that is not very useful, and not specific enough to be practical. Effective personnel manuals should include:

- Written policies.

- The process of how work must be conducted.

- Main authorities and responsibilities of certain positions.

- An overview of the organization, including a short history about the organization, its mission statement, and main objectives.

- Employment policies and general information in regards to introductory periods of employment, work hours, terms of employment, resignation, and termination of employment.

- Compensation and benefits, including performance and salary reviews, benefits package, overtime and sick leave, holidays, and vacations.

- Leaves of absence regulations, including family and medical leave, disability leave, and military reserve and jury leave.

- Guidelines on complaints and grievance procedures, conflict of interest, discipline, standards of professionalism, attendance, dress code, corporate communications, smoking, personal phone calls and E-mails, etc.

Table of Contents	- Overtime and Compensatory Time
The Organization	- Change of Employee Status
Introduction	- Salary and Performance Reviews
History	- Employee Benefits
Mission	- Social Security
Work Schedule	- Workers' Compensation Insurance
- Workday	- Unemployment Insurance
- Workweek	- Retirement Plan
- Lunch Period	- Benefits for Part-time Employees
- Holidays	Code of Conduct
- Personal Days	- Bulletin Boards
- Vacation	- Business Attire
- Sick Leave	- Emergency Procedures
- Family and Medical Leave	- Harassment
- Leave of Absence	- Housekeeping
- Bereavement Leave	- Personal Conduct
- Severe Weather Conditions	- Security
- Jury Duty	- Smoking Policy
- Military Reserve Duty	- Visitors
- Time Off Without Pay	- Vendors, Suppliers
Compensation	Recruitment
- Paydays	- Equal Employment Opportunity
	- Employment of Relatives

Figure 8-C
Sample Table of Contents for Personnel Handbook

XII. Assessing Your Situation

In order to practically benefit from this chapter, please consider your organization's situation. By asking yourself these questions, you would be assessing your situation as well as identifying the areas where making corrections would be beneficial.

- *Do your organization's financial resources allow for capable human resources, or is the opposite true?*

- *Would you characterize your staff as diverse, or do they all belong to a single ethnicity?*

- *When did your organization last conduct a thorough job analysis of all its personnel positions?*

- *What method(s) does your organization use to collect data on your HR needs?*

- *Does your organization have specific job descriptions for all paid and primary volunteer positions?*

- *Does your organization have a formal process to recruit, screen, and select staff for vacant positions?*

- *Does your organization have an evaluation process, and do all personnel go through a formal annual review?*

- *In your opinion, does your organization attract employees by paying competitive salaries, or are personnel attracted because of its mission and work environment?*

- *Does your organization retain employees for a long period? If not, why?*

- *What kind of training programs does your organization provide to its staff?*

- *Does your organization have a personnel plan to develop staff skills? If so, in what area and how will it be accomplished?*

- *How many volunteering staff members does your organization need? For what positions? How many does it currently have?*

- *Are there specific positions at your organization designated for volunteers?*

- *Does your organization have a complete and current personnel handbook that personnel follow closely?*

Chapter:

9.

Funding:

Sources & Strategies

I. Sources of Funding

- *Funding Categories*

- *What Funding Sources to Target*

- *Learning from Public Libraries*

II. Funding Strategies

- *Types of Funding, Donation Methods and Receiving Means*

- *Personal Solicitations*

- *Direct Mail*

- *Telemarketing*

- *Special Events*

- *Advertisements*

- *Getting Money from Grants*

- *Endowment Campaigns*

- *Planned Giving and Bequests*

- *Sponsorship Campaigns*

- *Corporate Sponsorships*

- *Joint Ventures*

- *Promotional Gifts and Programs*

III. The Development Team

IV. Assessing Your Situation

Funding development holds considerable importance for the nonprofit because this arena is where the lion's share of capital for their programs and operations begin. Built on organizational strength, fundraising is an active management process that requires commitment to an organization's mission and values. Any successful fundraising campaign is contingent upon the consideration of organizational form and relationship, directly reflecting organizational vitality. In this chapter, we will discuss seeking contributions through direct mail and online sources, and their importance to Islamic nonprofits in the US. We will also provide a bird's eye view of the available sources of funding, and offer a few strategies to seek funding from these sources. Two other major fundraising strategies will be covered in detail in other chapters.

I.   Sources of Funding

Every nonprofit needs funding for its programs as well as its own operations. Funding sources vary. These sources might be from grants provided by funding agencies or governments, public contributions received by mail or Internet, to public events held for the benefit of certain programs. Some organizations have a dedicated source based upon their particular program. One example of these are capital funds which target major gifts from individuals, as well as corporations and foundations, to support building campaigns or special projects such as establishing a hospital. Combining two or more of these methods will ensure a solid financial base from which any organization can draw. Not including public contributions, the following text outlines a few of the more popular methods.

FUNDING CATEGORIES

No fundraising campaign should ever begin before identifying the funding sources. Pinpointing not the specific donors but the five categories of donors is a primary concept that is critical to the entire campaign. Each campaign is unique and each source should be targeted accordingly—as a unique contribution goal to be achieved for that campaign. These five categories are:

· Board of trustees or board of directors of the organization

- Individuals

- Corporations

- Private and community foundations

- Governmental sources.

Board Members

As the board of trustees is a resource for an organization to draw on for carrying out its mission, it should be remembered that a great portion of a nonprofit's mission is to raise funds. This reasoning opens the door on board members, making them legitimate targets for an organization's fundraisers who can be counted on to give money, or freely of their time and efforts. Additionally, if an organization's trustees are not financially able to give, then the organization should seek out others whose pockets are deep enough to donate generously.

Individuals

Between 70 to 80 percent of all philanthropic contributions given in the US come from the individual donor. This source group is the most flexible and spontaneous in their giving, unlike foundations, corporations and governmental entities which put the nonprofit through a gauntlet before bestowing their funds. From 1978 to 1999, donations from individuals to private foundations in America grew seven-fold, from $4.25 billion to nearly $30 billion. As such, contributions from individuals, versus gifts from corporations and foundations, figure quite prominently in fundraising. According to the Giving USA 1999 Report, $174.5 billion dollars was given to charity in 1998 alone. From this total, individuals donated the lion's share of 88 percent, while foundations contributed seven percent, and corporations accounted for only five percent.

In the US, the economic growth enjoyed from the mid- to late-1990s helped to shape the production of individual wealth, with 95 percent of all contributions coming from only five percent of the population. Therefore, it is important to note that individual giving is crucial in advancing annual, capital, and endowment campaigns.

| 1978 | $4.25 |
| 1999 | $30 |

U.S. Growth of Donations of Individuals to
Private Foundations in Billions of Dollars

Figure 9-A

Corporations

Corporations look at contributions from a different point of view than does the individual. Before the cause, they first consider image enhancement for the corporation, and any indirect or direct benefits that may come from the contribution. The majority of philanthropic funding nonprofits usually receive from corporations are generally earmarked for annual fund campaigns and operational support, and are considered to be more of an atonement of community commitment and responsibilities towards their employees, shareholders and clients. Corporations rarely give out of altruistic concerns. Rather, their actions are an indirect public relations campaign. Additionally, name-recognition is usually a by-product of their support in the form of sponsorships for events or programs. The greater the exposure a nonprofit can give to the corporation, the greater the corporation's return on its investment. The caveat here is that the nonprofit will suffer from diminished funds, because of high out-of-pocket expenses connected with sponsoring the event or program. Therefore, the nonprofit should not put this kind of funding source at the top of its list.

Foundations

For the most part, private foundations are like money holders from one or few sources—mostly individuals or families. They typically donate to almost any type of organization, program and fundraising campaigns. Private foundations are often good sources for start-up and seed money, operating with a bit more freedom and more quickly than community foundations. Although some only give to specific subjects and causes, while others might limit grant-making to specific geographic areas.

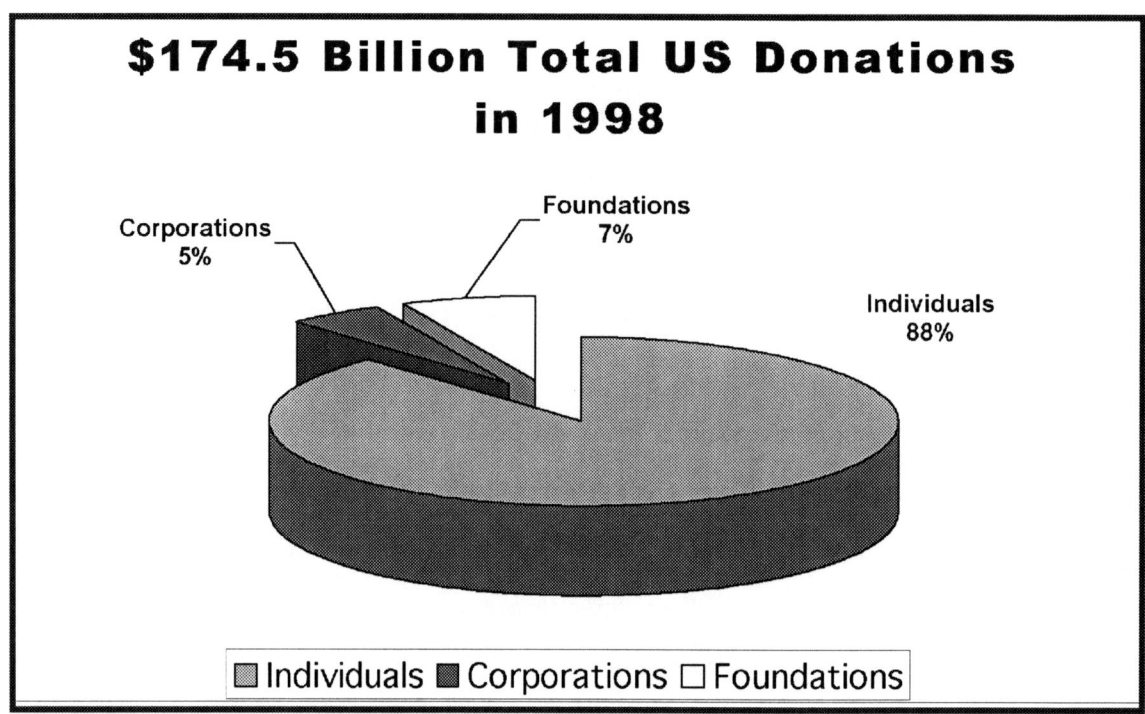

$174.5 Billion Total US Donations in 1998

Corporations
5%

Foundations
7%

Individuals
88%

☐ Individuals ☐ Corporations ☐ Foundations

Figure 9-B

The funding from community foundations generally comes from sources similar to those of private foundations as well as from corporations. Their funding is usually set aside to improve the quality of living within their community, which can cover a single city, region, state, or even an entire country. The money they give to nonprofits generally is from income earned on an endowment. Their funds can often be restricted to a specific interest area such as the arts, or to a specific organization such as a museum. Community foundation grant applications usually take time to analyze since they are generally reviewed by individuals and committees before they are accepted or rejected. It is not uncommon for months to pass before a grant is approved as most are usually only made on a quarterly basis.

Governmental Funding

Local, state, and federal governments also contribute funds to nonprofits. On the state and federal level, these are usually from area-of-interest grant-making agencies in an official or semi-independent capacity. On the local level, funding can come from a parks commission all the way up to the mayor's office. However, the general rule of thumb is that the lower the government level, the faster the turnaround time for the grant proposal. Even though local grants may not be on the scale of those from state or federal government, they probably will require that the organization making the request follow a set of predetermined guidelines. Elected officials are the ultimate controllers of government funds available for grants. It is important to not overlook the value of lobbying legislators, as well as informing and involving other pivotal government officials when an organization is seeking to have their grant proposal accepted. This is where the influence of the organization's board of trustees will come in handy—their sway within the community will prove invaluable at this critical phase, as their presentation to officials can make or break the funding.

WHAT FUNDING SOURCES TO TARGET

Each nonprofit must decide for itself which of the five funding sources will best serve their organization and its cause. In some cases, all five will be fair game. In others, maybe only one or two will fit. Taking a long hard look at the organization, its mission, community, philanthropic traditions, and the number of foundations, corporations, and governmental entities with a history for supporting organizations or programs such as theirs will help make this assessment. An organization must ask for money where the money can be found. It would not make much sense to approach a local government to help support a relief effort half a world away. Nor would it make much sense to jump through all of the hoops the federal government would require to obtain funding for a mosque's daycare initiative.

At times, it may seem more direct to ask a corporation for funding than a private individual. Although it is easier for a corporate officer to say "no", a fundraising campaign should not be based on the least painful turndown. Nor should a nonprofit funding strategy be based on a misinterpretation of wealth. Stockholders who are individuals own the corporation that said "no". Those individuals have wealth, and they often give to worthy causes. Nonprofits must choose their sources wisely by examining their tools, their cause, their arguments, and the means available to them while not overlooking the obvious.

LEARNING FROM PUBLIC LIBRARIES

When taking into account cross-sector partnerships, consider that in the United States, few nonprofit or other public organizations are like the public libraries which attract unprecedented charitable contributions from across the entire socio-economic spectrum.

Governmental cuts in the 1980's and early 1990's forced public libraries to address funding shortfalls by turning to foundations and library Friends' support groups to fulfill their needs. Built on contrasting management foundations, public libraries and private foundations faced inherent tensions. The two opposites were bound to clash; therefore, to work together, both require a dedicated stewardship of mutual support and cooperation.

II.   Funding Strategies

Of all the following strategies an organization may use for fundraising, there are definite advantages and disadvantages to each. In the next two chapters, we will discuss a few of these strategies such as direct mail and online solicitation. Here, we will emphasize those we did not discuss in detail elsewhere. Which strategy to use must be carefully considered, tailoring each method to a particular need while not exceeding the available budget.

TYPES OF FUNDING, DONATION METHODS, AND RECEIVING MEANS

Before we launch into discussing various strategies, we should first look into what types of funding are the most common, how they are usually received, and in what forms.

Types of Funding

There are five major types of gifts that come from programs that are designed to acquire revenue from existing or newly acquired donors. These are:

- *Annual*–Recurring funds from donors.
- *Major*–Planned and deferred funds that are nonrecurring.
- *Special Events*–Public events, sponsorships, etc.
- *Special Appeals*–Including any that are separate from annual gifts.
- *Grants*–These come from foundations, governments, etc.

Donation Methods

Most donations are made through the following methods:

1. Checks

2. Credit card

3. Stock donations

4. Electronic withdrawal

5. Cash

6. In-Kind.

Receiving Means

These donations are received by one or more of the following mediums:

- Postal delivery (paid for by the organization or the donor)

- Through the Internet

- Over the telephone

- Bank transfer (initiated by the donor or the organization)

- In person (at public events or by person).

In the following sections, we discuss those main strategies presented in the previous section while identifying means to raise funds from individuals, corporations, foundations, etc.

PERSONAL SOLICITATIONS

Person-to-person or face-to-face is probably the most effective fundraising tool that usually results in large or major gifts. Donors are more likely to give when someone takes the time out of their schedule to meet with them in person to enlist their support for a particular project. Additionally, the interpersonal touch more than likely will result in larger donation amounts than if that prospective donor were solicited by mail.

DIRECT MAIL

When addressing a much larger pool of prospective donors for individual donations, direct mail is the most effective tool to generate funding. It is best to start from a known list of current and past supporters and friends, and then add to it from other organizations. Targeted mailings usually yield less than $500 per person, while the donation request ranges from $30 to $1,000. The most prominent drawback of this sort of request is the postage and fees associated with printing the mailing. Since this particular funding strategy is very effective, and to some extent scientific, we have dedicated a chapter for this subject alone.

TELEMARKETING

A telemarketing campaign is best conducted as a part of a larger fundraising campaign, rather than as a stand-alone effort. Many nonprofits use telemarketing for contacting previous donors who fail to respond to repeated mail solicitations. Telemarketing is also an opportunity for a nonprofit to put the interpersonal touch on its fundraising, and gives the organization the chance to answer any questions donors may have. As well, a personal telephone call is a definite advantage when a nonprofit is trying to upgrade its donors. A prewritten script that addresses anticipated questions and provides accurate information about the organization should be provided to telemarketing staff. This method has the added bonus of doubling as market research because telemarketing calls can also do double duty by helping the organization determine its level of support.

SPECIAL EVENTS

Special events are limited only by one's imagination and vary from telethons, balls, marathons, silent auctions, awards programs to honor outstanding individuals or contributions, bazaars, bake sales, car washes, and the list goes on and on. Additionally, by inviting well-known personalities and the media, the organization will attract welcome attention to their cause. Never the less, whatever the affair, it should have a wide public appeal and be well planned, promoted, carried out, and assessed at the end. Useful byproducts an organization can reap from such events are heightened community awareness of the cause, and valuable Public Relations.

ADVERTISEMENT

Advertisement is one of the most supportive tools for any marketing and fundraising effort. It is important for Muslim nonprofits to maintain a certain exposure level in mainstream Islamic publications, TV and websites. Because Muslims are scattered all over the US, this type of advertising would make Muslims aware of their charities' existence, even if the nonprofits cannot reach them through mailings. Advertisements help keep the organization in the public eye, increasing visibility and exposure, and creating a corporate image and brand name.

Major Mediums for Advertisement

There are many mediums an organization can utilize for advertisement. The following are the three main areas of advertisements that are most useful for nonprofits:

- *Publications*–These are usually placed in either ethnic publications such as Arabic or Pakistani newspapers, or in Islamic publications read by Muslims from many ethnic groups.

- *TV*–Some television ad spots are very cheap, only costing $60 per spot commercial for localized stations. Obtaining ad spots on national stations such as ART (Arab Radio and Television) may very well be quite reasonable, while other ad spots obtained on international satellite stations such as Al-Jazeera could cost up to $7,500 per prime-time spot.

- *The Internet*–If used well, this medium could be very effective. The costs range from being totally free to completely unaffordable.

Keys to Capitalize on Advertisements

The following are some suggestions for an organization to streamline their advertisements:

- A balanced advertising plan must be developed and followed throughout the year for an organization to succeed in its advertisement campaign. First, identify the target market, and secondly, allocate the yearly advertising budget in a balanced way.

- If most of an organization's mailings and public events are done on the US West Coast, they should not advertise on local TV on the East Coast unless the organization intends to expand into this area in the near future.

- Approach different markets with different messages. An agency may want to advertise in Pakistan Times with a message about the Kashmiri refugees' need, but in Palestine Times about the Palestinian refugees' need.

- Advertisement works best with frequency. It is better to keep a constant presence in the market with some increase just before and during hot seasons such as Ramadan.

- Advertisements should be kept up to date, while bringing something new at least every quarter. An organization's main message should always be the same, while changing only minor details such as the photos, the headlines, and the data, if any.

- Negotiate yearly contracts with media outlets to save money on advertising. An organization can usually save up to 40 percent, and sometimes more, when they aggressively negotiate and sign yearly contracts with magazines, newspapers, websites, and TV.

GETTING MONEY FROM GRANTS

There are tons of money out there for nonprofits to take advantage of. A great deal of this is in the form of grants. What is a grant? Simply put, a grant is a monetary award given by a funder to pay for all sorts of things. Most funders are government agencies, foundations, or corporations. One can obtain this money by first filling out a grant application, which is a written request asking for the money. Most grants go to organizations with the IRS status of 501(c)(3) that write a winning grant application directed to the funding source. Some applications are reasonably short—the writer simply fills in the blanks. Whereas federal government grant applications can exceed 30 to 40 pages that require copious amounts of supporting documentation.

Where Do You Begin?

Since grant writing is a specialized field, what follows here is only a minimal guideline of where to begin the grant writing process. Grant writing is not an impossible task, nor is it for those of weak ego. It is, however, wise to take a course in grant writing before actually attempting it, or at least get a good book on the subject.

A grant application and a grant proposal are basically the same thing. One is an application to be filled out, and the other can be an exercise in creative writing if one does not go about it in an intelligent way: by using a national or regional template format. These are forms that have been accepted by regional or national grant writing associations as generic formats and can usually be downloaded from their websites. An invaluable place to look for available grants is in your public library. Two excellent resources available at most libraries are the yearly *Federal Register*, which is also available online, and the *Chronicle of Philanthropy*. Although, it is available online, it is a subscription-based source, but is free in the library.

How Do You Spell Success?

Grantors are drawn to ideas and solutions for problems that are innovative, and creative with a fresh spin, and although grantors will usually invest in supplemental programs, rarely will they fund operating expenses or risky investments. If possible, cite research that supports the program for which you are requesting funding. It cannot be stressed enough that when soliciting funding, the organization must comply with all stated restrictions, including geographic areas and funding purposes. Additionally, the vast majority of grants also have a funding guideline. For instance, a nonprofit cannot ask for a $150,000 grant written out in a ten page letter when the foundation from which it is being solicited limits the grants to $50,000 and has a standard two-page application. Do not forget to have the proposal proofread! Spelling and grammar errors certainly do not convey a positive image. Those agencies that do not wish to tackle the grant writing process on their own, and decide instead to hire a professional should know that the grant writer's fee must be decided upon from the outset. It is unethical and maybe illegal for the writer to charge or be paid on commission.

If your project is rejected, request reviewers' comments from the grantor, which may offer invaluable tips for improving your future grant applications. Even if you are rejected or receive only partial funding, never forget to write thank-you notes. Tenacity is another key to success. Keep at it. Your ego may take a serious blow, but in time a full grant will come through, and all of that hard work will have finally paid off.

Foundation Solicitations

When an organization is seeking funding from a foundation, they are generally seeking to acquire a grant that is given by that foundation. Thorough research should be conducted to conclude whether or not that particular foundation may support the proposed activity. Generally, foundation solicitations are comprised of interpersonal techniques executed through four successive actions:

- A one- or two-page letter of inquiry, submitted to the proper contact person within the foundation, followed up by a telephone call to determine the degree of shared interest.

- An initial interview can then be arranged, if the call's response is positive.

- A grant proposal is then written up consisting usually of ten components:

    1. Table of contents

    2. Executive summary should be limited to about three paragraphs which simply and directly explain the proposed project, and how it matches the foundation's interests. The amount of the request should be included in the first paragraph.

    3. Problem statement

    4. Objectives

    5. Project description should include a timeline and any methods or procedures which will be used to accomplish the objective, incorporating a viable solution.

6. Evaluation

7. Organizational expertise

8. Future plans

9. Budget must be realistic and concise, and encompass all direct and indirect expenses. A proposal whose numbers do not balance is almost definitely lost.

10. Appendix.

- A project interview, or on-site visit is a step that may be denied since some foundations limit or prohibit personal contact with solicitors. If an interview is granted, a timely thank-you letter should be sent afterwards.

The proposal is usually mailed to the foundation with a cover letter. Now comes the hard part: waiting for an answer. Some grant making cycles can take up to nine months, during which the fundraiser must continue business as usual sending out mass mailings, doing special events, etc.

ENDOWMENT CAMPAIGNS

Excellent approaches to acquire financial resources are endowment funds which support operational or capital budgets. Endowment funds are frequently the result of special interests, memorials, and planned gifts. The tangible gains of building an endowment usually lie in the future, and are the result of long-term efforts. An endowment includes capital and other assets, which are invested for long-term growth. The invested principal provides income, which may be reinvested or utilized. In Islam, an endowment is called "waqf", a continuous form of giving or gift set up by the donor for use over a long time.

Money raised for an organization to invest rather than spend is called an endowment campaign. This money is then put into an endowment fund, and the income from this is used by the organization to meet ongoing expenses, cover capital expenditures, or fund special projects and programs. When an organization undertakes the raising of endowment funds, it does so in order to lessen the annual need to raise money to cover operational deficits or extraordinary expenses. The income from an endowment fund is usually restricted to the purpose or purposes of that fund. The organization's bylaws generally make it hard or nearly impossible to invade the endowment fund.

PLANNED GIVING AND BEQUESTS

The category of planned giving is a gift committed during the present, but will not be received by the recipient institution until a period of time has elapsed, often many years. Nationally, planned giving is the second largest portion of institutional income only after capital campaigns, and is expected to increase. Because they are so complex or because their funds are usually deferred for so many years, charitable organizations tend to shy away from planned giving programs. Understandably, the services of a legal professional and a certified financial planner should be acquired to map out the details and run these programs and funds.

Planned Giving: Unlimited Potential

Current economic research suggests that by far, Americans over age 55 control the largest amount of individual capital, standing at nearly $10 trillion. Since 1990, nonprofit organizations have been the recipients of more than $40 billion in charitable gifts. As the American population who accumulated wealth after World War I ages and dies off, younger generations will inherit those financial resources, as will the older generations' favorite charities. This trend is expected to continue throughout a 55-year transfer of wealth period, from 1990 to 2044, and peaking around 2017.

Planned gifts can offer many advantages such as reducing estate taxes, provide a steady life income, and allow the donor to make a much larger gift than they thought possible. The donor also receives a current tax deduction for the gift, reduces or avoids capital gains tax, and supports the vital work of the nonprofit organization. Some of the most popular methods to accomplish this are to leave a bequest through a will, or one of many different types of trusts. Charitable Remainder Trusts can provide the donor or their heirs with a life income stream while also providing a gift to support the nonprofit's programs. A similar structure is found in charitable gift annuities, a type of contract that can provide the donor with payments for the rest of their life, while ultimately making a gift to support vital programs. As well, giving a gift of securities also has its advantages, allowing many donors to make gifts that will live on after they are gone. Stock that has been owned for at least one year that has increased in value can be donated to a charitable organization without having to pay capital gains tax on the increase. Presently, donors can take an income tax charitable deduction equal to the current market value of the securities (up to 30 percent of the donor's adjusted gross income). Different retirement plans including IRAs, pension plans, Keogh and 401(K) accounts can maximize a donation while allowing other property that is not subject to some taxes to be passed to beneficiaries.

SPONSORSHIP CAMPAIGNS

Funding donated for the support of a project, program, event, initiative, activity, or even a salary may come from a sponsorship campaign, and is generally donated by a corporation. Although, sometimes this type of funding can come from individuals, it is a relatively new fundraising strategy not unlike a capital campaign in that it raises money for a specific purpose. Unlike a capital campaign, though, the money raised is to cover an expense, not to purchase an asset.

Once an organization has made a practice of linking gifts from certain donors to particular activities, efforts, or programs, then these donors take sole sponsorship of those activities. The sponsor benefits by having its name exclusively and synonymously linked to that event or program, drawing in good Public Relations and exposure. However, before seeking the sponsorships, the organization must first identify likely projects, programs, events, initiatives, and activities to develop a general proposal for, and identify a prospective donor. Unique events should rarely be offered to two or more prospects for sponsorship at the same time since they are an effective way of increasing existing annual gifts and of drawing in new corporate donors. A secondary benefit is that the better known and regarded the sponsoring corporation is, the greater the endorsement is for the nonprofit, bolstering their credibility, and deepening the relationship with the sponsoring donor.

Corporate Sponsorships

Corporate sponsorships cannot be discussed without first discussing cause-related marketing. This is a strategy used by for-profit companies to sell products and services, whereby the company pays a percentage of the profits or a set amount to the charitable organization in exchange for use of the organization's name and mission. This method was initiated by American Express in 1981 when the company increased the use of its credit card in California. American Express advertised that it would give state arts groups a sum equal to one percent of its charge card sales. When American Express took the strategy national two years later by tying the use of its card to the restoration of the Statue of Liberty, card usage increased 28 percent. This resulted in an additional 45 percent more cards being issued, and netting $1.7 million for the project. Such a marketing strategy allows for increased exposure for the nonprofit. The company benefits by creating a unique image niche resulting from association with worthy projects and stronger ties to the community.

As the preceding point is a marketing strategy, corporate sponsorship is an advertising medium by which products or services can be marketed by companies who purchase advertising exposure, the same as they would in a magazine or on a website. Also known as event sponsorships, these are big business, and rely on borrowed imagery, as sponsors buy the right to associate their product or service with the goodwill and patrons a property cultivates. In 1991, General Mills sponsored a re-created shark exhibit at New Orleans' Aquarium of the Americas to sell its Shark Bites Fruit Snacks. The sponsorship cost General Mills $60,000 and included signage and identification on the exhibit. Children who brought along the snack food's proof-of-purchase got in half-price, further enhancing General Mills' exposure.

Joint Ventures

When a nonprofit enters into a marketing agreement with a for-profit company, it is entering into a "Joint Venture". This is for the dual purpose of generating low- or no-cost income for the 501(c)(3) organizations, and providing marketing advantages for the company. This "co-venture" allows for a quid pro quo relationship—an exchange of income whereby the nonprofit authorizes the use of its logo, name, mission and sometimes programs and publics for selling the company's products or services. In this type of relationship, the public is not making gifts as individual donors, but are buying the product or service offered by the company. The most common types of joint ventures are cause-related marketing, corporate sponsorships, collection canisters, honor boxes, and vending machines.

Promotional Gifts and Programs

Promotional gifts and programs such as discounts on Hajj or event sponsorships are not necessary, but are nice to offer occasionally. Some promotions have been proven to work well for nonprofits, such as convention sponsorships, and video documentaries; while others are criticized as expensive and unnecessary gifts. Although the following is only a brief guide, there are many types of promotions, with each having its own specific effectiveness:

- Convention and other public events sponsorship packages are useful because Islamic conventions bring in large Muslim populations for a set number of days, during which an agency can benefit from increased exposure. Designing some way to contact attendees after the convention, such as adding attendees to the organization's ML, can prove quite useful in the future.

- Audio and videotapes are very useful when given as a gift in return for a minimum set contribution. It is recommended that the message of such tapes benefit the causes being promoted.

- Book and publication sponsorships are widely used by nonprofits outside the US, where books on different subjects are donated to mosques, centers, contacts, and donors as a way of promoting the organization through gift giving. This method has not been tried for Muslim nonprofits in the US, but probably would be quite effective.

- Lecture series sponsorships are always a good idea, but only if they are accompanied by fundraising events. An example of this would be conducting a lecture in several cities by a well-known speaker. This method would be expensive and unjustified, unless the lecture topics and speakers draw in crowds.

- Gift items such as pens, bookmarks, pins, hats, shirts, T-shirts, diaries or planners, watches, etc., can be given to donors in appreciation of their support. Be aware that expensive gifts can easily backfire. Small and inexpensive gifts are always appreciated, as they are useful items that aid in keeping the organization in the donors' mind, while retaining a point of contact. It is recommended that the agency's logo, telephone number, and website address should be displayed on the gift item and, if it fits, their motto as well.

III.   The Development Team

The foundation of a successful fundraising program is comprised of those who raise the money, and those who provide it. Even if an organization cannot afford to keep professional fundraising officers on staff, they should at least budget for a professional development director. In some organizations, this person works in a voluntary capacity whose duties include the coordination and implementation of fundraising programs. They are also charged with creating numerous efficient and compelling opportunities for donors to support an organization, and to make the experience of giving a satisfying and rewarding one.

Although some organizations make their executive director handle these duties, this is not a good idea since the executive director has a specific role to play in carrying out the mission. The development director's time should be spent on planning and managing fundraising campaigns and activities, recruiting and training volunteer fundraising leadership, identifying and cultivating prospective donors, and staying abreast of community fundraising issues. As well as the forecasting and evaluation potential of fundraising campaigns and activities, producing solicitation materials, and the managing of personnel within the development department.

In the western world, Islamic nonprofits present their own array of specialized circumstances requiring skilled fundraising teams. The need here cannot be overstated. One cannot expect a volunteer with limited training to provide professional services. Additionally, as a volunteer, their time is severely limited. Hiring or contracting professional staff in the critical areas of fundraising, advertising or communications, financial planning, and management will pay off in the long-run, as a lack of skills in this area can mean disaster for the organization. If the nonprofit cannot afford to hire staff, then they should seriously consider seeking out consultants on a per-job basis, or outsource some of the more complicated or sensitive campaigns.

IV.   Assessing Your Situation

In order to practically benefit from this chapter, please consider your organization's situation, in light of what we have presented here. Answer these questions to assess and identify the areas where corrections are required. We encourage you to go back and review the specific materials of the chapter for clarification on some points.

- *Do your organization's board members have any financial responsibility to raise funds through their personal efforts?*

- *What types of funding do your revenues consist of, usually through what means are they received, and in what forms?*

- *Beyond the current funding sources of your organization, what do you see as other potential sources that your organization should tackle in the near future?*

- *Have any of your projects, events, or initiatives received any sort of sponsorships from corporations that benefit both organizations?*

- *Does your organization have a yearly detailed advertising plan that is balanced, covers your community, and is negotiated for the long-term?*

- *Does your organization have any kind of personal contact with your major donors, in person or by telephone, on at least a yearly basis?*

- *What special events does your organization hold that generate public awareness about what you do, and what type of funding and support you receive?*

  • *Does your organization have programs or services that are eligible for grants from foundations or governmental sources?*

  • *Has your organization seriously approached the issue of seeking grants, and has it done extensive research, enlisted professional help, and not given up when faced with rejection?*

  • *Does your organization have any long-term fund development programs such as endowment campaigns?*

  • *Do your donors have any opportunities for planned giving through your organization?*

  • *Has your organization entered into a cause-related marketing campaign or joint-venture with any other corporations, and what benefits did your organization receive?*

  • *What kinds of promotional programs does your organization offer donors as incentive to support a certain cause or program?*

  • *Does your organization have a dedicated department or committee for fund development with paid professional staff, and does it seek consultants when necessary to help develop new funding initiatives?*

Chapter

10.

The Missing-Link Cycle:

A Marketing Concept for International

Charities

I. *Fundraising's Role in Marketing*

   – *Fundraising's Evolution*

   – *An Additional Challenge for Muslim Charities*

II. *The Missing Link*

   – *How the Missing-Link Works*

   – *It's All About Effective Communication*

III. *Marketing and Fundraising Strategies*

IV. *Effective Internal Communication a Vital Key for Utilizing the Missing-Link*

   – *Tips on Useful Field Reports*

V. *Using the Missing-Link Leads to Growth and Stability*

   – *Growth & Stability at the Market Level*

   – *Growth & Stability at the Field Level*

VI. *Assessing Your Case*

This chapter addresses a major challenge commonly faced by Muslim-run international charities: they generally operate on one continent and raise funds in another. While some American Islamic charities obtain the lion's share of their funding from Muslims primarily within the US, the majority of their programs are implemented in third world countries throughout the Middle East, Africa, and Southeast Asia. These charities' potential donors are not freely able to visit the locales in which the charities operate, nor witness the implementation of the programs that help the needy. Giving to an endeavor such as this is not like that of a youth center established by a Muslim community that has intimate knowledge of the need and the project's achievements. Nor is it like a soup kitchen or food pantry where local donors can "drop in" to check how their donation is being used.

This chapter will provide a marketing concept as a plausible solution for charities whose donors and programs are in separate geographical areas by introducing "The Missing-Link" which will link the donors to the needs and achievements of the organization. It is all about creative communications and the effective use of multimedia strategies. It is about bringing the "field"—where the needs and the programs exist—to the "market", where your donors and potential supporters are. This is a tried and true concept that has produced outstanding success in growth and stability at both the market and field levels, allowing the practitioner to develop a professional image. We believe that not only will charities with international presence benefit from this concept, we believe that if other nonprofits apply this concept, they too will greatly benefit.

I.   Fundraising's Role in Marketing

Marketing is a management procedure aimed at fulfilling consumer needs and wants through a barter process. Until the 1970s, marketing had no role in nonprofit organizations, most of whom were content to sit in their ivory towers upon the cushy pillows of their ideals, waiting for the money to float in from donors. This flawed mentality lead to religious organizations losing members, while colleges failed to attract new students resulting in a few who were forced to close their hallowed doors for lack of students. Professional, cultural and trade society memberships were also declining.

FUNDRAISING'S EVOLUTION

Throughout the last 35 years, along with a downturn in the economy, nonprofits were forced to reevaluate their orientation, developing programs that were market-driven. Above all, fundraising has evolved into a form of marketing activity. Those nonprofits that had a vision for the future assigned marketing a major role within their organizations, allowing it to drive the daily work environment.

Even though there are those donors who are willing to give without much prodding, while others need some convincing, you still need to "market" the various causes and needs. Whether funds are needed for food aid amongst refugees in Darfur, or medicine for HIV patients in West Africa, various marketing tools must still be used to bring these situations to the attention of potential donors, encouraging their support.

AN ADDITIONAL CHALLENGE FOR MUSLIM CHARITIES

Most Islamic-based charities are dependent upon individual contributions, receiving neither government support nor major grants. This condition puts these charities in a situation of being responsible for obtaining their own independent funding, as well as for establishing programs. Such organizations must efficiently and effectively reach the Muslim donor population, which is scattered throughout the United States. A comprehensive media operation must be in place linking the fieldwork (which may be overseas) to our market in a way that brings the urgency of the field to our potential donors. They must earn their trust while keeping their beneficiaries' dignity intact, by not exploiting their needs. This requires a great deal of concentrated effort, an intimate knowledge of nonprofits, communication strategies, and experience in this complicated arena.

Muslims, as well as others, contribute after they feel the emotional connection to the needs and goals of the organization. Potential donors must also have confidence in the organization, understand its objective, appreciate its achievements, and feel that somewhere out there, their contribution is indeed making a positive difference in the field. For many Muslim charities, this is not easy since much of their fieldwork is in poor third-world countries in the Middle East and Africa, while their donors live all over the United States and other wealthy nations, such as in the Arabian Gulf and in parts of Europe. It is imperative to be able to identify, reach out to and convince potential donors in a timely and cost-effective way. This is where the need for a marketing approach comes in through the creative use of multimedia by establishing a link between donors and the beneficiary at the field. This continuous process is one that must be repeated constantly in an unbroken circuit we call "The Missing-Link".

Through years of dedicated experience and in-depth training in nonprofit charitable organizations, and after many trials and corrections, we have learned that an organization can maintain a continuous cycle linking the field to the market through creative multimedia strategies. The organization should be able to grow and prosper at a high rate, as well as operate in a highly professional manner.

Performance and Accountability

Muslim-run charities are faced with more challenges now that at any other time in history. Therefore, they must be acutely aware that their charities will have to perform better, be far more accountable, and act more professional than other charitable entities if they are to survive and best serve their humane goals.

II.   The Missing-Link

The Missing-Link rationally addresses the reasoning most international organizations fail to clearly demonstrate to their donors and that is what is really going on. Rather, they address their market in general and vague or over-used terms. We call this system the "Missing-Link" because most organizations fail to provide this link or connect their needy causes and programs to their potential donors. It is a "cycle" because once this link is established, it must remain continuously ongoing. This cycle is the medium through which field materials are processed and directed to your market through mail, advertisements, Internet publications, etc. These field materials convey what the needs are, and what the organization is doing about them. The information they carry will significantly increase the effectiveness of your fundraising.

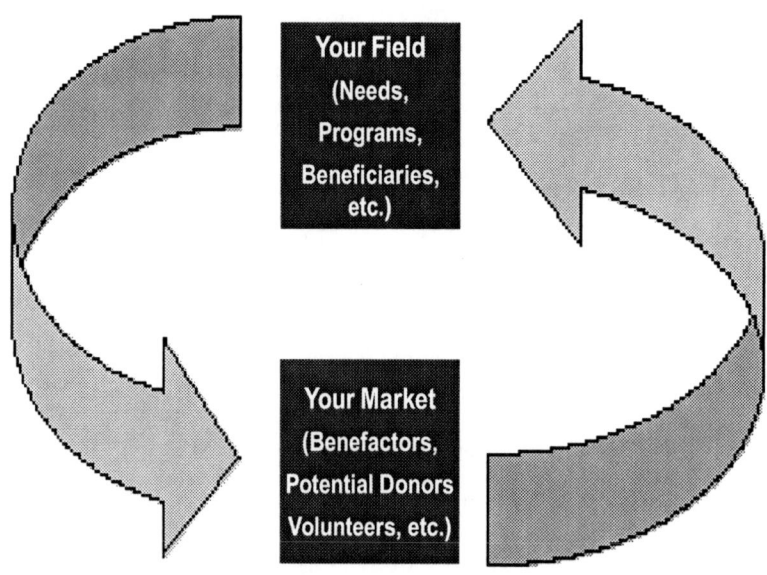

Figure 10-A The Missing-Link Cycle

This chapter concentrates on media and marketing operations in relation to this cycle, explaining how it works. A quick review of the major communication avenues your organization should go through to link your market to the field will be covered, but details will be left to other dedicated chapters.

In addition, in order to prepare your organization for employing this successful cycle, practical recommendations will be discussed for developing a communications system, which is necessary to establish and run this link. The whole cycle revolves around communicating with your market. Simply put, it is about managing the information from the field. Then, using multimedia to transfer this information to the people you wish to reach, mainly your organization's donors and potential donors, in order to convince them to donate, with the middle point being your organization.

All information contained in this chapter has been gained through practical use. Nothing contained in these pages is theoretical, since it is the essence and results learned throughout many years of work in this field. In practice, this concept has produced tremendous results. These concise Tips and practical Keys are a working guide for your organization to achieve a successful growth in your donor base and in your programs through the Missing-Link.

HOW THE MISSING-LINK WORKS

As illustrated, this is the cycle where *Your Field* (representing the needs where you operate and the programs you are providing to meet these needs) is linked to *Your Multimedia Department,* which is then linked to *Your Market* (representing your benefactors, potential donors and volunteers). The market is then linked to your field, and so on. It is a never-ending cycle as long as the organization survives. Your field provides your multimedia department with reports and raw media materials detailing what activities are going on, such as reports, data, images, and video footage. Then this information is processed and transferred to your market through direct mailings, the Internet, different types of advertisements, publications, audio- and video materials, CDs, DVDs, and promotional programs. All of these different mediums result in bringing funding to the field from your market. In the middle of this cycle sits your entire organization. Your dedicated and capable Human Resources, solid internal communication system, and your organization's management approach affect these factors. All of these are vital in guaranteeing the success of this cycle; therefore, it is an absolute must to staff your multimedia department with capable personnel possessing various levels of communication skills.

As a result of the Missing-Link as illustrated, your market will learn more about the needs your organization is targeting, and their associated programs, which will in turn provide increased donations to your organization. Your organization passes these funds on to these programs, as well as your overall operation, including your multimedia department. Consequently, as more funds come to the field programs, better and more effective programs will be instituted. The reports generated by these programs will be transformed by your multimedia department into effective communication pieces for your market, which will provide better funding to your field programs throughout your organization, and so on. In this process, your organization acts as a nucleus, where it represents a central role in the operation of the cycle, by proving staffing, communication standards, funding, and supervision.

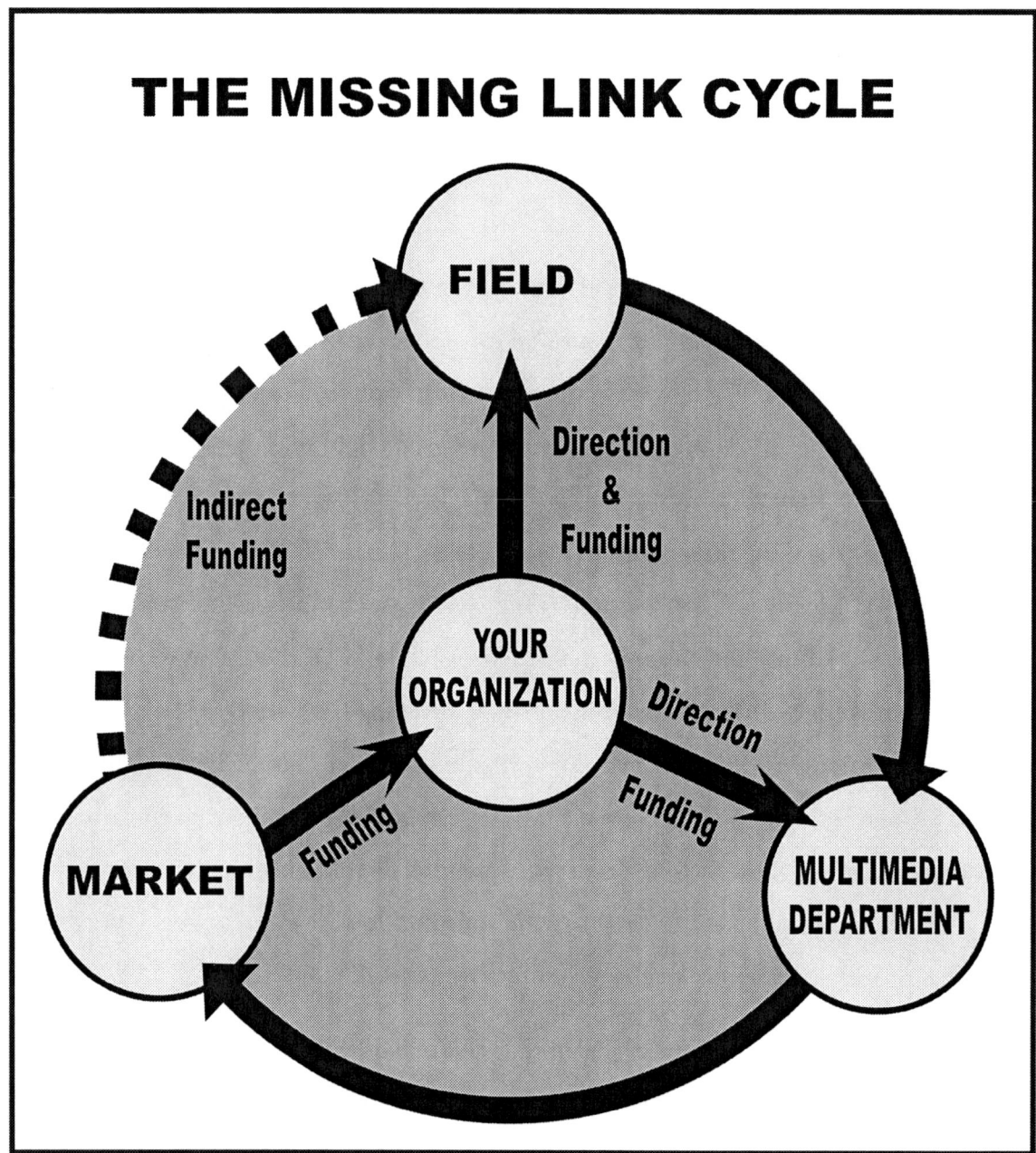

Figure 10-B

ITS ALL ABOUT EFFECTIVE COMMUNICATION

The most important matter to emphasize here would be for an organization to develop and maintain a clear and working understanding of the communication cycle of The Missing-Link Cycle. It is helpful to concentrate on one main idea that remains central while tying other ideas to it. The Missing-Link Cycle is a communication process, linking your market to your field.

Every day, some nonprofits fail to grow properly, yet others remain professional, experiencing growth and effectiveness. Much of this success is directly dependent on how the organization is perceived by their market. In addition, the organization's donors are key to being able to fulfill their mission, and should be nurtured. The organization should strive to gain the donors' trust and respect, while developing a sense of empathy with those who receive their donations in the field. Donors and potential donors should be given the right message at the right time, and they must be treated as "part of the team". The organization's relationship to their donors must be built on a solid basis of well thought-out multimedia communications.

Success will be dependent, to a large degree, on how effectively the organization can maintain the communication links within their agency. In other words, if the organization is able to efficiently bring all the elements together while working on applying the Missing-Link, they most likely will prosper and grow.

III.   Marketing and Fundraising Strategies

Only updated information about the needs and the achievements to meet these needs will entice donors to give and continue to give on a regular basis. This is achieved through high visibility, constant exposure, fundraising tools and a marketing mix. Although it maybe called the fundraising, marketing or development department, your multimedia department should aim to contact your potential market to raise funds. Your market is the pool of potential donors who you aim to reach through your marketing and fundraising activities. If you do not have a multimedia department, you should establish one. It should produce advertisements, newsletters, personal contacts, public events, as well as develop an Internet presence. Such efforts are all about reaching people and attempting to convince them to donate. At the same time, developing the corporate image and the organization's brand name, whether positive or negative.

There are many tools your media and communications department can use to raise funds; they are only limited by their imaginations. The following are the most important for publicly funded organizations:

- *Direct Mail Campaigns*

    Although we dedicated an entire chapter to direct mail marketing, we would like to say a few words here.

    Since the US is quite large, and with its Muslim population being scattered all over, it is not easy or very convenient to reach potential donors if you target them only at group gatherings. Therefore, a common fundraising tool for the nonprofit sector in the US, especially for Muslim charities, is direct mail marketing. It is the fastest, most effective way to reach many people using minimal effort, assuming that you are targeting the correct market with the right messages.

    Having a larger donor base will ensure that the organization's dependence on any single substantial funding source will not allow decisions to be tilted to the benefactor's advantage, thereby causing a loss of autonomy. Direct mail solicitation is the main strategy to acquire a broad donor base, despite most mail donations being in smaller amounts. Consequently, donor acquisitions are designed to persuade potential donors to make that first gift, which will most probably lead to a second larger donation, then a third, etc.

    Direct mail can come in many forms and for numerous different purposes. It could be for publications such as a monthly or quarterly newsletter used to report on programs, organization activities, etc. Alternatively, direct mail can be useful to update donors on the organization's achievements that will keep the donor funds coming in on a regular basis. Also, a more common form of direct mail campaign can be employed, such as a solicitation letter used in addition to a donation form and a return envelope promoting a certain program or cause.

    Other forms of direct mailings are self-mailer brochures, and various sizes of postcards, and annual reports. Additionally, these mailings are frequently sent for the purpose of emergency appeals, such as in the case of natural disasters, or for seasonal solicitations for Ramadan, Eid ul-Adha, or end-of-year campaigns. As these particular issues require more than a glance, we will detail them in a separate chapter.

- *Internet Marketing*

If used wisely, the Internet is a very successful tool that can readily allow people to know about your organization, and provide donations towards your programs at minimal cost. Online giving offers not only convenience, it answers people's heartfelt urge to respond immediately to others in need without having to send in a check or going through a more lengthy process. Currently, the vast majority of disaster response organizations are integrating online appeals with other methods. With online donations being larger on average than traditional gifts obtained by mail, technology is changing donor outreach programs to help find those willing and able to give more online. The web is allowing organizations to have ready access to Internet-savvy donors of all ages, and to cost effectively grow relationships online by collecting valuable data that can be used to communicate personal messages to constituents. To be successful in online solicitation, an organization must have an effective website with e-commerce capability where donors can give online by credit cards. However, this is not enough; the website itself must be marketed through Internet banners and E-mail updates, as well as all other marketing strategies the organization uses such as publications, direct mailings, and TV and publication advertising. These issues will also be discussed in detail in a separate chapter.

- *Advertisements*

Advertisement is an effective supportive tool for any marketing effort. Contrary to people that judge advertisement by its direct returns, advertisement pays off when you have another marketing mix in place. It is important for Muslim nonprofits to maintain certain exposure in mainstream Muslim publications, TV and websites. Because Muslims are a scattered population in the US, this type of advertising would make Muslims aware of these charities even if the nonprofits cannot reach them through mailings. Advertisements help keep your organization in the public eye, increase visibility and exposure, and create a corporate image. We will go into details about advertisements in another chapter.

- *Public Events*

    Public events are held to "market" a certain cause or program. Such events might be a fundraising dinner, a lecture or a short presentation. In any form, through this event, the organization must present to the attendees what the need(s) is, and what the organization is doing to meet that need. This should preferably be accomplished through a combination of multimedia presentations. These might be a PowerPoint presentation with a personal appeal or commentary, or a video highlighting a personal appeal or commentary, or in any other way that puts across to people the images and stories surrounding the message they want to present. A specially produced documentary can be very effective if done well. Public events also serve the public relations image of the organization. They might be held to introduce an organization to a particular community, or to meet the leadership of the community while aiming to solicit new benefactors and volunteers.

- *Promotions and Sponsorships*

    Promotions and sponsorships can be launched at conventions or public events with an objective of mobilizing people towards the organization. Nonprofits can carry out various promotions and sponsorships to market their organizations and their programs. These will be covered in detail in another chapter.

Additionally, since there are other proven marketing and fundraising means that have too much substance to cover here, we will go over these in upcoming chapters as well.

IV.   Effective Internal Communication a Vital Key for Utilizing the Missing-Link

In order to be able to utilize the Missing-Link Cycle effectively and grow with stability, it is recommended to pay extra attention towards your internal communication operation. Successful fundraising and marketing campaigns can not be achieved without an internal communication system in place. Such a system should be thorough enough to cover every aspect of the organizational operations. This includes all departments, branches, field offices, and different establishments or programs.

This communication system can be in the form of reports characterized as follows:

- *Periodic:* covering a specific period for which it is prepared. It is recommended that reporting should be done on a monthly basis.

- *Concise:* although thorough, it must provide the most important data and information necessary in a summarized format. If needed, any stories and details should be included as appendixes.

- *A Planning Tool:* not only should the report provide information about past and current projects and activities, but also about what are the planned activities in the near future. If it is a monthly report, then it should state last month's achievements, and the next month's plans in less detail.

- *Useful:* not everyone should write a report and not everything should be written about. Only that informative and useful information which requires reporting should be included. Reports are not meant to be filed without any future use, they are meant to somehow use the information they provide at some level, and then filed.

- *Not centralized:* if all reports come to top management from all departments, branches, and programs, they may never be read thoroughly, or processed in a useful manner. The communication system should include who receives what, or a copy of what to be precise. For instance, reports from three African field offices with several programs under their immediate supervision may be collected by a regional office there. The reports can then all be summarized into one regional report covering the operation of the three branches and their programs. After the regional management portion is added, the combined report can be sent on to the head office, possibly accompanied by copies of branch reports for reference. These regional reports citing achievements in the field may go directly to the Executive Director for quick review and transfer to the various departments for processing, including to the multimedia department. Reports from different regional or branch offices should be received on time by the multimedia department for purposes of marketing and reporting to donors. This garnered program information should be very useful in the different multimedia tools such as the website, E-mail updates, newsletter, advertisements, mailings, etc. The organization's accountant may benefit partially from these reports as well.

Good reports from the fields yield effective communications with donors. The reports generated ultimately reflect what the organization is doing, especially when the multimedia department translates that information into short articles, press releases, stories, tables, headlines, etc.

I.T. Department Report Data Example

An example of a monthly donations report from the Information Technology Manager or Development Department with IT support should be provided to management on a monthly basis. It should include the following:
- What is the current total active Mailing List size?
- Last month's total number of donations, New Donors, and Repeat Donors.
- Total donations and average donation of last month.
- Donation source analysis: what percentage came from what source or campaign? For example, the spring 2005 issue of the newsletter brought in 1,100 donations. One hundred and sixty are new donors, totaling $76,000, with an average donation of $145. This represents 75 percent of total donations received last month.
- It is recommended that a simple table should be followed for monthly reporting, with a fixed consistent format; however, more professional formatting, with visual presentations, should be used for quarterly or yearly report summarizing and analyzing the entire results.

For internal purposes to motivate and inform all staff on all issues at the organization, an organization's Communications Manager should be able to coordinate a monthly internal report which updates all staff at different levels. The report should also inform upper management about the kind of work being done, as well as what the main achievements were of the previous month. Including other pertinent points such as what new things are going on at the organization, who is in and who is out, the organization's new goals, and updates on future objectives is also a good idea. If management chooses, this report can be adapted into a tightly edited one- to two-page informational piece printed on-demand for donors. It can also be sent on a monthly basis, or used as an e-newsletter.

TIPS ON USEFUL FIELD REPORTS

An effective field report pays attention to specific data and materials. It should simply include:

- *What*—what kind of programs, what they offered or are offering, with a concise explanation of each program.

- *Where*—the location where each program was or is being executed or established.

- *Why*—the purpose behind each program, why it is crucially needed, some statistical data about certain situations leading to such a need.

- *Who*—who the beneficiaries are, exactly how many benefited or are receiving aid from each program, and what the status and situation is before and after, if applicable.

- *How much*—what is the size of each project in terms of amount of relief goods provided, how much it costs, and what are the projected future costs.

- *When*—when the program was accomplished—or begun if still in operation, and for how long it will last, if temporary. Provide a timeframe for each program.

- *Multimedia Materials*—provide enough photos and images for each program. Sometimes video footage is needed, which can be more effective.

V.   Using the Missing-Link Leads to Growth and Stability

Successful charities should not in anyway depend on crises for their survival; however, they can still benefit from them. One indication that a charity is dependent on emergencies and crises is organizational growth during a time of crisis. After the crisis ends, the organization's activities dramatically drop off. Their pace would go up and down without a steady and stable growth. To the contrary, successful organizations would see a boost during a crisis. Yet, they do not go back to their previous stage after the crisis ends. We have seen that the primary result of utilizing the Missing-Link is a steady growth at both the market and field levels on a continuous basis as long as the cycle in place.

GROWTH & STABILITY AT THE MARKET LEVEL

Year after year, more people are becoming exposed to your organization; therefore, the number of donors should steadily increase. It is well known that frequent exposure to the same market creates a brand name. When a potential donor wishes to contribute, this brand name is easily remembered. Time is the main factor here, since an organization can not build credibility and awareness overnight. For this reason, advertising and promoting the organization is a long-term investment.

An organization earns the fruits of its marketing efforts since the first time the market was exposed to that organization. For instance, if an organization has been frequently advertising in a certain magazine for the past five years, people's reaction to the last advertisement depends not only on this last issue, but on all advertisements over those past five years.

Keeping Donor Numbers from Declining

Steady growth at the market level means to have a certain percentage increase in your donor-base. It is important to stress here that this means in terms of donors, not donations.

Economic problems, lack of humanitarian crises and events such as 9/11 may cause a decrease in the overall total donations an organization receives. However, under no circumstances should the total number of active donors go down. At this point, the percentage of increase depends on the leadership of the organization, and whether the organization wants to grow quickly or slowly. Each has its pros and cons. To grow quickly, you must commit more resources towards the marketing or fundraising efforts. From this, the percentage of management and fundraising expenses would usually be very high.

Steady growth does not mean 40 percent growth in 2001, 30 percent in 2002 and minus 20 percent in 2003. Over these years, there is a sizable growth. However, it would be better to see at least a 20 percent yearly growth in donor-base for the first ten years of the organization's life. At least ten percent for the next decade and at least seven percent in subsequent years should follow this. Steady growth requires careful consideration of several sensitive issues. The following are some recommendations to consider while utilizing the Missing-Link:

- *Devise new fundraising methods as the organization grows older and wiser.* In the first year or two, an organization may start raising funds through personal contacts and small public events. Then, it starts to build its mailing list for direct mailings, followed by large events such as fundraising dinners. Later on, as the mailing list grows and more public events are being held covering a larger geographical area, there must be other innovative ways to get more exposure, raising even more funds from new people and through various methods. These funds can be generated from direct mail campaigns, advertisements, automatic monthly withdrawal programs, Internet presentations, conventions, sales for nonprofit causes, promotional programs, Infomercials, investment, etc. The use of multimedia marketing techniques such as the Internet, E-mail blasts, videotapes, DVDs, and website banners are able to reach more people more effectively. Television advertising, although expensive, can also be a qualified springboard for the organization to reach a much wider market by designing and producing effectual ads and/or infomercials.

- *Budget a fixed percentage of annual income towards advertisement purposes only.* These funds are neither for direct fundraising activities (such as mailings), nor for reporting to current donors (such as newsletters). Doing this will enable the organization to gain constant growth in exposure as their income grows. For instance, an organization allocates next year's advertising budget at five percent of this year's forecasted income of five million dollars, totaling $250,000. If this organization maintains a yearly income growth at a rate of ten percent, then the organization would maintain increasing market exposure year after year at the same rate.

- *Do not jump from one potential market to another.* Organizations make a big mistake when they try to enter a new market and increase exposure by jumping from one market to another. For instance, advertising on Al-Jazeera this year, and on Pak-TV and ART next year is an extremely bad strategy that results in draining the resources of the organization, leading to inefficiency and waste of financial resources. At the end of the year, the organization will find that advertisement costs are 25 percent of their income. In addition, other expenses such as management and fundraising will be an additional 25 percent, leaving only 50 percent for programs. A much better way is to grow into a new market while still maintaining coverage in the market the organization already has. For example, an organization has been advertising on ART for three months. For the coming year, they have a larger TV advertisement budget, but the increase does not allow them to advertise on both ART and Al-Jazeera. They then have two choices: the first choice is to either continue advertising on ART by allocating additional funds for more ads, or the second to advertise only on Al-Jazeera. Clearly, the wise choice is to stay with ART.

- *Reach more people every year by direct mail.* This means you must reach more and more people by growing the mailing list you have. However, building ML is a very sensitive and scientific process. The mailing list should grow wisely as much as possible, as long as the organization is able to afford it.

A good rule of thumb is that the agency must be financially able to keep in touch with their current mailing list for at least seven mailings. Sending several mailings to a particular ML is more effective than only sending a few mailings to a larger ML.

GROWTH & STABILITY AT THE FIELD LEVEL

Since the main purpose behind creating nonprofit organizations is to provide programs and services to people in need, there must be steady growth in such services either in size, geographical distributions, or quality and kind of programs. Many organizations miss this issue by concentrating totally on growth at the market level. For US-based Muslim charities operating internationally, the reasoning behind concentrating on marketing and fundraising is that their management and decision-makers are away from the field, which is usually overseas. Additionally, their boards are in the US, so naturally they will concentrate more on what they see within their own offices, and what happens in the US markets. However, a more careful look finds that the other way around can be more effective by paying closer attention to the main mission. By giving more at the field level, then these agencies will grow in a much easier way than they could have ever imagined.

Donors are becoming far more careful about how and for what purposes they contribute. There are many choices out there, and they tend to give to the organization they trust most. Trust and credibility depend on the programs and services the organization offers, and how efficient the organization is in allocating resources. Spending too much on marketing and advertising can backfire. Savvy donors know that all these expenses come at the expense of those in dire need. All the exposure at conventions, and advertising on costly satellite stations are sometimes deemed as being luxurious.

It "Ain't" Rocket Science

Growing at the field level is not rocket science. Naturally, when and if an organization grows at the market level, and they allocate financial resources fairly, they will be able to grow at the field level. Hopefully, the following advice will help while utilizing the Missing-Link:

- *Keep a ceiling on the total expenses spent on management and fundraising so that a sizable percentage of income can go towards programs.* For instance, it is understood that in the first two to four years of an organization's life, management and fundraising expenses can be high—sometimes reaching 50 percent or more of income. However, it should not remain that high after the organization has established its name and initial market. USAID standards are that only organizations with management and fundraising expenses of less than 40 percent may be considered for membership. A US-based charity with an income of five million dollars or more can live wisely, and still grow steadily with up to 20 percent of its budget (one million dollars or more) allocated for non-program expenses. To be more generous with such spending, it would be surprising to consider truthfully what remains for programs. Consider management costs of branches and field offices, personnel in the field, and logistics costs such as transportation, travel, storage and others, which are usually considered as indirect program expenses.

- *Do not rely totally on local humanitarian organizations for implementing your programs.* Clearly in many cases, it is impossible to do it all alone. Local charities do give help in many areas, but it is a huge mistake to rely totally on them. An organization has to build their own field offices, establish their own programs, and supply experienced staff. Otherwise, they will have nothing once a program is gone, and they will be out of the loop once an emergency is over. Unless the organization is a granting agency, they should grow by building their own field programs and field offices as they continue to grow at the market level.

- *Establish more developmental programs.* Developmental programs tend not only to benefit people more, but also last longer with a small on-going budget. For instance, during the Kosovo crisis, an organization spent $1.4 million within three months on refugee emergency relief efforts. Subsequently, it spent $300,000 over the next 12 months for developmental programs with more lasting effects, resulting in programs more valued by donors.

- *Always keep at least $300,000 in reserve funds in the bank for emergency situations.* Crises such as natural disasters will not wait a single day while worrying about the availability of the agency's initial funds to react. An agency must move to the field level first, then directly to the market level. Unfortunately, many inexperienced organizations do it the other way around. Once an emergency arises, their total concentration is devoted towards how to raise funds, and then as funds start to arrive they would react. This proves to be quite ineffective at both the market and field levels.

- *Have two to three program officers at the head office whose responsibilities would be coordinating and supervising programs at the field.* This includes determining how funds are allocated, coordinating programs, and traveling to the field on a frequent basis for evaluation and reporting back to headquarters. This team would be considered an emergency task force set to immediately travel once an emergency occurs. The team would not only be first responders in a time of crisis, but it may also be the organization's communication channel with other grant agencies and international relief organizations. Experience shows that such staff can have very powerful PR advantage over those agencies that talk about a cause, but have no practical experience.

VI. Assessing Your Case

In order to practically benefit from this chapter, please consider the situation of the organization you are a part of, in light of what we have presented here. By answering these questions, you would be assessing your situation as well as identifying the areas where corrections are required. Also, you are encouraged to go back to review the specific materials of the chapter for clarification on some questions.

- *Is it possible for your donors or potential donors to witness first-hand your organization's programs and achievements?*

- *When your organization is faced with a needy cause, is it successfully able to present this situation knowledgeably and with measured emotion to those who may donate towards it?*

- *Can your organization effectively report to your donors what their contributions are doing through reports and multimedia materials, allowing you to bring "samples" of these programs to them?*

- *Do you have an individual or department responsible for all media activities such as writing reports, news stories and press releases, designing graphic print media, maintaining your website and issuing E-mail blasts, and producing multimedia presentations?*

- *Can you easily and specifically identify your organization's market? Do you focus your marketing efforts only on that market?*

- *How do you keep high visibility and constant exposure in your market?*

- *Do you have a broad donor base? If not, what strategy would you use to acquire significantly more donors?*

- *Do you have presence on the Internet where people can visit your website and learn about your organization, what it does, where it operates, as well as make online donations?*

- *Does your organization have an internal communication system where all your organization's programs, departments, and branches report on a monthly basis, and in a standard format, to senior management on past achievements and future plans?*

- *Does your organization see a boost during a humanitarian crisis, then experience a dramatic drop off after the crisis ends?*

- *Does your organization budget a fixed percentage of annual income for advertising purposes?*

Chapter

11.

Direct Mail:

Maximizing Revenue

Nobody likes to receive junk mail. Most people simply toss it into the "circular file" the minute they get it. Direct mail, which includes leaflets, brochures, catalogs, and other printed advertisements that are delivered by a postal service, is usually considered to be junk mail. The cost of reaching each individual consumer is more with direct mail than with other forms of advertising or fundraising. So why concentrate on a medium that will probably be thrown away? Because of its effectiveness: with specialized mailing lists, the solicitor is virtually assured that their product will reach its target more efficiently.

A slightly higher cost factor is not the only cautionary issue with direct mail. Direct mail communications can help or hinder an agency's fundraising efforts as well as all of its achievements by over-saturation, bookkeeping oversights, and poor communications. An organization's work and credibility can be damaged when it issues too many "emergency appeals", does not issue receipts on time, or sends out conflicting messages to potential donors and/or constituents. Confusion, and sometimes anger, can be the results when the organization fails to keep its supporters up to date through a newsletter, or sends out the same message too many times.

I. Getting Started in Direct Mail

Direct mail is not cheap, nor is it an easy way to raise funds. It takes money to make money. It also requires marketing skills, patience and a particular type of management ability. Despite all of this, direct mail solicitation is still one of the most effective ways to build and cultivate a financial base. Over time, this will provide a nonprofit with predictable continuing support.

Getting started in direct mail is not an easy task, especially if one has exaggerated expectations. The general rule of thumb to determine a successful initial mailing is having a return rate of one in a hundred; on subsequent appeals, second gifts from those who initially responded are usually one in ten. An organization should be prepared to lose money on its initial appeal. This is inevitable; however, despite this loss, the investment will help build the donor list yielding continuing dividends over time. The newly acquired donors should continue giving for years. Many will increase their giving frequency, and may even increase the size of their gift. Achieving this enormous potential takes hard work and perseverance through a carefully orchestrated schedule of additional mailings, as well as telephone contact. In most cases, this means that an organization's most active donors should receive six or more mail communications per year.

Since the United States is very large, and with Muslims being scattered all over, it is not easy or convenient to reach potential donors only at group gatherings. Therefore, for Muslim nonprofits, direct mailing constitutes one of the most common means of reaching potential donors. Despite increases in postage costs, the US Postal Service is still the cheapest and most reliable worldwide.

Direct marketing is a very common fundraising tool for the nonprofit sector in the US. Yet, it can be the most expensive, least efficient fundraising tool if not done correctly. However, it can also be the fastest, most effective way to reach a large number of people with minimal effort. Direct mailing can easily fail if it does not target the correct market, if it uses the wrong data (mailing list), or if it is done without long-term commitment and persistence.

In short, the characteristics of direct mailing are:

- Reliability

- Fast and effective

- Requires initial capital

- Long-term.

BUILDING A BROAD DONOR BASE THROUGH MAIL SOLICITATION

An organization that seeks gifts from a diverse pool of sources is not only promoting its own financial health, but is making itself more resilient to downwards trends in giving. This organization is also making itself more aware of the market requirements, more sensitive to changes within its environment, and more responsive to the service and support requirements of its donor base. When an organization depends on a single type (i.e. grants) or a single source of funding (i.e. a particular foundation or corporation), it is eventually limiting itself, and possibly sealing its own doom. While only the smallest of agencies might be able to get away with this type of funding strategy, it is simply too risky. There is also a danger that a single large donor may have undue influence on the priorities of the nonprofit. Having a larger donor base will ensure that the organization's dependence on any single large funding will not tilt decisions to the benefactor's advantage, causing a loss of autonomy. Direct mail solicitation is the main strategy to acquire a broad donor base, even though most donors give small amounts by mail, usually between $25 to $150, depending on the organization's credibility and ability to convince donors to give large amounts.

Money is not the only focus of direct mail. It is often used to cultivate and recruit volunteers or prospective venues for fundraising activities. Direct mail is a flexible tool that can be used to serve a number of organizational strategies, including:

- Growth—by building a large donor base or membership list

- Involvement—by persuading supporters to become actively involved

- Stability—by reaching and maintaining an optimum level of direct mail fundraising activity

- Visibility—by publicizing the organization's work among the general public or a particular constituency.

DONOR ACQUISITION

Donor acquisition, also called prospect mailings or cold mail, is designed to persuade potential donors to make their first gift. With a few exceptions, acquisition mailings are relatively expensive, and are often produced in quantities from 50,000 to more than a million, and costing from 25 to 50 cents each. These mailings are also sent rather infrequently—at perhaps two to four times per year—with a response rate typically ranging from one-half to two percent. Although less than that can also happen, this should not be considered a failure. The costs associated with this type of mailing can easily add up to be greater than the contributions received. Their success or failure is generally evaluated in terms of "donor acquisition cost" which translates to the difference between the cost of the mailing and the amount of return generated in contributions, divided by the number of donors acquired. For example, if a $50,000 mailing generates proceeds of $40,000 and 2,500 new donors, the acquisition cost is $4 per donor. Although there is a net loss of $10,000, the key is to calculate the donor's value over time.

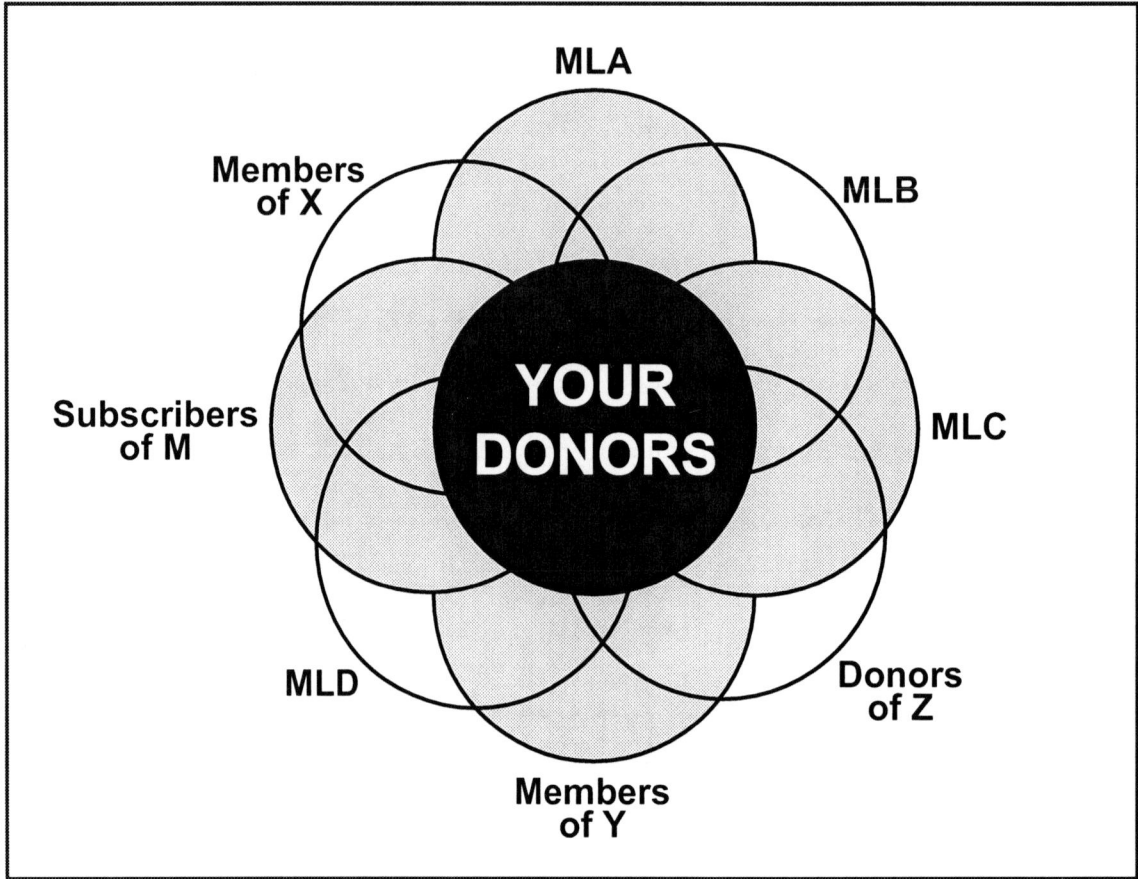

Figure 11-A

DONOR RESOLICITATION

By contrast, donor resolicitation, or donor renewal mailings—often called seasonal or special appeals—have a time value. Usually, these are written afresh for each appeal, and are sent in smaller quantities to a select group of donors, costing more. Their response rates typically fall between six to 12 percent when sent to current active donors. The following is a summation of the broad differences between acquisition and resolicitation mailings:

	Acquisition	Resolicitation
Purpose	*(Build Donor Base)*	*(Generate Income)*
Cost per piece	$0.25-0.50	$0.40-0.75
Quantity per mailing	50,000-250,000	1,000-25,000
Response rate	0.5%-2%	3%-12%

Prospecting for Donors

Those who are willing to give their money for a nonprofit's cause usually fall into two groups: those who are personally inspired, touched, or motivated by the organization's cause, programs and/or services; and, those who are not personally touched by the organization, but are impressed by its professionalism. It is for this very important reason that an effective fundraising mailing must know who cares about their organization, and who shares in the organization's belief that it benefits a particular community and deliver its message to those potential donors.

Once an organization is able to determine who will give and why, then the question of when they will give can be answered. For Muslims, the why is for religious reasons, and the when is because there are seasons for the bulk of Muslim giving. As well, soliciting for money requires some form of talent. Donors need to be convinced, cajoled and compelled to give through the right message with which you approach them. This means that the communication piece delivered in person or by mail asking for the funds must earn the donor's respect, and make a credible case for support.

After all of the convincing has been done, the issue of "in what form" a donation should be addressed. Cash is the universally accepted and expected form, whether by check or credit card; however, donors at times prefer to give whatever commodity works to their best advantage. This could mean stocks, bonds, property, etc. An organization should never refuse donations in any form, since almost anything can be turned into cash eventually.

II.   Elements of Successful Mail Campaigns

For an organization to succeed in its mailing campaigns, it has to pay attention to:

- which market it targets

- the contact list it uses

- the message it wants to deliver

- the medium and presentation of the message

- the timing.

TARGETING THE RIGHT MARKET

Since the percentage of return for a particular mailing depends primarily on the quality of the Mailing List (ML) used, this first condition deals with how to acquire the right ML, and how to maintain it. There are many sources to acquire new MLs. Some are free, which only require special contacts; others are not. Before mentioning several sources for MLs, it is best to define what could be considered as a good mailing list for Muslim nonprofits. Since potential donors to such organizations are in their majority Muslim, mailing lists of primarily Muslim names should be targeted. However, not all Muslims donate. For instance, some American Muslim groups may have their own local challenges and/or specific causes for which they donate to. They also sometimes have limited resources; therefore, these groups should not be the primary focus for overseas programs.

It is not an easy task to focus on a specific ethnic group. However, traditionally, higher donations are seen for certain regional programs or causes because of heightened sensitivities of Muslims from those regions. For instance, experience shows that Palestinians react more to Palestinian causes than to poverty in the Horn of Africa or to the Kashmiri issue. Therefore, some selection must be made among the general Muslim population depending on the cause or campaign the organization is launching, if possible. Successful campaigns would always zoom-in to select the best ML for each mailing.

Sources of Muslim Mailing Lists

• Purchasing of Muslim mailing list (ML) from commercial corporations such as InfoUSA and ethnic technologies based on ethnicity and economic situations.

• Acquiring data for members of professional Muslim associations such as Pakistani Physicians Association, Arab Physicians Association, Muslim Scientists and Engineers Association.

• Acquiring ML of Muslim umbrella organizations such as ISNA, ICNA, and MAS.

• Advertising in publications, websites and TV that Muslims read, access or view. Advertisements in Muslim media outlets are an expensive selection process that let you slowly gather the right donors for your fundraising causes.

• There are many ways for an organization to gather personal information to help increase donors and base. The two most important methods are through Udhiya and Fitrah programs, since most religious Muslims perform Udhiya and pay Fitrah every year, allowing these Islamic organizations to act on their behalf. Additionally, information can be harvested when Muslims visit an organization's website to access prayer schedules, for instructions on how to calculate Zakat, find addresses and directions to mosques, and so on. To be successful, an organization must be creative in ways to invite potential donors to give their personal information and mailing address.

• Making some promotions at conventions or on websites offering certain gifts or incentives attractive to Muslims can be used to invite visitors to join a ML or an E-mail list.

• Collection of attendees' addresses at public events such as fundraising dinners.

• Obtaining names and addresses from membership lists of Muslim Students Associations (MSA) and mosques directly from their management or indirectly through public events.

• Exchanging MLs, especially with non-competing organizations, is a proven way to obtain this information. However, do not exchange with similar organizations that direct mail for similar causes. Organizations should not give or exchange the donor list of the organization. This surely would have a long-term negative affect on both organizations.

It is best to be aware that attempting to get a new ML for potential donors does not necessarily mean that the organization will get a clean mailing list. An organization's reliable ML has two characteristics: first, it is dynamic—it is always maintained by adding potentially good contacts and deleting proven bad contacts. New ML contacts are in, while others are out on a continuous basis. Secondly, good mailing lists grow in the quantity and quality of information contained in them.

Maintenance of Mailing List

There is nothing more wasteful or disheartening than sending out a mailing of 50,000 pieces and have hundreds, or even thousands, returned for incorrect addresses or names. Organizations can save money, time and effort by avoiding such incidents through simple maintenance of their ML, which should include:

• *Correction:* Correcting addresses through comparing personal information provided in the donation card against the original information, Presorted First Class postcard, and specialized agencies that provide this service.

• *Updating:* Cleaning the ML for duplications. Quite frequently, for many reasons, more than one record is created for the same household. According to the US Postal Service, approximately ten percent of the US population relocates every year (the rate might be higher for students and immigrants). Therefore, there must be a constant effort to update the ML for any newly acquired information.

• *Completion:* An organization's records might start with only the address of a potential donor, but with time the telephone number, ethnicity, E-mail address, donation history and any other useful facts might be added.

• *Addition:* Mailing lists should always be added to and kept current. Additionally, it is important to always have a key with every record regarding the source of the ML, such as ISNA_Con2003 or Dinner92004. This comes in handy for periodic evaluation purposes of its return for different sources, enabling the organization to know when the information was added, and when it should be removed.

- *Deletion:* Many organizations add to their ML, yet fail to have a policy or process to delete ineffective portions of it. Research indicates that retiring or deactivating any ML portion which did not donate or respond after receiving seven mailings is recommended. The organizations might choose to do so after six, eight or ten mailings. However, to keep a name indefinitely is very unprofessional and wastes resources. There must be a policy and process to junk an ineffective ML. As previously mentioned, not all people donate, so sending one mailing after another will narrow down those who do and those who do not.

- *Certification:* It is helpful to certify every ML yearly, such as CASE certification and Zip + 4. This step is important not only to clean and sort the ML for lower postage rates, but also for frequent scrutiny to sort out bad addresses.

AT THE RIGHT TIME

Sseasonal programs require careful timing such as Zakatul-Mal, Zakat-al-Fitr, and Udhiya. Imagine a Zakat-al-Fitr mailing reaching people six weeks before 'Eid al-Fitr, or Udhiya reaching people after 'Eid ul-Adha. In both cases, it will not work. Being prepared for the unexpected and having a plan of action in place develops donor trust and ensures a quick fundraising response.

Also in cases of crisis or religious obligations, launching an appeal at the right time is important for its success. The failure experienced by some Islamic organizations in dealing with the Bosnia crisis came because most organizations were not prepared. They started their campaigns late; therefore, donors did not respond. In contrast, the Kosovo emergency relief campaign was quite successful for other organizations. Correctly anticipated, the situation in Kosovo erupted in a similar fashion to that in Bosnia. With this information, agencies began to prepare for the situation early. In anticipation of the crisis, one organization was able to found a field office at the Albanian border, and then opened an office in Tirana and hired enough people even before the crisis began. They also dispatched a media crew to shoot a video documentary and collected footage. Within three months, the tape was produced, duplicated, and stored for release at the right time. The same day the situation erupted, a letter was written and readied to be sent via a presorted first class mail, which took two days within the postal service's system.

Altogether, within three to four days after the crisis erupted, a letter was in the hands of people telling them that a plan was in place. The letter stated the agency's immediate appeal seeking a large budget to achieve a list of short-term goals. Following this, the previously prepared videos were mailed to all listed mosques, Islamic centers, and MSAs. A letter inviting them to hold fundraising events accompanied the video. In this way, they could help to raise funds, or they could contact the agency to provide a speaker. Additionally, the video was sent to all donors. The response was tremendous! All of the agency's available speakers were subsequently booked for four to five months in advance. Although the agency prepared well for a positive response, it needed additional staff because it did not anticipate the high level of reaction. This was such a success because the agency learned from a past mistake, in addition to correctly evaluating a developing situation through careful insight.

Another case that needs to be addressed is a sudden crisis such as a natural disaster. The 1999 earthquake in Turkey is such an example. No one can anticipate and prepare for disasters like this. The situation might be compounded if the organization had no operations in the country in question. Most relief organizations project themselves globally. In a crisis such as a severe earthquake or a tsunami, most organizations would aim to create a brand name by seeking to have potential donors connect them with an "immediate response". In these situations, the agency should react immediately. On that same day, a direct mailing should be written and printed to go out in the next business day's mail by Presorted First Class. This letter should include a general message stating that "the need is great and we require your financial help to implement emergency relief efforts". A team should be dispatched to the devastated area for immediate needs-assessment, and to provide the necessary aid.

As timing is very important, the organization's website should be updated to contain direct information from the team in the field about what relief is being provided. If not enough information is immediately available, the website content does not have to specify too many details at first, but can be updated as information trickles in. Additionally, it may become necessary to relocate a few staff members to that area from the organization's closest outpost. It is important to have photos taken to document relief activities, such as pitching tents and handing out food. These photos should be posted on the Internet within days to update donors or potential donors. By the time people received the letter and accessed the website for more information, the organization's volunteers would be there in pictures, making it clear what is needed and at what cost. Donors usually react when a crisis presents itself in the mainstream media, which could be a great support. After a week of media coverage, most natural disaster cases and updated information dwindle, and charitable donations for the event drop off sharply. Therefore, in these situations, your main objective must be to reach your market and your potential donors within two to four days of the disaster while the mass media—especially TV—is still covering the situation.

WITH THE RIGHT MESSAGE

Even if you deliver your mailing to the right market and at the right time, the message itself and the way it is presented has a great impact on the reaction of that targeted donor. The mailing's message is what you say and how you say it in terms of what you intend to raise the funds for. That is the cause or the program behind the marketing piece. A well-presented piece states what you will specifically accomplish, what justifications you offer to sell it with, and how you can do all of this.

The Message

Choosing the right message in term of contents and presentation accounts for over 70 percent of the success of the campaign. For instance, in early 1993 when the Bosnian crisis started, one agency's board decided not to shift their attention to this situation, but keep focusing on its current programs at hand which required lots of effort and funding. However, the media bombarded donors with what was happening in Bosnia; for two years, their emotions and attention were focused on what they saw on TV. The organization paid dearly for these two years of bad strategy, losing many of their donors, because their main message was focused other regions and causes.

There is no typical fundraising letter. They do not follow the same form or function as a business letter, personal correspondence or even advertising copy. Direct mail has its own rules and rhythms; therefore, the following five ingredients should be essential components of the solicitation letter:

- It establishes a one-on-one relationship or identification between the letter-signer and the person to whom it is addressed
- It presents an opportunity to participate in the organization by supporting a particular program
- It makes a compelling case for the program
- It establishes urgency
- It asks for a specific sum of money.

So, How Much Should You Ask For?

Making the fundraising campaign goal known to prospective donors is a very important strategy. Even though it is not acceptable to tell donors how much to give, it is a good idea to impart a campaign goal and a suggested amount, or provide a few options that are in line with a prospective donors' capacity to give.

If a fundraising campaign is to have a realistic chance at succeeding, an organization must:

- Evaluate donors' giving history
- Seek a realistic goal for the campaign
- Provide donors with a suggested gift amount or a few options.

People almost always want to know what the price is of something that they are going to buy. The same is true for charitable giving. Prospective donors need to be given an idea of what is appropriate and what the organization needs. The organization's solicitors must be ready with an answer of a specific dollar amount determined by a rating and evaluating process. Telling someone "to give whatever you can afford" is not a good answer. It is, after all, quite silly to ask a multi-millionaire to "give what you can afford". As is saying "give what you are comfortable with", as someone may only give $10 when the organization is in need of $100. "We would appreciate a gift in the range of $10 to $1,000" tells the prospect that the organization has not fixed their real needs. These responses are ambiguous at best. Setting a specific number, or a few suggested numbers, is giving the prospective donors something to shoot for. You must remember that the suggestion has to be presented in such a way that the prospective donor finds to be neither annoying nor demanding. Most donors will welcome and consider a request when it is made in the manner of the following example:

We are reaching out to the brothers and sisters of our Muslim community to raise $250,000 that we plan to use in the expansion of our daily Islamic school. These funds will assure that our community will continue to meet our children's educational needs; that we will be able to maintain, improve, and enhance our current educational programs and services, and have the opportunity to implement new ones to meet the growing needs of our community.

To help us meet our campaign goal, we hope that you will consider making a gift of $1,000. We are suggesting this amount because, as you can appreciate, a campaign of this magnitude and limited timeframe requires a certain number of leadership gifts at significant dollar levels. While this suggested amount was developed with that premise in mind, we recognize and understand that in the final analysis you will consider what is right for you. Of course, whatever you can give will be deeply appreciated.

However, there is another method that can be applied to donors from different levels. From past evaluations, how much you should know what to ask for is based upon your specific market. A rule of thumb is that you should never ask for an amount that is less than the average donation you receive. It is recommended that the agency ask for an amount that is at least four times the average donation, reducing this to the average donation. For instance if your average donation is $250, you can say something like:

... Please rush a contribution in the amount of $1000, $500, or $250 for the relief efforts in Southeast Asia for Tsunami victims, ... etc.

American statistics recommend asking for a very small donation amount from non-donors such as $10, $20, or $30. Although asking for these modest amounts is not recommended, this approach is acceptable for those who are first-time donors. In subsequent mailings, the request should be for a significantly higher figure. It is also recommended to ask for varying amounts from different categories. For instance, ask those who have donated $20 to give $40 or more next time, those who donated $30 to give $60 and more, those who donated over $100 to give $200 or more, and so on. Since Muslims are quite generous and donate well, we recommend not being conservative in the amounts requested.

Additionally, inform donors what their contribution will accomplish, or what it will be used for. Use a bulleted format if more than three programs are stated, such as:

- *Your $50 will provide a food basket for a needy family in Iraq for a complete month.*

- *Your $750 will provide a clean water well to a village in Ethiopia.*

- *Your $100 will provide five needy orphaned children with school supplies and clothing.*

Tips for a Successful Message

Writing a successful message is not an impossibility. Even those with little prior experience in writing a campaign letter can still gain a modest return if these recommendations are observed:

- **Motivational:** Most contributions result from either a religious obligation or an emotional cause. An effective message and style should be mindful of that. A fast paced style with short sentences that address the heart of the issue is recommended. It is recommended to use an example that anyone can relate to, such as a brief story to describe the need and suffering of a victim. The message should make the reader feel the pain the needy faces, as well as their responsibility towards the victim. Build empathy.

a. *Islamic Message:* This is mainly why Muslims give; therefore, the message should have a clear Islamic touch, such as an Islamic cause or obligation. Zakat and Sadaqah are the two primary reasons behind Muslim giving. It is very important to use the right Islamic terms, and clearly explain why it is an obligation, or why it is highly recommended to give for a particular cause. A well used verse or Hadith can be effective and meaningful.

- *Concise:* Although many western NGO training books recommend long letters with liberal use of underlined text, our own experiences show that the opposite is true when targeting Muslim audiences, as they have a tendency to be drawn to concise text. To guarantee that more of a piece will be read, make it relatively short—no longer than one page in length.

- *Bilingual:* If targeting the Arab market where English is the second language, it is proven to be more effective to present the message in English and Arabic. However, if the targeted ethnic market is the Indian-Pakistani community, we recommend presenting the message in English only.

- *Personal:* It is always important to have a style that communicates and relates to the reader. If it is in Arabic, do not use a plural style as is commonly used when talking to a group. Direct the point at one person: the reader. As well, the letter should be signed by a recognizable personality from the organization. If possible, greet the addressee by name. However, if it is technically not possible to do so, you might say: "Dear Supporter" or "Dear Donor", etc.

- *Clear:* It is important to clearly and repeatedly state what you want your reader to do. Ask the reader to donate in as many as three places within the letter but in different styles. For example: "your contribution is highly needed"; "please, rush your donation of at least $100 today", or "PS: Please note that we just dispatched an emergency relief team to the victims of this disaster, and we cannot do much without your participation. Please mail your gift today in the return envelope".

- *Specific:* Ask for a specific dollar amount or amounts as stated earlier.

The Presentation

A piece can be very well written, but presented so badly that it fails. Therefore, write a smartly presented piece aimed to make the receiver want to read it, or at least presented in a way that they get the message without reading the whole text. Also, clarify what you are asking of him/her without them having to do much thinking. Some tips for a successful presentation are:

- *Comprehensive packet:* The most recommended package includes the letter, the return envelope, and the donation form mailed in an outgoing envelope. However, all of this can be incorporated into a self-mailer, such as a multi-panel brochure. The four pieces above must be designed with a comprehensive concept sharing one focus. The outgoing envelope should have a statement and/or image about the mailing. The donation card should repeat the same message in different wording. The letter should have a related headline, etc. All should use the same colors (preferably only two colors), and share the same concept, cause and style.

- *Emphasis added:* All of the material must be laid out in such a way that the message presented is clear to the reader, without them having to put too much effort into reading the entire text. In the letter, this is accomplished by underlining a few selected statements and presenting a headline, a caption or a quotation, and/or an image that immediately captures the reader's attention. Use a postscript message below the signature that imparts an urgent message aimed at the reader for an instantaneous response. It is recommended that the PS statement be hand written, or in a different font and ink color. Statistics show that even if readers do not read the entire letter, they are generally drawn to read the underlined text and the PS statement.

- *Use Bullets:* If you want to relate some statistical figures, put them in bullet format at the top of the letter before addressing the donor. Use sources for more authenticity if you prefer, and be aware that it is not necessary to use complete sentences. Some examples:

- 75% under poverty line

- Over 50% unemployed

- 5,000 children below 5 years of age die monthly.

• *Use Images:* To put it bluntly, a photo is worth a thousand words. The use and impact of an effective image can quickly relay the message, especially when accompanied by a good caption. It is not recommended to use more than two images per mailing. However, even when no images are used, a mailing can still be effective. This can be achieved by using an alternative method like an effective headline, quotation, statistics, or a visual presentation such as a chart.

• *Be Creative:* The layout of the materials and the graphic design of the whole packet provides the reader with their first impression. Do not try to save money in this area. Make sure you give this work to a well-qualified artist, and work with them to emphasize the intended message. Outsource the work to an experienced person if necessary. The effective use of graphics, general layout, colors and fonts are able to clarify and emphasize the points where you want a reader's attention. For instance, a donation card can be confusing, especially when trying to include all the necessary information in a limited format. With a good layout, the reader should easily be able to understand the presented information, such as method of donation, programs donated for, and personal information.

III.   How to Maximize Your Returns

To increase the percentage of returns on Mailings, the following is highly suggested:

• *Donors' Update:* Keep donors informed about programs through newsletters, PR events, advertisements, reports and brochures.

• *High Exposure:* Keep a constant presence in the targeted market. Potential donors must see the agency so frequently that it sticks in their mind that they should donate towards its promoted causes.

• *Marketing Mix:* This is the most effective marketing strategy an organization must follow if it wants to keep its donor base growing. In short, it means using different marketing tools to target the same market. Spreading marketing resources thin is highly discouraged. An example of this would be targeting a very wide market with only one campaign, such as sending a 400,000-piece mailing one time to a single large market, without any other marketing campaign to target that same market. Additionally, it is not recommended to target different market sectors through different methods, such as advertising only on TV for the Pakistani community and only sending mailings to the Arab community. Be visible to your target market. Be seen in the mosques, in publications, by mail, and in the websites they visit. To further illustrate this example, consider a campaign that targeted the Pakistani market by highlighting a humanitarian cause in Kashmir. The strategy was designed to reach a mainly Pakistani market through a few select channels with a budget of $200,000 that was used for two large-scale mailings to about 300,000 Muslim households. Alternatively, the campaign can more effectively concentrate on a smaller targeted market with a mixed marketing strategy:

1. Over the next 12 months, send out four mailings to 75,000-ML of Pakistani ethnicity.

2. For the entire year, advertise the campaign in Pakistan Times, Islamic Horizon and The Message which are primarily read by Pakistani communities.

3. Advertise on PakTV during Ramadan when donations are expected to pick up.

4. Choose 15 mosques of primarily Pakistani membership to hold fundraising events during the same period.

IV.   Types of Direct Mail Campaigns

There are five major types of Direct Mailings. The following will discuss each one, as well as how to capitalize on them in order to receive the maximum return.

ANNUAL CAMPAIGNS

Although a nonprofit's regular ongoing expenses are offset by an annual campaign which is conducted each and every year, the funds raised by these campaigns is also applied to its programs. This campaign's funds are usually the organization's primary source of unrestricted contributed income, and should be a mainstay of its fundraising efforts whose goals ought to include:

- Stimulating the contribution of unrestricted funds

- Raising awareness and acceptance of the charity

- Developing a base of knowledgeable volunteers

- Cultivating donors for future giving.

Annual campaigns are more common for Islamic centers and other membership-based organizations, not necessarily humanitarian charities. However, every nonprofit in need of contributed income should conduct an annual campaign each year. The organization should estimate an obtainable goal for each source of annual fund income by listing the previous year's achievements, identifying what portion of that income will not be repeatable, and estimate expected new gifts and increases. From this information, the organization should be able to project the total amount of contributions that can be realistically achieved.

A pool of proven donors and a predictable base of supporters can be built upon the foundation of a well-planned and executed annual campaign. Most first time donors give during an organization's annual campaign. Repeat contributors are identified as a loyal and established group who shows caring and concern for the organization.

The annual campaign is so important to an organization's annual funding that if a non-profit does not have the money to do both an annual and a special-purpose campaign, the special purpose should be set aside for the annual campaign. Since the annual campaign is a broad-based fundraising effort directed at a large number of prospective donors, both the overall goal and the average gift are usually significantly smaller than those of other campaigns. Annual campaigns are broad-based in nature, and typically have thousands or tens of thousands of potential donors.

Nonprofits should never assume that it is better not to ask for more money with each year's campaign. Expenses are bound to go up; therefore, failing to target an increased amount is the single most devastating mistake an organization can make in its annual campaign. To increase a donor's contribution to an annual campaign, a very useful tool is the creation of a membership program where donors who give at a certain level attain the designation of "Friend of (organization name)". This pseudo title can be inflated with each higher stage of giving such as going from "Contributing Friend", to "Supporting

Friend", to "Sustaining Friend". For very large gifts, an organization can impart the honor of "Benefactor", "Founder", "President's Circle", etc. Be creative in appropriately recognizing donors for their generosity, while making certain that the distinction bestowed upon the top donors is recognized in the annual report. An organization might even place their best donors' names on plaques on a wall dedicated for this purpose in their organization's building. Not only does this type of recognition please the donors, but it may also elicit further donations from them or others who may want the same honor.

SEASONAL MAILINGS

Whether Muslim or non-Muslim humanitarian charities, most of these organizations have seasonal mailings. We know that all western nonprofits have their Christmas mailing as the single most important mailing of the year. For many of these organizations, this is their only mailing sent out during the year. For Muslim organizations, the most important two seasonal mailings are the Ramadan and the Udhiya mailings.

RAMADAN MAILING

Since most people pay their Zakat in Ramadan, during which Sadaqah and Fitrah are also paid, Ramadan is the most important season for Muslim nonprofits. If invested wisely, one-third to one-half of the yearly income typically comes during this season. The following are a few tips to capitalize on the Ramadan season:

• Increase your organization's visibility a month before Ramadan, and lasting through the end of Ramadan

• Do two mailings to your donor-base for this season, which can be done in one of two ways:

– Mail your newsletter so that it reaches people two to three weeks before Ramadan, with Ramadan and its programs as the main message. Then send out a separate Zakat/Ramadan mailing so that it reaches people around the 10th of Ramadan. The newsletter serves as preparation for people by promoting the organization and reporting on its achievements, by delivering a message, and by sending a direct invitation to give;

- Send the Zakat/Ramadan mailing so that it reaches people around the first day of Ramadan with a direct invitation to give, including information about the different programs in Ramadan. Follow this up by mailing a Presorted First Class postcard so that it reaches people around five days before 'Eid. This post card's message of "'Eid Mubarak" will serve as a reminder that if they have not paid their Zakat, Fitrah or Sadaqah, it is not too late. "Mail it today; call us to pay it over the telephone, or pay it online". This card has three purposes: First, it is a good final reminder to the target market before the end of Ramadan, and is proven to work. Secondly, it is a good gesture to deliver 'Eid greetings to those people on an organization's ML. Thirdly, sending a Presorted First Class postcard is the most effective way to clean the ML. It is highly recommended to send a mailing once a year. Although an agency can do this for either occasion of 'Eid al-Fitr or 'Eid ul-Adha, it has been found to better serve more of a purpose during 'Eid al-Fitr.

- The organization must prove that they are ready for Ramadan by being specific about their Ramadan programs. Provide donors with complete information about what the goals in Ramadan are, what areas the organization will concentrate on, and what the cost of such programs will be. For example, a statement such as 'This Ramadan we will provide food aid to over 50,000 families in Iraq, Afghanistan and Ethiopia' illustrates the agency's specific objectives for Ramadan.

- Provide information about what Zakat and Fitrah are, and how to calculate Zakat-ul-Mal. Provide a tool to help people estimate their Zakat dues. Establishing a Zakat Hotline to answer Zakat related questions is a proven success. Additionally, providing a Zakat calculation worksheet and an automatic Zakat calculator online will not only draw donors, but will help add to an organization's mailing list.

Successful Udhiya Mailing

This is another seasonal mailing that could be a financial liability. If not done carefully, the program will not break even; although, it does bring new donors to the organization. A few tips for a successful Udhiya season are:

- Estimate how much you expect to receive in Adahi, and send the money to where you expect to perform the Udhiya about a month before 'Eid. Then calculate and supply the corrected fund amounts as soon as you know by how much donations have exceeded the estimates, if any. This facilitates the logistics as the costs of sheep and cattle increase just before 'Eid. Being proactive saves money in terms of cost and transportation. Do not be afraid to purchase more animals than projected. If fewer funds are received (which can be the case for Udhiya in most countries), it is permissible to allocate part of Zakat towards this project to make up the difference.

- Add at least $5 per lamb and $10 per cow for operational costs.

- Suggest an additional general Sadaqah with each Udhiya, since it is proven that most people will add an additional $10 to $30 to their donation. This will help defray the extra costs accrued from this project.

- Neatly lay out the different choices and costs per Udhiya per country. The organization should invite people to give multiple Udhiya by suggesting a country or two where the need is greater.

EMERGENCY APPEALS

Emergency or urgent appeals are special mailings that are not seasonal; they are intended to be a reaction toward a certain crisis, either sudden or developing. These kinds of appeals are used when a quick emergency relief operation is vital, such as when cases of a natural disaster like an earthquake, flood, and severe drought occur, or when refugees or civilians are displaced in an armed conflict.

Tips for Maximum Return of Emergency Appeals

Following are some suggestions that make all the difference in the response of donors with such mailings:

• Do not overdo them. Urgent appeals are supposed to be an invitation to support the organization in coping with an emergency. If overdone, readers will not take them seriously, and such appeals will lose their urgency. How often such an appeal should be done varies depending on the need and crisis. This ranges from none in certain years, to as many as three per year. More than that is too much.

• Synchronize your appeal with the mass media coverage. A rule of thumb is that your emergency appeal will be successful if it reaches people while mass media is still covering a certain disaster; therefore, issue the appeal as fast as humanly possible. For instance, in cases of natural disaster, an appeal should go on the press the same day the disaster happens and should preferably be mailed by First Class that day, but no later than the next day.

• Use human faces and stories, as they are the most effective way to have people relate to disasters. A photo of the devastation that is actually happening is very effective.

A Case Study Example:
Drought in the Horn of Africa

In 1999 there was an anticipated drought developing in the Horn of Africa, mainly in Ethiopia. The media rarely addressed the issue. The drought was in Africa after all! One agency decided that they had to get involved. However, doing it the usual way—by issuing an emergency appeal and waiting for the money to come—would not work. In response, they dispatched a relief team for need assessment, sending along a TV crew to document the urgency and the situation. In the meantime, the agency issued an alarming article in their newsletter, followed by another in the next issue with a message from the Director about this developing crisis. For the next several months, an effective flier about the situation was inserted with every donation receipt. Within this period, their market was primed for an alarming appeal. How could potential donors feel the scope of the disaster if they did not see it? This quandary resulted in the production of a documentary entitled "Ethiopia: the Face of Hunger" which was sent out with an appeal letter. This method was effective because it brought the situation to the people front and center in their own living rooms. The donations received from this marketing strategy were quite helpful in setting up a $240,000 feeding center for three months. A secondary trip by doctors and additional relief workers, along with letters from the doctors documenting what they saw, ensured continuation of the programs for a while longer. In this situation, because mass media ignored the crisis, the organization created its own media campaign. This example illustrates that using creative methods to bring attention to causes not given adequate media coverage is quite effective.

- Have an emergency task team who are able to mobilize at a moment's notice. In a crisis, they could be an organization's best chance to be able to react effectively. Two to three people must be functionally trained to deal with humanitarian emergencies. Someone at your organization should be well trained in crisis management skills.

- Sometimes multiple crises happen at the same time or within relatively short time-frames. This is an important area to discuss: how to handle not only multiple crises, but also multiple programs. However, an agency must not launch two different appeals within the same period, targeting the same market. Rather, they must either concentrate on only one, or target a different market with a different appeal. One example of this was a military aggression that occurred in India's Gujarat province at the same time that one occurred in Palestine. In this instance, the agency targeted the Arab ethnicity with an appeal to help the victims of the Jenin refugee camp, and then separately targeted those of Indo-Pakistani ethnicity with another appeal to help the victims in Gujarat, India. During such a time, the data analysis an organization has at its disposal is one of its best assets. As well, the organization should not shy away from focusing on both issues in their newsletter or website for fear they will confuse or scatter people's attention.

- An agency must create media efforts to bring attention to an anticipated disaster. For example, a drought does not occur suddenly, but takes time to develop, and may not draw media attention until it is too late.

- Build a news dissemination network for literature distribution at mosques, special gatherings, Muslim student associations, and conventions, which could be a very effective method to reach people in case of crisis. This might be the fastest and most effective way to give a handout to many people, such as after Friday prayers. A well-established volunteer network can reach tens of thousands of people in the right target market within a day. In this era of the Internet, by keeping a current E-mail list, people can be notified quickly when a disaster occurs, directing them to your website.

PROGRAM CAMPAIGNS

Not all nonprofit mailings are either Seasonal or Emergency Appeals. Some mailings deal with non-emergency situations such as large developmental programs. For instance, it costs a great deal of money to establish and operate a vocational training center that serves 500 orphans or founding a hospital. As well, a program mailing can promote aid of 1,000 metric tons of rice or 100,000 blankets to refugees somewhere. Such projects require awareness and frequent promotion. The problem with long-term programs is that raising funds for them can be a challenge. Unfortunately, Muslims nowadays choose what cause to give to depending on their emotions, not the campaign's effectiveness. Most contributions are a reaction to one crisis after another, not as a proactive action to avoid the crisis. Consequently, when promoting developmental programs, more effort and careful strategy have to be applied.

TIPS FOR SUCCESSFUL PROGRAM MAILINGS

The following are a few suggestions to make sure such program mailings will succeed.

• *Make sure to keep donors or potential donors frequently updated about large projects or programs.* The organization must introduce the project clearly stating its justification, beneficiaries, and a budget. This can be done through a newsletter, and only then should a mailing be launched to raise funds for it. It is best to always mention the main highlights behind this project; but do not stop at that. The market should be kept abreast of what establishment stage the project is in, and what fundraising target needs to be met. From the beginning, the organization should specify a financial target to meet (i.e., two million dollars), and frequently inform donors how close this goal is to being reached. Get donors involved in the entire process by mentioning larger donations in the newsletter, as well as who volunteered to hold a benefit dinner for the cause, etc. For example, the organization can divide the funding required to establish a school into bite-sized pieces of 1,000 shares at $1,000 each. Then promote the fundraising process, and update donors based on this formula. The organization might want to mention who donates, and for how many shares, and so on.

- *When opening a large project such as a school, a hospital or vocational center, make certain to publicize this event very well.* Although the establishment cost might be met, there are operational expenses the organization needs to keep the project alive, and in the minds of donors. The running expenses should then be estimated by sponsorship shares, such as "$500 to sponsor the vocational training for a needy child for a year", or "$1,000 sponsors the treatment of 100 patients", etc.

- *Run an update report in the newsletter every quarter, six months, or yearly, depending on the project.* Together with these updates, promote the sponsorship of beneficiaries of this project.

- *Use fliers that are specifically designed to promote the project, and insert them with your routine mailings such as receipts and pledge reminder letters.* Such inserts are proven to work well without incurring any extra postage costs.

- *Promote the philosophy of self-sufficiency and long-term effectiveness when helping people to help themselves, by providing developmental programs to equip them with education and training.* This is the case especially when it comes to vocational training centers and schools. As the Chinese proverb says, "if you give a hungry man a fish, you feed him for a day; but if you teach him how to fish, you feed him for a lifetime". Also, stress the concept that it is more efficient in terms of cost to deal with the routes of poverty and diseases, than to provide relief to those affected with them.

OTHER TYPES OF DIRECT MAILINGS

Brochures, fliers and inserts are other types of materials which can be direct-mailed. There are two types of brochures: general-purpose corporate brochures, and program campaign brochures. Every organization should have one general-purpose brochure that represents what the organization is all about. It should include the organization's mission statement, and the main objectives the organization aims to fulfill, such as the services it provides and in what geographical areas. It is important to mention very concise and sum-marized data of previous years such as a table or chart stating the organization's achievements. This should also include one or more messages from beneficiaries whose lives were touched by the organization. There also must be a point of contact in the brochure for the reader to get more information such as telephone number and website. As well as an address where donations should be directed. Some brochures are self-mailers with a return envelope attached, which would definitely pay off, especially when used as handouts in public events and conventions.

General-purpose brochures or corporate brochures should not be too detailed about the programs. Additionally, they should not require frequent updating. The ideal situation is to update such a brochure once every year at the most, possibly using it for as much as three to five years. In contrast, a program brochure that promotes a particular program is specific and detailed, focused on one campaign, and used for a designated timeframe. A brochure of this kind usually states the objectives behind the program, what kind of services it would offer its beneficiaries, the stages of the project, the budget, and how donors should participate. It is more important here to have an attached self-mailer envelope than with the general-purpose brochure.

Fliers, posters and inserts are widely used for nonprofits. They are usually hand-distributed at public events such as Friday prayers and conventions, or prominently displayed for presentation. Items such as these can be printed in various sizes—from an insert small enough to fit inside a regular number nine envelope that does not require folding, to larger items such as posters. Regular letter-sized fliers are frequently used as inserts paired with a letter, or they are hand-distributed.

TIPS FOR EFFECTIVE BROCHURES, FLIERS AND INSERTS

Aside from hiring a professional marketing agency, most organizations can get the most mileage out of their mailers by using the following guidelines for successful fliers, brochures, and inserts:

– Use effective images. In most situations, one good photograph would be enough; however, sometimes more than one photo can be used on a larger flier.

- Fliers and inserts should not contain too much text. Brochures, however, should have detailed text.

- Use effective headlines, quotations, or statistics that deliver the message at a glance.

- Use bulleted format statements such as:

  - 2,500 MT of Rice Delivered

  - 1,500 Tents Provided

  - 2 Mobile Clinics in Operation

- Or use situation figures such as:

  - 3 Million People Displaced

  - Over 150,000 Civilian Victims

  - Over 60,000 Homes Destroyed

- Use practical benefits that specific donation amounts would bring, such as:

  - Your $150 provides shelter and feeds a family for a month

  - Your $2 provides an Iftar meal for a needy person.

- Include donation information—tell readers how to donate. The address, telephone number, and the website address must be included.

V. The Seven-Mailing Rule

Mailing lists are costly but provide large returns. However, organizations need to be careful what ML to add, when to delete a ML from their core list, and how to maintain it. This is a complicated matter requiring Information Technology skills, data analysis, and generous budget allocations for long-term direct mailing companies. An analytical research done by professional NGOs showed through important scientific data analysis that the response to an organization's mailings is affected by the number of different mailings sent to the same ML. The percentage of returns grows with every mailing sent to the same ML up to the seventh mailing. This means that with the first mailing, the ML recipient barely knows the name of the organization. With the second mailing, the recipient knows what the organization is all about and remembers the name from the first time. With the third mailing, they think seriously about donating, about the credibility of the organization, and so on. The percentage of returns changes from one organization to another, depending on the quality of the ML used and the campaigns. An example of this is depicted in Figure 11-B. Additionally, another issue which involves other variables is the increase of average donation per mailing to the same market due to increased credibility and trust; however, this factor changes with the effectiveness and cause of every campaign.

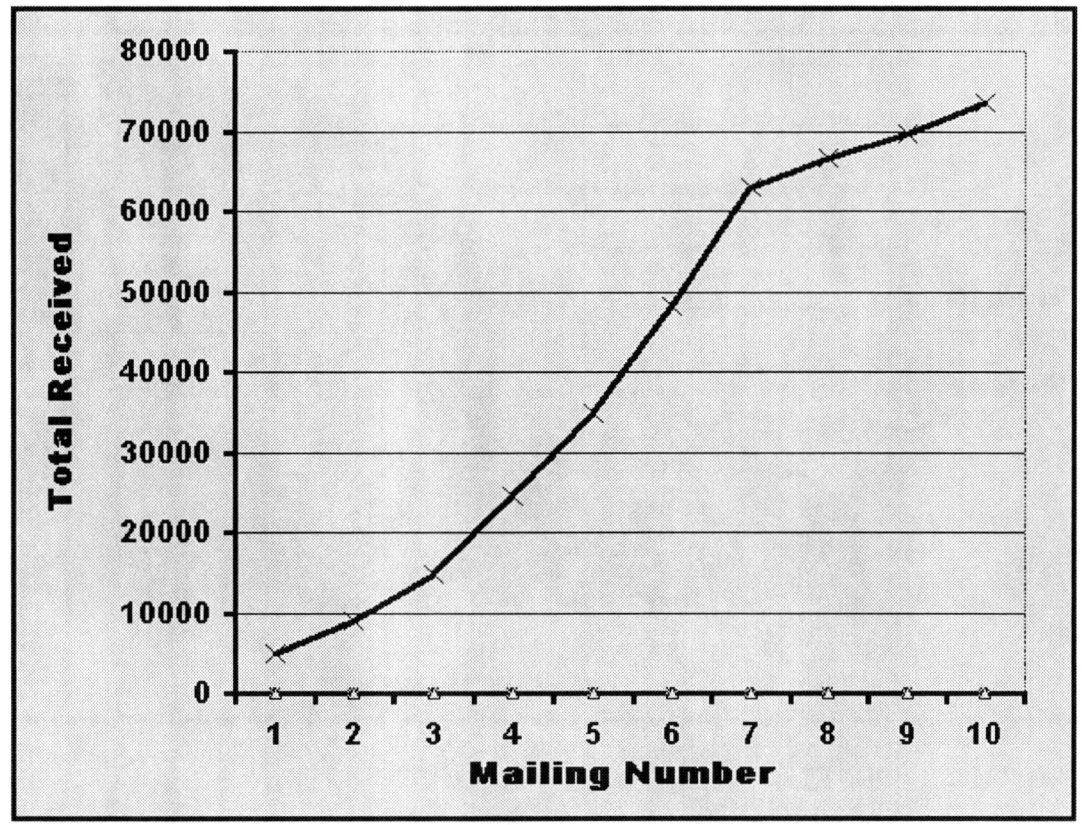

Figure 11-B: Mailing Totals Received Per Mailing Number

The mailing list illustrated in the graph in Figure 11-C shows a very good return of around four percent after seven mailings. However, the average donation is low, which can be increased by modifying the message of the campaign. To capitalize on the above ML, the organization should end mailings to non-donors after the seventh mailing. They should try concentrating instead on how to increase the average donation, and how to receive repeat donations from at least 1,000 people who made donations during this period of time. Those people are part of the organization's backbone permanent donor list. As the graph clearly shows, the growth of donations rise dramatically from the first until the seventh mailing; however, after the seventh mailing, the growth noticeably slows.

Obviously, this growth of total donation per mailing is due mainly to growth in the return percentage for every mailing. Although the average donation per mailing grows, it is not the main variable affecting the growth of total donations. As we can see below, the percentage of return increases steadily as expected until it reaches the seventh mailing.

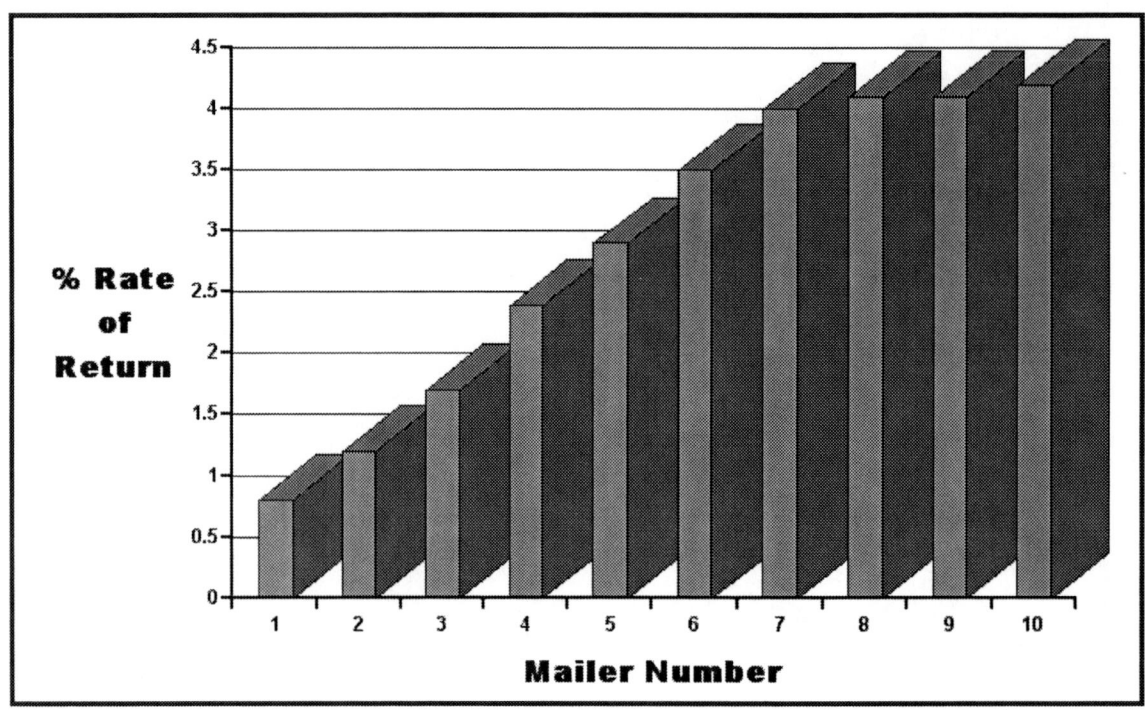

Figure 11-C: Mailing List Percentage Rate of Return

VI.   Working with Direct Mail Consultants

Saving money is a good thing—except when it leads to failure. Direct mail takes time and a certain managerial expertise, not to mention that it is not an easy task. Some organizations that decide to manage their own direct mail in-house fail to realize their full potential. Even though these organizations may feel that they need to save money, or that they know their cause better than anyone and therefore are their own best resource, they often lack the full range of skills and resources necessary to survive. Essentially, they are deluding themselves. Nonprofit marketing goes much deeper than simply having an intimate understanding of the organization and its cause. Special marketing and communications skills are required that are seldom found in nonprofit managers. As is the ability to work with a host of specialized vendors such as a network of list brokers, printers, writers and other production entities which enable the mailings to be cost-effective and on time. A mailing's success can come down to something as simple as its design, list selection, packaging, or timing. Additionally, a professionally designed piece can lift an appeal head and shoulders above that of other organizations, raising its response rate from five percent to eight percent, resulting in a donor base that is 20 to 30 percent larger. Only under certain circumstances should an organization attempt to manage its own direct mail in-house. These might include:

• The organization cannot afford professional help because their annual fundraising budget is less than $100,000.

• Their constituency or market is too small for aggressive donor acquisition.

• They have been in direct mailing for years, and follow along well-established, easily handled scenarios.

• The agency's resources are large enough and lucrative enough to afford to hire a full-time professional staff.

SELECTING THE RIGHT CONSULTANT

Although there is no special licensing or certification process associated with becoming a professional direct mail fundraising consultant, a few national organizations have established a code of ethics for the field. One of these is the Association of Direct Response Fundraising Counsel (ADRFCO) which has approximately 50 member agencies located throughout the US and a clientele of more than 600 nonprofit organizations, including some of the largest and most visible charities. For a list of its members, they can be contacted at www.adrfco.org. One other similar agency is the American Association Fundraising

Counsel, which can be reached at www.aafrc.org.

Many of these consultants are solo operators representing only a tiny handful of clients and may offer services ranging from copy writing to full-service management and consulting, to data entry as well as being brilliant fundraisers. As with the larger agencies, their skill and number of years in the field may vary and cover a broad range of clientele. Therefore, it is important to rely on a firm's reputation and experience, while also considering the following points:

• *Understanding*–Do they speak the same language as the organization? Does the consulting staff understand what the organization is about and can they motivate the organization's constituency? Sometimes you need to deal with Muslim consultants because they better understand the Muslim market.

• *Range of services*–Can they do the whole job and do it right?

• *Contract terms*–It is illegal in many states for a consultant to take only a percentage of the returns in compensation. It may also be illegal in some states for the firm to offer financial incentives such as capital to finance the organization's program with a guarantee of profit. The nonprofit should look closely at any special contract terms regarding financial matters.

• *Creativity*–Specially created packages and "winning" formulas bear watching as well. Although there is no right or wrong way, custom-tailored programs can be incredibly expensive, while inexpensive templates that have proven successful for other organization's fundraising efforts may not be one-size-fits-all.

• *Decision-making*–Who will make the key creative and financial decisions? The nonprofit or the consultant?

• *Accessibility*–The consultant should be available to address concerns in a timely fashion whenever necessary.

• *Compensation*–Aside from consulting fees the firm charges, what other fees will be incurred. It will pay off to know how a project will be billed (i.e. hourly, per project, etc.).

VII. Assessing Your Case

In light of what we have presented here and in order to practically benefit from this chapter, please consider your organization's situation by answering the following questions, which will allow you to identify the areas where corrections are necessary. Additionally, you are encouraged to go back to review the specific materials of this chapter for clarification on some questions.

- *Do you have an updated and complete mailing list of your members, potential donors or constituency?*

- *How many and what type of direct mail campaigns do you have per year?*

- *Do you take advantage of special not-for-profit permit/postage for the majority of your mail campaigns?*

- *Do you have a written, well-defined procedure to maintain your ML?*

- *Do you keep track of who on your ML received what mail campaigns and when?*

- *Do you continue mailing to non-donors on your ML even if they have not responded to seven mailings?*

- *Do you have a broad donor base, or do you rely on a small number of large donors?*

- *Do you apply marketing-mix strategy to solicit donations, or do you target your market through a single strategy?*

- *What is the percentage of response rate for your annual mail campaign for each of the last three years?*

- *What is your average donation received for each of the last three years?*

- *What is your average cost per donor acquisition for each of the last three years?*

Chapter

12.

Effective Online

Donations

If used wisely, the Internet is a very successful fundraising tool. For minimal cost, it easily and conveniently allows people to know about your organization and donate towards your programs. The possibilities of the web are limitless, reaching the most distant lands, and into the homes of every connected person on the planet. Online fundraising goes beyond just having a donation button on your website. Much like your direct mail campaigns, your website is an integral part of your fundraising strategy; however, you need to manage it well.

Therefore, by applying the ideas and strategies in this chapter, a nonprofit can actively seek out its intended audience, and attract them to its site.

In this chapter, we will discuss the steady growth of use by nonprofit organizations for online fundraising campaigns. As well as the main guidelines for building and maintaining an effective website, and how to generate traffic to your website. We will also present the future trends of online giving and, as usual at the end of the chapter, we will leave you with a set of questions to help you evaluate the situation of your organization in regards to its internet presence.

I.   The Nonprofit Use of the Internet

As the number of people using the Internet continues to dramatically increase, online philanthropy is gaining ground in the nonprofit sector. Online giving has been steadily increasing over the last few years. For instance, The Chronicle of Philanthropy reported that contributions made in the days following the attacks of September 11, 2001 overwhelmingly exceeded all previous Internet fundraising campaigns. It estimated that more than $70 million of the $676 million in contributions to relief organizations have come from online sites. Just two weeks after the disaster, the American Red Cross—the largest recipient—reported $60 million in online gifts. These online figures accounted for almost 30 percent of the total $211 million raised during that time.

Technology companies have played a major role in helping raise money for many charities and relief funds that respond to various tragedies. After raising more than $57 million through their own Web sites, six Internet companies (Amazon.com, AOL Time Warner, Cisco Systems, eBay, Microsoft, and Yahoo) joined together to form the American Liberty Partnership. The creation of the their website, Liberty Unites, was announced by President Bush at a ceremony in the White House's Rose Garden a week after the attacks.

According to the Chronicle of Philanthropy, before 2001 the most money any charity had ever raised in a single year online was $2.7 million, which was raised by the Red Cross in 1999. This included donations for the relief efforts in Kosovo.

Clearly, the amazing amount of money raised online is the result of the extraordinary nature of the disasters, as well as the increasing use of online philanthropy. An online campaign can be generated within literally minutes after the occurrence of an earthquake. In contrast, the fastest Presorted First Class Mail can take a minimum of three to seven days to reach its recipients, while the disaster's impact has dulled. This timeframe does not take into consideration printing time, mail preparation, and its duration in transit. Nor does this address the issue of the cost involved for First Class mail campaigns.

WHAT ARE E-CAMPAIGNS?

Increasingly since 2001, more nonprofit organizations have used online campaigns—or e-campaigns—to formulate their web-based communication strategies. The Internet provides a number of communication opportunities that are still under-utilized by most non-profits. The cost of conducting an e-campaign depends on the type of campaign. But, since the expenses associated with printing and mailing are excluded, it will generally be at a much lower cost than traditional media communications, resulting in a greater percentage of donations going toward the organization's programs.

E-campaigns include contextual ads, search driven ads, and of course e-mail. Contextual ads are inserted as paid placements on popular Web pages based on matching the ad to the content of a publisher's Web page. Search-based ads appear in search engine listings from Google, Yahoo, AOL, MSN and more, based on matching search terms to an ad's keywords. These ads can be priced based on the number of times the ad is viewed, which is measured in "impressions". Pricing can also be based on a pay-per-click (PPC) basis. PPC e-campaigns are becoming more popular, and preferred above other campaigns, as they are based on including a link back to the organization's website. This assures that payment for the ad has resulted in someone seeking additional information from the organization, and can lead to some type of transaction.

II.   Websites that Work

Online giving offers not only convenience, but it also answers people's heartfelt urges to respond immediately to others in need without having to send in a check, or having to go through a more lengthy process. Offering online giving opportunities is often a cost-efficient option for nonprofits because the per-transaction cost of online donations is far less than maintaining a toll-free telephone number that is available 24 hours a day. Donors can make a contribution earmarked for a specific disaster or program, and receive quick confirmation. However, before donations can be taken online, an organization must first have an effective website.

GUIDELINES FOR SUCCESSFUL WEBSITES

Developing a great website is not necessarily more expensive than creating a bad website. Usually, website quality does not depend nearly so much on the technical skills as on the strength of the information, the site's layout, and how well it all supports your objectives and your visitors' needs. The main guidelines for successful website functionality, content, navigation, and graphic design are as follows. These guidelines can help nonprofits to evaluate their existing website or think through a new one.

- *Provide comprehensive content:* Complete information about the organization, its history, past and current programs categorized by type of program and regional areas are essential to satisfy this point. It should enable benefactors to contribute by credit card, electronic check, or direct debit from their checking account, as well as allowing them to give one-time or monthly donations, gifts of stocks, or other contributions.

- *Customize the site to visitor's interests:* Above all, your website must meet the needs of those who will visit it. Most of those needs are likely to be basic—for instance, to find organizational contact information, or to answer a specific question about your organization. Ensure to facilitate quick lookup for those who know exactly what they are seeking. Doing so may also easily provide detailed information or functionality to those with deeper concerns. To ascertain what your visitors' needs are, study your potential online market, and then determine why they may visit your site. During Ramadan, Muslims may visit your site seeking to pay their Zakat; therefore, providing a way for them to calculate what they owe will be beneficial for both the user and your organization. Additionally, there is no better way to determine what features patrons want than to ask them. By conducting a periodic usage survey, you can discover what are the most prevalent issues that bring visitors to your website.

By being donor-driven, your organization's website is utilized as a marketing and fundraising tool, not a technological tool disclosing pride. The driving force behind the website content should be the fundraisers and marketers, not the web developer. It is also wise to keep perceptive donors updated about what they may be interested in, especially how their funds are being used. It is important to build effective relationships with your visitors and donors.

- *Make desired actions User-friendly:* Common and desired actions should be easy, and not at all confusing. This means your website must be laid out in a way that visitors can retrieve information, find what they want, and donate without confusion and without investing too much time. If you want your users to take a particular action, display an obvious call-to-action. First, identify what actions you would like your visitors to take. Would you like them to donate? Sign up for your newsletter? Sign up for a membership? Fill out a survey? Once you have defined your objectives, ensure your site includes content and functionality to make the actions as easy as possible for your visitors. To entice people to make a donation, include information about how your organization will put the money to use. Additionally, if you want them to sign up for your newsletter, do not ask them to supply too much personal information—just the basics will suffice.

Make sure to place important links to your content or functionality on key pages related to the action. Placing the links in too many places increases the chances that your visitors will tune them out. The top of the content area is generally regarded as the most prominent area on a page. Items at the very top may be ignored as advertising, while information that the visitor needs to scroll down to see may simply never be viewed.

- *Keep your site current:* Nothing is more important than the quality of the information on your site. No matter if it is the most beautiful and technologically advanced site, it is worthless if the information it contains is out of date. Write your content carefully to begin with, and plan for frequent updates. If you do not have the resources to frequently update your site, make certain that you do not include information that will soon be out of date. It is highly important that your site should be maintained and updated frequently. This can be difficult for many organizations if a proper communications system is not in place. The website should be updated at least on a weekly basis; however, it is understood that in a crisis, it is prudent to update more frequently.

- *Make your site fully automated:* Keeping your site fully automated (from Zakat calculation, donation processing, to online donation receipts) will pay off in the long-run. It is also better to make the site interactive; for instance, depending on the visitor's preference, they should be able to find out what programs the organization offers.

- *Write text in concise and easy-to-read formats:* Writing for the web is somewhat different than writing for offline media because few visitors actually read all the text on a page. Instead, the vast majority of visitors only scan pages. This makes it critical that the text be as concise as possible and provides headings, subheadings, bullet point lists, and topic sentences to allow someone to find information quickly. Make certain that your text is understandable to your audience by avoiding technical language, slang, and abbreviations that might not be familiar to your visitors.

Any reports or articles that you wish your visitors to carefully read should be in a format that can be printed without effort. Many web pages are too wide to print on a standard piece of paper. It is quite common to furnish readers with a "printer friendly version" of specific web pages, which provides a version of the page that is scaled down to fit standard paper size.

- *Provide impressive visual design:* Visitors assess your site, and surely your organization's credibility, from their first impression, mainly through the site's visual design more than any other aspect. A clumsy graphic design can cast doubt on the entire organization.

This is not to say that your graphic design needs to be flashy. Rather, a good design should be pleasant to look at, gives a respectful impression to the organization, and calls attention to your content, not to itself. The visual design should be aligned with your offline materials. Also, successful use of font sizes and styles, colors, lines and boxes, and positioning on the page can dramatically improve your visitor's understanding, while directing their attention where you want it to go. Therefore, it is worth investing up front in a solid, professional graphic design that you can be proud of.

- *Put your visitors in control:* Visitors expect to be able to control what they do on your site. Forcing them to do things like watch an introductory animation or register before they can see any information on your site is likely to backfire by irritating the user, prompting them to leave the site prematurely. Instead, inform your visitors as to what the possibilities are and let them choose. Encourage them to explore your site contents and functionality. Provide some interactive features on your site so that visitors can feel they have some control.

- *Ensure accessibility to all:* Your visitors may access your site using many different types of browsers—Microsoft Explorer, Netscape, etc. As well as on different computer platforms (Macs, PCs, cell phones), and connection speeds (dial-up modems, DSL, etc.). Each of these methods may result in a different experience. Ideally, each site would be optimized to account for all these possibilities. Think through the needs of your particular audience. Test the site for those configurations. Do not frustrate your audience with long downloads, hopefully no larger than 20K. Think about whether you want to accommodate wireless users—like those on PDAs and cell phones, and whether your audience is likely to have plug-ins such as Flash, ShockWave, or Real Audio that facilitate site viewing.

- *Make your site visible:* Building the best and most comprehensive website does not ensure potential donors will visit. On its own, your website will do nothing. It takes time to build an online brand name. It also takes all types of online and offline promotions and advertisements to entice Internet users to visit your site. Online success means identifying your audience, and targeting their attention to the wealth of information and services offered by your website. By integrating your Internet address and promoting your site in everything you do, you will be able to drive traffic to your site. This includes all organization publications, mailings, advertisements, Internet banners, and E-mail blasts.

- *Be consistent with other sites:* Your visitors have been to many other sites before, and have learned a lot about how websites work. Be sure not to break the most established norms:

  - Placing the navigation bar on the left or at the top of the site
  - Your organization's logo is in the upper left corner, with links to your homepage
  - Horizontal scrolling is not required, but vertical scrolling might be needed
  - Not using frames in the site
  - Links are underlined or in a different color
  - The Back button always takes you to the previously viewed page
  - There is a section which describes specifics about your organization labeled "About Us" (or something similar), some of your staff, and how to contact you.

EFFECTIVE WEBSITE WRITING

Although printed materials have a long, proven record of accomplishment, the Internet is still quite new, and studies of how people read online are few. This reality is double-edged in that nonprofits have no standard from which to measure their online content.

This is where studies about printed materials become relevant, as the rules for these can help to set the standard for Internet materials. Following the examples set forth for direct mail in the book Type and Layout, the following golden rules can also apply to a nonprofit organization's online written content:

- Use of elegant typefaces is more comprehended by readers than sans serif faces.

- The use of high-chrome colors, such as hot red or process red in the headlines will increase comprehension.

- Printed pages are typically read from top left to bottom right. This rule holds true for the video screen as well; therefore, headlines and more important information should be at the top left.

- Text in high-intensity colors is difficult to read; therefore, text color should be black.

- To increase comprehension, page background tints should not exceed 10 percent.

- Although lacking character, black text on a white background is the most legible.

- Reversed-out text is harder to read than non-reversed text.

- Text that is justified is easier to read than text that is ragged-left or ragged-right.

When developing your website's contents, following some quick and solid rules will allow the page to load faster:

- Keep the main page simple, and create links to other pages behind the first.

- Keep files as small as possible, while keeping the size of graphics to a minimum.

- By including height and width tags with graphics, text will appear before the graphics finish loading.

- It is a waste of memory and effort to include images with resolutions greater than 72 dpi (dots per inch) because computer screens cannot project pictures more detailed than this.

- Because better graphics do not look any better than lower standard graphics on a website, save low-quality photos and pictures as .GIF or .JPEG files.

- Also use as few colors as possible and use .GIF files for any solid colors, text art, cartoons, and poster art.

Good web writing is short and to the point without clichés and an excess of verbiage. Text should be well written with excellent use of bullets, and pertinent links. The site map should be well thought out, taking into account the unique qualities of hyperlinks and the architectural relationship between the page, its text, audio, video, animation, and color usage.

III.   Generating Traffic to Your Website

Congratulations! The website is built and it looks terrific. The message is concise and catchy. The graphics are cutting-edge, and it is completely relevant to the organization's mission. But, there is one little problem: it is not on paper. An organization cannot just drop it into a mailbox and wait for replies. The website is just a whole bunch of bytes zooming around in cyberspace, bouncing off the cosmic void. Now what?

Where does the organization go from here? How can they generate traffic to the site? Every nonprofit needs to develop a strategy to bring the public to its website, reaching those for whom the organization originally built the site. Unlike broadcasting a wide signal like in television, the Internet has a narrow, private and personal cast even though the Internet has opened up an entirely new world which is still in its infancy. This can be done successfully by using an online marketing strategy organized similarly to one used in the real world. Some of these strategies should include publicizing the website in all of the organization's real world publications, TV, public events, etc. Also, deciding who the audience will be and understanding how they are different than those outside cyberspace.

Then, plan incentives to have your potential donors visit your site to get needed information or services. Also, an effective way to generate traffic, other than applying all forms of offline campaigns, is to advertise your site online through banners and targeted E-mail blasts.

MAKING USE OF INTERNET BANNERS

The type of website to advertise on, banner placement, and the materials presented in banners are very sensitive, and can greatly affect the results. Usually, an organization's IT staff can track sources of donations on their website—or at least the sources of visitors—so that the organization can concentrate on the most effective banners which work for them. A common mistake that many nonprofits make is to put their name and logo on the banner, but not a cause or a program. This is only effective if they want exposure for their organization's name. Even then, it is more effective to promote a cause using a good picture with a link to your website, where donors will see the organization's name, logo, and details about their programs. For instance, for the seven days prior to 'Eid al-Fitr, they might just want to say 'Pay Zakatul-Fitr Before 'Eid. $7 per Family Member', along with an appealing 'Eid image of the organization's volunteers providing food to needy people.

One effective model can be seen in case of natural disasters, where scores of people are left homeless and in need of aid. An agency must first choose the proper website that provides news about this situation, then choose effective wording, such as 'They Greatly Need YOUR Help. Your $450 Provides Temporary Shelter and Food for a Homeless Family', accompanied by a photo of a homeless family on the side.

WHY MASS E-MAIL?

Attention can be drawn, and traffic generated to a website promoting a certain cause or a program by regularly sending an E-mail blast monthly. To do so, an organization must generate an E-mail list of their donors and potential donors. E-mail lists can be also purchased or leased from companies that specialize in mailing lists. Similarly, E-mail blasts should be very concise and neatly designed. Only an image and a few statements are recommended. The purpose of the E-mail campaign should solely be to have those who receive it click a link taking them to a particular page on the organization's website.

However, using mass E-mail to send messages has been overused lately by some non-profits. The proliferation of unwanted E-mail (known as Spam) is an annoyance to many. Most Internet solution providers are gaining an upper hand over Spam by directly deleting them before they reach the intended target. Therefore, nonprofits should only send E-mail to people who have agreed to receive it, such as those who subscribe to the organization's E-newsletter. So, rather than buying mass E-mail addresses, it is much better to be consistent in your attempts to collect E-mail addresses by communicating with people through other traditional means. It is also beneficial to assure them that you will honor their privacy and will not sell their E-mail address to anyone else.

## IV.	The Future of Online Giving

No matter how convenient or cutting-edge, until quite recently, online contributions did not approach the dollar amounts raised by direct mail. For example, in November 1998 out of the $3 million raised by CARE after Hurricane Mitch, only $120,000 was raised online. Additionally, for every $14 million the American Red Cross raised, only $450,000 came from online donations on average.

However, online donations in the U.S. in 2004 exceeded $3 billion. This figure was up 58 percent from the $1.9 billion raised in 2003, according to a recent study by technology provider Kintera and Luth Research, Inc. which can be found at www.kintera.org. Released in 2005, the study indicated that more than 8.6 million US households gave online donations in 2004. Results also show that more than 65 percent of all donors visited at least one of the websites of the nonprofit organizations or fundraising events to which they gave.

Internet Donation vs. Mail Donation

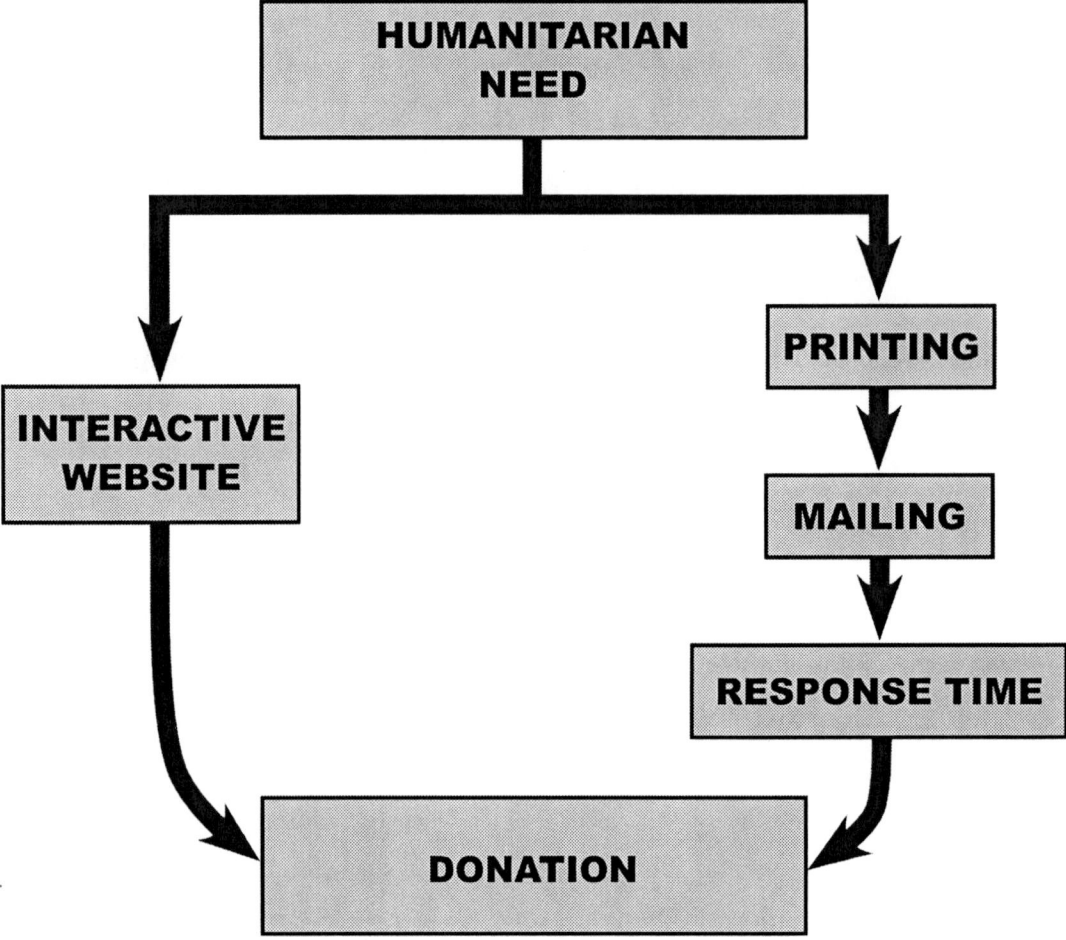

Figure 12-A

Other noteworthy results from the Kintera/Luth Nonprofit Trend Report include:

- On average, online givers donate in total (both online and offline) more than 50 percent more than those donors who do not give online.

- More than 12 percent of all donating households in 2004 made some online donations.

- Approximately 35 percent of all online donors gave at least half of their donation amount online; 22 percent of all online donors gave all of their donations online. This means that approximately 3 percent of all donors in 2004 gave all their donations online. Furthermore, a lesson is learned from current disasters that the best and fastest response comes online. For instance, following the devastating tsunamis that struck South Asia on December 26, 2004, nonprofit organizations mobilized quickly to help victims of the disaster via the Internet. In fact, Kintera, Inc., a provider of online technology to nonprofits (including U.S. Fund for UNICEF, and Doctors Without Borders) estimates that within two weeks of the disaster, their clients alone surpassed the initial $350 million pledged by the US government for relief efforts. Additionally, according to CBS Marketwatch's January 3, 2005 release on www.marketwatch. com, hundreds of millions of dollars were contributed to websites soliciting tsunami disaster relief funds.

Currently, the vast majority of disaster response organizations are integrating online appeals with other methods. Most are just beginning the process of tracking online donors and analyzing the trend. When an organization offers online giving, it is offering a vehicle to support its work. It will give people who may not participate in conferences or mosque activities the opportunity to help support a worthwhile effort. Future technology is changing donor outreach programs to help find those willing and able to give more online. The web is allowing organizations to have ready access to Internet-savvy donors of all ages, and to cost effectively grow relationships online by collecting valuable data that can be used to communicate personal messages to constituents. Online giving will continue to grow at a very high speed (no pun intended), and those who delay their Internet presence will lag behind.

FEAR OF ONLINE GIVING

The biggest obstacle to online giving is convincing donors that the process is safe. Fear of hackers, identity theft, unauthorized credit card charges, legitimacy of the organization, etc. keep some people from taking advantage of this unique and convenient form of donating. Potential donors generally want to know two things:

1) Is the organization they are supporting legitimate, and will the funds they are giving be used in an appropriate way, consistent with their intent?

2) Is my online contribution secure, and how can I be certain that my personal and credit card information will not be stolen or misused?

Surely, nonprofits should make certain that their website is secure so that personal information cannot be seen or stolen by others. In addition, they should aim to make the donor feel comfortable making their gift. These perceptions may not be totally unfounded or irrational, in light of the fact that multi-billion dollar corporations are being hacked; however, online giving is generally a safe environment. For many, no matter what manner of security the nonprofit invests in, they will not give online. Therefore, to expedite giving, it is wise for the nonprofit to provide alternative information on their website where a gift can be sent, or inquiries can be made. This information should include mailing address, fax number, telephone numbers, and contact E-mail address.

In the future, by utilizing some of the following items, giving can truly be at the click of a mouse:

- *Tailored Donation Forms*–Easy to create yet highly customizable donation forms that can be integrated into an organization's website, or linked to E-mail communications. As an option, they can be pre-populated with demographic information.
- *Multi-Level Donation Forms*–Associate giving levels with premiums and benefits to encourage larger gifts.
- *Dynamic Ask Levels*–Use past giving history as a basis for a nonprofit to know how much to ask a donor to give.
- *Multiple Giving Options*–Provide for donors' different payment options, including credit card, online checks, PayPal, and pledges with single and recurring donation options.
- *Bookkeeping and Reporting*–Extensive back-end accounting and analytic capabilities can be utilized with processing of transactions. Also, with the ability to study donations as related to the initiatives that generated them.
- *Matching Gifts*–Access to databases for study of matching gift options.
- *Donor Management System Compatibility*–The ability to synchronize donation data with offline databases.

TAILORING YOUR APPEALS

The objective of nonprofit organizations' online campaigns is to attract new donors, and to create online reply devices for repeat online donors. Often, direct mail fundraising response devices are personalized for the past donor. For instance, a response may show when he or she last made a gift, how much was given, the donor's name and address, and possibly noting a particular area of work the donor has indicated interest in. Websites can be customized to a donor by the organization instituting a donor-only area accessed by a password system. The organization will know who has accessed the site, and the donor can make a gift by filling in their name and password, thereby accessing a reply device unique to them.

Utilizing personalized pop-up screens, the reply device can give the donor up-to-date information on a new program area in which the donor may have shown previous interest. The donor's giving choices array on the reply coupon relies on a matrix based on the donor's past giving history (both online and offline) with the organization. When the donor logs onto the website, the donor's name, contact information and giving history can be instantly reviewed. By clicking on the current gift amount, everything else is taken care of.

V.   Assessing Your Situation

In order to practically benefit from this chapter, please consider the situation of the organization you are part of, in light of what we have presented here. By answering these questions, you would be assessing your situation as well as identifying the areas where corrections are required. Also, you are encouraged to go back to review the specific materials of the chapter for clarification on some questions.

- *Does your organization have an up-to-date useful website? If not, when does it intend to develop one?*

- *How many visited your organization's site in each of the last five years, and is the number of visitors growing at the same rate as people utilizing the Internet?*

- *Can your organization process secured online donations and issue receipts online, without any manual interventions?*

- *How much in online funds did your organization receive during each of the past five years, and are these numbers growing at the same rate as other successful organizations' online giving?*

- *In case of a disaster or an urgent situation that requires immediate communication with your community or donors, do you use the Internet as the first means to deliver your message?*

- *What types of E-campaigns does your organization utilize?*

- *Is your organization's website thorough enough to answer most visitors inquires easily and clearly, such as your mission, history highlights, information on current programs and services, and answers to frequently asked questions?*

- *Does your organization have an E-newsletter, and how often does your organization issue it to your subscribers?*

- *How does your organization generate traffic to its website?*

- *Do you characterize your site as being customized to your typical visitor's needs, and does its contents always stay current?*

- *What are the three most impotent features your organization's website lacks?*

- *Do you promote your Internet address and online features throughout all of your organization's publications, advertisements, public events, etc.?*

- *Do you have any types of customized online campaigns that are tailored to different individuals, depending upon their giving history and interests?*

- *Can your organization conveniently evaluate the responses to various campaigns by knowing what initiatives generated what online funding?*

- *Does your website follow the common established norms for navigating and developing websites?*

Chapter

13.

Communication and Outreach:

Donors, General Public

and the Government

Successful nonprofit organizations strive for two objectives. The first of which, how to acquire new donors through targeted mailing campaigns, advertisements, public events and the Internet, is covered in other chapters. The second objective, how to keep those donors, is discussed in this chapter. Many organizations fail to care effectively for their main assets: the donors they already have. Gaining donors costs a lot of money and takes a great deal of effort. However, keeping donors happy is not a costly venture, yet it is greatly overlooked.

In this chapter, we will discuss effective communication, not only with donors, but also with the public and other organizations, including those operated by non-Muslims. In this chapter, we present a few ideas on building strong relationships with donors by forming partnerships with them, and respecting them as partners. We recommend an analytical management approach within the organization, whereby your donor's records are comprehensive and thorough enough that you instinctively know how to deal effectively with each donor. Additionally, we will discuss a host of public relations tools that help organizations present themselves as courteously and professionally as possible. Since Muslim nonprofits have frequently come under intense scrutiny in the aftermath of 9/11, we offer recommendations on how to deal with adverse publicity. Lastly, we will discuss an array of effective relationship programs with governmental and non-Muslim organizations that address many issues Muslim nonprofits traditionally ignored, but can no longer afford to.

I.   Effective Donor Relations

It seems that many organizations put a great deal of effort into acquiring new donors. Yet, these same organizations invest very little time in retaining their current donors, keeping them loyal to the organization, and giving year after year. To entice new contributors, it is clear that an agency must invest in aggressive marketing campaigns and high exposure fundraising. Even with these strategies, not every person targeted donates. In fact, those who donate frequently constitute a small percentage of the public. It takes time, effort, and money to identify this generous group of those who really donate and get them to contribute to your organization. Moreover, it takes a delicate quality of relationship with these donors to keep them once they donate for the first time. Remember, from simple Friday prayer announcements to direct mailings, tens of fundraising campaigns target donors throughout the year. It is more likely that donors who give frequently jump from one organization to another, and from one cause to another, demonstrating limited loyalty to one particular organization. We will discuss in the coming sections how to earn donors' loyalty and get them to remain steadfast with your organization for years to come.

FRIEND-RAISING IS AS IMPORTANT AS FUNDRAISING

The essence of raising money lies in an organization's relationship with its constituency. The importance of people to a cause is far more vital than money, for when people give the cause their attention, interest, confidence, advocacy, and service, their financial support is not far behind. Developing a relationship of shared values with its donors is vital to a nonprofit. Simply putting out the tin cup will not develop the long-term relationship that will allow the nonprofit to reach financial stability. One important aspect of developing a relationship is communication that imparts information from one party within the relationship to another party in the relationship. Communication helps the prospective donor and the fundraiser to know what to expect from each other, while reducing uncertainty about probable outcomes of future exchanges. Solid, long-term effective fundraising requires two-way communication for identifying, maintaining and building donor relationships. Even if someone who donates a few dollars thinks of the organization and its leadership as friends, this will not make fundraising easier. In the long run, a few dollars here and there may add up, but the organization probably needs hundreds or thousands of "friends" just to pay the bills each month. There is far more effort put into treating potential donors as friends and partners when fundraising than in keeping ongoing existing donor support. Therefore, if these contributors are not dedicated to the cause, they may stop being friends, and therefore stop being donors.

THE LADDER OF COMMUNICATIONS AFFECTS GIFT AMOUNTS

The larger the gift, the more personal the solicitation. In terms of fundraising techniques, the "ladder of communications" was developed by practitioners to illustrate that personal communication has the most powerful effect on the amount of gifts. Therefore, the less personal the communication, the less the effect.

The ladder is divided into two tiers: the top consists of major gifts resulting from the personal approach, or interpersonal communication. The midpoint to bottom consists of many smaller gifts, or annual giving, resulting from less personal approaches. The upper tier techniques include personal visits from a team or one person for the primary and/or secondary contact. The third contact in this tier is a personal letter and subsequent telephone call. In addition to all of the above, the lower tier includes phone-athons and special events.

**FIRST LEVEL:
MAJOR GIFTS**

• **PERSONAL APPROACH**
   - PERSONAL VISITS FROM A TEAM OR ONE PERSON
• **INTERPERSONAL COMMUNICATION**
   - PERSONAL LETTER
   - TELEPHONE CALLS

**SECOND LEVEL:
ANNUAL GIVING
& SMALLER GIFTS**

• **LESS PERSONAL APPROACH**
   - PHONE-ATHONS
   - SPECIAL EVENTS
• **SECONDARY CONTACT**

Figure 13-A

Ladder of Communications Gift Levels

LADDER OF COMMUNICATIONS FOR GIVING LEVELS

I. **Interpersonal Communication**
  • *Major Gifts Program*
    - *Face-to-face Conversations*
    - *Small Group Meetings*
    - *Speeches*
    - *Telephone Conversations*
    - *Personal Letters*
    - *Personalized Proposals*
II. **Media Communications**
  • *Annual Giving Program*
    - *Direct Mail*
    - *Special Events*
    - *Publications (Newsletters, Brochures & Flyers)*
    - *Phone-athons*
    - *Videos and Films*
    - *Computer: Internet & Websites*
    - *Telethons: Television & Radio*
    - *Paid Advertisements, Billboards, Collection Signage*

Note:
  • **Interpersonal:** Direct communication between people.
  • **Media:** Mediated communication through channels controlled by the organization.
  • **Mass Media:** Mediated communication through uncontrolled channels (e.g., newspapers, television & radio).

Solid communication theory provides the basis for these techniques. Fundraisers know from experience that in order to attain major gifts, they must focus on interpersonal communication as opposed to the mass communication efforts used to acquire multiple lower level gifts.

DONOR BILL OF RIGHTS

Donors have certain rights which are important to respect in the fundraising process.

Developed in 1993 by the American Association of Fund-Raising Counsel (AAFRC), Association for Healthcare Philanthropy (AHP), Council for Advancement and Support of Education (CASE), and National Society of Fund Raising Executives (NSFRE), the Donor Bill of Rights is a compilation of 12 values for ethical decision making in fundraising. These values are: honesty, integrity, promise-keeping, fidelity/loyalty, fairness, caring for others, respect for others, responsible citizenship, pursuit of excellence, accountability, safeguarding the public trust, and duty. The bill is based on uniform hypotheses underscoring acknowledgment, social responsibility, two-way communication, candor and interdependency. Although it is incomplete, the Bill of Rights represents a fundamental stand against unethical paid solicitors. We encourage you to adhere to these rules and publish your commitments with the set of rules to donors so that they know their rights.

The Donor Bill of Rights

Philanthropy is based on voluntary action for the common good. It is a tradition of giving and sharing that is primary to the quality of life. To ensure that philanthropy merits the respect and trust of the general public, and that donors and prospective donors can have full confidence in the nonprofit organizations and causes they are asked to support, we declare that all donors have these rights:

I. To be informed of the organization's mission, of the way the organization intends to use donated resources, and of its capacity to use donations effectively for their intended purposes.

II. To be informed of the identity of those serving on the organization's governing board, and to expect the board to exercise prudent judgment in its stewardship responsibilities.

III. To have access to the organization's most recent financial statements.

IV. To be assured their gifts will be used for the purposes for which they were given.

V. To receive appropriate acknowledgement and recognition.

VI. To be assured that information about their donation is handled with respect and with confidentiality to the extent provided by law.

VII. To expect that all relationships with individuals representing organizations of interest to the donor will be professional in nature.

VIII. To be informed whether those seeking donations are volunteers, employees of the organization or hired solicitors.

IX. To have the opportunity for their names to be deleted from mailing lists that an organization may intend to share.

X. To feel free to ask questions when making a donation and to receive prompt, truthful and forthright answers.

The Donor Bill of Rights was created by the American Association of Fund Raising Counsel (AAFRC), Association for Healthcare Philanthropy (AHP), the Association of Fundraising Professionals (AFP), and the Council for Advancement and Support of Education (CASE). It has been endorsed by numerous organizations.

II. Forming Partnerships with Donors

There is no doubt that without the donors' gifts, the organization will be unable to establish programs and continue its operations. Donors give their money with no expectations of direct return from the organization itself. Therefore, donors must be considered as, and treated as partners. To consider them as such, the organization must share information with them, tell them what their donations are doing, and allow them to feel that the organization cannot do it without them. Some suggestions are:

- Keep donors updated by sending them a professional newsletter aimed at keeping them informed about the organization's activities (we will discuss the importance of this point in detail).

- An annual comprehensive report with financial information summarizing the entire year's achievements will greatly impact how donors perceive the organization. It is important to inform donors about how their money is being spent by making your financial statements readily available on your website, or by proving them upon request.

- Put faces on the organization through PR efforts. We will discuss this later in a separate section.

- Post updates on the organization's website.

KEEP DONORS UPDATED

The most common way to update and inform donors of the organization's programs is through periodic publications—mainly newsletters and annual reports, and sometimes press releases and other forms of updates, such as website updates. Usually such dissemination of information raises awareness of the organization. Their aim is not to raise funds, but to build the credibility of the organization. They are more of a reporting than a fundraising medium. However, they provide important support for other fundraising activities because people tend to donate after becoming familiar with the organization and its achievements.

THE NEWSLETTER

Although it is common to judge the success of newsletters by how much funding they directly bring, a newsletter's primarily purpose is not to raise funds. Rather, the main purposes behind such publications are reporting to donors about where their money is going, what are the future objectives, what current programs are accomplishing, and why we deserve your continuous donations.

One of the most effective tools to build a credible, positive corporate image is to issue a well-planned newsletter. Smartly timed issues, along with an enclosed or attached participation form, can give the newsletter a secondary purpose of being a fundraising tool. For instance, although most American nonprofit newsletters do not include a return envelope, a return envelope included in a Ramadan issue promoting Ramadan programs can serve the organization well, especially if received during the first few days of Ramadan. Additionally, if a single issue of a newsletter brings in enough funding to cover its own cost, then it is considered a success. If it brings in more than double its cost, it is deemed very successful. Experience shows that most issues put out during the summer at a time when donations are very slow, do not recover their initial costs. In contrast, issues during Ramadan, which promote Zakat collection as well as Ramadan programs, are usually quite successful. Both of these examples serve the primary purpose of creating awareness and credibility for the organization.

Although a frequent on-time publication issued without interruption leads to building a good image for the corporation, we need to stress that even nonprofits that have been around for over a decade have difficulties maintaining a timely newsletter. The process involves a legion of staff to devote time and effort collecting the materials and data, writing the text, laying it out, then printing and mailing the piece. Furthermore, this difficult cycle must be maintained through a great deal of cooperation between those in the field who report on the programs, to those whose duty it is to process the reports, to those with the marketing skills to produce the newsletter, etc. Once an issue is created however, it can feed materials to all other communications medium such as the website, advertisements, mailings, and annual reports. Additionally, there must be an internal communications system in place in order to be able to issue newsletters on time. Therefore, using the MLC cycle discussed in a previous chapter is a system proven to lead to the overall success of the organization. Nowadays, the importance of a well-produced newsletter is greater now than ever before because of the serious doubts and accusations swirling around Muslim charities.

Guidelines for Successful Newsletters

A successful newsletter tells it all without too much text. Most people do not take the time to read newsletters, and even if some give it a glance, they would read titles, look at images, a few standout captions, and whatever charts it might contain. A successful newsletter takes this into consideration by allowing the reader to get enough information from an issue by merely flipping through its pages. This can happen with the following:

- *Effective headlines:* People tend to read them, if nothing else.

- *Complete story sub-headlines:* A complete summary of the whole story or article in the headline, such as "8,000 Udhiya Performed in Iraq Benefiting over 40,000 Needy Families".

- *Many images with effective captions:* An image can be understood at a glance, and can provide the whole purpose behind an article.

- *Charts, tables, or other visual presentations:* Making donors aware of pertinent data at a glance.

- *Numbers, numbers and more numbers:* Together with photos, numbers represent the most effective materials you should provide to your donors.

This does not mean we should not provide text. However, it must be emphasized that placing blocks of text one after the other would not help much without the above. Therefore, although text is rarely read in its entirety, it must still be provided to give details. As well, the style of the text should change depending on each piece. Style should vary from a reporting style when talking about achievements to a scientific and objective style when talking about assessing a certain situation, to a personal style when addressing emotions for promoting a needy cause.

Effective Newsletter Content

For an organization to make its newsletter effective, it must impart meaningful information to its recipients that addresses what donors—or prospective donors—need to know, what their funds will support, and what goals the organization has for the future. In order to present the information efficiently, there are a number of tried-and-true guidelines that are suggested to include in the newsletter and its format.

- A main message, usually presented by the president or the executive director. This item should summarize the primary achievement during the past period, the challenges, and/or the focus ahead. It should project the organization's vision and current course.

- Reports and stories of completed and on-going programs. Remember that headlines and sub-headers or subtitles should state the main points behind the story.

- Needs assessment or reports about situations that require future intervention, such as a developing drought in a certain region. Sometimes, quotes, news reports or press releases about developing needs from other recognized world relief organizations such as UNHCR may be used.

- Summary tables or charts about the organization's activities.

- News from both fundraising and field levels. Many pack their newsletter full of reports about their programs at the field level (which should account for about 70 percent of the newsletter), but forget to mention anything about the organization itself. People are interested in knowing about the organization, the staff and their activities. For instance, to launch a campaign to raise one million dollars for a hospital in Iraq, not only is it helpful to update people about the establishment stage of the hospital, but also about the donations received up to that time. It could be helpful to personalize the newsletter by adding sections such as 'Our Team', talking about a staff member in every issue. This relates to readers and allows them to know the organizations from a personal standpoint. Additionally, any internal news about who joined the organization, who left, and what staff positions are open lend a personal touch. Adding blurbs about who visited field programs, and little stories from the field that deal with issues other than strictly relief, bring even more insight.

- Future programs that develop a vision for the future, telling readers that the organization is proactively planning, and not merely set up for reactive behavior. A charity must be careful not to make promises, and then fail to deliver what has been publicly "planned". For relief organizations, sudden humanitarian crises always cause diversion from long-term goals; therefore, it is important to make sure not to publicize future programs unless they are certain to be delivered or executed.

- How a potential donor can join an organization's efforts should always be available, while suggesting various ways the reader can support the organization. Although the most common thing to do is to invite readers to donate, also inviting those with needed expertise or skills to volunteer their time is important. Requests such as these can be presented by asking physicians or teachers to visit field clinics or schools, or to help others with administrative work at the headquarters. Any requests for financial support should be specific. Do not simply ask for contribution towards "Palestine Relief Fund". Instead, it must be clearly stated that "three containers of medicine were shipped to Palestine at $12,000, and we still have five loads to be shipped". Invite generous donations to sponsor the shipping cost of a container at $4,000 each. It is proven that more money is given when redirecting the attention of the potential donors from a mere dollar amount, to an actual action of what this amount would accomplish.

How Often and How Big?

A good time to mail a newsletter is three to four weeks before a major mailing. For example, the Ramadan issue should reach people one to two weeks before Ramadan. Then, it should be followed by a mailing to reach people around the second week of Ramadan (the 10th of Ramadan would be ideal). This is one way to capitalize on the newsletter: stating actual achievements and Ramadan programs, and then followed up by asking people again to participate in the Ramadan campaign in a separate mailing three to four weeks later.

Newsletters must be issued in a timely fashion. Even producing a smaller issue is better than delaying it. Many organizations avoid committing to a rigid timetable by saying 'ABC is a Periodic Publication of XYZ organization', while avoiding designating it as a monthly or quarterly. That is not professional unless it is during the first year of publication. If the organization is not prepared to issue a monthly or quarterly newsletter, then it should go for semi-annual. If necessary, the organization could produce an annual newsletter and call it the Annual Report. Calling a publication a quarterly newsletter, then issuing it only three times a year makes the agency look unorganized. The size and frequency of the newsletter depends upon the size and level of activity of the organization. Generally, relatively active organizations with an income of less than ten million dollars per year put out a quarterly newsletter thorough enough to cover all their activities, and consisting of at least eight to twelve pages.

Newsletter Audience

Newsletters are expensive. A twelve-page, two-color newsletter printed on Matt paper with a return envelope included would cost approximately 72 cents a copy (45 cents for printing and 27 cents for mail preparation and postage). Since the cumulative cost can be quite prohibitive, newsletter distribution should be limited to those who must receive them: the agency's donors, a few copies to each Islamic center on the mailing list, Muslim leaders, the agency's contacts, Muslim Student Associations, and places where the agency's target market gathers. Additionally, the newsletter must be readily available and easily received by whoever requests it, particularly potential donors. Newsletters are also an excellent means for an organization to introduce themselves to others, including conference audiences. A newsletter or brochure would be ideal material to give out at a public event such as fundraising dinners.

When it comes to the actual printing, practical experience has shown that a printing of three times the number of donors is sufficient. This rule of thumb holds true except during the slow summer season, when double the number of donors would be enough.

ANNUAL REPORTS

The second most common type of periodic publications are annual reports. There are also periodic reports that address a certain situation or large programs such as monthly updates concerning a specific circumstance, crisis, or project. Reports are more rigid in their form and content than newsletters. Some follow one strict format that states project achievements, financial position, and future milestones. Others give detailed information with tables, spreadsheets, and analytical results such as financial reports. When considering the writing of materials for proposals, reports, and newsletters, it is highly recommended to hire professional writers, at least for final editing.

The annual report summarizes the entire year's activities for its donors: how much was raised, what was accomplished, how much it cost, etc. Some larger organizations spend a great deal of time, money and effort to make their reports glitzy and full of substance. However, for a nonprofit to spend too much on such a report would be counterproductive. Donors generally have contrary feelings about their gifts going to something so extravagant. Keep the structure of such reports concise by highlighting accomplishments and new programs, devoting a section to each with liberal use of photos, charts and financial information. Smaller nonprofits might even forego the annual report altogether; instead putting the pertinent figures in their year-end newsletter.

III.   Donor Management System

To earn the respect of their donors, an organization must have a professional management system that organizes all donor information neatly and accurately. The data should contain the donors' individual interests and preferred programs, their donation amounts, the appeals sent to them, and all administration and record-keeping issues relating to their contributions. Having such data is extremely useful, enabling the organization to analyze returns on every campaign and study how donors are reacting to different strategies.

In this section, we will discuss what data the information system should contain; however, just having the system and not using it to make these analyses will not be helpful. Therefore, the next step is to discuss the suggested analytical approach an organization should take to be able to become fully informed about their donors, and the organization's relationship with them to be more effective.

INFORMATION SYSTEM REQUIREMENTS

To deliver professional services to donors, and to be able to know how effective an organization's marketing campaigns are, the organization must have a detailed information system. This system should technically enable the organization to keep all data relating to their donors' personal information and their contribution history, including the means and sources of all donations. The information recommended to have in an effective database is the following:

Personal Data: What is available about donors and potential donors such as name, address, phone number, e-mail, ethnicity or primary language.

Mailings Data: This is information that knows which mailings are sent to individuals in an organization's ML. Smart direct marketing does not mail everything to everyone. To be able to track who received what, use a code for each mailing. This code can be two letters representing what kind of campaign, and four digits that represent the date. For example, IA0702 would be for the Iraq Appeal in July of 2002, RM1005 would be for Ramadan Mailing in October of 2005, and NS505 would represent the newsletter mailed in May of 2005. It is extremely important to track what mailings—or at least the number of mailings—sent to each person on the mailing list. This allows the organization to know who received what, and when to retire an inactive portion of the ML after several mailings. Note that there is no need to remove any unwanted portion of the ML—simply change status as Not Active.

Record Status: Tells whether certain listings are Active, Not Active, Wrong Address, etc. It is important to keep donors in the system even when an organization no longer has their addresses, or they can no longer be located. Experience has shown that even years later, agencies may locate or receive a donation from a person who was "lost". Their donation information can easily be reclaimed after correcting that person's address information.

Donations Data: The donations record for every donor should be laid out in chronological order containing the following:

- *Date* of each donation.

- *Amount* of each donation.

- *For what program*–If not restricted, it should say Unrestricted, General Fund or Where Most Needed.

- *In the Form of Check, Money Order, Credit Card, Cash, Direct Debit, Stocks, etc.,* with the corresponding check or credit card number.

- *Receipt Issuing Date and Number*–Many times, donors call organizations because they have not received receipts. This can be avoided by adding a feature in the system which automatically records the receipt issuing date (the date it was printed and mailed). As well as the receipt number so that if the donor loses the receipt or cannot find it at the end of the year, the agency can re-issue the same receipt with the same number.

- *Pledge Information* to track what pledges donors made, for what program, at what event (such as a code containing the speaker's initials and date; for instance KJ112505), Amount Paid, and Remaining Balance. Scheduled payments should also be listed. For instance, a donor might pledge $5,000 that will be paid in ten installments over a two-year period. The system should be able to schedule and issue reminder letters as well as update balances when payments are made.

- *Donation Copy Locator*–Sometimes donors dispute the amount stated in the receipts, claiming to have donated a different amount. The organization is able to confirm the donation amount via a Copy Locator record that has been posted for every donation. In less than a minute, hard copy for any donation can be accessed from amongst over 100,000 donations. This works by copying all checks that an organization deposits in their bank after sorting them from the smallest to largest amount. These bundled checks are then labeled with the deposit date. Additionally, every page is numbered. When entering the donation data on the computer for a certain donation, the bundle number and the page number are recorded. For example, a Locator can tell the operator that the hard copy of the requested check is 110501-9 (that is, page 9 of the deposit bundle made on November 5, 2001). Since all these bundles are neatly filed in chronological order by deposit dates, it takes only moments to locate and confirm the amount. For example, was that donation for $500 as the donor claims, or $50 as the receipt states? Donors are always impressed with such services, even if the organization makes a mistake.

- *Source of Donation*–This crucial step should be with every donation, verifying its source, the manner by which the donation was received (via postal service, public event, advertisement, website, etc.), and through what campaign. The organization would be better served to go into even more detail by recording such additional information as through what mailing (for example, RA1104), through what PR Event (for example, MC112504), and through what advertisement (such as ART1102). It is extremely important for the organization to be proactive and track the sources of donations in order to analyze what are the most effective marketing and fundraising efforts being undertaken. This is easily accomplished when donors use the organization's donation cards and envelopes that can be printed with a different code for every mailing. In the event that a donation is called in over the telephone or given online, one question that should always be asked is "How did you learn about us?" The caller's answer might be, "I saw your advertisement in the Islamic Horizons". This tells the organization which advertisements work and which do not.

- Naturally, there will be a certain percentage of donations received through unknown campaigns such as donations received in regular envelopes (not in the organization's return envelopes preprinted with a corresponding code). In these cases, the source should be marked as "Unknown". Usually, at least 85 percent of donation sources are easily tracked. Many donations are made due to a combination of marketing mix. For example, a potential donor saw an organization's ad on ART television station, but was reminded to donate by an ad in the Islamic Horizons. So, he called. Or, maybe a person listened to an organization's speaker at their mosque and decided then to donate, but did not until he received a letter three months later, etc. Nevertheless, this should not prevent an organization from tracking the sources of funds to the best of their ability with as many details as possible. Tracking these sources will no doubt tell a lot about how donors and potential donors are reacting to different fundraising tools and campaigns. By doing this, the organization better understands their donors, and consequently, the organization would be able to build a better relationship with them. This will definitely capitalize on an organization's efforts by enabling them to allocate their marketing budget in the most effective and efficient way.

Another important factor to note is that following the above procedures meets compliance requirements about knowing your donors. Although these newly enacted regulations may very well be perceived as targeting Muslim-run organizations, they are meant to fight terrorism and control the flow of funding to international terror organizations. Organizations that comply in totality with these regulations will also find some measure of protection under the increased federal scrutiny.

AN ANALYTICAL APPROACH

A little bit of analysis tells a lot about an organization and its relationship with donors. Their results should guide the organization into more effective and focused efforts. Without such a scientific analytical approach, an organization may grow, but haphazardly and at a high cost. The most important analysis an organization should address is the effectiveness of every campaign, how much every dollar costs to raise, and what portion of their direct market reacts to what area. These issues were discussed in details in another chapter. In the following, we will present some important data to carefully track and evaluate your organization accordingly.

Which Numbers Tell What?

- *Number of Donors:* The number of total donors of an organization simply tells about the growth rate of the organization. Surely, total donations per year tell about the growth of the organization as well. However, it is not necessarily true that a small dip in total donations means the organization did not grow. This is true unless one takes into consideration the increase or decrease in the overall number of donors and the average donation.

- *Number of Repeat Donors:* Another important piece of data to track is the number of repeat donors. The term "repeat donor" refers to any donor who has donated at least two times. This piece of information tells about the dedication of donors, and their commitment towards the organization. Extensive research shows that once a person donates one time to an organization, it is very likely that he or she will donate again, that is if the organization is maintaining a good relationship with these donors. Therefore, a lot of effort is put into getting a person to donate for the first time. This holds true no matter what the amount is and towards what program. The likelihood is that this person will donate again, and the amount of other donations he or she gives would grow. Therefore, the organization should dedicate extra effort towards having most, if not all donors, as repeat donors.

The number of repeat donors for effective organizations is usually about 70 percent of total donors. The organization that can boast of this statistic should be seen as being very successful in keeping its donors dedicated and committed, requiring no improvement. If the figure of repeat donors is between 50 percent and 70 percent of total donors, then that organization is within fair range, but some improvement can be done. However, if the rate is less than 50 percent, then the organization is failing in maintaining its donors, and it must totally re-think its approach by devising an overall plan to improve its donor relations.

- *The Average Donation:* The average donation is a good measure of how convinced the market is with the cause or program the organization is promoting. If average donation is low, the organization has not done a good job selling their programs, or being aggressive enough in its campaigns. This number also reflects the organization's credibility. If the donor is convinced of the organization's cause, and trusts the organization, the donor would give larger amounts. If the donor is not very sure about the credibility of the organization, the amount would be low.

As stated in an earlier chapter, depending upon the type of nonprofit organization, the average donation from individual donors (not corporations or grants) that come through mass campaigns to western nonprofits is very low, usually in the range of $30 to $60. By contrast, the average is much higher for Muslim nonprofits, ranging from $150 to $240. Nearly all Islamic charities in the US, have maintained an average donation of greater than $100, which speaks well of Muslim donors' generosity. It is important to mention here that the average donation amount is also directly affected by the organization's fundraising approach. For instance, donations from public events are much higher on average than those coming through mailings. However, the economy plays a major role in affecting these figures.

- *The Percentage of Cost from Income:* Another very crucial number management should track carefully is the percentage of management and fundraising expenses from total income. This percentage tells the organization and its donors how efficient or non-efficient the organization is. As stated previously, this percentage tends to be high in the first three years of the organization's life, before decreasing in later years. More than anything else, donors watch this number closely, as it is the first and most important indication of how management deals with public donations. It is also an indication of the organization's commitment to help those in need or merely build an operation.

- *The Donor Ethnicity Breakdown:* The ethnicity of an organization's market, which is easily identified by the mother language, is important to market multiple projects at the same time. For example, you might target Pakistani donors with a program in Pakistan, or you might have an Arabic report or newsletter that you want to send to Arabic-speaking donors. To address whether to go globally or regionally, the organization must analyze how their market, or portions of their market, is expected to react to such moves.

What if Analysis Is Not Done?

If it is not done monthly, analysis should be done on a quarterly basis. However, if the above data cannot be extracted from the organization's Information System, it means the organization does not have the minimum required information system, or it does not gather the needed data with donations. As a result, it will have problems growing wisely and efficiently, resulting in blind decision-making. The remedy for this is to hire professional IT personnel to redesign the entire Information System database including these features. One better option is to purchase a ready-made Donors Management System designed specifically for NGOs.

ADMINISTRATIVE TIPS TO KEEP DONORS CONTRIBUTING

How should an organization keep its donors satisfied and dedicated? This can be answered through the following administrative issues that deal with the way the organization conducts itself with its donors:

• Always mail the receipt with a thank-you letter within one week of receiving the donation.

• Mail receipts via First Class Mail with Address Correction Requested to get the donor's correct address if it is wrong.

• Mail donors' annual summary receipts in January of every year stating all donations made in the past year in a table format clarifying the date, the amount, in what form, and towards what program. This should be done for every donation made. Also, include a notable message of gratitude. Most importantly, all records and information must be correct without any mistakes.

• Make sure the mailing list information is updated and free of duplicates, because when someone receives two to three duplicate mailings, they feel annoyed and unimpressed with the organization. Additionally, cleaning the mailing list of duplicates once a year is important. This task can be out-sourced to professional mailing list updating agencies.

• When donors call to inquire about their donations, everything should be easily accessible in the organization's database system without any delay. The organization should avoid the answer "we will get back to you later". Accomplishing this requires an information system or database that is thorough and up to date

IV. Public Relations

Every nonprofit needs Public Relations. Public Relations is the practice of communications with individuals and groups, influencing an organization's success in its cause, constituency, profession or the industry it represents. Effective communications help to enhance an organization's image, increase participation, and lend support to fundraising. Since a nonprofit is often identified with its cause, the cause becomes an asset endowing the nonprofit with a measure of credibility. Many activities within a nonprofit are supported by Public Relations: fundraising, community awareness, donor recruitment and retention, lobbying and issue advocacy, and crisis management.

Public Relations is the management of communications between an organization and its public. It helps manage these interdependencies by various strategies, which influence or affect the public. Obviously, Public Relations are more than mere publicity or publications. It is also the overall planning, execution, and evaluation of an organization's communication with both external and internal groups that affect the ability of the organization to meet its goals.

Among communications professionals there is a maxim that says advertising is bought, while Public Relations is earned. To say that Public Relations are simply image-building is not a complete description of the term. Although one of its goals is to improve an organization's status with its constituency, it is all about accepting input from them. This input is then translated into directives and initiatives to address their concerns. An organization can spend millions promoting itself through an advertising campaign, but without coverage that draws subtle attention to its good deeds and public outreach that good PR brings with it, that money is wasted.

PLANNING FOR PR CAMPAIGNS

Public Relations is rarely a solo act. It is carried out most effectively through a group meeting to analyze the circumstances and consider the organization's Public Relations options with as broad an agenda as possible:

- What are the organization's strengths and weaknesses?

- How do perceptions compare to the facts?

- How do important donors feel about the organization?

- Is the organization trusted and respected for its efforts?

- How does the organization wish to be perceived?

The next step in this process is to set goals consistent with the organization's overall strategic plan, and to map out a course of short- and long-term action. Is there a message the organization wants to impart on the public? Does it wish to change the public's perception of the nonprofit? Which individuals or groups does the organization wish to impress? In this planning process, it is usually necessary to take an inventory of staff and resources to accomplish these goals. The organization should decide whether an outside Public Relations firm should perform some or all of the work. While the latter is not a cheap way to go, hiring freelancers to do the work could cut costs considerably.

Now that the organization knows where it is going with the PR, it should research who they will be targeting with the PR program, and what is the best way to communicate with them. If the nonprofit operates in a specific arena, it would be quite helpful to develop a list of all the media that targets that arena: newspapers, magazines, television, and radio. There are many print and online directories available that list outlets by type, city, and subject. If the target audience has a common demographic feature, magazines that specialize in that area are the perfect medium. For example, to target Muslim physicians, the organization might think about publishing an ad or article in a quarterly publication that goes to all members of a physicians' association. The nonprofit might also give a presentation at their annual convention, or co-sponsor a mailing to the association's members that includes a package from the nonprofit organization.

FORMS OF EFFECTIVE PR

Our Muslim nonprofits need to build relationships and communicate effectively. Nonprofits bring formidable resources to the PR arena, but they must be cautiously practiced.

Speeches

No other PR strategies work better than speeches, which are an essentially powerful tool to strengthen a nonprofit's standing. Speeches are written for the ear, not the eye. Speeches should cover a very narrow scope of basic points and be no longer than 20-30 minutes in length. Props are effective uses to boost the visual impact, but should not detract from the message or the speaker. Seek out key audiences that are identified in the nonprofit's PR plan. Have a few Public Relations staff who are highly qualified speakers with good PR skills available to put human faces on the organization's work. Their responsibilities should be networking at conventions and public gatherings, and giving khateebs at mosques and Islamic centers. This should be done whether for Friday prayers, or as speakers at special events, or for general lectures or specific presentations about a certain issue. PR events are important not only for the direct funds derived from them, but for credibility and long-term public support.

Mass Media

The freedom of expression is protected in the First Amendment of the Bill of Rights. In the US, no institution has more independence or power than the media; therefore, it is important to cultivate a good relationship with those reporters or outlets that cover a nonprofit's issues. View the news media as a vehicle for getting the message out to significant audiences while providing important information. Become their most valuable source by providing accurate and colorful quotes. Do not lie to them. Quid pro quo. You give it to them; they will give it to you.

Designated Spokespersons

Define one or two spokespersons to represent the organization. Be certain that those chosen are articulate, quick thinking, knowledgeable about the organization, and diplomatic. Having a designated spokesperson will avoid confusion and contradiction at critical times when they are needed most.

Broadcast Interviews

When put before a television camera, it is important to put every second to good use. Words should be chosen wisely, and never assume that the microphone is off. Although a taping can run more than a half-hour, only a few seconds of that interview will air. The remainder will fall to the cutting room floor. It is important to make good use of the visual dimension as well. Fidgeting hands, tense facial muscles, unkempt appearance, confused demeanor, gaudy clothing...these all undermine the message, and create fodder for critics.

Community Relations

For nonprofit organizations, community relations carry their own benefits. Nonprofits can make good use of community relations to raise funds and enhance their public image through programs that aim to serve community members, even if minimal fees are involved to cover expenses. Some activities that are excellent for community relations include:

- Health fairs offering free cholesterol and blood pressure checks.

- Fun runs or walks where the entry fee is donated to the nonprofit, or where sponsors give a certain amount for each mile completed.

- Publishing a theme cookbook where the sales price goes to the nonprofit.

- Litter cleanup or neighborhood beautification days coordinated with local youth.

- Constructing or repairing homes for low-income families.

- Distributing blankets, coats or sleeping bags to homeless people.

- Sponsoring youth sports leagues.

- Support for local food pantries or soup kitchens.

- After-school or youth mentoring programs.

Community relations programs require the same skill and attention associated with Public Relations programs, especially when the program involves more than one group or coordinating responsibilities among organizations.

V.   Crisis Communications

In today's political climate, being an Islamic-based nonprofit automatically comes with a suspicion of the organization. Occasionally, events may threaten the integrity of the group or its constituency. For circumstances as critical as these, effective communication is crucial. A nonprofit could suddenly find itself under fire, much like numerous American Muslim charities after the tragedy of September 11, 2001. Therefore, it is better to be well prepared should the ugly specter of accusation—and possibly closure and freezing or seizure of assets—arise. It is also wise to be very well versed in current laws surrounding nonprofit disclosure.

UNCLE SAM IS WATCHING

Any charity that does not comply fully with federal law and the provisions of the Patriot Act is subject to closure under the International Emergency and Economic Powers Act. Although the Patriot Act requires a "knowing" standard before action can be taken against an entity, the Executive Order does not. These expanded legal powers give the federal government the right to seize and freeze assets of a nonprofit "pending an investigation", without the opportunity for the nonprofit to learn the evidence against it or effectively challenge the designation. Additionally, there is no way to know whether these actions are justified because of the secrecy surrounding the decisions.

After September 11, anxiety over the embattled charities was compounded because many Muslims hesitated in giving to Islamic charities with global operations, fearing that those charities were still under heavy scrutiny by law enforcement agencies. It is in the charity's best interest and the best interests of those it represents, to practice diligent efforts to work within the laws and guidelines put forth, and maintain a totally open-book policy with full disclosure.

GAINING SITUATION CONTROL

Being proactive by designating speakers who can address issues articulately and intelligently without being combative or evasive will go a long way toward the organization's credibility should such a situation arise for the nonprofit. Often, circumstances will not allow a delayed or non-response to media queries; therefore, it might be beneficial for the organization to initiate contact to avoid suspicion of hiding something. This takes away the element of surprise from the media, and also puts the spokesperson in a position to control the information. In a crisis, all communications should be limited to verifiable facts offered within logical timeframes, steering clear of all forms of speculation:

- Immediately upon hearing of the incident or controversy, let the media know that your spokesperson is available to comment.

- After a preparatory investigation, provide an initial assessment of the incident or controversy.

- Issue information updates as soon as possible when new or significant facts are uncovered.

- After completing the inquiry, offer a full explanation of the incident.

HOW NOT TO HANDLE ADVERSE PUBLICITY

In the recent past, many high profile nonprofit organizations have had to answer charges that their CEOs were being overcompensated or that they were misusing the funds entrusted to them. Additionally, a number of Islamic charities have had politically motivated charges of supporting terrorism thrown at them by governmental agencies, news outlets and self-styled "terrorism experts". Although some reporters and puffed-up talk-show hosts thrive on controversy, they are bound by ethical standards to be "fair and balanced". It seems that prior to 9/11/01, American Muslim charities were so preoccupied with packing boxes of relief goods that they were caught off-guard. The events which have unfolded on September 11th suddenly threw the charities into the spotlight, where they found themselves being accused of terrible things. They had no spokespersons, no prior experience dealing with the mass media, and previously had minimal government relations. To add to the problem, they were not well known outside of Islamic circles, and as a result, they were feared and distrusted.

The typical situation that played out was that of media personalities tossing dreadful accusations at the charities. Not knowing what to do or how to handle this sudden attention, the nonprofits contacted attorneys who ill advised them not to talk to the media. As legal advice, not saying anything is a proper strategy. But, as a public relations strategy, it is a great mistake since this allowed others to paint their own biased picture of the situation. More importantly, after getting replies of "no comment" too many times, the media outlets began to interpret the accusations as being truthful. Sadly, it was too late when the organizations realized the attorneys had given them bad advice. By the time they wised up and hired PR professionals to answer the media queries, the damage was already done.

GUIDELINES TO FACING ADVERSE PUBLICITY

An organization that does not have its own Public Relations professional is at a definite loss since an outside PR person cannot answer everything about the organization without in-depth preparation and intimate knowledge.

Anyone representing the nonprofit who goes before the media should be well prepared, calm, professional and articulate. Those who are representing the organization should be someone who is fluent in the language. They should also be clever enough to turn a bad situation around to the organization's advantage without being evasive or obtuse. Additionally, it is a monumental mistake to allow someone to face the media if they have a pronounced accent and are hard to understand. Those who speak on the organization's behalf should be careful not to quote Qur'anic verses without translating them into English, or resort to non-English terms that are understood only by those who speak Arabic. Leave "yanni" at home.

Dealing with the Media

When more than one person from the organization must speak to the media, be certain to have a preset order of speakers. It is also best to know ahead of time about what subjects or areas each person will address. For instance, have someone who is versed in the law speak only about that issue, and someone who knows international affairs stick to that subject. A field worker, for example, should not address current terrorism legislation when someone else in the group has experience in this realm. If there is no one who can effectively and knowledgeably address the question at hand, tell the questioner "I do not have any information on this subject". Then offer to find out the answer and get back to them. Although the question may have been hostile, do not become combative or belligerent. Remain professional at all cost. A huge word of advice: resist the temptation to accuse these entities of conspiring to destroy the organization! Doing so will only make the organization appear less credible, or make it look as though the nonprofit is hiding something, and just might fan the flames. Instead, use the accusations to tell your side of the story while correcting any inaccurate information.

Gaining the Upper Hand

When an organization is faced with an adverse event and resulting hostile attention from a particular media outlet, turn it to your advantage by holding a news conference, or interviewing with their closest competitor before the adverse material is aired or published. Always remember to keep responses factual and unemotional. Sometimes it is not prudent to answer inaccurate reports. Several factors should be carefully weighed when considering this option:

- The issue may be one that the organization wishes would just disappear. This may call for dignified silence.
- The organization may wish to "set the record straight". Correcting factual er-

rors may be a wise thing to do if this issue is likely to come up again.

- Aggressive responses should be reserved for issues that threaten the integrity of the organization or its community members and donors.

VI. Government Relations

In a democracy, government is responsive to its citizenry. "The loudest squeak gets the oil." This old saying has been proven time and time again to be not only true, but rather prophetic. Although designed to represent all of its citizens, those who take the time to let their values and views be known are the ones to who the government listens. If one does not take the time and expend a sincere effort to have their issues focused on, then those who have positions diametrically opposed may very well be the ones who win the ear of their legislators, and thus the legislation they desire.

Simply being prepared to respond to actions and decisions detrimental to one's cause is not enough. By taking the initiative in lobbying for their cause, a person can exert influence on those who make the laws. This influence—through letter writing, or public testimony—shows the legislators that this cause is not easily dismissed, and is demonstrative of the citizen's influence. Often, a government public relations campaign is launched to respond to one issue, but is ended once the issue is resolved. It is essential to keep an ongoing relationship with governmental entities to direct a quick response to new issues. One individual can have an impact on public policy; a coalition of people with the same goals can help determine public outcomes to a large extent. What, one might ask, does this have to do with Muslim nonprofits? The answer is simple: knowing your government and how it works, and becoming involved and a part of the system leads to understanding, partnerships and shared goals, and less fear of Islam, Muslims and those issues important to Muslims.

ESTABLISHING A LOCAL GOVERNMENT RELATIONS PROGRAM

Although the events of September 11, 2001 was a horrible tragedy, it can be said that one phoenix has risen out of the ashes of this terrible day and its fallout. Muslims from across America have come been mobilized to become involved in the happenings of their towns, cities, counties, states and nation. They have found that town meetings, city council sessions, and school board meetings are all venues where they can speak up about public policies that affect their lives. Whether it is to protest a tax-rate hike, demand better garbage pickup or voice an opinion on the curriculum of their children's school, this is all a part of the constitutionally mandated exercise of free speech, and the right of citizens to seek accountability from their government.

These newly active Muslims, who once went quietly about their lives, have learned how to lobby the government to meet their citizens' needs. Frequently, a single voice can be lost in the wind; therefore, often people who share a cause or opinion form temporary or permanent coalitions of activism to achieve what they need or want from their government.

Nonprofit organizations usually work at the community level, and what affects the community often affects them. This is especially true for the hundreds of Islamic centers across the US. Therefore, a government relations program is a prudent investment to build bridges with local, state, regional, and/or nationally elected officials and agencies. Naturally, this cannot be accomplished without a thorough understanding of the decision-making process, and of the essential people involved. Unfortunately, before that tragic day in 2001, many Muslim nonprofits, humanitarian organizations, and local religious institutions had very limited government contacts which consisted mainly of fulfilling the basic legal requirements at the end of every year. Many Muslim organizations met with outsiders to help ease public fear and dispel media misconceptions. One nonprofit invited the local FBI to tour their facility, giving them a presentation on Zakat, its sources, recipients, and demonstrating how it works. For others, fear drove them to suspend their operations although they had done nothing wrong!

Finding Success through Lobbying

Generally, nonprofit organizations are not supposed to influence legislation. However, there is an exception to influencing policy related to the charity's work. Keeping this in mind, by forming a steering committee to design the strategy for creating a government relations program, a nonprofit is taking a significant leap forward in helping move government policy to an arena that is favorable to the nonprofit and its cause. Active lobbying efforts by Muslim and non-Muslim organizations in Illinois saw fruitful results through the passing of Illinois Senate Resolution 178. On May 11, 2005, about 35 members from the Mosque Foundation which consisted of attorneys, social workers, physicians, corporate employees, college students, business owners, housewives, and high school students traveled to the Illinois state capital in Springfield. The legislation, which was sponsored by Senator Jacqueline Collins from the 16th district, reaffirms the rights of the Muslim community to donate charity without fear and calls on the Federal Government to create a list of "safe" Muslim charities. The resolution was passed a week later, and was followed a few weeks after that by the passing of HR 438, a version in the Illinois House of Representatives sponsored by Representative John Millner. The full text of this bill can be seen in the Appendix at the end of Chapter 3.

Forming Steering Committees

To be successful in government and political relations, a steering committee should be comprised of those who know the political process, have a relationship with principal players and programs, and are truly bipartisan in their thinking. Once the steering committee has mapped out the strategy and has defined its position or arguments, then it is time to enlist member support, contact key people, and begin writing letters. Although paid lobbyists provide valuable experience, there is no need to have professional lobbyists—the only qualification is a desire to change the status quo, be committed to their cause, and possess enthusiasm. Since their constituency holds the key to being re-elected in the palm of their hands, most elected officials will take sit up and pay attention.

Building a Government Relations Campaign

An organization needs certain things to happen so that a particular problem affecting its constituency can be resolved. Simply by having a problem to solve, and mapping out a strategy, they have already started a government relations campaign. The organization should know as much as possible about those they are trying to influence, and those who oppose the proposal. What are their interests and backgrounds? What is their record of support on similar issues? What committees do they serve on and what positions do they hold? Who chairs the committee that will be considering the proposal? Who is leading the opposition? If the nonprofit's government relations committee does not know one or all of these things, pick up the phone and ask.

A successful government relations campaign must have clear, easily articulated goals framed to appeal to a wide scope of public opinion and beliefs. Not every important decision-maker will be favorable to the organization's position; however, they may be sympathetic to others that the nonprofit may present in the future. Also be aware that advocacy is a long process that will not be won or lost through one individual endeavor, but requires tenacity, organization, research, patience and enthusiasm.

One example of this is a long-serving Congressman from Iowa who was up for re-election in 2002. Never facing strong opposition, the Congressman had a tradition of voting along conservative lines in domestic matters, which pleased his Muslim constituents. Unfortunately, his voting record in international affairs was closely aligned with heavy influence from a foreign government, a detriment for Muslims around the world. In 2001, the Congressman's district was redrawn to include a large liberal population, and possible defeat. Knowing that a US invasion of Iraq was imminent, the Muslims invited the Congressman to a meet-and-greet at their mosque to hear their concerns. This educational effort, along with lobbying by other anti-war constituents, resulted in him being one of only a few in Congress who voted against the war.

VII.   Coalitions with Non-Muslim Organizations

WorldBook encyclopedia defines coalitions as "organizations working together in a common effort for a common purpose in order to make more effective use of resources". Coalition building is the creation of coalitions through lobbying efforts. Coalitions are only one of several types of strategic or cooperative alliances that vary in structure and function from informal exchange networks to more formal inter-organizational coalitions working toward a common goal. Coalitions often find their impetus with one agency that identifies a problem or a need greater than they alone can address. Each organization brought into the coalition brings its own following and reputation, broadening their individual organization's strengths and expertise within their own sector, and sharing resources and staffing duties.

Coalitions formed around a common goal have distinct advantages and disadvantages. Organizationally, they tend to be very tenuous. Coalition members bring along their own rules and protocols. While some organizations may bring diversity in membership—which at first look seems to be a strong advantage—there are times when it can also be an obstacle. Additionally, decision making is more complicated and harder in a coalition since everyone has to be convinced of the course of action.

BENEFITS OF OUTREACH OUTSIDE THE MUSLIM COMMUNITY

Many mosques that were targeted post-September 11 found astonishing support from local churches. One other minor miracle that has come out of the ashes of September 11 is the strengthened relationship that has been built between Islam and other faith communities. In many cities across the US, mosques and local Muslim organizations that were singularly minded have opened their doors to their neighbors, developing close contacts, and have co-sponsored activities and programs that were not around before that fateful day. As well, other faith groups that invited Muslims to visit are benefiting from this new relationship.

THERE IS SAFETY IN NUMBERS

A coalition of organizations creates community power, and brings authority and energy that are vital in influencing change. Through its broad-based membership, the opportunities for publicity are multiplied, resulting in an extended pool of resources. In one mid-west community, a riverboat gambling referendum had been introduced in 2003 by a consortium of investors who had nearly unlimited financial backing. Along with the local mosque, many religious and family-oriented organizations voiced their opposition to the referendum with the county supervisors. They argued that a gambling boat would cause hardships to families affected by gambling addictions, and result in financial loss to those who could least afford it. They also reasoned that having a casino in the county would drag down family values by increasing local crime, bringing prostitution and increased drug abuse.

Holding millions of dollars in investments over the commissioners' heads, the consortium countered the coalition's argument with statistics on increases in tourism, jobs, and other financial gains the county would enjoy. They also stressed that they possessed one of only three gambling facility permits issued to non-Indigenous people, and therefore, the facility was sanctioned by the state.

Individually, none of the organizations against the riverboat had the political clout to fight the consortium, so they joined together into an inter-religious coalition. In addition to lobbying their representatives at the statehouse to get the investors' permit repealed, they also bought airtime on regional television and radio, put up billboards around the county, and hired a law firm to handle legal matters. They also launched a massive letter writing campaign to the county commissioners and newspapers. After a six-month battle, they were able to force a public vote on the referendum, where it was defeated. In this case, their shared morals and family values brought together area churches, a synagogue and two mosques to fight a common battle. By linking all of their resources, they achieved their goal. Simply put, there is strength in numbers.

The previous is an excellent demonstration of how in give-and-take relationships, sometimes you need to get involved for the common good. By supporting another organization's cause, they in turn will give you support when needed.

Although many organizations do not share a common religious or cultural background, there are many instances of lobbying battles fought around shared moral and ethical foundations. This was recently seen in Chicago when area Muslims and non-Muslims banded together against a strip club that had moved too close to a family neighborhood. Albeit the group lost their fight, they gained enormously by the coalitions and the relationships forged, as demonstrated through the Charity without Fear legislation and the Congressman who voted against the war.

VIII. Assessing Your Situation

In order to practically benefit from this chapter, please consider your organization's situation and setting, in light of what we have presented in this chapter. By answering these questions, you would be assessing your situation as well as identifying the areas where corrections are required. Furthermore, we encourage you to review the specific materials of the chapter for clarification on some questions.

- *Does your organization treat donors as partners on the same mission?*

- *What percentage of your donors are repeat donors? In light of this ratio, how do you evaluate your donor relation effectiveness?*

- *Does your organization personalize communications with your donors?*

- *Does your organization inform its donors of and adhere to the Donor Bill of Rights?*

- *Does your organization provide its donors with a report of how their collective contributions are spent, and what achievements they helped accomplish?*

- *Does your organization publish a timely newsletter that update its donors and community on important matters such as strategic directions, new initiatives, program achievements, fund allocations, and news about your organization?*

- *Does your organization publish an annual report, and which audience receives it?*

- *Are your organization's financial statements available to anyone upon request?*

- *Does your organization have a Donor Management System that keeps detailed records on donors' personal data, communications received by every individual, donations data, sources of donations, etc?*

- *Does your organization analyze the response of donors to every campaign or communication tool, and then use the findings in future campaigns?*

- *Does your organization receive complaints about receiving inaccurate correspondence, multiple copies of mailings, or late receipts?*

- *What tools does your organization use for public relations, and what seems to be the most effective one in your particular case?*

- *Does your organization have an official, articulate spokesperson who is known to local media outlets, and is available at all times?*

- *Does your organization have a community relations program that aims to strengthen the relationship with its constituency through services and sharing their concerns?*

- *Does your organization have a plan that can be promptly implemented in case of adverse publicity?*

- *What types of government relations has your organization had, at what levels, and do you have a dedicated committee with a plan to conduct these relationships effectively?*

- *What coalitions has your organization had with non-Muslim organizations, and do you have consistent communications with those organizations that share part of your objectives?*

Chapter

14.

Financial Management

It does not matter if it is called financial development, non-dues revenue, or just plain old-fashioned contribution income, fundraising is a little science with just a touch of art thrown in for good measure. In order for an organization to achieve its vision, fundraising is the essential element for any nonprofit to continue toward its goals and mission.

Unless an organization has an endless well of readily available financial resources, without fundraising the light bill will not be paid, the telephone will be shut off, salaries will not be met, and programs and projects cannot be funded. Fundraising provides the lifeblood for an organization: money to operate.

Although most of the text in this chapter is drawn from the experiences of larger organizations, and the emphasized cases may not be suitable for your organization, they are applicable for nonprofits of all sizes. This includes mosques and schools, as well as humanitarian organizations.

I.   Financial Planning

One of the primary necessities of every organization is raising funds to cover its budget. Even if funds are readily provided on a yearly basis in the form of grants, these organizations still need careful budgeting to allocate funds appropriately and efficiently.

Primarily, the amount of funding needed, and how to spend those funds efficiently deals with budgeting and funding allocations. How to raise the necessary funds takes into consideration the method or combination of methods for raising the required funds.

FINANCIAL PLANNING TIED TO GOALS

Financial planning is tied to both short- and long-term goals. No organization can know with certainty what their future financial needs might be. Nor can they know how to cover those needs or how to wisely allocate the funds needed unless they know what they really want. Organizations are not mere operations with paid staff and offices. They must have objectives and programs to accomplish. It is crucial for organizations, whether they are Islamic centers, humanitarian relief organizations or social agencies to begin by asking themselves: What do we really want? What do we want to accomplish in the next six months, in one year and in five years? Once these questions are answered, and clear goals are set in a measurable and timely manner, then it would be natural to estimate the cost to get there. At the same time, it would be possible to plan for raising the budget requirement.

> Vital to the success of any organization, financial planning provides the answers for these common questions:
> - What funds do we need?
> - How do we raise those funds?
> - How do we spend them efficiently?

Consider the case of Al-Huda Youth Center, a project proposed for opening at the end of 2006. The center is to be housed in a building that requires renovation. The available equipment is decrepit, and needs repairs or replacement. To achieve the objective, it is necessary to specify exactly what is needed to get there. Mainly, the center must be renovated, and all exercise equipment needs to be fixed or replaced. More specifically, the staff needs to list exactly what needs renovation, what machines must be fixed, what equipment needs to be replaced, how much each item costs, and how long each repair will take, etc. Once the work specifications are clear, the budget requirements can be identified. Only then will this loosely defined objective become a well-defined goal. What we really want: the Goal. It would also be feasible to work on How to get there: the Plan. Likewise, the establishment of a school for 500 students, or a 50-bed hospital are both long-term goals. In both cases, each project requires detailed long-term planning, part of which is the financial phase.

II.   Identifying Fundraising Needs

Before any of the fundraising steps are attempted, the nonprofit must step back and ask, "What exactly is the money for?" Is the fundraising meeting a need? Is it marketable? Does it justify a donor's commitment? If the plan is not well thought out, failure is almost assured; therefore, it is essential to create a sense of enthusiasm about the fundraising idea and of the belief that the project will "make a difference". If prospective donors do not see or feel this sense of enthusiasm, they will not be inclined to reach into their pockets.

To receive maximum support for the project, the organization's fundraising goal should relate to their mission. Precious resources and time may be otherwise wasted if the fundraising is for a project that is markedly divergent from the mission. Once an idea is formulated, the donors will want to know if it is viable. Now is the time to clearly outline the project's goals, objectives, and budget in writing. Just how much money is needed? The fundraising staff must assess these needs by discerning all costs by soliciting estimates, developing in-depth cost analyses, estimating the actual fundraising costs, etc. Predetermining variable costs such as postage, printing, telephone, supplies, and staff time, as well as all fixed costs such as rent, accounting, data processing, etc. can help assure that expenditures do not exceed a reasonable percentage of the overall project expenses.

III. Planning for Fundraising

People need to be asked to give; however, an organization cannot decide that it needs funds today, and then ask for the money tomorrow. Fundraising takes time, effort and planning. Nonprofits must be proactive in their approach to raising funds. A fundraising campaign must be developed well before the need rolls around. A campaign plan is the fundraiser's road map, agenda, and explanation. It assesses campaign goals, develops strategies, and determines tactics about how much money is to be raised, by whom, using what means, in how much time, and for what purpose. Once a campaign is designed, and its leadership is in place, chances are the organization will only get one shot at pitching it to a prospective donor; therefore, the organization must be prepared! Poor planning and presentation will only get "no" for an answer. Prospective donors need to be treated like partners in a business, not as if they had a responsibility to give. They must be courted like a customer, told how important they are, and treated with respect and courtesy. It is also very important to thank them for their gift—they are the organization's lifeblood!

> Planning a fundraising campaign is not so difficult, nor does it take a great deal of time. It is a methodical process that should follow seven basic steps:
> - Settle on an achievable goal
> - Develop a case for support
> - Prepare a campaign funding projection
> - Decide what means of solicitation to use
> - Develop a campaign timetable
> - Define the required human resources needed
> - Finalize the fundraising plan.

A fundraising campaign must have a multi-layered plan that works within the general development plan, which in turn fits into the organization's strategic plan, or the organization's blueprint for carrying out its mission statement. A critically important element of successful management, the strategic plan is initiated and implemented by an organization's staff and board, and reviewed periodically. This process, which should be developed and understood, would ideally cover at least three years, and is a prerequisite for establishing a general fundraising effort and specific fundraising campaigns. A primary step in establishing an organization's budget, this plan identifies priorities, maps out a course for goal achievement and objectives, lays out performance assessment and provides for midcourse corrections. Discerning all of these objectives allows costs to be determined, and income balanced against expenses.

A general development plan identifies where and how an organization will get its funding. It outlines the game plan, and communicates that information to their staff, volunteers and influential supporters. Usually written by the person who is responsible for managing the process of achieving contributed income, the general development plan is subject to periodic review and updating, as is the strategic plan.

IV.   Yearly Fundraising Plan

Fundraising planning defines the effective combination of fundraising and marketing campaigns, and the activities to take. The costs and forecasted income are based on previous analysis. If the organization is new and has no previous data, an educated guess based on experience and data from other agencies may be necessary.

A yearly fundraising plan has one purpose: to guide the agency throughout the year so they are able to cover their budget needs. This can be much harder when considering Muslim charities that depend on public funding in the US, since in most Muslim countries their governments or large donors fund these charities. Others are spin-offs of large businesses, and many are funded totally by families, or "Waqf" funds. Fundraising tools for nonprofits in the West overlap with marketing campaigns, as you will see in the example below.

If the end result were to raise a total of five million dollars, the following questions are the minimum things those in an organization should ask themselves in order to have a yearly fundraising plan:

- What means of fundraising/marketing should we use?

- Targeting what market (potential donors)?

- At what expense?

- On what timetable?

- By what delivery means (to reach your market)?

- Forecasting what income?

For instance, some of the available means which would answer the first question for a Muslim charity in the US could be as follows:

I. Direct mailings

    A. Periodical Publications

        - Newsletter

        - Annual Report

        - Corporate Brochure

    B. Seasonal Campaigns

        - Ramadan Campaign for Zakat Collection

        - Udhiya Campaign

        - 'Eid Appeal

    C. Emergency Appeals

- Natural Disaster (Example: Iran Earthquake, drought)

- Manmade Crisis (Example: war, sanction)

 D. Program Campaigns

- Orphan Sponsorship Program

- Medical Appeal for a Hospital

II. Advertisements

 A. Publication Ads

 B. Radio Ads

 C. Television Ads

III. The Internet

 A. Website

 B. E-mail Blast

 C. Internet Banners

IV. Public Relations Campaigns

 A. Public Presentations (Khutbas)

 B. Fundraising Dinners

 C. Donors Relations

V. Promotions

 A. Video Tapes

 B. CD-ROMs

 C. Convention and Event Sponsorships

 D. Gift Items

The strategies and tools listed above are the primary means used by many successful charities in the US; however, not all of these means work well for charities in Europe or the Middle East.

The next step would be to consider each item separately. Whether or not to use these depends on previous data analysis. Careful details should be considered for the ones that will be used—namely how often, when, how big or small, at what cost, etc.

Naturally, each organization's strategies will be based on their particular fundraising objectives for the coming year. First, it is recommended that these objectives be identified clearly after careful study. Only then can an organization move forward.

A few of the goals or objectives for the coming year could be as follows:

- To reduce advertising by 15% less than the current year.

- To effectively introduce the charity to 60,000 new Muslims in the US.

- To increase our donor base by at least 10% over the current donor base —increasing by at least 3,900 new donors.

- To increase the number of donations by at least 15% over last year—that is to receive at least 17,520 new donations.

- To reach a total of $6.5M in income as a result of all new fundraising strategies used.

- To limit the organization's fundraising costs to 18% of income.

After careful analysis of previous data and studying of new strategies, the outlined fundraising plan should be a detailed document. For instance, when one considers direct mail campaigns, the relevant information needed is specified as the following primary fundraising and marketing draft:

Direct Mail

Periodic Publications

- Newsletter:

  - *Specifications:* 8-1/2" by 11", 20 pages, full color, self-mailer, with a Return Business Reply Mail (BRM) envelope, to report the organization's achievements as well as promoting future programs.

  - *Number:* Two issues per year.

- *Market Size & Delivery Means:* For donors by Nonprofit Bulk Rate (30,000 copies). For mosques and Muslim Student Associations (MSAs) by First Class Mail (15,000 copies @ 15 to each). For public events (10,000 copies). Total of 55,000 copies per issue.

- *Timetable:* The first issue to reach market on June 1st, and the second to reach market a month before the first day of Ramadan (September 10th) to prepare for Ramadan campaign.

- *Expense Budget:* $24,750 per issue ($0.45/copy for printing and postage).

- *Income Forecast:* $82,500 per first issue (forecasting 1% return @ $150/average donation), and $121,000 per second issue (forecasting 1% return @ $220/average donation for Ramadan/Zakat season).

Consider this additional example:

Seasonal Campaign

Ramadan Campaign

- *Specifications:* A complete packet that includes a personalized two-sided letter, in two languages, a mini-brochure about Ramadan programs and Zakat, and a return envelope.

- *Market & Delivery:* To the entire mailing list (200,000 people) by Nonprofit Bulk Rate. To mosques and MSAs by First Class Mail and for by-hand distribution (25,000). Also for public events during Ramadan (25,000). Total number of copies is 250,000.

- *Timetable:* To reach direct market by the tenth of Ramadan (10/14/05) and hand-distributed throughout the month of Ramadan.

- *Budget (Campaign Cost):* $60,000.

- *Forecasted Income:* $440,000 (forecasting a 1.1% return @ $160/average donation).

The same strategy outlined above should be used for all other campaigns such as Udhiya, emergency appeals and various other mailings.

Advertising and Advertisements

Each organization should also closely consider the above detailed plan for their advertisement strategies, whether those strategies are in print media such as publications, aired on TV and radio, or published on the Internet. Consider the following example where each periodical's ad is specified by objective, what messages to use, in what publication or medium, at what cost, how often, what sizes, etc. After documenting your reasoning, and without going into too great detail, your end result should be a table such as the one which follows. As shown, the codes represents pre-designed advertisements with different themes or messages, one general ad, another about Ramadan program, and a third about a certain program:

Publication Name	Frequency	Ad Code	Ad Size	Approx. Cost Per Year
Islamic Horizons	Every Two Months	AD_G11	Two different 1/4 page strips & 1/2 page in Ramadan	$9,000
Al-Jumua'a	Monthly	AD_R10	As above	$7,000
The American Muslim	Monthly	AD_S03	As above	$7,000
Mirror	Weekly	AD_M03	Large Color strip	$6,500
The Message	Monthly	AD_P17	2 different , 1/4 page strips & 1/2 page in Ramadan	$4,000
Business Link	Yearly	AD_G11	1/4 page, full-color in the first few pages	$5,000
Al-Talib	Monthly	AD_R10	Full page B&W	$5,000
Washington Report for ME Affairs	Monthly	AD_P17	1/4 page color strip	$6,000
Muslim Observer	Weekly	AD_S03	B&W 1/2 page	$6,000

FUNDRAISING THROUGH PUBLIC EVENTS

Public events are also effective forums for fundraising. Friday Khutbas, presentations at Islamic centers, fundraising dinners, and donor public relations have good track-records for this purpose. Careful consideration should be used to determine how many events to hold, when, where, by whom, for what causes or programs, at what cost, forecasting what income, etc. Although it might be possible that all of these parameters can be summarized using a table format, naturally it would not be solidified for the entire year until events are formally scheduled and proper arrangements are made.

The overall plan should specify the number of events to be considered, potential cities and gathering places, and other details such as potential speakers. The arrangements should be done during the plan's implementation, with the solid specifications not being completed until a few weeks, or possibly months before the actual events. These plans are usually dynamic because they depend on many variables, such as availability of known speakers who will attract larger groups of possible donors, the tentative schedules of the Islamic centers, as well as other factors.

Initially, an organization's goals in this regard might be:

- *Fundraising Dinners*–Six major dinner events, with an initial budget of $60,000 and targeted income of $450,000 (an average of $75,000 per dinner).

- *Presentations at Mosques*–120 Khutbas and lectures at available Islamic centers featuring four speakers at 30 events per speaker per year. Budget is $160,000 with a target income of $960,000 ($8,000 per event).

TRACKING RETURNS ON FUNDRAISING CAMPAIGNS

One mark of a successful organization is that it always carefully measures the return on its fundraising activities. If an organization were to go for multiple fundraising means, and then dumped all of their income on one source, then they surely would be missing a great deal. An organization can be more effective analyzing the return from each campaign or fundraising mean, then weigh the results to see what works better.

CONTINGENCY FINANCIAL PLANNING

Every organization must be totally aware that the implementation phase of any plan might not go smoothly. World events might change, which would prevent the charity from sticking to its plan. For instance, in an unexpected case of natural disaster, management might need to modify the plan, expand a project, or delay another.

Considering these parameters, it is suggested that management approve a budget of up to 5% in permitted additional expenses. Moreover, it is recommended that management set aside a certain amount of reserved funds for emergency situations. Such an amount should be sufficient as seed money to launch an unbudgeted program, or in the event that the organization has no income for as much as six months. For instance, a reserve fund might be set aside in the amount of $300,000. This money will come in handy when an emergency team must be mobilized in the event of unforeseen disaster, or to fund the operational costs of the organization for a few months. It is also recommended to add to this amount on a yearly basis so that as the organization grows, its reserve fund also grows.

V.   How Much Does it Cost to Raise $1?

Even fundraising activities cost money. The basic fact is that you need to spend money to raise money. Before you even raise a single dollar, a simple 50,000-piece mailing could easily cost $17,000. Additionally, organizations that depend on public funding should have advertising campaigns as a supportive strategy for its funding means. These campaigns should be aimed at promoting the organization itself and its programs. This strategy is to have a brand name among the organization's potential market, which is done through various marketing strategies. The term "marketing" is used loosely here because such organizations will find themselves needing to sell their programs the same as any for-profit company that must market its products. Although marketing costs money, the return for nonprofits is indirect, rather than direct, as it boosts the return on fundraising campaigns.

If $800,000 in fundraising expenses produces five million dollars in income, then the cost to raise one dollar is 16 cents. This is a good figure for an international Islamic charity in the US. However, the cost could be much lower for a mosque—possibly costing only a few cents on the dollar. This premise is because it does not require a great deal of effort to raise the funds necessary for the yearly budget of most mosques. The majority of mosques are usually able to cover their budget from collection boxes after Friday prayers. Simply by having a few volunteers holding theses boxes at the doors, their costs are nearly nonexistent. In addition to this, to cover other expenses most mosques have a yearly fundraising dinner which frequently also has a low overhead. The majority of mosques in the US do not have financial problems unless they start large projects and programs in addition to the mosque. It is when they endeavor to start such projects as youth centers, schools, social agencies, etc. that the additional funding is required. Whenever there is a need for additional funding, a common practice in US mosques is for the imam or president to ask people for donations after large gatherings such as Friday prayers. Since community members are already inside the mosque, there is no need for additional costs such as postage or printing.

On an annual basis, the fundraising cost ratio should not exceed 25 percent, while the national average for organizations represented in National Society of Fund Raising Executives (NSFRE) is 20 percent. Previous studies in the 1990s found even lower ratios of 16 percent for colleges and universities, and 12 percent for hospitals and medical centers.

Most probably, when the cost ratio for an organization is high, it is usually the result of hiring paid solicitors. Low cost ratios are generally seen when an organization's fundraising includes a major gifts program and has a prospect pool with a high proportion of previous donors. Obtaining new donors—as opposed to targeting renewed donors—increases the costs. The same is true for when the average gift size decreases. Several studies have shown that direct-mail acquisitions targeting new donors costs $1 to $1.25 for every dollar raised; whereas direct-mail renewal costs 20 cents for every dollar raised. Clearly, although maintaining donor relationships is cost-efficient, charitable organizations must continually invest in acquiring new donors so that their donor base does not eventually disappear.

For other nonprofits, no matter what types they are, it should never cost more than 25 cents to raise a dollar, because when adding other non-program expenses to that amount, it ends up costing a lot more. Assuming that the fundraising cost is 25%, then management costs might very well be 15%. Likewise, indirect program expenses at the head office might be about 10%. If the organization has regional or field offices, there must be additional indirect program expenses from those offices. Therefore, a very high expense of over 50% for non-program costs can easily be reached. In fact, one of the conditions of eligibility to join USAID is for the petitioning agency to have management and fundraising costs not be over 40% of income.

In general, we would like to suggest an organization's fundraising effectiveness ranking based on the percentage of how much it costs to raise a dollar:

- Excellent: if the cost to raise every dollar is less than 15 cents

- Average: if the cost to raise every dollar is between 15 to 25 cents

- Low: if the cost to raise every dollar exceeds 25 cents.

If an organization's management and indirect program expenses are low, some organizations can still do well even if they have high fundraising costs. For instance, if an organization pays 25% of their yearly budget towards fundraising expenses, while both its management and indirect program costs are less than 15%, then over 60% of its income goes towards programs. This is an acceptable ratio for international relief organizations, although such situations are rarely practical.

On the other hand, there are nonprofits which pay very little money, if any, to raise their budget funds. They can do this by receiving full grants that fund their programs. In this case, one cannot really compare such an organization to another that receives public donations. To keep their donors giving year after year, the nonprofit which takes in cash collections is required to report back to the thousands of donors who gave $30, $50 and $100 at a time. This situation is very costly, but these organizations are rarely threatened financially like those funded by grants. The nonprofits that receive grants can easily shut down if the funding agency or government cuts off their funding.

How much is reasonable depends really on what kind of nonprofit the organization is: a publicly funded international charity, an Islamic center or a mosque, a government-funded agency, a funding agency, etc.

TRICKY ACCOUNTING METHODS GOBBLING THE PIE

Many western organizations spend a lot on fundraising. However, the actual amount usually does not show up on their annual statements for two reasons: first, they categorize most of such expenses as indirect program costs; and second, they outsource fundraising activities. There are many for-profit fundraising agencies whose entire business is to raise funds for nonprofit organizations at a very high cost. In most cases, the nonprofit organizations do not have to pay a fee to the for-profit fundraiser. Rather the agencies raise funds marketing certain causes, and in return eat a big chunk out of every dollar they raise, leaving the leftovers to the nonprofit organizations.

For instance, it occasionally happens that a fundraising agency will raise $500,000 for a cancer research program, and then give the nonprofit organization conducting this research $100,000. Here the actual cost to raise a dollar is 80 cents. Since the nonprofit organization did not pay this agency a penny, it shows on the books as if the $100,000 income came at no expense whatsoever to the nonprofit. We have all heard many times those radio advertisements inviting us to donate our old cars for the benefit of a good cause. This practice is primarily by for-profit fundraising agencies that receive the cars and then resells them. Out of that money, they pay high salaries and expenses, make a good commission on the net income, and then give the nonprofit organization with which they have contracted a small percentage of the car's sale price.

VI. Where do Operational Cost Funds Come From?

Most funds are received as a result of fundraising activities are earmarked as restricted income which must be put towards various programs. Funding the general management and costs associated with fundraising (also known as operational costs) to run the organization becomes a bit troublesome to many nonprofits. Thus, how to fund overhead expenses becomes a pressing question for every organization's leadership.

Ultimately, the best option for an organization to meets these costs is to have "Waqf", an endowment fund dedicated to the main purpose of relieving the organization from any distress in covering its basic management budget. A well-established organization should have long-term planning that outlines the acquisition of Waqf funds. For instance, an organization with three million dollars in income might require $600,000 in operational costs. When the majority of an organization's income is restricted, or reserved for specific programs such as clinics and schools, where can the organization find the necessary funding to support their own operational backbone?

One way to defray these costs might be for the organization to own a large building where it houses the organization's offices. They could then generate an income by renting space to several other businesses to cover its operational costs. There is no doubt that such a building may very well cost several million dollars. Only a well-established organization with long-term strategic planning would be able to accomplish this. Another method would be through other investments, which then produce income to fund such costs.

There are three major benefits to both of these situations:

1. No money will be deducted from the restricted funds by the organization for operational costs.

2. The organization would be creating a safety net to carry them through lean years when income is low. Such proactive planning can help a Muslim charity survive dire financial circumstances such as those in the recent past when Islamic charities have been painfully subjected to factors such as politically motivated agendas, people in governmental power rushing to judgment, or media campaigns that make donors afraid to give, etc.

3. The Waqf would be the main asset of the organization.

However ideal, the establishment of Waqf is not very common for Muslim charities in America. Therefore, we must consider a more probable case where the nonprofit in question does not have Waqf funds, and must rely instead on contributions to cover both its own operations, as well as the cost of its programs. How might an organization fund its yearly budget of $600,000 in the above example? The practical solution is to deduct a certain percentage across the board from all income, restricted and unrestricted. This ten to twenty percent would go towards the management budget, depending on the organization's leadership policy. Assume that the 15 percent management deduction set by the organization's Board of Directors still is not sufficient. Since $600,000 is 20 percent of three million dollars, then the remaining amount could be funded from unrestricted contributions. In the example above, the remaining $150,000 is covered by the unrestricted contributions.

This percentage can be determined depending on the ratio of restricted funds versus unrestricted funds. For some situations, if the unrestricted income is large enough that it can fund the management costs, it would be a good option to not deduct anything from the restricted income. It would be better instead to fund the entire operational cost from unrestricted funds. However, publicly funded organizations have a very high percentage of restricted funds that are usually greater than 85 percent of total donations received; this is because donors usually like to give towards specific programs.

Many organizations design fundraising strategies that lead people to give more towards unrestricted funds in order to use part of those funds for the overhead costs of the organization. However, experience has shown that it is more effective to market programs aggressively, without worrying about the ratio of restricted versus unrestricted funds. After this, approximately 15 percent from all funds received may be deducted. Any remaining needs would be covered from unrestricted funds, because donors tend to give more money allocated for specific, defined programs rather than as general donations. Experience has also shown that the average donation of restricted contributions is much higher than those of unrestricted contributions. For some organizations, the average restricted donation is $190; whereas, the average unrestricted donation is $60.

VII.   Case Study: Funding A Mosque's Programs

A common yearly budget for a larger Islamic center could feasibly be set at $650,000. Half of this could be raised in a yearly fundraising dinner, and the remaining amount through collection boxes averaging about $6,000 per week.

Most usually, mosques have no problem when it comes to raising their operational budget. But they do struggle a bit and require careful fundraising planning when it comes to having weekend schools, youth centers or a gymnasium, and social programs such as providing counseling and financial support for families in distress. In this case, they need some planning. The lack of planning—financial or otherwise—leads to failing programs. Closing a youth center after years of operation, having to turn away all genuine cases of financial need, or Muslim women having to go to unsuitable public shelters are failures that could have been avoided had accurate plans been made.

> In the initial planning stages, it is generally valid to begin with these strategic questions:
> - What is the objective?
> - Where are we now?
> - How to get there?

Consider a simple case where a weekend school has a yearly deficit of $135,000 because collected fees cover only part of its operational cost. Additionally, the gym requires $43,000 per year to pay the salary of a part-time employee, and cover equipment maintenance. The social committee requires another $120,000 yearly mainly to cover direct financial support and a professional counselor. The Islamic center will continue to struggle if its leadership does not take the serious yet simple step of financial planning. In addition to funding the main mosque operations from donation boxes, and having a yearly fundraising dinner, what else can be done?

• *Funding the Social Committee:* Since the bulk of the social committee's expenses are financial support to families in distress, Zakat would be the correct funding source. All it may take from such a large mosque, is one full day of good planning during Ramadan. In a smaller Islamic center, raising these funds may take considerably longer. In any event, during his Khutba, the Imam can raise the issue of helping local families in need. He should remind the community that these are lawful recipients of Zakat, calling upon the members to estimate and pay their Zakat towards this cause. Additionally, literature (such as a brochure explaining Zakat and how to estimate them) should be distributed. This should be repeated after Tarawih prayer on the same day as well. In larger mosques, this amount is very well within reach when you choose the right time and method to collect it. Of course, not everyone will donate or pay Zakat for this. However, the last week of Ramadan is when most people pay their Zakat, and might be the most suitable time to approach the issue. There is no doubt that communities differ in their financial ability and generosity; therefore, planning should always take into consideration past experiences and data. What could be sufficient for one community might be irrelevant to another. That is why one particular method cannot be prescribed for all situations. Generally speaking, the organization has to choose:

- **The right message** (helping local families in need from their Zakat)

- **At the right time** (on a Friday during the last week of Ramadan)

- **In the right place** (what could be better than the mosque to reach the community?)

- **Through the right means** (personal appeal together with *pledge forms*).

• *Funding the Gymnasium Budget:* The Islamic center leadership may decide to fund the gym totally though yearly memberships at $200 per member. Since there are a few hundred youth who regularly come to the gym, it might be prudent to restrict access to the gym only to members. The Islamic center administration should plan for, design and implement an effective system to collect fees, issue membership cards, and promote this among the youth. Only 215 members are needed to cover the gym's yearly budget. This would relieve the Islamic center from having to cover this amount from the weekly collection money.

• *Funding the Weekend School:* After careful study, this might be done through a combination of a letter to all parents encouraging them to donate for this important program, and a benefit dinner for the same cause. Raising the tuition to cover the weekend school budget might force some families with lower incomes to withdraw their children from school. Therefore, covering the deficit can be done through donations from financially capable parents who appreciate the program. Assume 400 students attend the weekend school. From those students are 310 families who know about the weekend school's efforts, to who the mosque's administration would send a letter reporting what the tuition fees bring and what the expenses are. The letter will also invite them to give specific amounts such as $250 or $500. If 25 percent of those parents respond positively with an average donation of $350, then $27,000 can be raised. Imagine if this is done twice a year, then $55,000 is covered! In addition, a benefit dinner for parents should be planned.

AUTO-MONTHLY PLEDGE PROGRAM

The mosque finance committee might propose to the Board of Directors to fund all three of the above programs through one method: Auto-Monthly Pledge Program. AMDP is a method in which the mosque automatically withdraws a pre-agreed upon amount from a donor's checking account on a monthly basis.

STRATEGIC QUESTIONS

Since the total budget is $293,000 for these three programs, the mosque would need $24,416 per month for this type of donation. This method is quite challenging, requiring long-term effort to get enough participants. A simple solution would be to market the program as:

- $1 per day

- $2 per day

- $3 per day

All of which are an affordable amount for any mosque attendee, totaling only $30, $60 or $90 monthly. This method is quite possible for a large mosque, and is a wise way to allow Islamic centers to have long-term and stable income for vital programs. Different participants pledge different monthly amounts. Assuming that the average monthly pledge is $60, the organization would need a base of 407 participants to fund the weekend school, the gymnasium, and the social programs, possibly benefiting hundreds with vital services.

To reach the goal, the organization must consider every aspect of this program. It might be necessary to form a committee to take care of the whole project, or assign a person as the project manager. The implementation process involves promoting and marketing the program to convince community members to participate. They must also get the system ready for the process by making bank arrangements, settling technical software/hardware issues, and acquiring pledge agreement forms. After the planning, they must begin deducting the amounts monthly, issuing receipts, reporting back to the community on "Now vs. Target Situations", and possibly utilizing visuals to present progress to motivate people to participate. This last item might be accomplished through the use of a bar chart on the center's bulletin board. As long as it takes to reach the goal, it is important to continue requesting that people participate, especially at weekly Friday prayers. Another way to draw participation to this project is to set up a table in the Islamic center where people can pledge donations. This worthy goal will be reached in only three months if 30 people sign up weekly for this program!

A small quarterly newsletter can keep donors updated with reports on how their gifts are making positive changes within the community. Once the goal is reached, fewer efforts to promote the program will be necessary. It is inevitable that some people will stop participating; therefore, the door should be kept open to additional participants, so that the total amount received does not decrease. It is important to remember that overall efforts must be continuous so that the organization is always beyond meeting the basic needs for these three programs.

VIII. Assessing Your Situation

In order to practically benefit from this chapter, please consider your organization's situation. By asking yourself these questions, you would be assessing your situation as well as identifying the areas where making corrections would be beneficial.

• *Does your organization currently have a fundraising plan that is currently being implemented?*

• *Are you clear about your organization's financial needs to meet its objectives for the next three years?*

• *Does your organization have a plan to raise funds to meet its financial needs for the coming year?*

- *Does your organization have a system that enables you to identify how much it raises, and at what cost, for every fundraising source and strategy utilized?*

- *Overall, how much does it cost your organization to raise one dollar? What is its fundraising effectiveness rank according to our suggested scale?*

- *What are the ratios of your General Management and Fundraising costs from the total income for each of the last three years?*

- *How do you fund your General Management and Fundraising costs while still honoring your donors' restriction of contributions?*

Chapter

15.

Budgetary Process

Many of the financial problems that occur in nonprofits are due to lack of proper budgeting. A powerful tool used to allocate financial resources, budgeting is based on plans and knowledgeable expectations in terms of revenues and expenses. Without proper and thorough budgeting, funds will not be wisely allocated dependent upon priorities and needs, resulting in the over- or under-funding of different programs. On the contrary, with budgeting, an organization would at least know in advance what funds are needed and for what purposes, so that its fundraising efforts can be aligned with these goals in mind.

In this chapter, we will go beyond rudimentary bookkeeping methods by providing important basic financial skills that nonprofit managers should make an attempt to acquaint themselves with. We will discuss what budgeting is really all about, including how to prepare an effective budget. Additionally, we will discuss various types of budgets, as well as budgeting for revenues and expenses. Later in this chapter, the reader will be introduced to primary Internal Revenue Service forms and procedures that are imperative for every nonprofit. Additionally, we will provide an explanation of key financial statements and various financial terms that are useful for every organization.

I.   All about Budgeting

Since some nonprofits can live without it, budgeting appears to be a complicated process that many would rather avoid. It is true that an organization might be able to survive without proper budgeting, but its financial situations will definitely be riddled with reactive, haphazard decisions. This will result in ineffectiveness and a financial situation in crisis. The solution is not to avoid budgeting, but to learn what it is and how to do it.

WHAT IS BUDGETING?

Simply put, a budget is a blueprint for spending based on expected income for a defined fiscal period. The budget reflects the organization's thinking in terms of what they believe will happen financially, and what initiatives it plans to take in the coming fiscal term. When a budget is created, from the beginning it is presumed that resources are limited. There is never enough money to go around. The decision of how much to put where is always a formidable one.

```
┌─────────────────────────────────────────┐
│                                           │
│      Five Purposes of a Budget            │
│                                           │
│   1.  Puts strategy into operation.       │
│   2.  Allocates resources.                │
│   3.  Provides guidelines                 │
│   4.  Controls spending.                  │
│   5.  Communicates plans.                 │
│                                           │
└─────────────────────────────────────────┘
```

The process of creating a budget is in itself a good chance for the organization to take stock of its resources and their limits. As to how to allocate the money, the organization has many choices dependent upon its needs internally and externally. These needs can be broken down into units or departments, programs, and activities—all of which may be distinguishable by grants and/or restricted gifts. Some of these programs may be able to stand alone by their abilities to bring in new resources, have a dedicated fund especially for their needs, or have the opportunity to generate funding of their own.

Who Handles Budgeting?

Fundamentally, the executive level is where the budget process occurs, and where leadership creates a major tool to achieve its objectives. In most organizations, only the top administrative person has special formal authority over fiscal matters, including budgets. It is a commonly accepted rule that the senior officer must approve of budgets, financial reports, and other such documents before they are released internally or externally. Therefore, that person bears the ultimate fiscal responsibility for the contents of that budget or report, regardless of any lower tier personnel who may have actually made the decisions, or done the work.

Fiscal management should be relegated to the bookkeeper, accounting, finance director, and, possibly the board treasurer. Program planners and fiscal managers never speak the same language—their priorities are completely different, and they often do not take into account the importance of their peer's budget process. Program planning decisions are usually seen as failing to reflect economic realities, while fiscal management decisions are viewed as insensitive to the programmatic mission of the organization. For this reason, both program staff and financial staff should work with the executive director and board to develop budgets truly reflecting organizational priorities, acting as a guide for spending and decision making.

Some agencies generally handle budgeting through an administrative style where almost everyone assists during budget time. Certain people may handle cost estimation, others may write program descriptions, and yet others might be involved with allocations by function, and so forth. Elsewhere, a group may be put together from various sections of the organization whose specific purpose is planning and development for different parts of the budget. Finally, a few organizations may require outside help from firms that specialize in fiscal matters.

Once the budget has been created, someone must be responsible for implementing it to ensure that the entire process has not been wasted, nor are the funds. In the end, this person becomes the one who is accountable.

The Budget Cycle

It takes much longer than the fiscal year for the complete cycle of activities associated with the program/fiscal year to take place. Depending upon the program or reason for funding, some series of activities must be carried out well before the beginning of the actual fiscal year, while others occur during it and still others after the year is over. So, complete budget cycle activities overlap more than one year. This extended sequence is known as the budget cycle.

Every agency is individual in its size, mission, structure, programs, traditions, and so on; however, the actual budget cycle will remain remarkably consistent from agency to agency. Budget cycle's features are also very similar among agencies and typically include the following essential activities:

Program and budget planning

- Needs assessment and feasibility study

- Program planning

- Cost estimating

- Budget development

Funds procurement

- Budget request submission

- Fundraising

Fiscal management

- Designation of cost and responsibility centers

- Internal funds allocation and re-budgeting

- Establishment of restricted accounts

- Financial transactions, recording, and accounting

- Operations monitoring and reporting

Performance assessment, financial reports, audits

- End-of-year (EOY) financial statements

- Financial audit

- Performance audit

- Cost analysis

Generally, all of the above features may be condensed into three major steps, each with a distinctive time perspective:

- *Budget preparation*–takes place well before the specific budget year begins. Policymaking is a part of this phase, as are the primary activities associated with funding procurement.

- *Budget execution, monitoring, control and adjustments*–occur throughout the budget year.

- *Analysis of final results*–are analyzed after the budget year ends, and includes accountability.

One of the most important features that organizations must realize is the significance of setting schedules of dates and times for accomplishing all the tasks on the budget cycle list. These schedules should include timeframes for preparing, reviewing, deciding on, and submitting the materials for each task, as well as the beginning and completion dates, and who is assigned to do what.

II.   Budget Preparation

An organization should begin thinking about the budget for the upcoming year at least two or three months before the beginning of the fiscal year reflecting the organization's operating cycle. For example, an after-school program might have a fiscal year coinciding with the beginning of the school year.

PRELIMINARIES

The first step in budget preparation is the completion of an environmental statement. A nonprofit cannot effectively plan for the upcoming year without a clearly stated idea of what its position is regarding programs, and beneficiaries. An annual evaluation of nonprofit organization trends, changes in donor base, technological changes, and so on can help the nonprofit to better determine where it should be going.

Start at the Previous Fiscal Year

To achieve a basic understanding of the current financial situation, it is imperative to analyze the most recent fiscal year. In almost all but the smallest of organizations, there is some group responsible for budget planning which may include the organization leader, officers, staff, board members, or others. After the budget planning group has been formed, they should examine the previous year's financial results with respect to last year's budget:

- Did the organization make or lose money?

- Did the programs cover their individual costs?

- How did the organization do relative to its budget?

- What were the sources of variances (good or bad) from the budget?

- How did the organization do in its major sources of revenue and major expense categories?

- What factors drove variances?

Another primary step in the budget process is a review of program achievements over the past year, including reviewing objectives achieved, comparing budget to actual figures, and looking at the number of people served in each program. By dividing the true cost of each program by the number of people served, you can also analyze the cost per unit of service. Based on this review, new aims can be weighed and decided upon. These objectives should fit into your strategic, long-range plan, allowing progress towards the nonprofit's mission with the true estimation of the costs required to achieve your objectives, including staff, supplies, and other resources. Including both program management and financial staff in program cost decisions will ensure that all required departmental program resources are considered. When projecting future costs, be certain to take into account upcoming adjustments in areas prone to significant fluctuations.

Develop Objectives and Policies

The next step is for top management to develop a set of general objectives and policies. This statement should be a broad-based look at what the nonprofit hopes to achieve. Is the coming year to be a year of rapid growth? Is the nonprofit looking for domestic expansion or establishment of foreign branches? Does the organization expect to increase its existing programs? If top management communicates the desired direction of the nonprofit, middle management can set it into motion.

Finally, specific, measurable goals should be established. Here we are not dealing simply with the general direction of the nonprofit, but with the actual operating objectives. For example, service should increase by ten percent and beneficiaries of service by 15 percent.

These are two ambitious objectives—more often than not, a nonprofit that fails to budget, or that fails to control the budget will not have much success in achieving such goals.

A budget is a planning tool and should be prepared well in advance of the period of the actual performance. Plenty of time should be given for presenting the budget to the board of directors for approval, and for making changes.

FORECASTING

Although forecasts can be based on complex mathematical formulas, they can be quite simple, such as a projection that indicates what happened this year would happen again next year. An accurate forecast must also consider any changes that may make the future different from the past. These changes can be due to various decisions made, improved technology, changes in laws, world events, etc.

Computers make sophisticated forecasting techniques accessible to managers. Some software programs can take seasonal patterns into account. If a nonprofit has times of the year that are generally very busy (such as during 'Eid ul-Adha), a forecast for the year as a whole will not do the whole job. A manager gains a significant advantage by knowing which months are likely to be usually busy or slow, and by how much.

Forecasts Based on Historical Data

Information on how much service was required in the past five to ten years, and last year's actual vs. budget cost provides a basis for a future forecast. Once the basic historical data for services has been used to predict future need, that information can be used to predict the necessary materials, staff, and other expenses as well. When historical data does exist, forecasting is a bit easier. Knowledge about the past is often an excellent starting point.

The easiest approach to forecasting using a series of historical data points is to simply take an average. By adding up the data over the past five years, and then dividing that amount by five, you will arrive at the desired estimate for the coming year ($y6 = [y1 + y2 +$

y3 + y4 + y5] / 5). Although this is the simplest method, it is also the most elementary approach, leaving the results open to too many random factors, and ignoring any underlying patterns.

Another, more academic approach is the linear regression statistical technique which entails arriving at a trend line through plotting historical points. The points are then projected into the future to make a forecast, the results of which are generally more accurate than taking an average. The limitation of this method is that it is based on a straight line, which is notoriously poor for projecting seasonal trends.

There are quite a few reliable forecasting software programs in the retail market such as *SmartForecasts for Windows©*, which can produce curved-line forecasts that can more closely match a seasonal historical pattern. This results in a more accurate forecast, and may be used to forecast just about anything else that the nonprofit wishes using historical data.

Sometimes obtaining historical data to predict future trends is not available. This is generally the case when a new organization is in its startup phase, or when a new program is being developed. How does a nonprofit work around such a dilemma? To some extent, a "guess-timation" (guess or estimation based on individual instinct or experience) will get the nonprofit where it needs to go. At other times, an engineered calculation can determine the data necessary to make the forecast. However, in the absence of historic data, it is better to go through a thorough and detailed estimation of all expenses involved as well as expected income.

PRELIMINARY BUDGET EXAMPLE

Assalaam Youth Services is a nonprofit organization considering implementing a community youth center to provide counseling services, sporting programs and after-school programs for at-risk youths aged seven to 18.

Assalaam Youth Services Program: Community Youth Center Preliminary Budget	
Line Item	**Requested Budget**
Personnel	
1a. Center Director	$35,000
1b. Screening Superior	22,260
1c. Intake Worker	18,400
1d. 2 Full-time Custodians	71,400
1e. Counselors	41,310
1f. Secretaries	22,000
1g. Part-time Workers	3,000
1. Total Salaries/Wages	**213,370**
2. Employee Benefits & Payroll Taxes	42,674
3. Professional Fees	11,110
4. Supplies, Communications, and Reproduction	10,452
5. Occupancy: Rent	13,000
Renovation	2,500
6. Equipment	4,480
7. Total Direct Costs	**297,586**
8. Overhead/Indirect Cost (18% of TDC)	**53,565**
9. GRAND TOTAL	**351,151**

Figure 15-A

In the primary stages, a preliminary budget is drawn up for the Community Youth Center by the planning committee, allocating resources according to the model set by the umbrella organization.

At the first Budget team meeting, the AYS director reviewed the planning and rationale of the Preliminary Budget, provided background information, and answered questions. By the end of the meeting, the group was fully aware of the nonspecific status of some of the line-item costs in the Preliminary Budget. Clearly, the Revised Budget team would have to pin down and firmly fix many of the dollar figures.

Dar al-Islam Universal High School Expense Budget

Object Code	Description	Base (Current Budget)	Increase Factor (%)	Proposed Budget
3000	Faculty salaries	$652,000	4	$678,080
3100	Professional salaries	144,460	3	148,794
3200	Bimonthly salaries	105,062	3	107,184
3250	Overtime	13,132	0	13,132
Total Salaries		**$914,654**		**$947,190**
5000	Office supplies	31,500	0	31,500
5050	Lab supplies	52,500	0	52,500
5100	Computer hardware	31,500	0	31,500
5200	Postage	31,500	0	31,500
5250	Photocopying & duplicating	31,500	0	31,500
5400	Telephone–access	21,000	3	21,630
5410	Telephone–Long Distance	10,500	3	10,815
Total Other Expenses		**$210,000**		**$210,945**
TOTAL EXPENSE BUDGET				**$1,158,135**

Figure 15-B

INCREMENTAL BUDGETING

Seen as a rigid practice, incremental budgeting is not as widely used as in previous years, but is still very common and simple. The central budget staff builds a model of institutional revenues and expenses. After collecting some initial assumptions about revenue, an estimation guideline is calculated for future levels of expense increases the organization can afford in a few major categories, such as supplies, general expenses, equipment, furniture and travel. In addition, it is possible that some expense categories such as employee raises can be factored into this mix.

Departments receive a budget baseline, usually based on their current year budget, and the guidelines outlined above. Their total allocation for increased expenses is determined by multiplying the suitable guideline rate times the budgeted amount in each category. The budget may be presented based upon expense categories or object codes. The following example shows an illustration of an Islamic high school's expense budget using object codes. Increase factors are identified for each object code, and used to project a budget for each. The school then adjusts the guideline to move the funds where they are needed, with some restrictions: funds cannot be moved between salaries and other object codes. The school might choose to budget on the base of higher-level categories since it usually applies the same increase factor to all object codes within a category.

III. Organizational vs. Program Budgets

There are two types of budgets: the *organizational budget* and the *program budget*. The organizational budget is an organization's detailed funding plan for a period of usually one year. It specifies which funds are expected to come from what sources, and how those funds will be allocated between departments, accounts, and types of spending. To a varying degree, the budget then determines spending during its covered period. The organizational budget is a tool used by the organization's leadership to inform its board so that they might exercise its oversight role over leadership actions. Additionally, to the organization itself so that managers, staff, volunteers, and members can fine-tune the organization's financial management needs. Organizational budgeting has the deepest implications for organizational management, and many organizations use budgeting to increase their overall effectiveness.

PROGRAM BUDGETS

Program budgets are proposals prepared for specific fund sources requesting a certain level of funding, and identifying exactly how the organization will use those funds. The funding request is often paired with a service budget showing the types and volume of service the organization will provide with the resources funded from the request. This process allows the funding agency to make an informed decision in buying a certain number of units of service. Unquestionably, program budgets form a portion of the organization's overall budget; although, due to timing differences or policy decisions, program budgeting and organizational budgeting may occur separately.

Program budgets allow nonprofits to design and observe the use of resources by purpose including programs, administration, fundraising, and membership development.

Because nonprofits are mission-based, this provides a fundamental viewpoint for nonprofit managers and board members, allowing them to see the full cost of each activity within the organization.

Program by source budgets, on the other hand, indicate the information from a program budget, including the full cost of that activity, alongside the source budgets of the various funding sources that help to pay for the program. This format allows organizations to divide program costs by funding sources, determining which costs in a program are funded and which are not.

FUNCTIONAL BUDGETING

For every one of the many service programs an organization carries out, specific objectives are marked by a complex set of activities. Each of these activities is supported by its own particular line-item budget. Each activity, commonly referred to by the term "function", requires its own distinctive type and amount of resource. So how does an organization know how much funding to allocate to each activity?

Line-item budgeting does not explain for what program functions (categories or sets of activities) the line-items will be used. Nor does it tell how the line-item elements or objects are to be allocated among categories. Since nonprofit organizations exist to carry out programs, not just to pay salaries or incur expenses, functional basis forces the nonprofit to identify specific programs, identifying the costs associated with each program.

The functional budget serves as a major tool in planning, deciding, implementing, and monitoring program operations. Many federal and state funding sources require that a budget be submitted in both functional *and* line-item format.

The terminology of cost accounting and human services are very different; therefore, different words will be found to mean the same thing. Excellent examples of this are the words "functions" and "categories", or "sets of activities". These terms designate the same thing: groups of identifiable activities, personnel, and material resources that can be clustered together, and whose particular object costs can be specified. Moreover, the word "program" is used to identify all functions taken together as they pertain to a designated set of objectives.

	General	State Food Aid	After-School Program	Summer Program	Meals-On-Wheels Program
Community Food Bank					
Results for Fiscal Year Ended September 30					
Revenue					
Sponsorships	$2,400				
Grants	40,000	30,000			
Contracts			25,000	27,000	
Donations	5,500				800
Fundraising	5,000				1,400
Total Revenue	**52,900**	**30,000**	**25,000**	**27,000**	**2,200**
Expenses					
Salaries	27,200	30,000	16,600	14,200	
Benefits	3,100				
Rent	12,000				
Supplies	300				
Telephones	610				
Computer lease	2,600				
Contract services			8,000	12,000	
Delivery costs					3,300
Insurance	975				
Printing	600		400	1,800	
Advertising	2,300				
Total Expenses	**49,685**	**30,000**	**25,000**	**28,000**	**3,300**
Net Surplus/ (Deficit)	**$3,215**	**$0**	**$0**	**($1,000)**	**($1,100)**

Figure 15-C

In Figure 15-C, you see a simple budget for an organization with a few programs. The actual revenue and expenses for the Community Food Bank for the fiscal year ending September 30th are presented. Sources of revenues as well as expenses for its main programs are shown. These numbers might not totally agree with the budget of each program.

Variance in Food Bank Summer and Meals-on-Wheels Programs						
	SUMMER PROGRAM			MEALS-ON-WHEELS		
	Budget	Actual	Variance	Budget	Actual	Variance
Total Revenue	$30,000	$27,000	($3,000)	$3,000	$2,200	($800)
Total Expenses	$28,000	$28,000	0	$3,000	$3,300	$300
Net Surplus/ (Deficit)	$2,000	($1,000)	($3,000)	0	($1,100)	($1,100)

Figure 15-D

The Variances of actual vs. budget for every source and expense is the difference between the two. In Figure 15-D, we sum up the variances for Summer and Meals-on-Wheels programs, without stating the line item, just to illustrate an example of this concept.

IV. Budgeting Revenues

Over the past several years, the activities of many nonprofit organizations have increasingly been put under microscopes by donors, governmental agencies, the media and charity watch groups. Their primary reasoning is to guarantee that contributed money goes principally to providing direct program services versus supporting the administrative operations. Benefactors want assurance that their contributions are spent toward the program or charitable purpose they wish to support.

The nonprofit must budget for income as well as expenses. Past experiences can help estimate revenues with some degree of accuracy even though unpredictable events may influence contributions. Short of relying on a crystal ball, liberal anticipation of future plans and adjustments is important with any budgeting based on the past. Grants from foundations, corporations, and government agencies can be more difficult to predict. In collaboration with the executive director and the fundraising committee, the financial and fundraising staff must make the most realistic assessment possible for budgeting purposes.

An inevitably useful exercise is the development of contingency budgets reflecting more conservative or optimistic projections of revenue.

There are two philosophies of Revenue Budgeting:

- *Revenues drive expenses*–we expect X revenue, so we can spend Y;

- *Revenues respond to expenses*–we must find X revenue to support our basic expenses Y.

No matter which of these philosophies an organization follows for funding, the process of budgeting revenues should encompass three main elements:

1. *Identify all primary sources of revenue.* Usually, the primary funding sources align with the revenue categories used in the budget statement.

2. *Determine how to establish the budget for each primary source.* Sources of revenue will fall into categories that require different techniques for projection and budgeting.

- *Large items*–the best example of this is a grant, identified by the source. Also, its risk of failing to come through at a different level, and whether or not it might be reduced or eliminated within the timeframe of the designated budget.

- *Small items*–such as corporate or individual memberships, forecasted by taking an average from past years' memberships and revenue from sales of goods or services fees.

3. *Compile the Revenues.* After having developed a budget for each major revenue source, all of the items need to be brought together into a single, comprehensive view of revenues in the new budget as shown in Figure 15-E. The compiled revenue projections and targets will give the organization starting parameters for expense budgets. In most cases, revenue budgets are subject to revision in light of operating needs.

Budget for All Primary Sources of Revenue

Major Revenue Source	Budget
Memberships	$2,000
State Grant	30,000
Ramadan Appeal	40,000
Annual Dinner	52,000
Rentals	4,500
Sales	1,200
Online Donations	6,000
Advertising	4,000
Total	$139,000

Figure 15-E

V.   Budgeting Expenses

The opposite side of revenues (income) is expenses (costs). Sometimes revenues and expenses are tied together, such as in fundraising projects that generate revenue at a certain cost. Excess revenue over expenses usually can be used to cover other expenses of the organization. Examples of these are found in programs that do not generate revenue and administrative expenses.

Costs are associated with items that have a future benefit (e.g., desks, computers, and other assets are known as capital expenditures). Telephone service and postage are disbursements that generally do not have a future value. In either case, they must be budgeted.

In many organizations, expense budgeting is a paradox: while it requires the most time from line managers, it also seems perfunctory. Large organizations often engage in some form of incremental expense budgeting, while small organizations align their expense budget to the availability of revenue; however, the real effort goes into determining revenue availability.

To understand how the expense budget works, you need to approach it as if you were starting from zero and building up each element. Such an understanding forms the foundation for variances and for making cuts or reallocations when required or permissible.

COST DRIVERS

Costs are motivated by one or more of the following factors:

• *Activity*–Some costs are directly related to the volume of certain activities. Program budgets are formed on the basis of the activity they are supporting. The program budget is set up by determining how much of each expense category is required to support the suggested activities, such as office supplies, telephones, cost of rent or renovations, and personnel, etc. All of the expenses in an organization should be traceable to some supported activity. When expenses need to be reduced, it is helpful to determine what each program would cost at different service levels. Cutting a fixed percent amount across all expense lines is often not the most effective way to reduce expenses. For instance, do not assume that benefits and costs are interdependent with each additional dollar spent, resulting in an additional dollar of results.

• *Negotiated, Contracted, or Fixed Pricing*–Negotiated costs will drive some of the expense elements. This includes negotiated salaries, such as that of the director, and insurance coverage. There is little choice but to include these in the issues in the budget.

• *Revenue*–In some cases, revenue can drive a cost element. This comes into play when an organization reserves a certain percentage of their revenues for particular programs; such as when an Islamic center has a policy of putting at least 25% of its revenues into Da'wa programs.

• *Inflation*–Prices have a tendency to go up. Inflation is a concept based on the average increase of prices in a basket of goods: some items in the basket experience greater rates of increase. How will the organization respond to the pressure on costs? Some organizations often find the particular sources of increases more problematic. During a time of economic growth, wages may also go up.

TYPES OF EXPENSES

The following are some of the main expenses nonprofits face:

• *Personnel*–These costs often form the largest expense for most nonprofit organizations, often eating up 50 to 60 percent of the total operational budget. Primarily, for an organization whose cornerstone is its volunteers, the toughest question a nonprofit must ask itself is whether or not to add paid staff. The addition of salaried personnel brings more professionalism to the group as a whole; however, any decision to add paid personnel involves some degree of long-term commitment, and a variable cost of production regardless of output or level of activity. With this decision come other things to consider: salary increases for such things as cost-of-living, and health and retirement benefits which are optional and negotiable with the employee.

• *Other fixed costs*–This category can become the catchall for sundry other required expenses incurred by an organization on a regular basis, such as employer contributions to Social Security and Unemployment Compensation. Fixed expenses such as rent and utilities fall into this category as well.

• *Depreciation*–A sad fact of life is that the minute something leaves the showroom floor or store shelf, it begins to depreciate in value. The tax-based depreciation period allowed for business equipment rarely exceeds five years. The same is true for office furniture, company vehicles, etc. Nonprofits are required to record the purchase of long-lasting, real property and equipment (such as computers, vans, buildings, etc.) as assets in the financial records. They must then post a portion of the cost of those items to each year in which they have a useful life. This process is known as capitalizing and depreciating fixed assets.

For example, suppose that on January 1, an organization purchases a computer with a useful life of four years. Although the computer initially costs $2,500 the cash for the computer was disbursed in the first year. However, one-fourth of the expense for the computer will appear on the Statement of Activity (Income Statement) for each of the four years it is deemed to have a useful life. Therefore, in the three years after the purchase, a depreciation expense of $625 ($2,500 / 4 years = $625) will appear on expense statements despite no cash being used during those years. By the end of the fourth year, the computer will be fully depreciated, with the full cost of the computer having been recorded as an expense.

Since depreciation expense is a non-cash expense, it is important to plan for the replacement of fixed assets as they wear out or become obsolete. For example, some organizations set aside an amount of cash equal to the amount of their yearly depreciation expense so that funds will be available to purchase a new asset once the current one is fully depreciated.

- *Contingencies*–Funds that are set aside to cover unexpected expenses are known as contingency funds. These funds have no specified purpose and are at the disposal of the organization's higher echelon officers to allocate as necessary. It is important not to over-budget contingencies, because the organization loses the planning and control advantages of budgeting when a large proportion is allocated to discretionary funding. In most organizations, these funds are subject to periodic incremental increases, a luxury many smaller nonprofits do not have.

Allocating Expenses

Expense allocation refers to the practice of splitting an expense item or category and assigning shares of it to other departments or spending categories. Program services are activities that result in goods and services provided to fulfill the organization's mission. Program expenses will vary based on the type of not-for-profit entity. Program expenses include costs such as direct salaries, expenses related to children's programs in a youth organization, payments for art exhibits in a museum, or payments to the elderly or under-privileged in a community assistance organization. On the other hand, support services encompass all of the other nonprofit's activities that are not directly related to providing the established program services. These include general and administrative expenses, fundraising, and membership development activities. Generally, the field that comes under immediate examination is the percentages of amounts spent on fundraising and support services as compared to direct program services. Expenses benefiting only one program or a single service are straightforward to report. However, questions are bound to come up if an expense item (i.e., the executive director's salary) crosses many programs or functions. In many organizations, it is quite likely that the executive director may spend the morning at a fundraising breakfast, and then attend planning and administrative meetings throughout the middle part of the day. He might spend the remainder of the day directly participating in an organizational activity. Such a situation most probably occurs many times and with many different people in the organization; therefore, those expenses should be allocated among the appropriate areas.

The life cycle of the organization also directly affects these ratios. Additionally, administrative costs will likely be greater if an entity is in the startup phase. A nonprofit should be cautious throughout the year to maintain and allocate proper percentages of program, support, and fundraising expenses. It is wise to periodically review expense allocation methods for appropriateness.

VI.   Projected Budgets, Taxes and the IRS

There are a number of federal processes that must be diligently adhered to in order to comply with the law, and allow the organization to operate as a nonprofit. It is up to the organization to find out which ones apply to them, then familiarize themselves with these processes and comply with them. Although wading through these processes on their own is not unheard of, it would be wise for the organization to seek out the services of a certified public accountant to help them through.

IRS FORM 1023

Generally, when a nonprofit files for 501(c) (3) status, the Internal Revenue Service (IRS) requires that Form 1023–Exemption Application is filed with their agency detailing a three-year projected budget for the nonprofit. How can a fledgling organization that has not even begun work make a projected budget for the IRS? How should they approach budget preparation without having been in service for a couple of years? The smartest course, naturally, would be to consult a certified public accountant (CPA) who is able to steer the organization down the correct path. For those who insist on setting out without the immediate assistance of a CPA, it would be beneficial for them to:

- Set goals

- Figure out how much it will cost to accomplish these goals

- Figure out how to raise the needed funding.

An alternative approach to the problem could also be to ask themselves, "how much money do we think we can raise?"

The budget projections requested in Form 1023, and the numbers and amounts of funding sources will distinguish your agency between being a "private" foundation or a "public" charity. An organization can generally be considered a public charity if the organization stands up to a litmus test where revenues come from a wide range of sources.

IRS FORM 990

IRS Form 990 (Return of Organization Exempt from Income Tax) is the information return that must be filed by all but exempt nonprofits (e.g., religious organizations) with the Internal Revenue Service on an annual basis. The importance of Form 990 cannot be emphasized enough. Although some nonprofits are exempt from filing this form, they should do so anyway. Charitable 501(c)(3) organizations file Form 990 (along with a Schedule A) that reports financial information, including a statement of Revenue and a Statement of Functional Expenses (i.e., program services, management and general, and fundraising). It also describes program accomplishments for the year.

There currently are four versions of this form, including a short form for small nonprofits (990EZ), and a business income tax return (990-T). Another type of Form 990 that is filed by private foundations, and is used by fundraisers for prospect research on foundation donors, is Form 990-PF.

EMPLOYMENT TAXES

All entities doing business—whether nonprofit or for-profit—in the United States and its territories must file federal quarterly tax returns. Some states and localities also require similar forms. Ignorance of the law is no excuse; therefore, it would be wise to know the state and local requirements regarding this issue. It is never a good idea to ignore Form 941, "Employer's Quarterly Federal Tax Return," sent to you by the IRS. The form must be filed whether or not the organization had any payroll for the quarter, or even if there were no employees. The form must be completed and sent to the IRS anyway, with a copy of the return retained for the organization's records.

Who is FICA, and why did they take my money?

Face it. People hate doing paperwork. More contemptuous is paying taxes: Federal Withholding, FICA, Medicare tax, Unemployment Contribution tax, state tax, local tax, etc. As tempting as it may be when hiring staff to treat them as independent contractors rather than employees, there are few ways to avoid all that nagging paperwork. Tax withholding, quarterly deposits, etc. is by far the most common issue IRS auditors raise with non-profit organizations. To help an organization determine how an employee might be classified, it would be quite beneficial to the organization to consult IRS Publication 539 which discusses the factors the IRS considers in classifying workers.

For those times when workers really are independent contractors, it would greatly serve organizations at audit time not to overlook the necessity of reporting to the IRS compensation of $600 or more. Any person who passes the independent worker test set forth by the IRS, and works for an organization outside of the regular employee stable, or receives awards, fees, and similar payments must be supplied at the end of the tax year with Form 1099-MISC. These forms should be sent to the worker no later than January 31 and to the IRS—along with Form 1096 transmittal—no later than February 28. It is also important to note that if these advisories have not been followed as outlined by the IRS code, and the worker does not file the required income tax forms, the nonprofit can be held liable for any taxes due on that income. As the reader can see, being a nonprofit or not-for-profit organization is not truly tax-exempt. As the saying goes, "the only certainties in life are death and taxes".

VII.   Understanding Key Financial Statements

The most important financial reports include balance sheets, income statements, and statements of cash flows. A balance sheet shows a company's assets, liabilities, and net worth. An income statement is a report of a firm's revenue and expenses during a certain period. The bottom line of an income statement shows whether the company had a net profit or a net loss for that period. A statement of cash flows shows the amounts of money flowing into a company and out of it as a result of its operating, investing, and financing activities.

Organizations that do not seek a profit need many of the same kinds of financial reports. For example, private schools must keep track of their tuition income and their expenses. A government agency may wish to compare the cost of a program with the benefits. Possible donors to a charity may like to see how previous donations were utilized.

BALANCE SHEET

The balance sheet and the statement of financial position are two names for the same function: a financial snapshot indicating the financial position of an organization at a particular point in time. This is illustrated through the basic accounting equation *(Assets = Liabilities + Stockholders' Equity)* on a specific date which is at the end of the accounting period. Typically, the final day of the accounting period falls on the end-date of the organization's fiscal year; not including interim accounting periods (usually monthly) set for internal information purposes, and quarterly for external reports. Only by default does the accounting period end on the calendar year. The activities taken care of at the end of the fiscal year should include the organization's internal accountant and exterior auditor. Although quite time consuming, an audit must take place.

INCOME STATEMENT

The income statement compares the organization's revenues to its expenses, or more simply, revenues minus expenses equal its net income. Unlike the balance sheet—which deals with an exact moment in time, the income statement dictates what happened to the

organization over a period of time, such as over a month or a year. This is useful in helping board members or trustees see how the organization has grown financially from year
to year, and helping to determine whether or not an organization can afford to grow, add
equipment, venues, staff, and so on.

Darul Salaam Community Daycare Center
Income Statement
For the Year Ending December 31, 2003

Revenues	$20,000
Less Expenses	-12,000
NET INCOME	**$8,000**

Darul Salaam Community Daycare Center
Statement of Income and Retained Earnings
For the Year Ending December 31, 2003

Revenues	$20,000
Less Expenses	-12,000
NET INCOME	**$8,000**
Retained Earnings, January 1, 2003	4,000
TOTAL	**$12,000**
Less Dividends Declared	-0-
Retained Earnings, December 31, 2003	**$12,000**

Darul Salaam Community Daycare Center
Statement of Retained Earnings
For the Year Ending December 31, 2003

Retained Earnings, January 1, 2003	$4,000
Net Income for the Year Ending December 31, 2003	8,000
Total	**$12,000**
Less Dividends Declared	-0-
Retained Earnings, December 31, 2003	**$12,000**

Figure 15-F

A statement of income and retained earnings is a combination of both an income
statement and earnings held over from the previous year, and not distributed to an organization's owners or shareholders. Although a nonprofit organization has no owners

or shareholders, this combined statement is still useful in representing the organization's accumulated earnings or loss thereof.

THE STATEMENT OF CASH FLOWS

The statement of cash flows is the third major financial statement, which provides information about the organization's inflow and outflow of cash. At the end of each accounting period, the current assets section of the balance sheet indicates how much cash the organization has, and can be compared from year to year tracking how the balance has changed. Strictly speaking, relying only on the balance sheet for this information can result in erroneous interpretations of the financial statement.

Darul Salaam Community Daycare Center
Statement of Cash Flows
For the Year Ending December 31, 2003

Cash Flows from Operating Activities
Daycare Tuition	$19,000
Payments to Suppliers	(8,000)
Payments to Employees	(3,000)
Net Cash from Operating Activities	**$8,000**

Cash Flows from Investing Activities
Purchase of New Equipment	$(6,000)
Net Cash Used for Investing Activities	**$(6,000)**

Cash Flows from Financing Activities
Borrowing from Creditors	$2,000
Loan for Classroom Furniture	1,000
School Van Loan Payment	(2,000)
Net Cash from Financing Activities	**$1,000**
Net Increase/ (Decrease) In Cash	**$3,000**
Cash, Beginning of Year	1,000
Cash, End of Year	**$4,000**

Figure 15-G

Such an incident might happen when an end-of-year balance shows a greater amount of cash than usual. In a nonprofit organization, a scenario like this could possibly be the result of a sudden one-time injection of emergency donations, causing the organization to appear far more liquid and stable than it really is. As an integral part of the overall financial statement, the statement of cash flows will detail where the money came from, and how the money is to be used. Accounting numbers do not always tell the organization's entire story, as the financial statements tend to be inadequate to fully convey the results of operations and its financial position. Therefore, detailed notes fully outlining the origins of the figures used should accompany all financial statements.

VIII. Understanding Useful Financial Terms

In this section, we present useful financial terms that every manager should know clearly. Some of these terms have been explained further in the previous sections of this chapter.

Activity-based Budgeting: A budgeting system in which funds are allocated on the basis of the costs necessary to reach a desired production level determined by cost studies of services or goods. An activity-based budgeting system also looks at the types of costs consumed by those activities and the rate with which each unit of the activity consumes those costs.

Balance Sheet: The statement of an organization's liabilities, assets, and fund balances at a given point in time. It is also known as the statement of financial position.

Budget Base: Under an incremental budgeting system, the initial set of expenses and revenues to which increase (or decrease) factors are applied to calculate the total funds and revenue targets for the next fiscal year.

The Fiscal Year: The annual timeframe or cycle that parallels the one created by the government for appropriations and funding, which has become known as the fiscal year (FY). Most public and private organizational structures now reflect this flow for program and budgeting processes where plans and decisions are completed, operations are carried out, and reviews, reports and audits follow. Although the rhythm normally follows a twelve-month cycle, it does not have to coincide with the calendar year of January 1 through

December 31. The federal fiscal year runs from October 1 through September 30. This annual cycle establishes a powerful universal flow for policymaking, control and accounting functions.

Contingency: Funds to be used for discretionary or emergency purposes and that are not allocated for a specific purpose at the time the budget is established.

Control: A system put into place by an organization's board, management, and other personnel which give reasonable guarantee regarding the effectiveness and efficiency of operations, reliability of financial reporting, and compliance with applicable laws and regulations. This encompasses the overall control environment, risk assessment, control activities (such as reviews, reconciliations, information processing edits, physical controls, segregation of duties, and policies and procedures, and communication and monitoring).

Cost Allocation: The process of associating costs with or assigning them to departments, activities, or programs (cost objects). Some costs may be directly identified with a department, activity, or program, such as the salaries for personnel assigned to a department. Other costs have an indirect relationship to the ultimate cost objects, and are allocated according to activity levels, formulas, or some other method.

Endowment: Organizational assets held on a long-term basis whose use is limited to the income, or a portion of the income, earned by those assets. True endowments are established by stipulation of the donor of the asset and restricted to use as endowment on a permanent basis or for a specified time period. An organization's board may also set aside funds and treat them like an endowment, making a long-term investment of the asset and limiting use to income earned; these are often called quasi-endowment funds.

Operating Statement: An organization's state of its cumulative current operating revenues and expenses during a particular time period. The operating statement is one of the three basic statements used in financial accounting. Organizations use different names for this statement, including income statement, statement of activities, statement of changes in unrestricted net assets, and statement of current funds revenues, expenditures, and other changes.

Program Budget: The budget for a definite program within an organization. The program may be defined according to organizational characteristics (e.g., the activities and associated revenue and costs of a single department or director) or funding source, such as activities and costs funded from a particular group.

Variances: The mathematical difference between two values for the same expense or revenue factor within the same set of fund groups, account groups, departments, or programs. Variances can be calculated for the differences between any combination of budgets, projections, and actual results for various time periods.

Zero-based Budgeting: A budgeting system in which an organization builds up its budget from scratch, starting with a projection of revenues and service levels that are the basis for determining the organization's need for resources. In contrast to incremental budgeting (in which the organization's future budget is based on its current budget), every element within each of the organization's budgets must be justified each year.

IX.   Assessing Your Case

In light of what has been presented in this chapter, and in order to practically benefit from this chapter, please consider your organization's particular situation. By answering these questions, you would be assessing your situation as well as identifying the areas where corrections are required. It is also recommended that you go back through the chapter to review specific materials for clarification on some questions.

- *Does your organization prepare a methodical annual budget for its management operations, as well as for each of its programs?*

- *Does your organization involve both fiscal managers and program planners to prepare its budgets?*

- *What are the main stages of the budget cycle your organization follows on an annual basis?*

- *Does your organization thoroughly analyze the most recent financial results with respect to last year's budget, and then establish next year's goals in preparation for budgeting?*

- *What forecasting approach does your organization use in preparation for budgeting?*

- *Does your organization adhere strictly to incremental budgeting every year?*

- *When was the last time your organization went through the process of Zero-based Budgeting?*

- *Does your organization know the cost of a unit of service for each of its programs?*

- *What is the percentage range of variances between the Budget and Actual line items for the last fiscal year?*

- *Does your organization budget revenues for all primary sources of income?*

- *When budgeting for revenues, does your organization assume that revenues drive expenses, or revenues respond to expenses?*

- *How does your organization allocate expenses when an expense item crosses several programs?*

- *What percentage of total revenues is allocated for contingency annually?*

Chapter

16.

Managing Financial

Revenues and Expenses

Fiscal responsibilities do not end once budgets are prepared and approved. Nonprofits must constantly monitor financial resources, and compare actual revenues and expenses to budgets. Some nonprofits budget expenses carefully, yet fail to budget revenues because they find calculating revenue expenses for every source difficult.

There are two purposes of expense and revenue management that are widely used:

- Linking the use of resources to the achievement of objectives, and

- Adhering to accountability requirements that are commonly referred to as fiscal management.

Although summarized, the following sections describe the practical procedures for improving fiscal records, and for monitoring and managing the flow of resources. Gone are the days when aid can be given without knowing the name, age, family history, and fingerprints of the receiver. Additionally, funds received must have a total visible trail to their source. With more and more government scrutiny descending upon Islamic nonprofits, it is not only good business to keep open books and procedures, it is vital to the survival of the nonprofit.

Using simple financial management techniques, this chapter will guide those who are not professional fiscal administrators by providing assistance in effectively overseeing their economic resources. We will go through many of the difficult matters that international nonprofits face, such as maintaining clear program balances, considering various sources of funding per program, addressing direct versus indirect costs, and disbursements. Additionally, as we go through this chapter, we will provide practical recommendations for keeping resources safe, i.e., separation of functions, and authorization policies and procedures, etc.

I.   Revenue and Expense Management

Monitoring revenues and controlling revenues pose similar problems. Nonprofit organizations receive and are accountable for many types of revenue: grants, allocations, service fees, contributions, dues, and bequests. Some or all of these might be partially restricted or designated toward a particular purpose. Although the funding may arrive in lump sums, at specific intervals or just drop by drop, no matter what the source, they must be used judiciously, with every penny accounted for. Short of hiring a full-time and highly qualified accountant who specializes in nonprofits, the organization's administrators should consult with many of the numerous texts available on accountancy procedures directed specifically towards nonprofits. Through these resources, it can be determined which approaches will provide the most efficient and satisfactory methods for their organization, based upon its size and kind of revenue sources.

REVENUE/EXPENSE FLOW AND BALANCE

Nonprofit organizations face unique challenges and stress factors not seen by others in the for-profit sector. Cash flow balance is commonly interpreted in the not-for-profit sector to mean the balance between incoming revenues—whatever their sources—and outgoing expenses, a term which can be confusing if the agency operates strictly on a cash accounting basis. Especially for smaller agencies or programs, problems are usually found in balancing the inflow and the outflow of resources. This stems from the lack of sources from which to seek advice, since most information available on these topics is directed at the for-profit sector.

A simple chronological graph or chart projection showing what receipts align with what expected expenses can go a long way toward making the organization's management aware of its stress points and allow the necessary time for coping with any shortage. A chronological chart might address any "lead time" (often thirty days) for both paying obligations and revenue receipt. In today's times of financial and political troubles, sudden loss or cutbacks in funding can create unanticipated problems in balancing revenues and expenses, forcing organizations to shift to less reliable resources. This type of grave crisis can hit even the most historically solid organizations.

MONTHLY EXPENSE SUMMARY

Certain monthly expenses are a given: rent, utilities, salaries, taxes, etc. Knowing these is much easier than knowing the amount of revenue that will be taken in each month to cover expenses. With this in mind, a standard five-column format can be drawn for the Monthly Expense Summary as shown in Figure 16-A. In this example, an agency operates a fund that delivers humanitarian programs to children in Gaza, Palestine. The organization allocated a yearly budget for every program, which could be translated into a monthly budget for ongoing programs, and a few seasonally budgeted, like 'Eid Gifts. Here we see that in January, the Children's Clinic has a budget of $8,500, and a year-to-date budget of $30,000 which is the amount allocated from the start of the fiscal period through January. For this same example, actual expenses for this program are $8,480 in January, and $30,920 year-to-date. As shown in the variance column, the program is $920 over budget.

Monthly Expense Summary
Fiscal Period October 2004–September 2005

Account Name: Gaza Children Fund
Report for the Month Ending January 2005

PROGRAM	BUDGET		EXPENSES		VARIENCE
	Current Month	Year to Date	Current Month	Year to Date	Year to Date
'Eid Gifts	1,200	3,600	1,200	3,560	40
Back-to-School	4,000	15,000	4,190	15,964	(964)
Clean Water Fountains	500	1,500	500	1,450	50
Children's Clinic	8,500	30,000	8,480	30,920	(920)
Orphan Program	3,000	12,000	3,300	12,720	(720)
Food Aid	6,500	26,000	6,230	26,410	(410)
Total	23,700	88,100	23,900	91,024	(2,924)

Figure 16-A

MONTHLY REVENUE SUMMARY

The typical monthly revenue statement in most organizations parallels its typical expense statement. Each statement should show year-to-date and current month balances of how much money comes in, as opposed to how much money goes out, and show both budget and actual figures. Setting up a five-column Monthly Revenue Summary would prove to be invaluable in showing all transactions, including those that are anticipated or expected, as well as those that have actually occurred. After all, for organizations to survive, anticipation of funding to some degree of accuracy is essential. Nonprofits should at least know the cumulative total of expected revenue-per-source for the whole year. For organizations which survive on one funding source, this is a simple matter. For those depending on more than one source, clearly refining their expectations every month makes for a more total financial picture, and helps to stimulate efforts to collect that revenue. Therefore, monthly revenue summary changes according to each organization's needs. In the following example, the organization states what sources of revenues are fund producers for the Gaza Children's Relief Fund, including specific details on the number of donations, the average donation, and the cost of raising one dollar. This does not mean that the five-column summary is not needed. Instead, this organization chose to have this type of report monthly, while comparing the budgeted revenues to actual revenues on a quarterly basis, based on their objectives and needs.

Monthly Revenue Summary
Fiscal Period October 2004–September 2005

Account Name: Gaza Children Fund
Report for the Month Ending January 2005

SOURCE	RECEIVED YEAR-TO-DATE		CONTRIBUTIONS DATA			
	Current Month	Year to Date	Number of Donations	Average Donation	Campaign Cost	Cost per $1
Newsletter	2,200	6,200	60	104	4650	0.75
Back-to-School Appeal	5,250	18,220	202	90	255	0.14
Website	1,920	17,500	288	26	375	0.05
Ramadan Appeal	38,210	103,025	636	162	11,333	0.11
Orphan Sponsorship	3,030	12,120	346	35	1,090	0.09
'Eid ul-Adha Program	10,525	13,575	200	68	1,765	0.13
Total	61,135	160,640	1,732	93	21,763	0.10

Figure 16-B

In example 16-B, the organization is tracking the sources for different campaigns that generate revenue towards this fund. Clearly, this organization depends on public contributions, mainly coming through direct mail and online campaigns. We see, for instance, that the 'Eid ul-Adha campaign generated $10,525 during January, and $13,575 year-to-date, because it is a seasonal campaign. In addition, the average donation—which is the total received divided by the total number of donations—ranges from $26 for online donations to $162 for Ramadan donations. At the same time, the cost to raise one dollar—which is the campaign cost divided by the total received through it—varies for these two sources. The actual cost to raise one dollar online was found to be five cents, as opposed to the 11 cents it cost to raise one dollar through the Ramadan campaign.

MONTHLY BUDGET SUMMARY

Preparing a monthly budget summary is very useful and recommended, and reflects the anticipated timing of revenue vs. expenses per month, instead of dividing the full budget into twelve equal parts. Therefore, an organization's December fundraiser proceeds would be included in their monthly revenues to correspond with the one-forth to one-third of income received in Ramadan. At the same time, if the organization's insurance is due once a year rather than monthly, the entire insurance premium would be reflected in that month's budget, rather than divided into twelve equal parts throughout the year. By preparing monthly budget breakdowns and comparing them with actual dollars expended and received, you can more accurately spot real changes and revise the budget accordingly. In our example above, we would have budgeted expenses vs. actual expenses, and revenues vs. actual revenues, as well as the variances between them and the availability of funds.

II.   Management, Fundraising and Program Expenses

Nobody likes paperwork; however, when it comes down to survival of an organization, it is better to just bite the bullet and conform. Short of being a CPA, knowing when to file, what to file, what information should be retained, what needs documentation, what needs a report, and on and on, the goal of these next few items is to help the reader navigate these choppy waters.

MANAGEMENT AND FUNDRAISING EXPENSES

Most Muslim charities in the US disburse both management expenses such as salaries, rent, and insurance as well as fundraising expenses, such as printing, postage and advertising. For each of these expenses, supporting documentation should be filed along with a copy of the expenditure. For instance, payroll reports should be filed on a monthly basis stating gross salaries paid, tax deductions, employer tax, and net salary paid, along with the check numbers, dates and payee information to make the CPA's quarterly tax filing easier.

Infrequently repeated single payments should have a contract, an invoice or both. Annual advertisement deals ought to have yearly contracts along with an invoice for each payment made to the vendor. The same is true for Consultation arrangements. In short, you need to file all expenditures on a monthly basis along with supporting documents for all expenditures, whether they are contracts, invoices, or management reports. In addition, each branch of an international charity would record its own expenses.

BRANCH EXPENSES

The rules for domestic expenditures are not difficult when compared to those for branch office spending. These expenses may be divided into two categories:

• *Office expenses that are management operational expenses used to administer and supervise all aspects of programs being implemented abroad*–Such spending is usually budgeted on a yearly basis. Since these expenditures are fixed, it is suggested that this budget be disbursed on a quarterly or monthly basis, separately from any programs budget. However, the head office should receive from each branch a management report outlining management issues, including the actual expenses of the last period (whether it is monthly or quarterly), and a formal request for the next period's budget. Because budgeted expenses are simply estimations of future costs, it is important to detail all actual expenses. As well, management reports should include copies of the supporting documents for every item on the expense sheet. For instance, invoices of utilities, payroll reports, rent contracts, receipts, etc.

- *Programs expenses*–For this aspect, there are three stages:

Before–Proposal. The proposal must outline what the program is all about, who will be the beneficiaries, what services will be offered, how the program will be implemented, and the itemized program costs given in detail, etc.

Approval–Management approval and disbursement of funds. Management at the head office must evaluate the program, approve, disapprove, or modify it and file its response. If approved, management must have a form that summarizes the findings and decision, and a method verifying and control of funds, along with direct instructions to the accountant on how to disburse funds for the program.

After–Report. It is better to send the same management approval form or a letter noting this decision to the implementing agency, whether it is your organization's branch or a partner organization. The letter should also inform the recipient of the program's approval, the date the funds will be disbursed to the project's account, and any requirements for continuous support. Additionally, request a specified date the report should be received from the organization. For example, if the funding is for an Udhiya program in Ethiopia, request a detailed report to be received two weeks after the execution of the Udhiya. Reports should also include names and information for all beneficiaries with their signature and pictures, if possible.

The following are three program cases in regards to reporting:

- *A Seasonal Single Program*–A program that is conducted for a short time period in an area where you have no other current programs, i.e. Ramadan program in Azerbaijan. In this instance, it is recommended to follow the previous three stages: proposal, approval, and reporting.

- *An On-going Single Program*–A program that is continuous in an area where an organization has no other projects. For example, a clinic or a school. Before beginning such a project, it is recommended to have one proposal at the start with a clear agreement concerning monthly or quarterly budgets. These proposals must be followed by monthly or quarterly reports from the implementing agency or program management stating the last period's achievements. As well as the program status, how the last period's funds were spent, and a formal request for the next disbursement. It is important to receive copies of all supporting documents with each report. As well, a letter stating how much was wired and for what reason should be faxed or mailed after each disbursement.

•   *Various Multiple programs*—The most difficult case of this sort consists of having different forms of programs—while all are under the same management and usually in the same area, some are ongoing, yet others may be seasonal or one-time. For instance, in Bangladesh you might have two functioning clinics and a school, an orphan sponsorship program, and seasonal Ramadan and Udhiya programs. In this instance, the management team must decide whether to combine all programs through one monthly report from their branch office there, or deal with each program separately. If the collective monthly report is chosen, it must include a blanket summary report of all programs. This should contain the status of each program, number of those benefited (example: 300 orphans), total funds spent, funds requested, and other pertinent information of your choosing. It must also include a separate report for every program, along with all supporting documents, as well as detailed data. Using this method, funds may be disbursed monthly to all programs, along with a letter stating the disbursement reason, and for what programs the wired funds may be used. To ensure a well-organized operation, as well as proper record-keeping, it is strongly recommended having a policy of not disbursing funds for the next budget until a detailed report is received, along with all supporting documents for the previous period to verify how funds were spent.

Reports and supporting documents should include materials not only for the accounting department, but also for the media department, as these documents are very important for newsletters, website maintenance, brochures, and advertisements. They might include news articles from local newspapers, letters (if any) from beneficiaries, photos, video footage, etc. In short, you must coordinate with the media manager to request reports and supporting documents, and multimedia materials benefiting both departments' purposes.

INDIRECT VS. DIRECT PROGRAM COSTS

Since donors make contributions to further a nonprofit's mission, they are concerned that charitable dollars are used to achieve the organization's service goals efficiently. To help donors and boards, agencies such as the National Charities Information Bureau (NCIB) have established certain standards outlining the amount from an organization's budget that should be spent in each category. For example, NCIB recommends that at least 60 percent of annual expenses be assigned to program services. In addition, many of the larger accounting firms have developed industry standards for the arts, libraries, human service organizations, and others to show what percent of expenses are commonly devoted to programmatic services and what percent to supporting services. Generally, there is no set industry rule for measuring the appropriate proportion of expenses that an organization should maintain, but program expenses should make up the majority.

Program costs for nonprofits are categorized as direct and indirect program expenses. Many nonprofits make heavy use of an unethical strategy that presents the organization to donors as a very efficient organization whose bulk of financial resources goes towards programs, not other operations while the reality is contrary to this. Both direct and indirect program expenses are program costs, not management and fundraising expenses. However, this is a deceptive practice where the majority of the actual management and fundraising expenses are dumped into indirect program costs!

Practices and policies of how expenses are allocated among functional expense categories vary among sources. Therefore, within the nonprofit sector, expense allocation practices vary widely from organization to organization. The lack of standard allocation practices makes functional accounting a somewhat unreliable measure of nonprofit efficiency and effectiveness. Lacking clear guidelines, each organization defines for themselves which expenses are legitimately programmatic and supportive, and which are management cost. Auditors and donors are likely to accept the internal guidelines as long as they are reasonable and justifiable.

A primary example of legitimate expenses that could be categorized as indirect program expenses would be if a charity has an orphan sponsorship program. No doubt that the financial, services, and material support provided to the sponsored orphans are direct program costs. This support might be the provided monthly fund, the price of new clothes, the cost of medical check-ups, and so on. Although there might be a full-time program coordinator at the office whose main duty is as liaison between the sponsors and the orphans, mailing reports to the sponsors, collecting sponsorships, disbursing funds, etc., the expenses acquired by this staff member (such as his or her salary) could be categorized as indirect program costs. These might even be considered as fundraising costs by other organizations if the main duty of this staff member is to collect the sponsorship funds. As well, the salary and expenses of a social worker in the field where an organization supports orphans, and who monitors the orphans' conditions, delivering their sponsorship benefits is surely an indirect program. In general, indirect program costs are supervisory or supportive services to deliver the program itself. It is very effective for an organization that has many charitable programs in a certain area to have a branch office in this area to supervise the implementation of all its programs, and to assure their effectiveness. As a result, some expenses will be required to run this field office. Because of its supervisory role over the programs it carries out, the overhead costs of the branch certainly can be considered as indirect program costs.

On the other hand, consider an organization that is located in a city where it is expensive to maintain an office. The organization is housed within a very elegant building, and its staff is highly paid. Moreover, it is publicly funded, meaning it does not receive grants to easily fund its budget; rather it has to conduct public fundraising campaigns to raise its budget, which is a costly process. The nonprofit has a yearly income of about $4 million. To the astonishment of all, it claims that its management cost is only three and one-half percent of income, with over 90 percent of income going towards program expenses. Professionals in this field know that this feat is impossible. With a staff of about ten members at its head office, it would be safe to assume that their salaries range from $40,000 to $45,000 per year. The total salaries alone add up to at least $425,000 per year, exceeding ten percent of revenues. This amount still has not taken into consideration rent, taxes, and utilities. Nor does it take into account the organization's costly fundraising expenses such as printing and postage of newsletters, mailing campaigns, and advertisement costs. Upon further investigation, it is seen that the organization's low overhead is accomplished by assigning only the president's salary as part of management costs. All other costs are earmarked as indirect program expenses. Even their fundraising campaigns are mostly allocated as indirect program costs under the guise that they bring about cause and situation awareness for which they are raising the funds.

If Muslim charities can be proud of only one thing, it would be that they do not engage in "tricky accounting" like the organization above. Those who work for Muslim charities do so in the first place out of their feelings of responsibility towards people in need, and not to make careers out of this mobile profession. It is highly important for organizations to keep their records as true to reality as possible, even if management and fundraising expenses outpace expenses in other areas.

PROGRAM BALANCES

Nonprofit organizations differ in the nature of their work. Some are solely funding agencies. Others specialize in a specific field, implementing programs on the ground. They could be a one-program agency or a multi-program agency. The most difficult case is when the organization does all of the above—raises funds and implements multi-purpose programs. This no doubt creates an environment where there is a lack of focus, is less effective and is very difficult to do. Although the more specialized the nonprofit is, the better off it is. Currently, Muslim charities are not developed well enough to focus on different specialties. Our record of experience is short, whereas the need is overwhelming; therefore, we must do it all. Granted, this is not always an excuse. Sometimes it is a matter of survival for the charity. As people in this field know, if the charity specialized in very specific programs such as providing medical aid in Africa, the potential donors-market decreases, leaving the organization to struggle. The only way to cope with specialized efforts is to have long-term cooperative relationships among various charities.

A typical Muslim charity does not have only one program for which it must raise funds. Rather it is common, especially for international humanitarian charities, to have multiple programs launched and implemented concurrently. For instance, a charity might be establishing a school in Ghana, mobilizing an emergency team to bring earthquake relief to Iran, and implementing an Udhiya program in several countries across four continents. As well as having many other ongoing programs, such as an orphan sponsorship program, an adopted clinic in Palestine, and a feeding center in Ethiopia. While some of these programs or projects might be temporary, others are ongoing.

Charities such as these may also promote these programs through various means. As a result, they receive individual donations for different causes. Those organizations that depend on public donations receive many small contributions for various restricted purposes. At the same time, funds are disbursed to ongoing programs on a monthly or as-needed basis.

It could lead to great confusion if simple financial record keeping was not taken into consideration. The leadership of these organizations must always be aware of the following:

- What are the Monthly & Year-to-Date budgets of every program?

- What are the Monthly & Year-to-Date actual revenues and expenses of every program?

- What is the current balance for every program?

There could be also other data required, which are very beneficial to look at such as:

- What is the number of donations received per program?

- What is the total donation received per program?

- What is the overhead cost per program?

- What is the monthly disbursement per program?

There are many ways to present this data. Some means are complicated and full of irrelevant details—others are informative and simple. The worst case scenario is not having updated data, or data that is not provided on a frequent basis. Non-complicated data is better, because the more complicated they are, the more difficult it would be to come up with these data. Let us consider an example where the organization produces a monthly program report that tracks data that is basic yet vital for organized financial management.

Program Monthly Report
For January, 2005

Program	Previous Balance	Income	Overhead (10%)	Disbursements	End-of-Month Balance
Tsunami Relief	$947	$20,603	($2,060)	($32,500)	$14,904
Orphan Sponsorship	($347)	$8,425	($842)	($8,250)	$320
Salaam Clinic	$1,079	$2,000	($200)	($1,800)	$1,079
Niger Food Aid	$16,801	$13,438	($1,343)	($18,000)	$15,980

Figure 16-C

In example 16-C, the first column states the program funds that are expended for during the month of January. The second column refers to the indirect program costs that management deducts to cover its operations to run these programs. While the third column refers to how much money is put directly toward each program, which could be the funds transferred to the specific account or branch implementing each program. As for the last column, to get this amount, you follow this simple formula:

End-of-month Balance =

Previous balance + income – (disbursements + overhead).

A spreadsheet such as this should be automated by feeding data into it from other sources. Although it is simple, it provides management with numbers that tell a lot when taken into consideration with other data, especially at a time of evaluation and planning.

III. Budget Monitoring, Tracking, and Adjustments

As any line manager would probably say, monitoring the current year's budget usually consumes more time than the budget's actual development. The primary task involved with managing the current year's budget is not to spend more than you earn. If revenues exceed planning, it may be necessary and/or allowed to increase spending; however, in the case of revenue shortfall, it is far better for the organization to come in under budget.

The monitoring process is quite simple: do not spend more than the budget allows. In an ideal situation, if expenses fall evenly throughout the year, or the manager can control the timing of expenditures, then each month's expenditures should equal one twelfth of the entire budget. If the fiscal year starts in July and expenditures have consumed half the budget at the end of December, then the manager is staying on budget. Otherwise, the manager must find ways to slow spending.

MONITORING THE EXPENSE BUDGET

In order to ensure upkeep and control of expenses, the budget must be watched closely. The importance of the relationship between budget development and monitoring cannot be overemphasized. If an organization's costs are realistically projected through reliable and precise budget estimates, then spending patterns will conform to them, while the task of monitoring will be simpler. This holds true for both major and minor line-item object costs. For example, a travel item in the budget would be relatively simple to monitor if time and costs for each person traveling is well documented. However, a trip of indiscriminate time by an undetermined number of people is hard to control.

Successful monitoring requires management skills, ingenuity, tact and foresight. Obviously, larger organizations require techniques very different from those of a medium or small organization. Working through department heads and program coordinators calls for skills very different from those needed when the organization is small enough for one-on-one staff interaction.

When monitoring functions in a smaller organization, there are three dimensions that the administrator should understand and recognize:

• *The temporal dimension*–a specific attempt at observing which budget action might happen before, during or after a cost is incurred, or which action might happen at selected or haphazard times during the fiscal year. The administrator must decide when is the best time for which items to occur, a factor that impinges strongly on expense control.

• *The structural dimension*–included in this realm would be the organization's degree of independence from its board or funding sources, and the board of directors or outside funding sources' power and role. Additionally, it would also include the level of autonomy given to the fiscal administrator, and the amount of fiscal discretion given to individual staff members.

- *The discriminate dimension*–includes recognizing those budget items that are the most critical and those which can wait, and which monitoring tasks can not be delegated but must be dealt with directly by management. As well as what funding resources are still available for actions in the category, and the interrelations between the cost centers.

Along with these things, other factors such as experience, understanding of program operations, and knowledge of current situation fluctuations intermingle during the monitoring processes. This is where a good administrator earns their pay by being able to sort through all of these issues, ranking each action accordingly.

In carrying out each of these tasks, the monitoring process merges with the control process. Both procedures can benefit from gathering, tabulating, and classifying available data. An ongoing accrual Monthly Expense Summary is simple to set up and maintain, whether or not a sophisticated accounting system is in use. Once a routine is established, it can readily be aligned with expense records by cost centers, working hand-in-hand with existing accepted accounting procedures. For any organization that has sound fiscal management, all of the data required for the scenario should already be a part of its available basic financial information.

IV.   Financial Record Keeping

Presently, most nonprofits recognize the importance of keeping good financial records. Ultimately, how well and how sophisticated an organization keeps its records are based upon how much money it has to pay good accountants and/or bookkeepers. Most nonprofits realize that the funds put into their hands are given for a specific cause, and therefore they are entrusted to use those funds to the best of their abilities for that cause. They also realize that they are the custodians of other people's money with the responsibility to account for every penny.

Although there are few laws or regulations that directly state how nonprofit organizations must operate their finances internally, there are some important points requiring strong emphasis. Commonsense dictates that financial records should be as complete and accurate as feasibly possible. Maintaining good records does not necessarily require a sophisticated computer or complex software. Even if dealing with a minor program with a budget of only a few thousand dollars, good records and information are essential. All programs should be dealt with on the same level, regardless of revenue or expenses. Also, all financial records should be kept current, with solid documentation for backup.

Furthermore, since they are accountable for the programs and responsible for future planning, all the records must be of use to the director, executive committee, or board. No matter how detailed, if the information does not help tie fiscal and program records together, it cannot be useful for reviewing, assessing, and projecting the effects and results of these operations. The basic minimum of these records should include payroll journals, a voucher system, receipts journal, check register, accounts payable ledger, deposit slip journal and so on. Additionally, to ensure sufficient joint fiscal/program information, a number of non-fiscal supportive records and data can be useful. These items are essential for preparing financial and operations reports for external funding sources.

```
PETTY-CASH RECEIPT

No._____Amount_____

RECEIVED OF PETTY CASH

For_____

Charge to_____

_____

Approved by _____  Received by _____
```

Figure 16-D

One simple example of this record-keeping is the Petty Cash Receipt. This printed form, like the sample in Figure 16-D, is widely available in office supply stores and is viewed as one of the necessary—but not totally sufficient—tools in standard cash disbursement records. This little piece of paper provides invaluable activity information, and when amended, affords a practical means of tracking cash. Typically, the line *"For"* might say, *"trip for client"* or *"postage"*, or *"shipping envelopes"*, and so on. The *"Charge to"* line will show the account number and might say *"travel"*, or *"postage"*, or *"supplies"*.

Another good example is a purchase order that might include similar details such as account number, line-item, cost center, and other relevant information. Whenever possible, a transaction record should serve internal, funding source, and audit needs. The significance of gaining staff cooperation in saving receipts for documentation cannot be over emphasized. In the long-run, doing this small thing will make any accounting procedure or audit much less painful.

UTILIZING AVAILABLE TECHNOLOGY

As technology progresses, the procedures and forms have or will become more automated. The need for allowing experienced professional financial/management personnel to handle the lion's share of these duties is quite important. Not-for-profit organizations have distinct needs. Simply adapting a generic software package with industry-specific limitations may not be sufficient; although, organizations more often than not build tools for themselves from readily available applications such as spreadsheets. These tools are only limited by the users' expertise in the application. We will not recommend specific software solutions for nonprofit accounting because this depends greatly on the size of the organization, its technology budget, and its needs. However, it is highly recommended not to use those software systems that are made for for-profit corporations, rather you should choose a system that is made in the for-nonprofit organizations. Undoubtedly in the future, new and better software is bound to come along that will be more affordable, user-friendly, and easily adapted to nonprofits' specific requirements.

V.   Accountability and Internal Control

As stated before, having altruistic goals and a deep passion for your mission is just not enough. Building a sustainable nonprofit organization begins at the foundation—creating a thorough planning process. While this is very true, it is also true that to achieve the best possible results, the plans need to be carried out. This is where accountability raises its insightful head, assuring that departments and individuals are held accountable for their actions and their results.

MANAGEMENT CONTROL SYSTEMS

Management Control Systems (MCS) is the core of an organization's effort to bring its goals to fruition through a set of policies and procedures designed to keep operations going according to plan. These are also designed to detect deviations from the specific course, providing managers with information they will need to take corrective actions when necessary.

Furthermore, MCS establishes an environment in which it is likely that the organization will come as close as possible to its original plan. This means that management control systems are reactive as well as proactive. They are reactive to the extent that they monitor and detect if something is going wrong, and then initiate actions to correct the problem. As well, they are proactive in that they set into play incentives and controls allowing the organization to avoid negative results to begin with, providing managers with a clear route to identify and capitalize on opportunities.

Management control systems are often compared to thermostats. Although a room's thermostat might be set for a comfortable 70 degrees, a thermostat does not simply establish the desired temperature. It also monitors the existing room temperature. Likewise, a MCS assesses the organization's actual results.

One of the most important primary steps toward developing a MCS in regards to revenues and expenses is to set up the appropriate journals, ledgers, special bank accounts, and so on which will allow the administrator to:

- Ensure the timeliness and accuracy of records
- Follow the flow of money step-by-step
- Simplify reconciliation of bank statements with records.

This system involves planning transaction records, establishing routes for orderly processing, designating responsibilities and authorizations for each task, isolating custody and assigning authority, determining supervision and review measures, etc. Definite measures must be taken to ensure that the process guard against improprieties or fraud by maintaining accurate information for fiscal planning and management, and promotes accountability.

In the past few years, Islamic charitable and religious organizations have come under increased governmental scrutiny. The Internal Revenue Service, Justice Department and the Federal Bureau of Investigation have raided many of these organizations. Without warning, numerous Islamic organizations and charities have found their bank accounts and funds frozen. Their operations were closed pending investigations. Muslim charities will continue to be under a degree of scrutiny that other non-Islamic charities will never face. Therefore, investing in a bookkeeping system directed at cash accounting and management for nonprofits that is widely available on the open market would be wise. These resources focus on a broad range of duties: how to record receipts, client information records, accounts receivable summaries, daily/monthly journals, money disbursement, and recording line-items by categories, etc.

SAFEGUARDING RESOURCES

Two critical elements of internal control are management control systems and performance measurement. Internal control refers to systems designed to ensure efficiency and effectiveness of operations, compliance with all relevant laws, and reliable reporting of financial results. All of this is a part of ensuring that an organization's assets are safeguarded.

The foremost step in this protection process is to hire reliable, ethical people and to maintain a culture of forthright actions, creating an environment of scrupulous behavior. As a primary rule within the organization, any and all unethical and illegal behavior should be condemned. Even after taking these steps, it is still necessary to insure the organization's resources by outlining an audit trail, separation of duties, proper authorization, adequate documentation, proper procedures, physical safeguards, bonding, vacations, rotation of duties, independent checks, and cost-benefit analysis.

PHYSICAL SAFEGUARDS

It goes without saying that blank checks and cash should not be kept lying around. These items are an open invitation to fraud and theft. Backup copies of computer records should be made on a regular basis and maintained at separate locations. As well, controls should be instituted to protect valuable inventory.

PERFORMANCE AUDITS

Another system of review, that should take place on a regular basis, is the performance audit, or operational audit. This audit is usually divided into two subcategories: efficiency audits, and program audits. Efficiency audits are reviews that determine if the organization is acquiring, protecting and using its resources efficiently—essentially checking for waste. By contrast, program audits check for effectiveness to determine whether the organization's programs are accomplishing their goals.

Audit Trail

The most primary element in accounting control is to establish a clear audit trail, which is the ability to trace each transaction in an accounting system back to its source. For example, a charitable organization spends $50,000 a year on travel expenses, which at first glance might appear to be a large amount. Documentation should exist that would allow the determination of exactly what that $50,000 was spent on. Although the expenditures may have been legitimate, the travel might well have been unauthorized. The audit trail serves as a preventative device where the misappropriation of funds can be averted, not only through the knowledge that valid documentation must be provided, but that those actually spending the money will be held accountable. Both of these instances serve as inhibitions to inappropriate spending, thereby serving as an effective method of fiscal control.

Larger organizations have internal audit departments who are dedicated to working year-round on performance audits whose purpose is to review the financial and operating systems of that organization. Primarily for seeking out weaknesses in control that might allow for theft of resources, they are also charged with improving the system, reducing the chance that errors will occur in the reporting of financial information or its recording. At the same time, internal auditors focus their performance audits on trying to find ways that the organization might better achieve its mission, while evaluating the role and function of each unit or department.

Some organizations hire independent outside auditors who serve a crucial role. They have the benefit of experience from reviewing control systems in many different organizations. As a result, from their unique perspective they can offer suggestions for improvement in internal controls, catching flaws that might be missed by less impartial auditors.

SEPARATION OF FUNCTIONS

We have all heard the urban legend of the accountant who skips out to Rio with a suitcase filled with their hapless clients' entire bank accounts in tow. The once successful business person is now a destitute pauper with no means of support. Too bad that business person was not astute enough to insist on a separation of functions, an activity that relates to the disbursement of resources which should be separated so that no one individual controls too much of the process. As the business person would have found out, the individual who approves bills for payment should not be the same person who writes checks. Taking the separation of function control even further, the person who writes the checks should not be the same person who signs the checks.

One other advantage of having such a system would be that each individual might catch mistakes made or missed by another, further lessening the opportunity for problems to arise. Unlike the accountant who is now soaking up the sun in Rio, an employee who tries to embezzle funds in an organization that uses the separation of functions system is more than likely soaking up to his elbows in the prison laundry.

Granted, no system is foolproof. Separation of function can still be defeated if dishonest people collaborate to steal. This all comes back to hiring ethical people whose basis in life is moral value. It also comes back to the organization setting up an environment of ethical behavior, adhering to the law, and the critical elements of an internal control system.

PROPER AUTHORIZATION

Setting and adhering to spending policies within an organization is another control element related to proper authorization. For example, an organization's policy is that all travel be done in coach. By not allowing first-class air tickets to be purchased through the establishment of formal authorization mechanisms helps the firm to adhere to policy. Allowing reimbursements of expenditures made only with the proper authorization is a good impetus for an employee who tries to take a first-class trip at the expense of the organization to remain honest. By the same token, having to get authorization for every single purchase can be suffocating; therefore, some predetermined purchases can be given a general authorization. This allows for certain items under a set dollar amount or for a certain purpose to receive authorization through standing approval. Those items that cannot be purchased through general authorization must have specific authorization, requiring an individual to obtain written permission to override the general authorization policies.

This set of standards does not only apply to purchases. They are also applicable to different types of disbursements of funds and to the signing of contracts. The ultimate source of authority lies with the board of directors. The board provides letters of delegation to senior managers, providing them with the authority to undertake a variety of functions on behalf of the organization—delegation of authority. These managers, in turn, report back to the board.

PROPER PROCEDURES

A procedures manual is a standard in most organizations, providing a heavily relied upon internal control system. However rigid this system may seem, it provides for clearly documented procedures that are less likely to produce errors, and even less time to correct those that do occur. Clearly, this system requires that it be kept current and relevant with frequent review and updating.

ADEQUATE DOCUMENTATION

Accounting processes have changed rapidly with the times. Organizations at one time maintained all financial activities by using canceled checks. If a question arose about a transaction, the canceled check could be produced to verify the transaction. These days, most transactions are made through electronic transfer rather than by check, including payroll, which can be electronically deposited to the employee's account.

It is essential that organizations carefully think out what documentation will be available to them allowing transactions to be traced back, explained and proven to have occurred. Paper receipts such as purchase orders, petty cash receipts, sales receipts, and so on are integral parts of the audit trail. Whenever possible, paper records should be digitized, verified and then stored for retrieval at a later date.

ROTATION OF DUTIES

Employees are assumed to be honest from the outset; however, a few employees who deal with significant amounts of money are in a position to steal. It would be better for all involved if those employees were bonded. Other ways to guard an organization is by vacations, and staff rotation. If money is being pilfered from the accounts receivable cash stream, then it is possible that the perpetrator could use checks received later on to cover for the misappropriated cash. Furthermore, by requiring vacations, employees are moved into other roles on a temporary basis possibly providing for any discrepancies to be uncovered. Since the employee will not be doing the same job day to day or month to month, it allows them some respite from mundane jobs, and lets it be known that a rotation in duties could discover any problems.

LEGAL CONSIDERATIONS

In the 1970s, the Foreign Corrupt Practices Act (FCPA) was instituted to reduce certain abuses of internal control systems. Although the law was put into effect to stem certain international activities by American firms, it actually applies to all organizations, without consideration of whether or not they do business internationally or domestically. The law requires maintenance of a system of internal controls and accurate accounting records, and to review their system while being specific in the cost-benefit concessions made that limit the system. They are also required to assess the scope to which the internal control system works. The failures of organizations such as Enron, MCI, and Adelphia, among others since early 2000 until the present, will surely usher in new legislation, as well as rules for doing business and the tightening of internal controls.

VI. Assessing Your Case

In light of what we have presented here, please consider your organization's situation when answering these questions. This chapter will not only provide practical benefit for your organization, but it will help in identifying the areas where corrections are needed. Additionally, you are encouraged to go back to review the specific materials of the chapter for clarification on some questions.

- *Does your organization compare its actual revenues and expenses to its monthly budget?*

- *How many sources of revenues does your organization track?*

- *For the past three years, what were your organization's total fundraising and revenues, management and general costs, and total program expenses?*

- *What are the percentages of management, fundraising and program expenses from total expenses for each of the last three years?*

- *What kind of reports and for what period (how frequent) does your organization produce or receive on each program?*

- *Can your organization know at any point of time what is the actual balance available for every program or fund it runs?*

- *What procedures do your management follow to keep financial transactions going according to budget?*

- *Does your organization perform a financial audit by an independent accounting firm every year regardless of whether or not required by law?*

- *Does your organization maintain clear separation of financial functions by different individuals?*

- *Does your organization maintain adequate documentation for every financial transaction that is easily traced it to its origin? This includes for what program and budget line item, who au-*

thorized it, who actually made it, and its supporting documents such as invoice, contracts and/or authorizations?

- *Do you have a Management Control System that clearly spells out all financial policies, procedures and levels of authorization?*

Concluding Remarks

Writing this book has been a challenging and rewarding experience. It has allowed me as the author to impart my knowledge and experience. Tremendous time and effort went into the process of researching, writing, and rewriting. As with any other creative work, numerous individuals contributed in many ways to this endeavor. I wish to thank those who helped me to focus my thoughts, as well as sensitize me to a number of issues.

Harvesting great benefits from my more than 17 years of experience in the field of nonprofit management, this book has addressed important issues facing nonprofit organizations today. While experiencing the creative process of authoring a book, I was forced to think deeply about many issues, and critically consider matters that I have been dealing with practically, but never before had the chance to study academically.

I trust that this book will provide countless individuals with vital help in the area of nonprofit management.

I have two main goals in this book. The first is to discuss Muslim charity in a comparative perspective. The second is to benefit nonprofit organizations, regardless of mission type, to become more professional and effective. It is a call for them to grow professionally, and apply strategies of excellence and success by providing a practical operations guide. At the very least, it is my hope and expectation that this book will become a must-have reference tool and that its readers will learn the Islamic perspective on charity, as well as how Muslim organizations operate in the US.

Charity is one of the five pillars of Islam. Therefore, the importance of charity in Islam cannot be underestimated. Muslims will always give money to charities. It is a testament to the glory and universality of the religion that Islam recognizes poverty as a serious problem and elevates dealing with it to the level of an article of the faith. While American law enacts rules that govern charities, Islamic jurisprudence in many ways has developed far more strict regulations on charitable work.

Unfortunately, some important people view Muslim charities as a liability. These charities collect donations that are spent not only within the confines of American and international law, but within the confines of Islamic law. Muslim donors entrust that their Zakat donations will be spent according to their intentions. If these charities did not exist, Muslims would have to trust their Zakat money to channels that are informal and much harder for the government to regulate and monitor. Therefore, American Muslim charities, to Muslims and non-Muslims alike, are an asset and not a liability.

I have one word of advice to Muslim charities: engagement. The saying, "No man is an island" should be held true for all, whether it be an entity or a charitable organization. I advise American Muslim charities not to fear engagement with the government or the larger civil society. Engagement with both helps charities become more transparent. In the Muslim culture, charity is supposed to be low key, to the point of anonymity. However, it is important to publicize such deeds in order to remove the aura of mystery currently surrounding work conducted by Muslim nonprofits.

For Muslim nonprofits, engagement in the form of government and civic society out-reach is not a threat to maintaining their identity. Nor is partnering with other charities, whether or not they are operated by Muslims. My experience has shown such partner-ships are of great importance, with non-Muslim organizations being very receptive to the practice.

Charity work is not easy. It does not simply consist of getting donations and delivering those donations to the recipients. However, it is about properly obtaining the donations, managing them, appropriately spending them, and then publicizing the fruits of those financial gifts. The field is challenging and always changing. Staying current on trends in charitable work and the regulations surrounding this work is an ongoing process. Be-ing a member of professional organizations such as InterAction, as well as subscribing to resources such as BoardSource are two methods of accomplishing this.

When the world changed after 9/11, it also severely disturbed charitable endeavors around the globe. In the post-9/11 era there are many issues facing charities in general, and in the Muslim charities in particular. I would have liked to address them within these pages, but am unable to since they go beyond its scope. God willing, I will deal with these issues in another publication.

This is the first edition of this book. I understand that perfection is an attribute of God, but human beings and their work are far from perfect. I am open to readers' ideas, suggestions, or comments, which may be sent to the contact information below.

Khalil Jassemm, Ph.D.
LIFE for Relief and Development
17300 Ten Mile Rd.
Southfield, MI 48037
Ceo@lifeusa.org
(248) 424-7493

Index

media queries 395, 396
Medical Appeal 414
medical care 4, 17, 32, 48, 125, 200
medical centers 420
medical procedure 96
medical research 69
Medicare tax 454
Medina 67, 70, 90, 95
meet-and-greet 401
meeting information 229
membership-based organizations 335
membership body 227, 228, 232
membership cards 426
membership program 335
mentally pre-occupied 46
mercy 57, 62, 75, 76, 92
mere suspicion 108
Messenger of Allah 25, 41
metals and petroleum 78
metamorphosing 177
methodical questioning 170
methodologies 118
methodology 80
methods of assessment 254
method of donation 333
me generation 257
micro-economy 73
micro-manager 194
micro-managing 221
Micro-Managing Board 222
microphone 393
Microsoft 354, 358
Microsoft Explorer 358
Microsoft Project 212, 217
Middle East 33, 128, 295, 296, 414
Middle East oil 128
Milestone Charts 212
Military 98, 123, 124
Representative John Millner 400
mini-plans 190
Ministry of Islamic Affairs 68
Mirror 417
Miskin 60, 77, 89
mismanagement 22
mission 240, 242, 249, 250, 253, 257, 258, 261,
    262, 263, 264, 265, 267, 268, 269, 270
Mission Board-Staff Retreat 165
mission driven 153, 249
mission focused 153
Mission Statement 224
mission statement 101, 412
mistreated employees 263
ML 322, 323, 324, 325, 334, 337, 344, 345, 349
MLC cycle 378

mobilizing 9, 304, 476
models for boards 227
modernizing technology or equipment 186
Mohammed Bin Muslimah 83
monetary act of worship 19, 38
monetary award 282
monetary income 69
money 4, 8, 9, 12, 14, 15, 20, 22, 24, 25, 36, 38, 51,
    52, 54, 56, 58, 59, 60, 61, 64, 74, 76, 77, 78, 79,
    81, 82, 83, 90, 92, 93, 94, 95, 112, 132, 155,
    162, 163, 164, 187, 188, 203, 204, 241, 261,
    274, 275, 276, 277, 282, 285, 287, 290, 295,
    317, 321, 324, 328, 333, 335, 338, 339, 341,
    346, 353, 354, 356, 371, 372, 376, 377, 380,
    382, 391, 409, 410, 411, 419, 421, 422, 423,
    424, 426, 434, 437, 446, 453, 454, 455, 458,
    467, 477, 479, 482, 483, 484, 487, 491, 492
money trail 132
Monitoring and Control 175
monitoring and measuring progress 170
monitoring process 477, 479
Monograph on Terrorist Financing 108
monotheistic religions 3
Monthly & Year-to-Date actual
    revenues and expenses 476
Monthly & Year-to-Date budgets 476
monthly budget breakdowns 469
Monthly Expense Summary 464, 466, 467, 479
monthly or quarterly newsletter 302
Monthly Revenue Summary 467, 468
Moralists 16
morals 39, 403
Morocco 126
Moses 73
mosque 386, 401, 402
mosque's administration 426
mosques 409, 416, 420, 424, 425
Mosque Foundation 400
mosque of Quba' 67
mosque operations 68, 425
motivational programs 241
Mu'az Bin Jabal 74
Mua'th Bin Jabal 94, 95
Muhammad Ali 70
multi-layered plan 412
Multi-Level Donation Forms 366
multi-organization initiative 179
Multimedia Materials 308
multimedia strategies 295, 297
multimedia tools 306
multiple fundraising means 418
Multiple Giving Options 366
multitude of constituencies 230
Muslim-affected areas 134

unwanted E-mail 363
UN Department of Humanitarian Affairs 122
upkeep and control of expenses 478
USAID 134, 135, 137, 139, 145, 312, 421
User-friendly 356
Use of elegant typefaces 360
use of font sizes and styles 358
using frames 359
US Agency for International
        Development (USAID) 134
US Constitution 101
US government 365
US government guidelines 22
US markets 311
US Pacific Command 134
US Postal Service 324
US postal service 318
US tax code 14
US Treasury 32, 98, 109, 110, 112,
        130, 132, 140, 143
US West Coast 282
US work force 11

V

vague areas 182
value-based marketing 151
values of freedom 134
value based 153
Variances 446, 460
Variances of actual vs. budget 446
variance column 467
vending machines 289
vendors 110, 117
venues 163
Verse 49, 50, 52
verse or Hadith 331
vertical scrolling 359
viable alternatives 18
video-conferencing 259
video documentaries 289
video documentary 326
video footage 299, 308
violent act 107
vision and qualifications 223
visual dimension 393
visual presentations 306, 378
vocational training center 341, 342
Vocational training programs 21
voicemail 106
voluntary charity 6, 20, 21, 38, 61, 85
voluntary giving 8, 19
voluntary groups 10
volunteerism 265, 267

Volunteers 239, 258, 265, 266, 267
volunteer coordinator 267
volunteer fundraising leadership 290
volunteer hours 8
volunteer network 340
volunteer support 76
voter registration 29
voting record 401
voucher program 132
voucher system 480

W

"We exist because hunger hurts" 149
"we exist because life is precious" 149
waajib (obligatory) 87
Waqf 22, 62, 63, 64, 65, 66, 67, 68, 69, 70,
        71, 72, 73, 89, 413, 422, 423
waqf 285
Waqf assets 67
Waqf for injured or old animals 69
Waqf Systems 62
Waqf trustee 64
war 414
wars 32, 67, 120, 128
Washington Report for ME Affairs 417
Water and sewerage systems 21
water tunnels 63
WBS 213, 214, 215
wealthy people 45
Website 163
website 353, 354, 355, 356, 357, 359,
        361, 362, 363, 366, 367, 368
Website Administrator 208
Weekend School 426
weekend school budget 426
weight of law 106
Welfare 2, 4, 5, 7, 39, 84, 90, 96
welfare budgets 7
welfare recipients 8
welfare reforms 8
welfare system 3, 7, 8, 39, 65, 83, 85
well-defined systems 45
wellbeing of society 24
western nonprofits 336
western philosophy 19
West Bank 129, 132
Whistle-Blower Protection 106
White House 130
White House's Rose Garden 354
who serves on their boards 224
Who Should Be Involved 189
Why do we exist? 149
why were we founded 149

Printed in the United States
67346LVS00006B/151

9 781425 931605